1L OF A RIDE:

A WELL–TRAVELED PROFESSOR'S ROADMAP TO SUCCESS IN THE FIRST YEAR OF LAW SCHOOL

Second Edition

By

Andrew J. McClurg

Herbert Herff Chair of Excellence in Law
Cecil C. Humphreys School of Law
The University of Memphis

AMERICAN CASEBOOK SERIES®

WEST®

Mat #41309291

American Casebook Series is a trademark registered in the U.S. Patent and Trademark Office.

© 2013 LEG, Inc. d/b/a West Academic Publishing

    610 Opperman Drive
    St. Paul, MN 55123
    1–800–313–9378

Printed in the United States of America

ISBN: 978–0–314–28305–4

To my students—past, present, and future.

ACKNOWLEDGEMENTS

It's appropriate that a book written for and about law students was shaped every step of the way with the help of law students. Students who provided direct assistance are thanked below, but I'm indebted to all of my students collectively. Even after a quarter century as a law professor, I learn something new from law students nearly every day.

Of the many fortunate aspects of being a law professor, few rival the privilege of working daily with talented research assistants, all of whom epitomize what it means to be a great law student. Research assistants at the University of Memphis Cecil C. Humphreys School of Law who helped with this book include Joshua Baker, Shea Barker, Chelsea L. Brown, James Duckworth, Lindsey Gill, Russell Hayes, Sally Joyner, Julia M. Kavanagh, Jane Marie Lewis, Natalie Fox Malone, Johannah F. O'Malley, Elizabeth Rogers, Meredith Blake Stewart, James Stone, Mary L. Wagner, and Todd V. Williams.

Special thanks also to the students who shared their case briefs, class notes, and course outlines so that readers can learn from authentic samples of these crucial law school documents. All of those students were either research assistants or are listed below.

Since beginning work on the first edition in 2006, I've solicited comments from hundreds of law students, mostly through formal surveys, but also via email, Facebook, and conversations in and out of the classroom. Most of them are current or former students at the University of Memphis, but they also include former students at the University of Arkansas at Little Rock School of Law, Florida International University College of Law, and Golden Gate University School of Law, as well as a handful of students from other schools.

Realizing I'm probably leaving some people out, thanks to the following students and former students for their comments and other assistance: William D. Albright, Lauren M. Armstrong, Monica Barba, Shea Barker, David Barman, Jennifer M. Baum, Christopher N. Bell, Willem H. Bermel, Jonathan E. Bettis, Matthew K. Bishop, Anna Vergos Blair, Daane J. Blocksma, Peter G. Bolac, Bianca F. Brasher, Christopher G. Britt, Chelsea L. Brown, Kimberly G. Brown, Wilson S. Bryan, Katie Burch, France Caldwell, Amanda G. Carpenter, Joseph D. Cassidy, John C. Catmur, Jessica H. Chandler, Courtney Clothier, Christopher B. Connolly, Aaron B. Crafton, Caroline W. Crawford, Edwin Cruz, Kyle R. Cummins, Anne B. Davis, Tamara Davis, Adam R. deNobriga, Andrew S. DeShazo, Carolan M. Deutch, Rachel D. Dyer, Carl T. Eppler, John M. Escue, Jamie Ewing, Libba Fyke, Charles F. Fleet, Sharon A. Fortner, LaTaya Franklin, Caroline E. Gabriel, Matthew P. Gabriel, Tyler C. Ginn, Whitney Goode, Michele B. Gwinn, Jennifer D. Haile, Blake W. Hazlerig, Kevin P. Henson, Katherine L. Herriman, Jayniece R. Higgins, Richard T. Hoehn, Mackenzie R. Hogan, Amy L. Holland, Megan R. House, Laurence B. Howard, Taylor Hughes, Sheryl T. Hurst, Christian R. Johnson, Michele L. Johnson Spears, Sally Joyner, Yael Julian, Christine Jurado, Terri Keinlen, Erica R. Kelley, Marissa A. King, William Kruse, Erin Kubisiak, Cloteal LaBroi, Denise Lambert, Laura J. Lee, Ashley M. Levins, Erno D. Lindner, Jonathan A. Lindsey, Abigail M. Mabry, Chandra Madison, Tanesha L. Matthews, Kevin M. McCormack, Brandon F. McNary, M. Elizabeth McNinch, J. Bradley Mercer, Jonathon M. Meredith, Matthew E. Miller, Kate L. Moore, Robert G. Morgan, Charles M. Molder, J. Aaron Mullis, Katie Myers, Benjamin R. Newman, Donald P. Nicholson, Zachary S. Ogale, Daniel L. Owens, Holly Palmer, Alexander Y. Pao, Lacy Papadeas, Brian A. Parker, Laura Partlow, Laurie Peterson, Bryce H. Phillips, Galen P. Pickard, William M. Plosser, Joshua C. Powell, Susan Price, Adam C. Ragan, Allison S. Raines, Debra Reece, Emma J. Redden, Horace A. Reid, Monica R. Rejaei, William A. Roach, Carson L. Rogers, Schaefer K. Rowe, Ashley Jordan Russell, Caroline E. Sapp, Erica J. Scott, Benjamin T. Seamon, Seth M. Segraves, Reginald E. Shelton, Steven D. Shirley, Lakeisha D. Sisco–Beck, Jeffrey S. Smith, John D. Smith, Shayne Smith, Dylan M. Spaduzzi, Ryan J. Spickard, Allison J. Starnes–Anglea, Bridgett L. Stigger, Kendall F. Stivers, Brittany L. Strung, Matthew A. Thomas, Neely Campbell Thomas, Sarah M. Turner, Christopher J. Tutor, Pablo A. Varela, Gregory H. Wallace, Bridget M. Warner, Cameron M. Watson, Rachel D. Whitaker, Chad M. Wilgenbusch, Joanna L. Williams, Smith Nall Wilson, Dina Windle, Justin Wojciechowski, Jason J. Yasinksy, and Erin C. Young.

The comments from law students and their significant others in Chapter 23, addressing the impact of law school on outside relationships, are borrowed from my book, *The "Companion Text" to Law School: Understanding and Surviving Life with a Law Student* (2012). They were obtained from surveys administered to more than 200 students and their partners at the University of Memphis, California Western School of Law, and Seattle University College of Law. All of those contributors are named in the acknowledgements to *The "Companion Text" to Law School* so I won't relist them here, but I want to say thanks again!

I also received help from many law professors. Particular thanks to the five legal writing professors who generously contributed so much of their time and expertise to Chapter 18: Kimberly K. Boone, Christine N. Coughlin, Sandy C. Patrick, Joan Malmud Rocklin, and David Walter. Mary Pat Treuthart read and commented on a draft, offering her usual insightful, blunt, and often hilarious wisdom. Other professors who shared input or gave other help include: Thomas E. Baker, Coleen M. Barger, Sara R. Benson, Leslie Burton, Markita D. Cooper, John M.A. DiPippa, June F. Entman, Barbara Glesner Fines, Judith D. Fischer, Elizabeth P. Foley, Jose Gabilondo, Larry Howell, Barbara Kritchevsky, Nancy Levit, Ernest F. Lidge, III, Jana R. McCreary, Kathleen A. Miller, Steven J. Mulroy, Martha M. Peters, Lawrence A. Pivnick, Janet L. Richards, Ruth Anne Robbins, Ediberto Román, David S. Romantz, Daniel Schaffzin, Eugene Shapiro, Sheila J. Simon, Kevin H. Smith, Stephen Smith, Andrej Thomas Starkis, Meredith A.G. Stange, Brenda L. Tofte, Grace C. Tonner, Barbara J. Tyler, Nicholas L. White, and Jodi Wilson.

Several administrative, library, and other staff members at the University of Memphis law school also provided assistance, including Howard E. Bailey, Callie Caldwell, Patricia Collier Crowell, Cheryl Edwards, Yolanda D. Wesley Ingram, Karol Landers, Sue Ann McClellan, and especially Linda H. Hayes, the University of Memphis law school "mom."

Lindsay Paige Watkins went out of her way to answer questions and provide other help regarding the 2012 Law School Survey of Student Engagement. Professor Catherine Carpenter did likewise for the 2012 ABA law school curriculum survey.

Finally, I'm grateful to the great folks at West Academic Publishing for all of their assistance and support. It's an honor to be part of such a distinguished publishing family.

A few passages were borrowed from my previous books, *The "Companion Text" to Law School: Understanding and Surviving Life as a Law Student* (2012) and *The Law School Trip: The Insider's Guide to Law School* (2001).

PROLOGUE

For more than two decades as a law professor, at several schools across the country, I've watched first-year law students—"1Ls"—make the same mistakes: in their approach to studying, behavior in and out of the classroom, exam preparation, exam performance, and overall mindset toward law school. Sometimes these mistakes result from following bad advice, but more often they occur simply because students don't know what to expect or what is expected of them when they arrive at law school.

The consequences of these missteps vary. Some students flunk out, of course, but more often the mistakes prevent students from maximizing their potential, meeting their own high expectations, and living reasonably happy lives. Even many students who end up excelling in law school struggle dispiritedly to cope with the stress and anxiety that come from having to compete in the high-stakes 1L race without prior training and on a route lacking clear road markers.

My partial remedy, and the goal of this book—both when the first edition appeared in 2009 and now in this updated, revised, and expanded second edition—is to provide new students with a candid, beginning-to-end roadmap to the first year of law school, along with the navigational and other tools to complete the sojourn scholastically accomplished and emotionally intact.

But if you've done any looking around, you know that a bunch of other "how to succeed in law school" books already exist. What makes this book distinctive?

- **Written by a law professor with a wide range of experience teaching different kinds of students at different law schools.**

As you approach law school, lots of people—lawyer acquaintances, other law students, and authors of books like this one—will be giving you advice about how to succeed. Your first question to any of us should be: "Who are you to be giving me advice?"

I've taught thousands of students at six law schools, from
the West Coast (San Francisco) to the East Coast (Miami),
and points in between (Boulder, Little Rock, Memphis, and
Winston–Salem). These include law schools in each tier of the
U.S. News & World Report law school rankings. I have
experience teaching every kind of law student: affluent students, poor students, private-school students, public-school
students, young students just out of college, older students
with families and established careers, single parents, brilliant, average, and struggling students, kids whose parents
were law school deans and those first in their family to
attend college, urbanites, ruralites, full-time day students,
part-time night students, minority students, and students
with disabilities. I've taught students who went on to become
great judges and students who went on to become great
bartenders.

My teaching credentials include six teaching awards,
excellent student evaluations at six law schools, articles and
book chapters about law teaching, and teaching presentations
for organizations such as the Institute for Law School Teaching and Association of American Law Schools. My publishing
record includes six books and numerous scholarly articles
that have been quoted and cited in more than 500 books and
articles and by more than thirty courts. As a legal expert, I've
been interviewed and quoted by sources such as National
Public Radio, the *New York Times*, *Washington Post*, *Time*,
and *U.S. News & World Report*.

Additionally, I once was a successful law student. In
1980, I graduated third in my class at the University of
Florida College of Law, where I was a member of the law
review and Order of the Coif, an honor conferred on the top
10 percent of graduates at select law schools. While my
memories of the first year of law school are distant, some of
them remain quite clear, which says a lot about the impact of
the 1L adventure. I still remember my first day of law school
orientation, first class, first Socratic interrogation, and first
exam. That my own law school memories still have relevance
tells you something important to know about U.S. legal
education: it's deeply rooted in tradition. As noted—with
disapproval—by the authors of the *Best Practices for Legal
Education* report, "[t]ypical classroom instruction at most

law schools today would be familiar to any lawyer who attended law school during the past hundred thirty years."[1]

I don't claim to have the only right answers about succeeding in law school. Be skeptical of anyone who does. Any advice-giver who would make such a claim knows little about the wide variations in the learning styles of law students and teaching styles of professors. As with the law itself, many of the relevant questions about how to succeed have more than one answer depending on the particular student and professor. Indeed, the very definition of "success" is subject to different answers. I base my advice on what will be most helpful to the largest group of students.

- **Provides a candid beginning-to-end roadmap of what to expect in the first year.**

A large part of what makes the first year of law school so stressful and frightening is not knowing what to expect. For several years, I asked my entering Torts students this online poll question:

As you begin your 1L quest, what is your dominant feeling?

- Confidence
- Excitement
- Lack of confidence
- Pride
- Stress
- Fear or anxiety
- Uncertainty

"Uncertainty" was the most common answer. "Stress" and "Fear or Anxiety"—much of which is generated by uncertainty—also received many votes. To reduce your uncertainty and enlarge your comfort zone, this book explains what to expect as a 1L and how to respond when it happens. Essentially, it answers the questions, "What is the first year of law school really like and how do I make the most of it?"

The first year is the most important year in the three-year U.S. law school curriculum (four years for part-time

1. ROY STUCKEY ET AL., BEST PRACTICES FOR LEGAL EDUCATION 133 (2007) [hereinafter BEST PRACTICES FOR LEGAL EDUCATION].

students). The first year is where students acquire the basic knowledge and tools of legal analysis that carry them through the rest of law school and beyond. Think of it as the foundation on which all subsequent building blocks for becoming and being a lawyer are laid. It is also the year that tends to define students, both academically and in terms of their overall attitude and approach to law school.

While virtually all of the advice applies to the entire first year, we'll concentrate on the all-critical first semester. The first semester is where students learn to read cases, write case briefs, take class notes, compose course outlines, deal with the Socratic teaching method, and develop either good or poor classroom, study, and exam strategies. Those first fourteen weeks forge the critical-reasoning skills that law professors like to call "thinking like a lawyer."

I try to be candid in depicting the good, bad, and ugly of law school. To keep myself honest in that regard, I approached the book from this standpoint: If my daughter decided to go to law school, what advice would I give her? I wouldn't necessarily tell her everything law professors would want her to hear. I'd be bluntly honest.

- **Addresses each aspect of academic success, including the top five habits of successful law students, effective class participation, case-briefing, note-taking, outlining, exam preparation, and essay and multiple-choice exam strategies.**

You may already be aware that grades, particularly early grades, are important to opportunities both within and outside of law school, more important than in other graduate programs and employment sectors. Any suggestion to the contrary would be a misrepresentation. The finding of a 1980s national study of higher education remains true today: in no other educational discipline do early grades have as much impact as they do in law school.[2] This isn't to say that people without high grades can't or don't succeed in the legal

2. In a survey of stress in undergraduate, graduate, law, and medical students, a report by the Association for the Study of Higher Education concluded about law school: "[I]n no other university setting do grades have the importance at such an early point in one's education." NEAL WHITMAN ET AL., ASS'N FOR THE STUDY OF HIGHER EDUC., STUDENT STRESS: EFFECTS AND SOLUTIONS, ASHE–ERIC HIGHER EDUCATION RESEARCH REPORT NO. 2 53 (1984).

profession. Quite the contrary is true. Many of the wealthiest and most successful lawyers in America were *C* law students. I laughed when a colleague told me her law school has a nice basketball court for students bearing a plaque that says "Donated by a *C* Student."

But it's a fact that high GPAs and class rankings open doors not available to students who lack them, both in law school and in the real-world job market. Within law school, students with good grades have better opportunities to obtain scholarships, positions as research assistants to professors, and law review and moot court membership. Outside of law school, many law firms and judges won't interview people who are not in the top quartile of their class. At the end of an academic year, I asked my students to name one thing they wish they had known when they started law school. One student responded: "I wish I had known how important law firms find class rank to be."

Most law schools, albeit not all, hold rigorous attitudes toward grading. As covered in Chapter 14, a large majority of schools have formal grading policies, many of which impose mandatory curves. Even at schools without mandatory curves, law school grades in first-year courses usually follow a well-defined, bell-shaped curve.

The result is that high grades in law school are much harder to come by than in most other graduate programs. Because grades play such a crucial role in law school, a large portion of the book is devoted to helping you "make the grade." I can't promise that if you follow my advice, you will ace your courses or finish at the top of your class. Mathematics dictates that in every law school class since the dawn of time only 10 percent of students finish in the top 10 percent. Ninety percent don't. But I do firmly believe that following the advice in this book will substantially improve your chances of succeeding at a higher level than you would otherwise.

If you're looking for shortcuts to success in law school, this may not be the book for you. While it does offer important tips for being efficient—a critical time-saving attribute of successful law students—I'm sorry to report that students who make a habit of cutting corners simply do not succeed at the highest levels in law school. Most students "succeed" in law school in terms of not being academically dismissed, including many students who cut corners. But if your definition of success is something higher, cutting corners isn't a viable option for most students.

But don't take my word for it. In response to a year-ending question to list one piece of advice students would give to someone starting law school, one student wrote:

> I read some books before I started law school: [*Title omitted*] and [*Title omitted*]. Both were helpful, but it seems that most of the pre-law, self-help books are geared toward helping students find the easy way out. For example, one of the books I read had a whole chapter on book-briefing and gathering outlines from others. Well, the people who book-brief and don't do their own outlines usually don't do well. I would emphasize in your book that there is no easy way through law school.

And this came from a kid I jumped all over on the second day of class for arriving late. Law students, God love 'em.

- **Focuses on practical advice that can be followed by any student from day one.**

One of the problems with a lot of advice about how to succeed in law school is that, while it's good advice, as a practical matter, it can't be readily followed. I learned this in seeking feedback from other law professors. Reduced to its essence, much of their advice amounted to "learn to read better," "learn to write better," and "learn to think better." Easier said than done. This book focuses on practical advice that can be followed by any student from the first day of law school.

- **Addresses "emotional success" in addition to academic success.**

> People are starting to lose it a bit, egos flying, etc. One girl started crying the other day because she threw a french fry at this kid, just playing around, and he flew off the handle because it hit his laptop.

> —Mid-first semester update from a 1L

Here's an early warning: law school takes an emotional and physical toll on a substantial percentage of students, even those who enjoy it and perform well. Studies of law student psychological distress, as you will see, do not paint a pretty picture.

Most advice in law school prep books, including this one, is geared toward maximizing academic success by traditional barometers: grades and class rank. That makes good sense because those evaluations play vital roles both in law school and in obtaining legal employment. But as important as grades are, they are by no means the only measuring sticks of law school achievement. Success as a law student also comes in the form of happiness, well-being, learning for its own sake, empowerment, pride in accomplishment, relationship building, and a belief that one made the right decision in deciding to devote every bit of energy and resources to pursuing a law degree as opposed to doing something else.

At many stops along the road to academic success, this book offers advice for reducing stress and leading a healthy, balanced law school life. Several chapters are specifically devoted to these issues. Don't let this book or law school make you lose sight of the most important goals of life, which do not include writing the top exam in Contracts.

- *Shows* **with anecdotes and examples.**

Showing is more effective than telling, so many anecdotes and examples are used to make and illuminate points, including samples of authentic Socratic dialogue, student case briefs, student course outline excerpts, student class notes, and exam questions and answers.

Nearly all of the examples come from the subject of Torts. Simplistically, Torts is the study of monetary liability for personal injuries, both physical and mental. Torts is a good subject to use as a vehicle for exploring law school's first year because it is a required first-year course at all schools and many of the basic principles and fact patterns of tort law are comprehensible without extensive background or explanation. It is also a subject with which incoming students have at least some familiarity due to the widespread coverage of tort lawsuits and the tort system in the mainstream media and blogosphere.

A cautionary note: I picked and constructed simple examples that can be followed and processed by pre-law, admitted, and new students. Don't be misled into thinking law is as straightforward or easy as some of the examples might make it appear.

- **Includes a student voice with comments from real 1Ls.**

To stay in touch with the modern 1L experience from a student perspective, I've sought input from many law students over the past several years. Their interesting, insightful, and frequently poignant comments add confirmation as well as balance to (and relief from) the drone of teacher talk that will be bearing down on you for the next many pages.

Most of the comments are from students who attend or attended the University of Memphis Cecil C. Humphreys School of Law, my current institution, but I also obtained input from students at several other law schools, including the University of Arkansas at Little Rock School of Law, Cal Western University School of Law, Florida International University College of Law, Golden Gate University School of Law, and Seattle University School of Law.

Obviously, these limited student populations do not scientifically represent the entire universe of law students, but in terms of student reactions to the trials and tribulations of the 1L experience, they come very close. This is attributable to the remarkable uniformity in the basic structures and institutions of the first year of law school throughout U.S. legal education. In teaching at schools in different parts of the country, I've always been struck by the core likeness of law students. At schools great and small, all 1Ls struggle to learn the same material under the same teaching methodologies and evaluation formats.

I made style adjustments and punctuation and grammar corrections in the comments, but did not change their meaning.

- **Backs up advice with empirical research.**

Scores of studies have been conducted about law students, legal education, and teaching and learning in general, yet this research is often overlooked in giving advice to law students. To boost confidence (yours and mine) in my recommendations, I researched and discuss many of these studies. Did you know that students who sit in the front of classrooms get higher grades than those who sit in back? That women voluntarily participate in law school class discussion at lower rates than men? That the conventional wisdom to not change initial answers to multiple-choice questions is backwards? Some of the research on these and other points might surprise you.

• Includes input from other law professors.

To broaden my own view, I solicited input from other law professors all along the way. In particular, in Chapter 18, five experienced legal writing professors from different law schools answer important questions about legal research and writing courses, required in the first-year curriculum at all law schools. As you will soon learn all too well, no 1L courses generate more attention, angst, and complaining from students.

• Written in a reader-friendly voice.

Who wants to read several hundred pages of boring law professor advice? I wouldn't, so I try to keep you engaged with a lively voice and touch of humor. My credentials for attempting to occasionally amuse you include four years as the monthly humor columnist for the *American Bar Association Journal*, editor of Lawhaha.com, and author/editor of two books in the seemingly oxymoronic genre of "legal humor."

* * *

Like all roadmaps, you'll want to keep this one close by during your 1L trip. If you were taking a real one-year road trip, you wouldn't just glance at the map once before you backed out of the driveway then toss it aside. You'd review it each time you entered new territory or faced a new fork in the road. Consider this book to be a companion text to your entire first year, a handbook that should be kept handy for convenient reference.

If you haven't started law school yet, read the entire book to get the big picture, then return to consult particular chapters as they become more directly relevant in your 1L journey. Much of the advice is very specific. If you haven't started law school yet, you won't be able to remember or process it all. For example, as scintillating as the subject is, reading the chapter on course outlines (Chapter 13) before law school is unlikely to permanently imprint in memory all the details you'll need to know when it comes time to start preparing your own outlines in week three or four of the first semester. The same holds true for several other chapters, including those on case-briefing (Chapter 11), note-taking (Chapter 12), exam preparation (Chapter 15), essay and multiple-choice exam strategies (Chapters 16 and 17), legal research and writing (Chapter 18), maintaining well-being (Chapter 20), dealing with the second semester (Chapter 21), and co- and extracurricular activities (Chapter 24).

Buy some highlighters and mark the heck out of key passages as you read. That's what you'll be doing with your other law school books, so it will be good practice. Consult the index for answers to specific questions. It is extremely detailed for that purpose.

I hope you enjoy reading and learning from this book as much as I enjoyed writing it. Most important, I hope you'll actually *follow* the advice. I sometimes receive student comments ending with statements like "I learned that lesson the hard way." Learn the easy way! It's all in here.

TABLE OF CONTENTS

1L OF A RIDE:

A WELL-TRAVELED PROFESSOR'S ROADMAP TO SUCCESS IN THE FIRST YEAR OF LAW SCHOOL

CHAPTER 1
DESTINATION LAW SCHOOL

Get ready to embark on a wild ride unlike anything you've ever experienced, packed with thrills, chills, and probably a few spills. Being a 1L will challenge you like you've never been challenged. Law school and a law degree offer the potential for great rewards, but at a cost. The first year of law school will be one of hardest years of your life, if not *the* hardest. Law school will profoundly alter the way you think, view, and interact with the world around you, in ways both good and bad. Your 1L experience will literally change who you are, whether you want it to or not.

But you may already be tired of hearing or reading these kinds of dire proclamations and predictions. Perhaps you've encountered them in other prep books. Maybe they even sound like clichés to you by now. "Yeah, yeah, law school will be hard. I'll be changed. Whatever. Everyone says the same thing. I can handle it."

The best analogy I have for explaining how law school will both take you by surprise and forever alter you involves becoming a parent. When I was an expectant dad many years ago, friends and family told me the same kinds of things about becoming a parent. "It will change your life forever." "It will be the hardest thing you've ever done." "Say good-bye to your old life."

I thought they were exaggerating. It wasn't like I was uninformed. I'd read all the essential baby and parenting books. I even attended parenting classes. I cruised blissfully through the entire event thinking, "I'm prepared. I'm prepared. I'm prepared." Then five seconds into my first encoun-

1

ter with infant projectile vomiting, it was, "Augh! I'm not prepared! I'm not prepared! I'm not prepared!"

Like being a parent, one can truly understand and appreciate the first year of law school only by experiencing it, so let's start by looking at some reactions from those who did. On the last page of my first-semester Torts exam, I sometimes insert this bonus question: "Write the name of a song or a song lyric that best describes your feelings about the first semester of law school." It doesn't really count for any points, so don't get your hopes up that law school exams are that easy. Below are some of the responses. Lyrics are in quotation marks.

While we can't attach deep psychological meaning to these answers, dashed off hastily and perhaps in jest, the students' spontaneous associations are nevertheless revealing. Their first-semester jukebox reflects the rollercoaster ride of emotions inherent in being a 1L, including:

Stress, anxiety:
- Help!—The Beatles
- Chalkdust Torture—Phish
- Under Pressure—Queen/David Bowie
- I Wanna Be Sedated—The Ramones
- Panic—The Smiths

Disorientation, madness:
- Highway to Hell—AC/DC
- "They won't let me out, they won't let me out (I'm locked up)"—Akon
- Basketcase—Green Day
- Welcome Home (Sanitarium)—Metallica
- Crazy Train—Ozzy Osborne

Exhaustion, frustration, hostility:
- A Hard Day's Night—The Beatles
- Welcome to the Jungle—Guns N' Roses
- "I'm gonna knock you out. Mama said knock you out."—LL Cool J
- Rat Race—Bob Marley
- We're Not Gonna Take It—Twisted Sister

Melancholy, depression:

- A Hard Rain's A–Gonna Fall—Bob Dylan
- The Loneliness of the Long Distance Runner—Iron Maiden
- Paint It Black—The Rolling Stones
- "Reflections of the way life used to be."—The Supremes
- Bittersweet Symphony—The Verve

Self-doubt:

- "I fought the law and the law won."—Bobby Fuller Four
- Livin' on a Prayer—Bon Jovi
- Should I Stay or Should I Go?—The Clash
- Should Have Been a Cowboy (instead of a lawyer)—Toby Keith
- Another One Bites the Dust—Queen

But don't let these answers bring you down. They were solicited at the end of a long, tough semester, seconds after students completed a grueling three-hour exam. And even then—even in the very worst of times—many students expressed excitement, hope, optimism, and pride, as in:

- I Feel Good—James Brown
- I Will Survive—Gloria Gaynor
- "Here I am, rock you like a hurricane."—The Scorpions
- Nothing's Gonna Stop Us Now—Jefferson Starship
- We are the Champions—Queen

Every time I use the song question, one or more students quote the Grateful Dead, describing the first semester as a "long strange trip." And indeed it is. So what are we waiting for? If you haven't already started, law school is probably looming on the not-too-distant horizon. It may be just months away, perhaps only weeks. You're probably wondering what you should be doing and feeling. Let's find out.

CHAPTER 2

PRE-TRIP PLANNING: WHAT TO DO BEFORE YOU ARRIVE

Incoming students naturally feel like they should be doing something to get ready for law school before they get there. They should be, but not necessarily the things they think they should be doing. Below are two pre-arrival "To Do" lists, one for intangibles and one for tangibles. Law students and law student advice usually focus on the tangibles, but the intangibles are just as important and some of them are harder to accomplish.

Pre-Arrival "To Do" List: The Intangibles

Be excited!

Be excited about going to law school. It's a big deal and you should treat it that way. Approach it with enthusiasm, not dread (distinguishing dread from a healthy apprehension), and certainly not apathy—nothing would be worse than that. My experience observing law students has taught me that President Harry Truman got it right when he said he had studied the lives of great people and "found that the men and women who got to the top were those who did the jobs they had in hand with everything they had of *energy and enthusiasm.*"

Law school is an entry pass to an exclusive club offering unique challenges, opportunities, and rewards. Your degree will grant you the power to single-handedly change people's lives for the better. That's what ordinary lawyers do every day.

4

In my original draft of this chapter, to inspire you, I talked about some big, important lawyers and how their big, important cases changed history. It was all true. Experience has shown time and again that lawyers are the only group with the conviction and courage to consistently stand up and fight for justice when it's unpopular to do so. Lawyers created the liberties we cherish and have fought to protect them for more than two hundred years. Thirty-three of the fifty-five framers of the U.S. Constitution were lawyers. An astonishing 60 percent of U.S. Presidents studied law. Tales about lawyers who altered the path of America could fill this and many other books.

But a conversation in the hallway with a 2L caused me to change course. As I was walking into class, he came up and recounted a dispute he'd been having with his landlord. He said he was able to resolve it because a lawyer offered to help him without charge because he was a struggling law student. The student told me: "Professor, I'm going to remember that when I become a lawyer. I'm going to remember what it felt like to have no money and no power and no voice and how that lawyer helped me."

That brought back to me the real heart and soul of what it means to be a lawyer. Big cases change history, but the smallest and simplest cases often have the biggest impact on ordinary people. I decided to cut the history lesson and tell you instead about a very tiny case I handled as a young lawyer. It was a pro bono case, meaning there was no fee involved. The Jacksonville, Florida legal aid organization called and asked if I would help an elderly man being sued by a home improvement contractor for breach of contract. I was tempted to say I was too busy—which I was, such is the life of a young litigation associate as many of you will learn—but I accepted the case.

My client was a man in his eighties whom I'll call Clarence Jackson. Mr. Jackson had shown up at the legal aid office clutching a packet of papers, explaining to the intake interviewer that he had signed a contract with a home improvement contractor to have some repairs done on his house for $1,000, a lot of money back then, especially for a man living on Social Security. He said the contractor didn't complete the work properly, so he refused to pay. The contractor hauled off and sued him and, in a letter, threatened to take his house away.

I drove out to the house on a hot, humid summer morning to meet Mr. Jackson. The house was in a neighborhood on "the other side of town" that I had never visited. Honestly, it wasn't much of a house. It was very small and very old, but exceptionally well-kept. Mr. Jackson greeted me at the door and I took an instant liking to him. He was a gentle, soft-spoken man of diminutive stature. He wore overalls and I felt ridiculous standing on the porch sweating in my lawyer power suit. He invited me in, showed me pictures of his kids and grandchildren, and gave me some iced tea. We sat in the living room looking over the contract and the legal complaint, then he took me on a tour of the premises.

He pointed out the shoddy workmanship by the contractor: bare, wrong-size fascia boards nailed haphazardly at the roof line, a toilet that poured water out the bottom every time it was flushed, a window several inches too small for the opening, etc. I remember getting mad. The nerve of that contractor to not only do such slapdash work, but sue Mr. Jackson and scare the heck out of him by threatening to take his home away.

I took some pictures with a Polaroid camera (this was long before the days of digital cameras) and went back to my office to prepare an affidavit for Mr. Jackson to sign and a motion for summary judgment in the lawsuit. Summary judgment is a way for a court to dispose of a case without a trial. We had a hearing on the motion in the judge's chambers. At the end, the judge granted our motion—dismissing the case—but with all the legalese the old man misunderstood. He thought we lost. When the judge adjourned the hearing, Mr. Jackson put his hand on my shoulder and said, "Thank you, Mr. McClurg, I know you did a good job. I guess some things just can't be helped." I said, "Mr. Jackson, it's okay. We won."[3]

He couldn't believe it. Literally. Maybe he went in believing the system would be stacked against him. When the victory finally sunk in, he just kept repeating "Thank you, thank you, thank you." I was embarrassed. I was still in my

3. I don't recall the exact words of the conversation in this or other anecdotes sprinkled throughout the book. I recount their substance to the best of my ability.

twenties. Here was a man who had done and seen far more than I ever had. But for just *a little bit* of my time, I'd changed his life.

A few days after the hearing, the receptionist buzzed me and said "There's a man out here who says he's your client." Mr. Jackson did not fit the profile of the firm's usual well-heeled clientele. I walked out to the receptionist area and there stood Mr. Jackson, still wearing overalls. He said he wanted to pay me and pulled a wad of bills from his pocket. He said it was a hundred dollars. I explained again that his was a pro bono case and that he didn't owe me anything. But he kept insisting he had to do something for me. Finally, he said, "Mr. McClurg, I'll tell you what. You come over to my house on Saturday and I'll cook you supper." (I had insisted he call me by my first name, but he never did.)

I went. And to this day I've never felt more proud to be a lawyer than that afternoon, sitting in that old man's blazing hot kitchen—he didn't have air conditioning—eating the dinner he made for me.

America is filled with "Mr. Jacksons"—people who desperately need help with legal problems that may seem small from the outside but which dominate their lives. Our system entrusts the awesome responsibility to give that help to one group: *lawyers*. People tend to think of doctors as being the primary life-saving profession, but make no mistake: lawyers have people's lives in their hands every day.

Start law school feeling proud about becoming part of a noble and honorable profession. Don't let the people around you sour you on studying to be a lawyer. The public has a love-hate relationship with lawyers. On the one hand, they're fascinated with the law and lawyers, as shown by the nonstop supply of books, movies, and television programming about them. On the other hand, people are quick to malign lawyers. Even total strangers will feel comfortable telling you lawyer jokes.

True story: I went on a canoeing trip with a group of law professors. You can imagine what a rollicking adventure that was. The woman at the canoe rental place asked what I did and I said, "Law professor." Without hesitating, she said, "I hate lawyers." Without hesitating, I said, "I hate people who rent canoes." She was shocked and appalled I would say something so rude. Although the irony escaped her, I felt good about standing up for my profession. Plus, I really do hate people who rent canoes.

Lawyers aren't perfect, and there are rotten apples in the bin of every profession, but as a fellow named Harrison Tweed said more than half a century ago: "With all their faults, [lawyers] stack up well against those in every other occupation or profession. They are better to work with or play with or fight with or drink with than most other varieties of mankind." Trust that the haters and joke-tellers will be the first ones running to a lawyer when they get in trouble.

Let the power of the law to right wrongs invigorate you. Let the grand tradition of lawyers in America make you proud. Be excited! If you're enthusiastic about law school, the workload will be more tolerable and you'll enjoy the experience much more. If you're not enthusiastic about law school before you get there, reconsider your decision to attend.

Get your life in order.

The first year of law school is all-consuming. The workload and volume of material you will be expected to master will be unlike anything you've ever encountered. To maximize your chances for success, you need to enter law school with your full focus on it.

Life distractions should be resolved before you get there. Don't be a procrastinator when it comes to getting your housing situation or financial aid firmed up. Having to work out kinks in either while starting school will not only take away needed time and energy, it will add extra stress you don't need. Law school will provide plenty of that.

If you're in a turbulent intimate relationship that you know deep down is going to end at some point anyway, the summer before law school is a good time to say goodbye. Don't drag it out until after law school starts. Law school takes a heavy toll even on good relationships. (Chapter 23 is devoted to the impact of law school on outside relationships.) No reason to jeopardize your success by wasting emotional energy on a relationship you know is already on life support.

For part-time evening-division students, employment conflicts are the biggest challenge and number one reason for failing to succeed. "Ti-ii-ii-ime is *not* on your side"[4] if you're going to be attending law school at night while working full-time. You will need a very specific time management plan before you get to law school. Chapter 22 addresses the unique challenges, including time management, faced by part-time evening students and nontraditional students generally.

Health issues are another source of interference with law school success. Unfortunately, people have less ability to control them than many other potential life distractions. If you face serious health issues as law school approaches, consider the prognosis for the immediate future, recognizing that the stress of law school can aggravate health conditions. If the prognosis for improvement before law school starts is unclear or not good, consider postponing law school until your health issues can be resolved. Schools often will grant deferments to admitted students for health reasons, meaning you can enroll in the next academic year without having to reapply.

Do not plan weddings, extended vacations, or pregnancies during the first year of law school. To the fullest extent possible, clear your calendar of major non-law school events from August through May of the first year.

Develop a financial plan.

Related to the above, you need a plan for financing your legal education, paying particular attention to ways to keep your student loan debt as low as possible. You have heard, or soon will, about the daunting financial challenges facing new law graduates. Many law students graduate with unmanageable debt-load, and, as of this writing, are doing so in a period where the legal employment sector remains precarious following the 2008 recession.

Predicting, as the saying goes, is always difficult, especially with regard to the future, but there is a suspicion in some quarters that the weaker legal job market is part of a

---

4. *See* THE ROLLING STONES, TIME IS ON MY SIDE (Verve 1963). This song became the Stones' first top ten single in the United States. Notice those big and small capital letters? Virtually unknown to the rest of the printed universe, they are vitally important to correct legal citation style per *The Bluebook*. You'll hear more about *The Bluebook* in future pages, but for an early insight into the compulsively detailed world of legal citation style, *The Bluebook* even has specific rules for referencing song titles. *See* THE BLUEBOOK: A UNIFORM SYSTEM OF CITATION R. 18.7.1, at 174–75 (Columbia Law Review Ass'n et al. eds., 19th ed. 2010) (setting forth rules for citing to audio recordings).

permanent paradigm shift in the profession rather than a temporary result of the recession. Technology advances, globalization, competition among lawyers, legal system reforms, and demands by business clients for lower costs all have been given as bases for forecasting permanent alterations in legal employment. Hopefully, rosier economic tidings for lawyers are on the horizon. In the meantime, take the following data to heart.

According to the American Bar Association (ABA), 2011 law graduates borrowed an average of $76,000 to attend public law schools and nearly $125,000 to attend private schools.[5] Data collected for the 2012 Law School Survey of Student Engagement, to which nearly 26,000 students responded, revealed that 31 percent of participating students anticipate graduating with more than $120,000 in loan debt, up from 18 percent in 2006.[6]

Meanwhile, the economic downturn inflicted a blow on the legal job market. ABA data showed that only 55 percent of 2011 law graduates were employed in permanent full-time jobs requiring a law degree within nine months of graduation (the standard measuring period).[7] The overall 2011 employment rate after nine months was significantly higher: 84.7 percent according to data gathered by the National Association of Law Placement, but even that seemingly high figure was the lowest since 1994.[8] The lower ABA percentage reflects new employment reporting rules that require law schools to distinguish between permanent full-time jobs requiring a law degree and all other jobs. It is underinclusive to the extent that it excludes some good jobs that don't require a law degree, as well as the growing number of lawyers who work for firms on a contract basis (some by choice and some because those are the only jobs they could find) and are not considered fulltime employees. On the other hand, the old

---

5. ABA Section Legal Educ. & Admissions to the Bar, *Average Amount Borrowed for Law School 2001–2010*, STATISTICS, http://www.americanbar.org/content/dam/aba/administrative/legal_ed ucation_and_admissions_to_the_bar/sta tistics/avg_amnt_brwd.authcheckdam. pdf.

6. LAW SCH. SURVEY OF STUDENT ENGAGEMENT, *LSSSE 2012 Overview*, *in* LAW SCHOOL REPORT 2012 [hereinafter 2012 LAW SCH. SURVEY OF STUDENT ENGAGEMENT].

7. The complete 2011 Employment Summary Report, including data for individual schools, can be accessed at http://employmentsummary.abaquestion naire.org/.

8. Press Release, NALP, Law School Grads Face Worst Job Market Yet—Less Than Half Find Jobs in Private Practice (June 7, 2012), http://www.nalp.org/uploads/PressReleases/Classof2011ERSS SelectedFindingsPressRelease.pdf.

rules were overinclusive because they did not distinguish between legal jobs and working at *Starbucks*.

Assuming you're committed to law school and becoming a lawyer, don't let these admittedly daunting figures deter you, but *do* let them influence your behavior. As explained in Chapter 20, I'm convinced most students could shave off a significant percentage of their loan debt simply by making it a point to live more frugally. If you're living on borrowed money, attend law school with the mindset that you will do everything *reasonably* (law's favorite standard of conduct) within your power to keep your debt low.

In choosing a law school, don't rely solely on the *U.S. News & World Report* rankings, as too many students unwisely do. Take into account the costs of tuition and living. Attending a private law school in an expensive locale can double or even triple your loan debt compared to attending a public school in a city with a low cost of living. Depending on the school, it might be worth the extra outlay, but in many cases it isn't. Estimate your consumption expenses in advance and do everything you can to minimize them. Strongly consider living with roommates or even with your parents if that's feasible, to cut down dwelling costs—the largest consumption expense of all.

It's almost impossible for most students to escape law school without debt, but the lower the amount, the better off you will be. Heavy debt will weigh down not only your bank account for as long as twenty years, but press heavily on you psychologically. Chapter 20 gives more details about this major un-doer of student well-being, including some tips on how to minimize your debt.

Approach law school like a full-time job.

The single most important thing you should be doing prior to law school is developing the proper mindset. Transposing a classic U.S. military recruiting slogan, law school's not just an adventure—it's a job. If every law student approached law school as they would a full-time job, more would excel at it. Accept that law school is going to be a full-time endeavor marked by long, sometimes tedious hours. Accept that you're going to have to sacrifice a lot of the leisure time you enjoyed in your pre-law student life.

Think about it. Suppose instead of going to law school, you accepted a career-type job in your field of study from undergraduate school, a job offering potentially great rewards for good performance, as well as the possibility of getting canned for poor performance. Would you:

- Show up late for work?
- Browse the web and send Facebook messages to friends during important company meetings?
- Arrive unprepared for a meeting with your boss?
- Skip work on days when you have a conflicting social event?
- Stay out late drinking and partying on weeknights when you know you have to get up early and go to work?
- Search for ways to cut corners in completing important job assignments, rather than giving them your best effort?

Presumably the answer to each question would be *no*, yet some law students follow exactly these behavioral patterns in law school. If you approach law school as a full-time job, you will have already charted a course toward success.

Forget what you think you know about law.

You've heard the adage that a little knowledge is a dangerous thing. Nowhere is this truer than when starting law school. On the first day of Torts, I tell my students that if they think they know something about the law, *please* try to forget it. Why? Because everything people think they know about the law when they get to law school is wrong, incomplete, taken out of context, or not in the form that your professors will want you to know it.

Beginning students without any legal background are sometimes alarmed when it seems that some of their classmates already know a lot about the law. Perhaps these students took a few undergraduate law courses. Some may have worked as secretaries or paralegals at law firms. Don't worry. The latter may know something about how law is practiced in real life, but no one without a legal education really knows anything about "the law." Most important, no one coming to law school knows anything about law that will be useful in helping them perform academically in the first year.

Trust that law school will teach you what you need to know, or at least give you the tools to acquire that knowledge. That's why you can go to law school with an undergraduate degree in religion or art history, but can attend medical school only with a background in science. Arrive at law school imagining your brain as a fresh sponge, right out of the package, ready to absorb a whole new world of information and way of thinking.

Expect and embrace uncertainty.

New law students arrive expecting the law to be a neat and tidy catalog of rules that they can memorize and, by doing so, become successful students and lawyers. They're perplexed and frustrated to discover that so much of law is awash in shades of gray rather than black and white. "It depends" is the most accurate answer to many legal questions. Students also struggle with the fact that the complex pieces of law do not fit neatly together like a jigsaw puzzle.

Part of this indeterminacy stems from the fact that the U.S. is a "common law" legal system. Most of the rest of the world, including all of Europe and Latin America, follows what is known as the "civil law tradition." Common law is judge-made law, derived from and developed through case precedent. In civil law systems, law is derived primarily from codes—i.e., books of neatly organized statutes promulgated by legislators. In theory, judges have no power to make law in civil law systems. Their job is to follow the rules set forth in the codes. (It doesn't really work that way in practice, as all legal language requires interpretation.)

Exasperated by the indefiniteness of the law, U.S. law students frequently utter comments such as, "Why don't they just write all the rules down in one place? That way, we'd know what the law is!" Without realizing it, they're advocating for a civil law system. Someone actually tried to do that once. In the eighteenth century, Frederick the Great implemented the Prussian Code under Prussia's civil law system. The Prussian Code stands as an attempt to install what so many U.S. law students desperately wish for: a detailed compendium of rules intended to foresee and govern the entire range of human conduct. The Prussian Code contained more than 17,000 provisions setting forth specific rules designed to govern specific fact situations. It didn't work. Even 17,000 provisions proved to be insufficient to cover all varieties of human conduct. Seventeen million provisions would not be enough.

When I workshopped a chapter of this book with a group of law professors, I asked them to name the most important traits of successful law students. Immediately, one of my colleagues blurted, "The ability to embrace uncertainty!" Accept before you arrive at law school that much of law is vague and malleable, as it must be to address the infinite permutations in facts that comprise legal disputes.

Here's an example, from criminal law, to prepare you for the abyss of ambiguity that is law. A federal statute, 21 U.S.C. § 924(c)(1), imposes a mandatory minimum enhanced sentence of five years for one who uses or "carries" a firearm during and in relation to the commission of a drug-trafficking crime. Sounds clear enough. Everyone understands what "carries" means, right? If you have your phone in your pocket, purse, or backpack, you're carrying it. If you forget it and leave it at home, you're not. Surely such a simple word could not lead to a protracted legal dispute. It did.

In *United States v. Foster*,[9] the police pulled over the defendant and arrested him for drug-trafficking when they found methamphetamine in his pickup truck. They also arrested him for "carrying" a firearm during the commission of a drug-trafficking crime. But the gun wasn't found on the defendant's person. It was in the bed of his truck under a buttoned-down tarp. Was he "carrying" the gun within the meaning of the statute? It took years to find the answer. The trial court ruled he was carrying it, but nine years of appeals and many pages of judicial opinions later, a U.S. Court of Appeals held that the defendant was not carrying the gun within the meaning of the statute. His conviction on the firearm charge was reversed. Nine years of appeals over the meaning of *a single word*. Well, at least the issue was finally settled once and for all ... until the U.S. Supreme Court came along and ruled in a different case that transporting guns in vehicles *does* constitute carrying them.[10] Oh well.

---

9. 133 F.3d 704 (9th Cir. 1998).

10. Muscarello v. United States, 524 U.S. 125, 126–27 (1998) (holding that

Students who fixate on searching for *the* answer to every legal question can drive both themselves and their professors mad. Arrive open to the idea that the answer to many legal questions is a range of possibilities, frequently dependent on the facts of the case, rather than a single rock-solid right answer. Embrace uncertainty.

Define "success" for yourself.

Figure out what you want out of law school before you get there. "Success" can mean different things to different people. For most incoming students, success means achieving at a high academic level and this book operates on the assumption that "grade success" is at least part of the goal for most readers. But not all students come to law school with the goal of graduating in the top echelon of their class. Many part-time students with existing careers, for example, attend law school to advance their lives and careers in a practical way. They're interested in getting a law degree, not necessarily a law degree with honors.

Of course, every student has a goal of succeeding at an academic level high enough to avoid being academically dismissed, so advice pertaining to academic success applies to every student at some level. Hopefully, your academic aspirations are higher than the bare minimum necessary to avoid getting booted out of law school, but if they're not, filter the advice herein in accordance with your own goals.

But success also has meaning beyond academic achievement. Many students care about *more* than just grades. In addition to academic success, they care about things like justice, exploration, enlightenment, general happiness, and becoming a "professional."

Define success for yourself. Literally. Put it in writing. Begin the sentence with "My definition of success in law school is . . ." and complete the sentence. Or make a list if your idea of success includes several components. Putting it in writing will force you to think more concretely about what you really want and need out of law school. Revisit the definition as you progress through the first year. If you notice it changing, stop and consider why. As discussed later, law school has a way of changing people's goals and values.

one "who knowingly possesses and con- them within the meaning of the en-
veys firearms in a vehicle" is carrying hanced sentencing statute).

Pre–Arrival "To Do" List: The Tangibles

Some tangible tasks also should be on your pre-law school "To Do" list, although not as many as you might think. Let's take a look.

Buy some books (but not as many as everyone wants you to buy).

Books, books, and more books. Everywhere you turn. Piles of books. Thick books. Expensive books. Complex books. Distinctively colored red, blue, black, brownish-red, and gray books. If the law could have intimate relations, it would be with a book. It wouldn't be pretty, but a lot of things in law aren't. This section breaks down the different types of books associated with starting law school and offers advice on what to buy and when to buy it.

● **Law school recommended reading lists.** Law schools may inadvertently perpetuate a belief among incoming students that they should be trying to learn about the law and legal analysis before getting to law school by distributing or posting lists of recommended prelaw reading lists. The lists sometimes include more than fifty books. One law school recommends more than three hundred books.

Many of the recommended books are deep, dense tomes about jurisprudence and legal history. Some of the works that regularly appear on these lists, such as Karl Llewellyn's *The Bramblebush: On Our Law and Its Study* (1951) and Edward H. Levi's *An Introduction to Legal Reasoning* (1949), are classics that should be read at some point in every lawyer's life. But laboring to comprehend this dense material, especially without any context, may spike your anxiety level and fry your synapses before you ever set foot in the door.

Certainly, much good would come from reading the great books about American jurisprudence and legal history. In a perfect world with unlimited free time, every law student, lawyer, and law professor should read them all. We'd be smarter, better-informed, and more capable readers and thinkers. But, of course, most people don't have that kind of time. The good news is that you don't need to read any of the heady tomes to do well in law school.

If you insist on doing serious legal reading prior to law school, select books that explain the institutions and functioning of American government, particularly the structures and roles of courts. Because legal writing is so important to success as a law student and lawyer, another good choice would be Bryan Garner's *The Elements of Legal Style* (2002), a legal version of Strunk & White's classic writing handbook, *The Elements of Style*. Avoid all books that purport to teach law per se.

● **"How to Succeed" books.** Many of the recommended reading lists include less lofty books from the "how to succeed in law school" genre. A variety of these books exists. Most of them offer good information and advice. Some of the books written by law professors are excellent. This one, of course, is indispensable. (Successfully fought off urge to insert smiley-face emoticon, for which I know you are grateful.)

I intentionally did not look at any of the other law school prep books while composing this one because I didn't want to be influenced by them, even if only unconsciously. After I finished the manuscript to the first edition, I did scan several of them. What I discovered was affirming. Much of the advice is not only consistent with my advice, but remarkably identical to it. Not all of it though. I came across advice in books written by non-law professors that was at times amusing, without intending to be, and at times downright scary. Sift through all advice in law school prep books, including this one, with a discerning eye. Be wary of books that offer shortcuts to success.

● **Inspirational books.** For enjoyable inspiration about your new pursuit, check out one of these page-turners showing the power of lawyers and the law to change lives:

● Jonathan Harr, *A Civil Action* (1996). A tenacious, flamboyant lawyer gives his all in taking on a large corporation accused of dumping cancer-causing solvents into the groundwater in Woburn, Masschusetts. John Travolta and Robert Duvall starred in an inferior 1998 movie version.

● Anthony Lewis, *Gideon's Trumpet* (1964). A small-time criminal named Clarence Earl Gideon changes history by appealing his burglary conviction to the U.S. Supreme Court, resulting in a landmark decision establishing the right to counsel for indigent criminal defendants. Henry Fonda played Gideon in a 1979 movie version, but the book is better.

- Harper Lee, *To Kill a Mockingbird* (1960). Friends chastised me for leaving this classic out of the first edition. I assumed all students would have been made to read it before escaping high school, but that apparently is no longer true. This Pulitzer-winning tale of Southern lawyer Atticus Finch's defense of a wrongly accused man in a racially charged rape trial is not only the best legal book ever written, but one of the best books, period. In a questionnaire, I ask incoming students: What made you want to become a lawyer? A recent 1L said she read *To Kill a Mockingbird* as a high school freshman and Atticus Finch's courtroom speech set her on her legal career path. The movie version won three Oscars. Gregory Peck's depiction of Atticus Finch earned him the ultimate cinematic accolade. In 2003, the American Film Institute named him the number one movie hero of all time. Imagine that: a lawyer is America's top film hero.

- **Study aids.** You will become very familiar with law school "study aids." A study aid is a book that, unlike your casebooks, clearly explains the law in a particular subject area, either in an outline or treatise-like format. Study aids have traveled an interesting journey through legal education. When I was in law school, our professors threatened us with mayhem if they laid eyes on a study aid in class. Professors referred to them derisively as "commercial" study aids, as if expensive casebooks are distributed by non-profit organizations. While some professors still look down on study aids, many actually recommend particular study aids to students.

Law school study aid series generally break down into four basic types: (1) outlines of the law in particular subject areas, sometimes keyed to popular casebooks; (2) treatise-like works that explain the law of a subject area in an expository non-outline format; (3) exam-prep series containing practice essay and/or multiple-choice questions and analyses (many of the outline series also contain practice questions); and (4) "canned brief" series containing case briefs of all of the cases appearing in particular casebooks. Good news! One of the best and most frequently used study aids—CALI (Computer–Assisted Legal Instruction) computer exercises—is free to law students. CALI is a non-profit consortium of law professors, who have prepared sets of online practice questions in just about every subject area.

The overall quality of modern law school study aids is high because most are written by law professors who are experts in the particular field. At last count, there were more than fifty different *series* of law school study aid books. Several of the series feature dozens of titles. The long-running West Nutshell Series has books in more than 160 subject areas. The sheer length of the list of available study aid series should convince you not to rush out and start buying any of them until you acquire more information about what you really need.

That so many study aids exist flags one of the oddest aspects of legal education. Law is the only educational discipline where students feel compelled to routinely buy external books to explain what they're supposed to be learning from their assigned books. I surveyed a 1L class asking how many study aids they purchased during the first year and the answers ranged from zero to twelve, with an average of four. One student said he snatched up twenty-five study aids from a 3L in exchange for paying the 3L's bar tab at the annual Barrister's Ball, one more reason to socialize with your colleagues. My strategy in law school was to find one good study aid for each course.

Study aids can be helpful not only in elucidating legal doctrine but in casting what you're learning into a coherent framework that makes it easier to see the big picture. Depending on the professor, they can be a lifesaver. Frankly, some professors just aren't very good at or concerned about conveying the law they expect you to know for the exam in a complete or organized fashion.

Just don't make the mistake of substituting study aids for reading your casebook assignments and taking good notes in class. Study aids are only useful as a supplement to, not a replacement for, your casebooks. In grading exams, professors want you to present the law in the way they taught it to you. It's always obvious when students are regurgitating something they read in a study aid because the content and presentation will be different from the way the professor taught it. That doesn't mean the answer is necessarily wrong, although it can be, but it won't fit the professor's conception

of how the issue should be analyzed and, thus, their precon-
ception of what they're looking for in exam answers.

• **Books required and recommended by professors.**
The only books you absolutely must buy are those your
professors assign as "required." Your law school will post a
list of these books on its website and probably also email you
or give you a hard copy list. For most courses, your main
required book will be a "casebook." See Chapter 7 for a
discussion of casebooks and the case method of teaching.

Some casebooks come with paperbound supplements (sold
separately, of course) containing new cases and statutes
designed to keep the book up-to-date until the next edition
comes out. It's easy to overlook the supplements, so take your
time when reviewing the list and make sure you get everything you need.

Buy all required texts and make sure you buy the *correct
edition*. Casebooks are updated in new editions every few
years. Because the page numbers always will be different, an
outdated edition is worthless even if 99 percent of the content
stays the same. You won't be able to follow the assignments
and you won't be able to follow along in class if you don't
have the correct edition. When the professor says, "Let's read
the case holding at the top of page 825, four lines down," you
don't want to be lost. Required texts simply are not an item
to skimp on.

An age-old quandary faced by higher-education students
at every level is whether to buy new or used books. Law
school texts are expensive. New casebooks can cost more than
$200. 1Ls can expect to fork out up to $1000 for new first-
semester books. Used books cost less, but even when I was a
destitute law student, I opted for new books, and you should
do the same if you can manage it financially. You want to be
able to learn the law and legal analysis without the distraction of someone else's (and maybe several persons depending
on how old the book is) thought pattern memorialized by
highlighting, underlining, and marginalia. For all you know,
that someone could have flunked out of law school. As one
student put it, "I advise people coming to law school to not
buy used books because some idiot will have highlighted
everything you don't want to know in every case." But even
if you could lay your hands on the used book of the person

who wrote the top exam for the course, you're still better off learning from a clean slate.

If you buy used books, look through them to find the ones with the least markings. As one former student wrote:

> As a 1L, I bought "used" as much as possible, but my Property book taught me the hard lesson that it's worth the time to sit in the bookstore and rifle through all the used options before buying. I didn't think it would bother me, but several generations of different colored highlighting and writing in the margins made the reading much more difficult. I probably looked weird in later years spending thirty minutes in the bookstore looking through the used books for the ones with the least writing in them, but I think it was worth it.

Law school book buying is much more complicated than it used to be. In the not-so-distant past, all law students bought their required texts at the law school or university bookstore. Today, many students buy their books online. I consulted a student who is an entrepreneurial book-buying expert. He advises buying online as a way to save money, cautioning that "you need to buy at least a few weeks before classes start or the market will spike and you'll pay about the same price as in the bookstore." Other students stress ordering online books well in advance for a different reason: to avoid expedited shipping costs.

Amazon and other booksellers list used copies at greatly reduced prices, but one problem with buying used books online is that you can't check their condition in advance. Students tell me that "good condition" to a used law book seller does not mean the same thing to law students (see student comment above about overly highlighted and scribbled-in books).

A recent development in law school book marketing is the renting of books by law school bookstores and publishers. It seems like a good deal. Students can rent books at a substantially lower cost than purchasing them new, use them during the semester (and are even allowed to write in them), then turn them back in. But my source says, "Not so fast." He explains that while you can rent books cheaper than you can buy them, students can come out ahead by buying books online at a discount, then selling them back when they're finished with them.

It also should be noted that many law students like to keep their books rather than resell them after the course, thinking they will be useful to consult in the future. In truth, that rarely happens, but they do make sharp-looking additions to any bookcase. Once you're a law student, you will notice when watching television or movies that office backgrounds often have law books in the bookshelves, even if it's not a lawyer office. I kept my casebooks for years before selling them at a garage sale.

Finally, some law book publishers offer online versions of casebooks, a trend sure to expand, at lower prices than bound copies. Some of these are downloadable, but many are non-downloadable and can only be accessed online. Check with your professors before going the electronic route. As we'll discuss, some professors ban computers in class, so electronic books won't be an option. And food for thought: A 3L who used electronic books in most of his classes said he got called on in class a lot more often because his professors thought he was just playing on his computer.

Electronic books are, no doubt, the future of publishing. I wouldn't be surprised if when the time comes for a third edition of *1L of a Ride*, you'll have no option but to purchase an electronic version because paper books will have ceased to exist. I prefer hard copies of reading material because I learn better reading from and marking on paper than from a computer screen, but the times, as Bob Dylan sang, they are a-changing. While I would have thought reading comprehension from electronic books would be lower than for paper books, some recent research shows no difference in learning outcome between electronic and hard copy books.[11]

Consistent with what I've already said, don't attempt to read even required books prior to starting law school, other than your first assignments, of course. Not only will it be a waste of time, it will be counterproductive because you won't have a proper foundation or context to understand what

---

11. *See* Rey Hernandez–Julian & Christina Peters, *Does the Medium Matter? Online Versus Paper Coursework*, 78 S. ECON. J. 1333 (2012) (finding no difference in learning outcomes in study of college economic students randomly divided into two groups, one which learned from electronic text and one which learned from paper text).

you're reading. Nor will you remember any of it. I once had a student who spent the summer before law school reading and briefing the cases in her casebooks. When she boasted this fact to me at the beginning of the semester, I cringed. I respected her for being so motivated and diligent, but knew she had made a grave error. I told her to throw away everything she had prepared and start fresh, but she didn't listen. She attempted to rely on her pre-prepared briefs in the first semester. Sadly, because she was a dedicated student and nice person, she did not make it past the first year.

At most, skim through your casebooks to get a feel for what a casebook is. Look at the table of contents. Read the preface. Okay, I know you won't be able to resist taking a peek at some of the cases, but don't try to understand them until you get to law school.

In addition to required texts, many professors list one or more *recommended* texts. Some of them might be study aids. With regard to books that are merely recommended, even by the professor, it's generally wise to hold off buying them until you get more information. Some professors may list several recommended books, none of which you really need. Or they may list several study aids, any one of which would suffice. Since you won't need any of these books until law school starts, wait until you arrive before shelling out cash for them. The exception is if the professor has recommended a *single* study aid for the course. A professor generally would do that only if he or she had personally reviewed and approved of the content as consistent with the way the prof teaches the course. Buy it.

● **Law dictionary.** At the beginning of law school you'll be inundated with words and phrases that are foreign to you. Some professors will expect you to look up all unfamiliar legal terms and express disapproval if they call on you to ask the meaning of a term and you don't know the answer. An important part of the first year of law school is learning the language of the law.

In the past, virtually all new law students purchased a copy of *Black's Law Dictionary*, the classic legal dictionary. I still recommend buying a copy. It's a book with a long practical shelf-life. Even experienced lawyers have to look up legal terms from time to time. The hardcover version (ninth edition as of this writing) makes for a nice long-term bookshelf acquisition, but the paperbound version (fourth edition) will suit most of your needs, sells for half as much, and is much more portable.

Definitions of legal terms can be found online, of course, and many modern students opt for Google over *Black's*, but be aware that online definitions are not always accurate or complete. Westlaw, a legal research database with which you will become very familiar, offers *Black's Law Dictionary* online. Depending on the school, however, you might not be granted access to Westlaw (or its rival LexisNexis, which features a different legal dictionary) at the very beginning of law school.

If you buy a legal dictionary, as with all law books, you're better off with the latest edition, but if you're on a tight budget, you can scrimp here and get by with a used, older edition. Most of the terms you'll be looking up have been around for a long, long time.

Discover your "law-learning personality."

Most law students are bright people. Beyond that, it's hard to generalize about them. As is true of any large group of people, an entering law school class contains a wide variety of personality types. Teaching and learning styles that work best for some students don't work as well for others. Similarly, not all law school advice works equally well for all people. If you're interested in figuring out your own law-learning style, a couple of excellent tools are available to do just that.

Many years ago, a college English professor auditing Torts introduced me to the Myers–Briggs Type Indicator (MBTI), an instrument for measuring personality preferences based on Swiss psychologist Carl Jung's research into psychological types. The MBTI is designed to help people understand certain core personality preferences that affect the way they gather information, make decisions, organize their lives, and interact with people and the world around them. If the name sounds familiar, it could be that you've already taken the MBTI in a different educational or career context. The MBTI is the world's most widely administered personality measuring instrument for mentally "normal" (if there is such a thing) people. Roughly two million people take the MBTI each year.

The MBTI identifies sixteen psychological types based on eight paired personality preferences:

Extraversion vs. Introversion (how we direct and develop our energy—inward or outward—and interact with the world around us)

Sensing vs. Intuition (how we perceive and take in information upon which to make decisions)

Thinking vs. Feeling (how we make decisions)

Judging vs. Perceiving (the ways we organize our lives and operate in the world)

A person's type is a four-letter combination of their preferences as to all four pairings. For example, I'm an ENFJ (Extraverted, Intuitive, Feeling, Judging). Each type has strengths and weaknesses for adapting to different education, employment, and relationship settings.

Several excellent books have been written about the MBTI and psychological typing, but law students have the benefit of an outstanding MBTI book written just for them: *Juris Types: Learning Law through Self–Understanding* (2007).[12] Authors Martha and Don Peters are MBTI gurus who have spent decades researching the MBTI and its application to law students. *Juris Types* is filled with practical information about the learning strengths and weaknesses for each of the sixteen MBTI types in tackling the core challenges of law school: studying, classroom participation, and exam-writing.

Let's use Extraversion and Introversion as an example. The Peters' research shows that Extraverts find it easier to participate in class and enjoy working in study groups, while Introverts may not be able to access and demonstrate their knowledge as easily when called on in class and need and prefer solitary over group study. Extraverts tend to write more on exams, but may analyze problems at a superficial level due in part to an absence of external verbal cues. Introverts may engage in deeper internal analysis, but may not write down everything they've mentally processed.[13] For each type, the Peters offer strategies about how to maximize strengths and overcome challenges. If you're curious about how your personality is cut out for the different ways of

---

12. MARTHA M. PETERS & DON PETERS, JURIS TYPES: LEARNING LAW THROUGH SELF–UNDERSTANDING (2007).

13. *See id.* at 26–30.

learning law, take the MBTI (it's available online for a fee) or track down your old results if you've taken it before and read the Peters' book.

Even if you don't take the MBTI or read the Peters' book, it's important to recognize and be aware that students have different learning styles. As Professor Chris Coughlin recommends in Chapter 18, one way to bolster your self-understanding is to look back on your educational experiences and "determine whether there is a common denominator in the teachers, environments, situations, and subjects in which you responded most positively and successfully." While Coughlin's suggestion is directed at legal writing courses, it applies across the board. Think also about the other side of the coin: to which kinds of teachers, environments, situations, and subjects did you *not* respond positively?

In addition to helping you succeed at a higher level, developing an awareness of your learning preferences can help you overcome confusion and self-doubt arising from differences between the ways you and your classmates are experiencing law school. You'll better understand, for example, why some of your classmates love the way Professor X teaches, while you find her impossible to follow, or why you love contract law and hate constitutional law when your best friend feels exactly the opposite.

Another important aspect of learning styles involves students with learning disabilities. If you have or think you might have a learning or other disability, you could be entitled to accommodations such as, depending on the type of disability, longer time for exams or being permitted to take them in an isolated room. A student who suffers from ADHD (Attention Deficit Hyperactivity Disorder) urged me to address this issue in this second edition and offered some useful information and suggestions:

> For 0Ls who have or might have a learning disability and are still in undergraduate school, I recommend they call the disability services office at their undergraduate institution and inquire about the cost of doing the requisite disability testing there. If testing is expensive or unavailable, then call the law schools to which you've been accepted and inquire about testing there. Testing can cost between $200 (at a school with a graduate psychology department and an active psy-

chological counseling and testing center) to upwards of $2,000 (at a private psychological testing office). If you are moving great distances and are on anti-anxiety or ADHD meds, you'll need recent testing so that a psychiatrist in your new location will treat you. Particularly in the case of ADHD meds (colloquially regarded as "steroids" for the brain) and law students, psychiatrists are reluctant to prescribe these drugs because of abuses. Because of a presumption that law students are seeking them for performance enhancement, rather than genuine need, *you must get the testing done before you set foot in orientation*. Work with your disability services counselor and develop a plan that works for you. Don't be too proud, and don't worry about what others say about any testing accommodations you might receive.

Buy a notebook computer and become adept at using it.

By the time you're about to enter law school, it's too late to perfect the most important skills you will need—such as reading comprehension and writing skills—but one important ability you might still have time to hone is your computer adeptness. Notebook computers are standard appendages for modern law students. By notebook computer, I'm referring to any type of portable computer with a keyboard.

Here's why you will need one and need to be proficient at using it:

• **Note-taking.** Most undergraduate students already own notebook computers, but might not have used them on an everyday basis to take notes in class. Effective note-taking is essential to succeeding in most law school courses. The avalanche of complex material covered in class comes at students quickly. If you can type faster than you write by hand, you'll be able to capture more of the key points. This does not mean that you want to try to transcribe every word spoken. Some students make that mistake, but, as covered in Chapter 12, most students err on the side of taking too few class notes rather than too many.

Computerized notes also are easier to add to, edit, and reorganize. Moreover, much of the content of your course outlines (see Chapter 13) will be inputted from your class notes. Taking class notes on a computer will save the time and effort of having to transcribe them for outlining purposes later. (On the other hand, some students report a strong benefit in having to retype their class notes as a form of periodic review, which is a crucial component of law school success.)

Be aware that the use of computers in classrooms is controversial among law professors. Some professors ban them, citing as reasons: (1) Computers turn some students into stenographers who attempt to transcribe the entire class, an ineffective note-taking strategy; (2) Too many students abuse their in-class computer privileges by browsing the web, checking email, etc.; (3) Due to the first two reasons, computers cause students to disengage from class and class discussion; and (4) Computer users—especially misusers—are a distraction to the students sitting around them.

Some students reject using computers for note-taking for some of the same reasons, including this student who was number one in her class:

> I do not find computers helpful in the classroom setting, although I'm sure I don't speak for most students. I never use mine in class. I know I am in the minority here, but I have always written much faster than I type. Even after becoming more proficient on the keyboard, I continue to retain much more information when I write. I have talked to a number of people who notice a similar difference in their retention of material when they write as opposed to type. For example, our Civil Procedure class last year did not allow laptop usage. Despite the difficulty of this class, some of my classmates did better in Civil Procedure than in their other classes where laptops were permitted. As a result, these students have made the decision to no longer use laptops to take notes in class and have indicated to me that they are already noticing an improvement in retention. Additionally, I think there is a lot of merit to the argument that laptop usage in class gets in the way of students engaging with the material.

Her points are well-taken and hard to argue with since she performed so well. But note, significantly, her statement that she writes "much faster" by hand than by keyboard. If that is true about you as well, it undermines one of the principal advantages of computers for note-taking. On a broader level, her comments reaffirm the point that there is no single right answer to many of the questions as to the "best way" to do things in law school because students and learning styles are different.

- **Exam-taking.** Regardless of whether you choose to take class notes on a computer, you will want to use a computer to take exams. Almost all students do. Only two students out of seventy in my most recent Torts class hand-wrote their exams.

The same basic reasons why computers can be valuable for taking notes—faster writing and more efficient editing and reorganization—also support using a computer for exams. Accurate, complete legal analysis requires much more depth than most students allot to it on exams. While longer is not always better, as discussed in Chapter 16, in reviewing Torts exams, I found that the top-scoring essay-writers wrote, on average, about 40 percent more words than the lowest scorers.

Using a computer to type essay exam answers also facilitates clarity and organization. Law schools require students to install anti-cheating software on their computers for exams. Basically, these software programs convert your computer into a high-tech typewriter by blocking access to files, programs, and the internet. The security software gives schools the flexibility to enable or disable various word-processing functions. Most schools, for example, disable the spell-check function to avoid giving computer users an advantage over hand-writers, but they usually leave the cut-and-paste function enabled, which is a much bigger advantage. Because organization counts big-time on essay exams, being able to easily rearrange text is a tremendous luxury.

Taking exams on computer also avoids problems that arise from illegible handwriting. Several non-law school studies have shown that students with better handwriting get better grades than students with poor handwriting. Typed words beat the best handwriting in the world. Anything you can do to make your exams more presentable and readable gives you a boost.

In 2001, three professors at Brigham Young University published a study in which they empirically tested the proposition that computer users have an advantage over hand-writers on law school exams. While more extensive and updated data would be needed to draw reliable conclusions, the study found that computer users received higher grades.[14]

● **Miscellaneous other uses.** Apart from note- and exam-taking, a notebook computer with wireless capabilities will be essential to your everyday law school life. While at school—but not in class!—you will be doing online legal research, working on legal writing assignments, briefing cases, reviewing notes, composing course outlines, checking email, etc.

Buy other essential school supplies.

In addition to books and a computer, I recommend obtaining:

● **A three-ring binder with tabbed dividers.** Three-ring binders are an efficient way to organize and keep track of all of your course materials (e.g., notes, case briefs, out-lines, course handouts). Some students use a separate binder for each course, while some opt for a single binder wide enough to include materials for all their courses. More and more students rely on their computers as digital binders, using computer note-taking programs such as Microsoft One-Note to organize and manage their course data. (See Chapter 12 for a discussion of OneNote.) But even if you go the digital route, you are going to end up with hard copies of some items, such as course handouts, that you will need to keep track of in an organized fashion.

● **A heavy-duty three-hole punch.** If you go the three-ring binder route, spring for a three-hole punch. You don't want to be jamming holes in the paper with the binder ring like we did back in elementary school. Get a heavy duty one. They don't call it "the paper chase" for nothing.

---

14. *See* Kif Augustine–Adams, Suzanne B. Hendrix & James R. Rasband, *Pen or Printer: Can Students Afford to Handwrite Their Exams?*, 51 J. LEGAL EDUC. 118 (2001). Reviewing 2,588 first-year exams, the authors concluded that both mean and median grades were higher for students who typed their exams over students who handwrote them. Although the difference was small (roughly one-tenth of a point on a 4.0 scale), the authors said it was enough to make a significant difference in class rank for many students at BYU. Possible explanations offered by the authors for the higher grades by computer users included the easier readability of typed exams and the ability to write longer answers.

• **A heavy-duty stapler.** Similarly, you'll be turning in legal writing assignments and printing out a lot of cases and articles for research that will require stapling. Invest in a heavy-duty stapler that can drill staples through at least fifteen pages without crumpling.

• **A box of highlighters.** You'll need more, but one box will get you started. I still stick with monochromatic yellow, but many students use a color-coded highlighting system when reading cases.

• **A large backpack or airline carry-on-type bag with wheels.** You're going to be carting around a ton of stuff in law school. Casebooks are thick and heavy. You'll also have your computer and accessories, study aids, research for your legal research and writing course, notes, briefs, outlines (preferably neatly organized in three-ring binders as described above), and personal items to carry. Most students opt for large backpacks, but many go for luggage on wheels. Today's law school classrooms look like a combination of a Sierra Club backpacking base camp and a gate area at LaGuardia.

Forget style. Functionality is the key. This comment from a 1L about things she wished she knew at the beginning of law school made me smile:

> I remember the first day I brought this cute laptop bag thinking of how professional I looked. When I got to school I realized that I couldn't fit any of my books in it. And after seeing everyone with their huge back-packs the first day, as soon as I got out of class I went and bought a huge backpack of my own. I think I ended up with one of the biggest backpacks in the class!

• **A day planner.** One of the top habits of successful law students is that they are organized. Chapter 10 explains why you need to assiduously keep track of the many events and deadlines in your new law school life. No surprise to you that an old guy like me still prefers keeping track of life on a day planner made of real paper, rather than on a smart phone or computer. I figured I was a dinosaur in this regard until a recent office meeting with three law review editors (all top students) during which I set a date for a future event and watched in surprise as all three pulled out their old-fashioned day planners to write it down. If you follow suit, make sure you get one with pages and calendar spaces large enough to pencil in several items per day.

Of course, keeping track of schedules on electronic devices is perfectly fine if you're adept at using—and *will* use—the calendaring function.

Relax and enjoy!

Finally, here's a "To Do" task that's easy to get behind. Surprising as it may sound, one of the best ways to prepare for law school, assuming you have your life in order, is to just kick back and enjoy your summer. Unless you plan on attending another graduate program after law school, the summer before law school may very well be your last chance until retirement to enjoy an extended break. After the first year, there will be pressure to clerk at a law firm or do an internship during the summer. Write-on competitions to become a member of the law review are held in the summer after your first year. A substantial percentage of students attend summer school. On graduation, you'll only have fifteen minutes to celebrate before knuckling down to start studying for the bar exam.

Take a vacation. Exercise. Eat well. Get in good physical shape. Enter law school rested and ready to go. One of my 3L research assistants, assigned to proofread the final draft of this second edition, wrote to say he remembered reading *1L of a Ride* in the summer before law school while floating in a swimming pool. That sounds good to me (assuming you don't get it wet, because you will need it later).

CHAPTER 3

FEAR FACTOR: TOP FIVE LAW STUDENT WORRIES

"Come to the edge," he said. They said, "We are afraid." "Come to the edge," he said. They came. He pushed them . . . and they flew.

—Guillaume Apollinaire

If you're stressed out about beginning law school, take comfort in the fact that you have lots of company. Every 1L you meet, whether they show it or not, will be feeling the same feelings you are. Two weeks into the first semester, I asked a group of students to name their "biggest surprise" about law school. One student wrote: "My biggest surprise is that everyone feels the same way that I do. My insecurities are shared among most of my 152 peers. That provides tremendous comfort in that I am not the only one feeling overwhelmed, scared, stressed, and excited all at once."

Not only are your new colleagues as anxious as you are, they're stressing about the same issues. Law students tend to think their fears are unique, but they're not. Evidence to support this conclusion comes from an entering-student questionnaire I've been distributing for more than two decades. One question asks: "What is your greatest fear about law school?" Everywhere I've taught, all across the country, the answers repeat themselves. From reading thousands of these questionnaires, I've identified five of the most common worries shared by new law students:

- Failure/failing to meet personal expectations.
- Socratic method/getting called on in class.

- Not understanding the material.

- Detrimental impact on non-law school life, especially relationships.

- Not being able to keep up with the workload.

I'd like to assure you that all of these fears are baseless, but I can't. Each of the fears listed above has a legitimate basis in reality. The problem is that students don't properly calibrate them. They exaggerate some fears, while underestimating others. Let's look at them individually.

Failure/Failing to Meet Personal Expectations

Failure is the most common answer to my fear question. Here I have some good news. If failure is defined to mean failing to achieve and maintain the GPA necessary to remain a student in good standing (generally a 2.0)—i.e., getting kicked out of law school—the picture isn't as bleak as most imagine. Because admissions standards at most ABA-approved law schools remain high, the average attrition rate due to academic reasons is quite low.

Analysis of data in the 2013 *ABA–LSAC Official Guide to ABA–Approved Law Schools* showed that in 2010 (most recent data available), just 3 percent of the nation's 52,448 first-year law students attrited for academic reasons.[15] The 3 percent figure is somewhat misleading because it is common for struggling students to see the handwriting on the wall and withdraw from law school before they are academically dismissed. But even when attrition for all reasons is considered, the overall average attrition rate for first-year students in 2010 was still only about 10 percent.

These figures should help alleviate fears you might have about "flunking out," *assuming* you fully apply yourself. The bottom line is that in most law school courses, in a typical 1L section of seventy to eighty students,[16] you generally have to

---

15. Law Sch. Admission Council & A.B.A. Section of Legal Educ. & Admissions to the Bar, ABA–LSAC Official Guide to ABA–Approved Law Schools: 2013 Edition (2012). National attrition data is not calculated. Research assistants arrived at the overall percentages by compiling attrition information for both academic and all reasons for each accredited law school, and dividing the

figures by the total number of first-year students.

16. The average size of a first-year law school section in 2011 (most recent data available) was seventy-three students. Research assistants calculated this figure using information reported by individual schools in the 2013 ABA–LSAC guide. *See id.* This figure may decline. Roughly half of law schools cut out-perform only about ten to fifteen students, sometimes fewer, to be assured of receiving grades that will enable you to remain in law school.

A common variation on the failure fear is the fear of not living up to one's own expectations. Most students in law school have performed well academically their entire lives. For students who have been good pupils since the first grade, failure doesn't just mean flunking out. It means not excelling.

One student answered the "greatest fear" question in my questionnaire by saying: "Failure, not as in failing a class or performing poorly. My fear is primarily that I will not successfully meet or exceed my own expectations." Another lamented: "Not being smart enough. I have always been the smart one and the one everything came easy to. What if I don't stand out like I always have? What if it doesn't click with me?" A third student set a specific bar: "Failing (as in anything below a *B-*)—and yes, I know that is an unreasonable standard for my first year of law school!" Yes, that is an unreasonable expectation for most students at most schools. Don't be shocked to see one or more *C*s on your first grade report.

Here's a tale about a recent 1L who suffered a major law school reality check in terms of expected grades. In my new student questionnaire, the student confided boldly, "I wouldn't tell my classmates, family, or even my girlfriend, but I think I have the ability to finish at the top of my class." But in an end-of-the-year survey, the same student wrote, "So long as I get at least *C*s, that seems to be O.K. with me."

The fear of not living up to high personal expectations is much more well-founded than the fear of being academically dismissed. Law schools are full of high achievers. Instead of competing against students like your undergraduate roommate who sat in his dorm room smoking a bong and listening to Pink Floyd all night, you're competing against motivated, talented people with lifelong track records of academic accomplishment. Okay, some of them may still be smoking a bong and listening to Pink Floyd, but only after they've read and briefed all their cases for the next day.

the size of their entering classes in 2012–13 because of a nationwide drop in applications. It is too soon to know whether this is a temporary phenomenon or, as some have suggested, part of the "new normal."

Many fine law students who will become excellent lawyers do not get the grades they want and expect. If you come to law school expecting *A*s, you're likely to be disappointed. At most law schools, high grades are much harder to come by than in undergraduate or other graduate programs. Typically, only about 10–15 percent of the students in a first-year law school class receive any form of *A* grade (i.e., *A*+, *A*, or *A*-), which translates to only seven to twelve *A* grades in an average-size first-year section. Often the number is fewer. Thus, if everyone's standard for success is to make all *A*s and be in the golden top 10 percent of their class, the vast majority of students are doomed to feel like failures. The good news is that it doesn't take *A*s to be a successful law student.

I always tell students that a *C* in law school is a certification that they have demonstrated, among a group of talented people, the ability to be a competent lawyer, which is no small feat. I go on to emphasize that any form of *B* grade (i.e., *B*+, *B* or *B*-) in law school is a cause for breaking open a bottle of champagne and celebrating. In law school, I tell them, "*B* is the new *A*." Still, they don't listen.

Once I was in my office working at my computer. I had just posted the Torts grades (by anonymous exam number) outside the door, which was common in the days before grades started being posted online. Out of the corner of my eye, I could see students coming and going to check their grades. Working at my computer, I pretended not to notice, both to give them privacy and avoid having to deal with their disappointment until they had time to process it.

I noticed a young man I'll call Devin standing in the hall studying the grade sheet. He stayed there a long time. I liked Devin. He overcame a lot of odds to get to law school. He participated in class, seemed well-prepared, and struck me as a serious student. After a couple of minutes, I finally turned to look at him. His disappointment was palpable. He appeared to be wiping a tear from his cheek. He must have flunked, I thought. I felt terrible. Our ensuing conversation went something like this:

Me: Hey, Devin, how're you doing?

Him: [disconsolately] Not too good, professor.

Me: What's wrong? [As if I didn't know.]

Him: I—I didn't do very well. I'm really disappointed in myself.

Me: [hesitantly] What grade did you get? That's if you want to tell me. You don't have to.

Him: I only got a $B+$.

Me: A $B+$? Devin, you got a $B+$? That's B as in boy?

Him: [hangdog face] That's right, professor.

Me: Devin, I want to jump across this desk right now both to give you a hug for doing so well and also to strangle you for scaring the bejeezus out of me.

Lower your performance expectations or you'll drive yourself and those around you insane even if you're a good student. Since many students don't listen to this "lower your expectations" advice when I give it, maybe it will help to hear it from a 1L:

> It's hard to have this image of yourself as a Top Student crumble. I hear that from many other students, and I think that if one doesn't realize that EVERYONE is feeling this, it may seem that everyone else has it all together and you're the only one struggling. Most people who come to law school have probably heard all their lives, from first grade onward, that they are "smarter." In college, scholarships get thrown your way, you win special fellowships or work for your professors on special projects. You have this feeling of being "good" at this school thing and feeling competent.
>
> I think the Socratic Method (hearing someone give an answer that seems so much more intelligent than whatever you were thinking) and the evaluation method (not having feedback through assignments and midterm tests and what not) can really mess with you. I received an email from a fellow student. She's a student I think people assume "has it all together," and she said, "I feel like I'm hanging on by my fingernails." My personal metaphor for law school is one of a mouse running on a wheel. You've seen mice running too fast and the next thing, they're spinning around with the wheel. I feel that if I stumble, the wheel will fling me off.

I know this is turning into a long answer, but I'm trying to think of how to explain this feeling to someone who hasn't begun the experience (or who is in it and feels like they're drowning). We've all heard, "This isn't like being an undergrad ... This is going to be different from anything you've known ... The playing field is now leveled ..." which is true, but I think everyone lets it go in one ear and right back out again. Law school is different than simply continuing on to grad school or some other "tougher than college" environment. In the way that the military is a "different world," I think the law school experience has that element of complete and utter "forget your expectations; forget what you thought you knew."

While the student's comments may sound bleak, once again, take comfort in the fact that the feelings he expressed are nearly universal among first-year law students. In the meantime, while it sounds platitudinous, just be the best law student you can be. You have no way of predicting what kind of a law student you will be grade-wise because, except in your legal writing course, you're unlikely to receive much performance feedback until the first semester is over. Trust that if you apply yourself Consistently, Rigorously, Efficiently, Diligently, and Organizedly (see the C.R.E.D.O. for law students in Chapter 10) from the very beginning, you will maximize your opportunities to succeed at your highest potential—the most that any person can do. Academic dismissal of students who follow a committed, sound approach to law school is uncommon.

Socratic Method/Getting Called On

Another great fear of law school, which I vividly recall experiencing as a beginning student, is being victimized by the Socratic teaching method, which emphasizes cold-calling on students to recite and analyze cases from the assigned reading in a question and answer format; i.e., being publicly interrogated. As one student articulated it:

I was terrified of being called on—not of the act itself, but of the all-consuming silence that would follow the calling of my name, as eighty other people waited to see if I would sink or swim. Having a multitude of witnesses to a potential humiliation was a very unpleasant thought. Yet though my hands shook the first time I heard stentorian tones say "Ms. _____," and I felt sick with nervous apprehension with every question the professor posed—one after another after another—when he turned to someone else, I felt as if I had passed some test.

The student's reaction to the Socratic method mirrors that of most students, both her initial fear and subsequent relief and satisfaction when she realized she could, in fact, "pass the test" of this unique rite of passage in American legal education. Chapter 7 explains the Socratic method, so we'll postpone in-depth discussion of it. For now, just let me assure you that the horrors of the Socratic method are greatly exaggerated and that being terrorized by professors should be among the very least of your concerns.

Not Understanding the Material

A third frequently expressed fear is not understanding the material. While this anxiety could be seen merely as a variation of the failure theme, it falls into a discrete category. The *no comprende*-fear is much more immediate. Students worry they will arrive in this new academic world and find that the legal rules they're supposed to be learning are unintelligible ciphers and, worse, that they are the only ones without a decoding manual. The fear is commonly reflected in answers to the "greatest fear" question such as "that I would be the only person to not understand the reading" and "that everyone will 'get it' and I won't."

I'm happy to report this fear is also overblown. Coming into law school, the law naturally seems inaccessible and unfathomable because it's a complete unknown. Some of the first cases students are required to read confirm their worst fears about not being able to grasp the law.

Below is an excerpt from a famous Torts case decided in 1616 by the King's Bench in England commonly assigned in the first weeks of law school. The case, *Weaver v. Ward*,[17] is the earliest known decision expressly recognizing that a defendant might not be liable for damages for a purely accidental injury occurring without fault. But it's doubtful many students ever figure that out from the opinion itself, which reads like this:

17. (1616) 80 Eng. Rep. 284 (K.B.).

And upon demurrer by the plaintiff, judgment was given for him; for though it were agreed, that if men tilt or turney in the presence of the King, or if two masters of defence playing their prizes kill one another, that this shall be no felony; or if a lunatick kill a man, or the like, because felony must be done animo felonico; yet in trespass, which tends only to give damages according to hurt or loss, it is not so; and therefore if a lunatick hurt a man, he shall be answerable in trespass; and therefore no man shall be excused of a trespass (for this is in the nature of an excuse, and not of a justification, prout ei bene licuit), except it may be judged utterly without his fault.

Er, could you run that by us again? Why couldn't those old English judges speak ... well, English? Don't worry. Modern opinions aren't nearly as bad. Once you get past the moldy-oldies still included in casebooks because of their historical significance, the reading gets easier because most modern judges write lucidly and in plain English. Take a look, for example, at the judicial opinion in *Robinson v. Lindsay* reprinted in Chapter 11 as part of a case-briefing exercise. Compared to *Weaver v. Ward* it reads like a *My First Reader*.

As with so many other challenges that seem overwhelming when we first encounter them, learning the law becomes less intimidating with each passing day as students begin to figure out basic legal terms and procedures. One of my favorite parts of teaching 1Ls is watching the satisfaction, even joy, as the light bulbs start to go on, as students start to realize, "Hey, I really can understand this stuff! I really can learn the law!"

Don't get me wrong. A lot of the material is difficult and not all students grasp the law equally well. Some legal topics (the law of "future interests" in Property comes to mind as a quintessential 1L example) do approach utter incomprehensibility, but even those riddles can be unraveled by most students if they're willing to put in the necessary effort.

Have faith that you've been carefully prescreened by the admissions committee of your law school, which has determined you possess the ability to understand law.

Damage to Non–Law School Life, Especially Relationships

A fourth oft-repeated fear is the toll that law school will take on a student's outside life, especially their relationships with friends, families, and significant others. This fear is well-grounded. Not only does law school put your relationships at risk, stormy relationships can put your law school success at risk. In one study of stress in law school, the number one "crisis" cited by students for falling behind in their studies was a relationship crisis.[18]

Because the first year of law school is so all-consuming, law students somehow manage to both drive their loved ones crazy with obsessive talk about law school and neglect them at the same time. Quite a feat! Resentment, conflict, and sometimes even dissolution of the relationship can result. Chapter 23 addresses the problems that being a law student can present to outside relationships, so we'll wait until then to cover the topic.

Not Being Able to Keep Up with the Workload

This last fear deserves, in real rather than imagined terms, the top ranking on all law student worry lists—by far.[19] Students obsessing about getting called on in class or not understanding the material are worrying about the wrong things. In the 1992 presidential race, matching Bill Clinton against President George H.W. Bush, political consultant James Carville came up with Clinton's election-winning campaign strategy. To keep the campaign simple and on message, Carville instructed campaign workers to remember: "It's the economy, stupid." Adapting Carville's slogan to law school, "It's the workload, stupid." Memorize this and repeat it when you find yourself obsessing about less important things.

Effectively managing the workload is likely to be your main law school challenge. Asked how law school differs from undergraduate school, one student explained:

18. Marilyn Heins et al., *Law Students and Medical Students: A Comparison of Perceived Stress*, 33 J. LEGAL EDUC. 511, 520 (1983).

19. We're talking here exclusively about fears of law school itself. As students make their way through school, two related external fears assume dominance: landing a good job and paying back mounting student loans.

About the only similarity between undergraduate
school and law school is that it is school. Other than
that, law school is an entirely different caliber—requiring so much more than undergrad that it does not even
compare. When law students say we must get ready for
class, it doesn't mean the same thing as it did in
undergrad. When people ask "When will you be done
studying?" there is actually no good answer because
we could probably spend every waking hour outside of
class studying and still not be done. The only answerable question would be "When are you going to stop
studying tonight?"

The vast majority of the people who do not succeed in law
school or who succeed at levels below their potential do so
because *they weren't prepared to handle the overwhelming
workload*. They did not arrive at law school with either the
mindset or an organized plan to carefully read (and reread)
from 100–150 pages of dense legal analysis in casebooks each
week, compose case briefs for twenty-five or more complicated judicial opinions each week, attend 14–16 intense class
hours each week, prepare lengthy course outlines, learn an
entirely new language, research and write (and then rewrite
and rewrite) intricate legal memoranda and briefs in their
legal research and writing courses, and still manage to juggle
the other parts of their lives, including family and other
relationships and, for part-time students, full-time employment. They get behind early ... and never catch up. Nothing, I repeat, nothing will portend lack of success more than
falling behind.

Recall the student quoted earlier in this chapter who
started law school convinced he would be at the top of his
class but ended his first year saying he was happy with Cs.
What the heck happened to him? In his words, "I simply did
not have the mental endurance to complete every daily reading assignment, research and writing project, and then outline and prepare for exams simultaneously." Sound familiar?
Reread the preceding paragraph.

* * *

Overall, a healthy trepidation starting law school is not
only a good motivator, but appropriate given the reality of
what you're about to embark on. I'm not talking about
counterproductive paralyzing fear, which inhibits learning,

but an informed apprehension that law school is going to challenge you in ways you've never been challenged before.

To not have some anxiety about law school doesn't make one brave, but foolish. It means the person is clueless about what they're getting into. In every entering class, at least one student responds to my fear question with an answer such as "No fear" or "Nothing scares me." Heed the warning from this formerly fearless student:

As a U.S. Army Major, I was used to long hard work. The work in law school is very different and in many ways harder. In retrospect, I wish I had more fears and concerns than what I did as I was not overly concerned about anything. Fear is a very powerful motivator, and had I been more fearful I probably would have worked harder and done better.

We'll talk more about the sources of 1L stress, including tips for reducing and managing it. In the meantime, if you find yourself feeling alone in your fears and doubts, find solace in one of my favorite quotations, from motivational educator Stan Dale:

It all changed when I realized I'm not the only one on the planet who's scared. Everyone else is, too. I started asking people, "Are you scared, too?" "You bet your sweet life I am." "Aha, so that's the way it is for you, too." We were all in the same boat.

So buckle your life preserver and get ready to climb aboard the 1L boat, secure in the knowledge that you will find many passengers feeling just like you do.

CHAPTER 4

WHAT KIND OF STUDENT DO YOU WANT TO BE (AND BE KNOWN AS)?: TWENTY LAW STUDENT TYPES

Most students arrive at law school with at least some hope that they will become a great law student. Generally, their perception of "great" is quite limited, corresponding with a high GPA. Many attributes apart from grades work to define students, both to their peers and to the faculty and staff of the law school. The good news is that, unlike grade performance, students have more control over most of these other defining qualities.

This chapter contains a list of twenty types of law students. There's spillover among the categories, with students usually displaying traits from more than one type. Some of the types evoke positive associations, while some carry clear negative connotations. Several of the types, however, are two-sided coins, with both positives and negatives.

It's worth thinking in advance about the different types of law students and which type or types you would like to become. Just as important, it's worth thinking about which type of law student you would like to be known as by others. Because 1Ls take the same classes from the same professors throughout the first year, everyone gets to know everyone else. More accurately, everyone *thinks* they know everyone else, with opinions often based on limited evidence derived from short classroom performances, social exchanges, and rumor. From the moment you arrive at law school, people—

students, faculty, and staff—will be forming opinions about you based on how you conduct yourself. Many of these opinions may be off-base, but one's perception is their reality. Thus, in perusing the list below, think not only about the type of student you desire to be, but how you want to be perceived by others. Here are twenty law student types:

1. The Frequent Participators. The Socratic method of law school teaching involves a lot of questions being asked by the professor, including many "What do you think?"-type questions. Most first-year law school class sections include a small number of students who are more willing to volunteer answers and comments than the other students.[20] And I say to them: Thank you! Someone has to answer those questions. From a professor's perspective, a Frequent Participator beats the heck out of the students who sit silently all year long never engaging in the class. The most interesting and exciting parts of law school classes always involve class discussion.

Unfortunately, people who participate frequently sometimes get labeled by the law school slur, "gunner." It's unfortunate because the fear of being labeled a gunner deters too many students with good ideas and answers from participating in class.

Do not worry about being labeled a gunner! A 1L came to my office and said he was afraid to participate in class discussion on a regular basis because he didn't want to be labeled as a gunner. He explained that during orientation an upper-level student assigned to his group as a mentor warned them not to participate frequently in class because they would be marked as gunners whom no one would like or want to study with. A month or so later, another student from the same class came to see me and expressed concern that his classmates might perceive him to be a gunner. I told him he most definitely was *not* a gunner. Rather, he was a much-appreciated, reliable participator who helped me and his class by being willing to raise his hand when others wouldn't. Other students have expressed the same fears to me. Most everyone, it seems, is afraid of being labeled a gunner, except for the gunner.

20. Frequent Participators usually are guys. As discussed in Chapter 7, studies show women voluntarily participate in class discussions at lower rates than men.

True gunners are rare. They usually are students who not only volunteer frequently, but do so obnoxiously, with a misplaced air of superiority. Or they may routinely offer extremely conservative or extremely liberal viewpoints with a "My position is the only right one" attitude that offends one-half of the class. Students need to understand, but don't, that being a gunner is more about attitude than frequency of participation. Recently, I had an older full-time student who *loved* to raise his hand, several times in each fifty-minute class. But he did it out of an almost-childlike wonder and excitement for the law, not because he liked to hear himself talk. He was beloved by his classmates and professors alike.

Ideally, everyone in a class would participate at a roughly equal level, but that's just not the reality of group dynamics in large law school classes. Many students never volunteer at all. Someone has to pick up the slack. When in doubt, choose to participate. The benefits of regular class participation, as explained in Chapter 8, are many, and far outweigh the risk of being stamped as a gunner. Leave it to the professors to identify the gunners. They'll deal with them appropriately, generally by simply overlooking them when they raise their hands.

2. The Regular and Occasional Participators. Between the extremes of the Frequent Participator and the Stealth Student (see below) are all the other students who make some effort to voluntarily participate in class discussions. Since the Regular and Occasional Participators include a large percentage of the class, they're not really discrete types. Nevertheless, they're worth identifying because voluntary class participation of any type—as it involves a public display of courage, preparation, and analytical ability—does help define students. Even occasional voluntary participation will earn you most of the benefits that come from class participation.

3. The Stealth Student. The Stealth Student is a student who manages to blend into the surroundings so well that the student's very existence remains unknown, at least to the professors. Needless to say, Stealth Students don't voluntarily participate in class. They don't do *anything* in class that would draw attention to themselves. They don't arrive late, don't talk to their neighbors, don't shuffle their books or other belongings. For all I know, they may hold their breath and fail to blink for the entire class hour.

In professor-speak, Stealth Student sometimes has an added meaning as the student who manages to remain completely anonymous during the semester, only to blow everyone else out of the water come final exam time. Every class seems to have a curve-busting Stealth Student of this type. For reasons I've never figured out, the top-ranked student in a law school class, if not anonymous, is often a quiet type. Of course, you can't really choose to be a Stealth Student in this sense of the term. You can elect to seek anonymity (see Backburners below), although I recommend against it.

4.   The Backburner. In Chapter 6, I recommend sitting in the front of the classroom for a variety of reasons. Here, I merely list Backburners as a type of law student and explain how they may be perceived by professors.

By necessity, large first-year classes are held in large rooms. Depending on the design of the room, students who sit in the nose-bleed seats are sometimes so far away from the action that they barely seem to be a physical part of the class. They often camp behind their computer screens, sometimes wearing baseball caps that shield what little could otherwise be seen of their faces. Many students in the back— not all—voluntarily participate in class discussions infrequently or never. They're essentially invisible, which indeed may be their goal.

Professors may interpret the Backburners' seat choice and corresponding disengagement as part of a bad or bored attitude toward the course and learning the law. This is not always an accurate or fair assessment because some excellent students choose to sit in the back. I asked one good student why she sat in the back and she said, "I just don't feel comfortable with everyone behind me, looking at the back of my head."

Understandable, but the physical arrangement of the room may create a barricade even for Backburner students who want to be engaged. The Backburners don't necessarily generate bad reputations with professors. The bigger problem is that unless they make an effort to participate they don't generate *any* reputation because they remain faceless and anonymous, unlike . . .

5.   The Front Row Crowd. From an alternative universe, or at least the other side of the room, are students who choose to sit toward the front of the room. Professors like the Front Row Crowd because they appreciate them sitting there and also because professors *get to know* these students. Part of this connecting may be attributable to the personalities of people who choose to sit in front, but a larger part of it is simply a matter of proximity. I usually arrive to class at least ten minutes early to get set up. With nothing else to do, I chat with the students in the front while I'm hanging out at the podium. We talk about music, sports, their current law school gripes—a variety of matters. I get to know them and they get to know me. See Chapter 9 on the importance of getting to know and getting known by your professors.

6.   The Know–It–All. You can imagine what law professors think about students who believe they know more about the law and legal education than their professors. Know–It–Alls sincerely believe that within weeks or even days of starting law school, perhaps due to supernatural phenomena, they know the law and understand how to succeed in law school better than people who have devoted their lives to these endeavors. These students can be amusing, but are mostly irritating. I remember a student who, after three days of law school, bopped into my office, plopped down in a chair, and said: "Professor, you do a pretty good job, but I'd like to give you some suggestions on how to improve your teaching." Come exam time, the Know–It–Alls are usually exposed as Turns–Out–They–Didn't–Know–Much–At–Alls.

7.   The Chronically Late. Every first-year class has a couple of students who, left to their own devices, will regularly arrive late for class. Because their arrival is disruptive in a very public way, it won't take you long to spot this type. Most professors will not tolerate the Chronically Late, although some do, to the annoyance of the rest of the class. See the section on classroom etiquette in Chapter 6 for more about the importance of being punctual.

8.   The Slacker. Regrettably, despite careful screening by admissions committees, every law school class includes its share of Slackers, students who do not read their assignments, brief their cases, attend class regularly, etc. In the 2012 Law School Survey of Student Engagement, 7 percent of participating first-year students reported they either often or very often failed to read assignments prior to class.[21]

Even worse than the regular Slacker is the Bragging Slacker; i.e., a student who actually takes pride in boasting about how they don't read their assignments or brief the cases, as if there were something appealing about being lazy and irresponsible.

No surprise: professors have a natural lack of regard for this type of student. As one would expect, Slackers flunk out of law school at disproportionate rates.

9. The Overconfident Without Cause. Most first-year law students are fearful and intimidated—with just cause—by the Jupiter-size amount of foreign, dense material they're expected to master, but every entering class has a few students who approach law school from a "What, me worry?" perspective. They're marked by their casual attitude toward diligent studying. While other students are preparing case briefs or outlines, the Overconfident Without Cause shrug it off with "Briefs? Outlines? Who needs 'em?" Overconfident students often are bright, and perhaps sailed through undergraduate school with minimal effort. They seem to be unaware of the fact that the same holds true for most of their classmates.

Overconfident students rarely achieve at high levels academically in law school because their cavalier attitude diminishes their motivation to study hard. No person has cause to be overly confident about succeeding in law school.

The Overconfident Without Cause are distinguishable from the Know–It–Alls. Unlike the KIAs, the OWC don't assume they know all the answers. Their laid-back self-assurance keeps them from even thinking about the questions. One reason they're overconfident is because they haven't thought deeply enough to know what they don't know.

10. The Insecure Contrary to Evidence. At the opposite end of the continuum from the Overconfident Without Cause are the Insecure Contrary to Evidence. These are students who worry themselves sick—sometimes literally so—because they're convinced that everyone around them is

---

21. *Frequency Distributions, 1L Students*, in 2012 LAW SCH. SURVEY OF STUDENT ENGAGEMENT, *supra*.

smarter than they are. They have a tendency to preface statements about the future with "If I don't flunk out...." Their self-deprecation is sincere. They really doubt their ability, even when their credentials would suggest such extreme insecurity is unfounded.

Here's a confession I rarely share: I was a certified member of the Insecure Contrary to Evidence crowd as a first-year law student, to the point where I sought medical treatment in my first semester for stress-induced gastrointestinal issues. I even considered quitting law school. Despite entering law school with a high LSAT score and undergraduate GPA, I was convinced I was a total dolt as I sat in class listening to my brilliant classmates expound. "How did they think of that? Why couldn't I have come up with that? They're so much smarter than me!" I tormented myself with these thoughts.

When the first set of grades came out, I was pleasantly surprised to discover that my insecurities were misplaced. I landed in the top five percent of my class and stayed there throughout law school.

My student experience is common. Many of the Insecure Contrary to Evidence end up as top students. One reason is that, because of their insecurity, they are motivated to work harder to overcome their perceived shortcomings. Another factor is that they see and worry about all the little details and complexities of the law—the same fine points that escape the notice of the Overconfident Without Cause and which are so important to performing well on law school exams.

11. Mr./Ms. Reliable. How professors love these students. It takes a while to figure out who they are, because they tend to volunteer infrequently (some of them may overlap with the Insecure Contrary to Evidence). But once they become known to the professor, everyone else will know who they are because professors will call on them disproportionately. These are diligent students who are *always* well-prepared. They're life preservers when the class is wallowing in a mire of cluelessness or unpreparedness. When the going gets tough in terms of getting an answer to a question, the professor will turn instinctively to a Mr./Ms. Reliable. They're the "go to" guys and gals of the class.

No great shock, members of this group usually do well in law school. If you're already a law student and find yourself getting called on disproportionately for no apparent reason, maybe you've been identified by the prof as a Mr./Ms. Reliable. Of course, you might also have been identified as a Slacker whom the professor wants to make an example of, so don't start patting yourself on the back until you've figured it out. Because of their generally quiet demeanor, more Mr./Ms. Reliables exist than are identified by the professors, which is yet another good reason to contribute voluntarily in class. You want the professor to know if you're a Mr./Ms. Reliable.

12. The Nattering Nabob of Negativism. Borrowing a phrase that former Vice–President Spiro Agnew (under Richard Nixon) used in 1970 to describe the media, in all social environments we regularly encounter people who whine and complain about everything. Nothing is ever right for these folks. A disproportionate number of injustices seem to befall them. In law school, they complain about their professors, their books, their assignments, their classmates, their lunch. You name it, they're unhappy with it.

For some people, complaining is just a bad habit, but some individuals are bitter and unhappy by nature. Law school is going to be stressful enough as it is. Letting it consume you with negative energy is not only unhealthy, but an unattractive quality. If you're unable to develop a positive attitude, at least try to minimize your outward manifestations of negativity. Like our parents taught us, if you can't say something nice, you're better off saying nothing.

A tangible downside of bad-mouthing people is that just about everything one says about a classmate or professor will get passed along to others because of the marble-size world that is law school. Some comments find their way back to the object of the comment.

Be positive. Keep a sense of humor about everything, including yourself. People who can laugh at themselves are healthier people. Continual complaining about your trials and tribulations and constant bad-mouthing of others is just going to make you and those around you feel worse.

Avoid associating with confirmed Nattering Nabobs of Negativism, lest they drag you into their drag of an existence.

13. Curious George/Georgette. Curious George was a children's book character created in 1941 by H.A. Rey and Margret Rey. A mischievous ape, Curious George's defining characteristic, as his name suggests, was his unquenchable curiosity. Curious George was a lovable character, as are most students who fit into this type. Whereas many students want to know the bare minimum they need to know to succeed in law school, Curious Georges/Georgettes always want to know *more* than they need to know. Their curiosity leads them, for example, to look up the note cases following the principal cases in their casebooks, track down the unabridged versions of the principal cases to learn more facts, or research the actors, places, and history surrounding the cases and case events.

A classic example is the Curious Georgette who, on reading an old case about the consent defense to intentional torts involving a woman who was vaccinated against her wishes on board a ship sailing "from Queenstown to Boston," decided she needed to know more about Queenstown. Because the plaintiff claimed not to understand the vaccination proceedings, the student was curious about what language the woman spoke. Her research turned up the factoid that Queenstown was the final port of call for the Titanic on its doomed, maiden voyage. Interesting tidbit, but not the type of information that will be helpful come exams.

Professors appreciate CGs. With too many students uninterested in learning anything beyond "the rules," how could they not? On the other hand, while intellectual curiosity is an admirable quality that should be encouraged, students need to be careful about how they allocate their scarce time.

A subcategory of the Curious Georges/Georgettes includes students obsessed with the great "What if?" These are students who, instead of focusing on the case facts or the hypothetical facts posed by the professor, insist on exploring their own extreme fact scenarios to test the application of legal principles. Within reasonable bounds, this is a valuable mental exercise, as a large part of learning to analyze law does indeed involve applying legal rules to changing fact patterns. Many what-if inquiries are excellent questions that lead to interesting and illuminating class discussion, so don't be discouraged from posing them. They become a problem only when a student repeatedly flogs issues with what-ifs taken to absurd lengths. If a Civil Procedure professor discussing personal jurisdiction queries "What if the defendant was served with process in another country?", a What–If

Curious George/Georgette will want to know "What if he was served with process on another planet?"

14. The Party Animal. Despite the heavy workload, most law students seem to find plenty of time to socialize. This is healthy, of course. The bonding that occurs among first-year students is one of the great byproducts of the "trial by ordeal" method of legal education. But some students quickly become known as partiers first and law students second, sometimes a distant second. Since most law school socializing involves consuming alcohol, being known as the class Party Animal often carries other negative associations with it. Party Animals are rarely top-performing law students, although they often are quite popular.

15. The Star of Rumor Central. Because law schools are cloistered, competitive environments, everyone likes to know and talk about other people's business. Rumors, some of them fantastical, swirl with frequency. Sometimes they contain a kernel of truth, but like the old pass-it-along game we played in elementary school, the stories get more distorted each time they're retold. Reading this, a research assistant wrote in the margin: "Rumor passing in law school is worse than it was in high school!"

In response to a survey question asking students to identify their biggest surprise about law school, another student wrote:

> Honestly, my biggest surprise has to do with my fellow classmates and all the students in law school. I almost feel like I am back in high school again. There is so much drama between guys and girls as well as just between girls. I thought at this age, people would be over worrying about who likes who, etc., but that does not seem to be the case. I guess that's what happens when you are with the same seventy people every day all day!

With everyone watching everyone else, you need to be cautious in your behavior, both academically and socially, to avoid ending up as a target of gossipmongers. Frequently, the wholly innocent get caught up in the gossip web. If you regularly hang out and study with a person of the opposite sex (or possibly even the same sex), do not be surprised if rumors begin circulating that the two of you are "sleeping together."

Not all law school rumors are unfounded. Often, gossip attaches itself to people who behave in ways that predictably lead to gossip. Be cautious about alcohol, drugs, and sexual activities. Very little remains private in law school. Avoid letting people take untoward pictures of you at social gatherings. In a world where nearly everyone carries a camera phone, embarrassing pictures can come back to haunt people. Most employers, including most legal employers, routinely scour the internet for information about recruits when making hiring decisions.

16. The Evaluator/Judger. These two closely related types are sometimes the same person, but not always. Both spend a disproportionate amount of time sizing up the competition, the Evaluator by keeping close tabs on everyone's progress and the Judger by overtly rating his classmates as smart or not smart, often based on their classroom comments. Evaluators are obsessed with knowing everyone's grades and comparing them to their own. At one school, in the days when grades were still publicly posted on the "wailing wall" or "wall of shame" (as students called it), we had to change the entire anonymous grade-number system because an Evaluator took the time to collect and chart the grades of every 1L by exam number.

As for the Judger, who may also qualify as a Know–It–All, it is presumptuous in the extreme for any 1L student to believe he is qualified to evaluate the knowledge and analytical abilities of his classmates. It probably goes without saying that overt Evaluators/Judgers are not well-liked by their classmates.

17. The Class Joker. As someone who appreciates humor and the value of it for bolstering the sense of community and energy level in law school classrooms, I love Class Jokers. Most first-year sections will include at least one real character. These are people who like attention and appear to enjoy being the subject of good-natured ribbing from the professor. When the going gets tough or tedious, an appropriate Class Joker can add a much needed spark of energy to a class.

By "appropriate Class Joker," I am excluding students who go overboard in trying to be funny, diverting the focus of the class discussion. Appropriate Class Jokers know their place in the hierarchy. Think of the appropriate Class Joker as the law school equivalent of a sidekick to a late-night talk show host (e.g., Paul Shaffer to David Letterman). They can get away with some gentle limelight-seeking, but remain cognizant of their primary role as the "straight man."

18. The Lightning Rod. As with the Class Joker, most law school classes have at least one Lightning Rod, a person willing to express strong and sometimes outrageous opinions about the issues being discussed in class. Often, these views can be associated with either the far left or right of the political spectrum. Sometimes their opinions are politically incorrect. Not all professors share my view, but I like having Lightning Rods as students, even when I disagree with their views, because their opinions prompt other students who normally would not participate to jump into the fray. The surest identifier of a Lightning Rod is a person whose classroom comments ignite an immediate sea of waving hands. Some Lightning Rods offer their opinions with a wink and a nod to the professor, knowing full well the role they're fulfilling.

A truly passionate Lightning Rod may open himself to derision from classmates in much the same way as a true gunner, and, in fact, these categories sometimes overlap. Unfortunately, fear of peer disapproval for expressing strong opinions, similar to the fear of being labeled a gunner, deters many non-Lightning Rod students from offering honest opinions about charged issues, of which there are many in law.

A classic example from Torts is the famous Iowa "spring-gun case," *Katko v. Briney*,[22] which you are likely to study. Marvin Katko sued Edward and Bertha Briney after he broke into their unoccupied farmhouse intent on stealing their property and ended up losing a portion of his leg to a shotgun the Brineys had wired to the bedroom door. The jury awarded Katko substantial compensatory and punitive damages. The Brineys had to auction eighty acres of their farm to pay the judgment. Katko won on the principle that the law values life over property. From teaching this case for many years, I know that a large percentage of students in every class vehemently disagree with the result that a criminal can recover damages from a homeowner whose property he unlawfully invades, but they're often afraid to express their disagreement until a Lightning Rod opens the door with a comment such as "That S.O.B. got what he deserved!"

---

22. 183 N.W.2d 657 (Iowa 1971).

It's bad enough that students shy away from expressing opinions about charged legal issues, but it's even worse that many professors are so apprehensive of offending the overly delicate sensitivities of some students that they avoid ever raising hot issues in class. That is a darn shame. Law school classes should be vital and exciting. When sensitive legal issues can't be discussed even in law school, we're in trouble as a society. But I digress.

19. The Cheater. From a professor's perspective, the only student type worse than the Slacker is the Cheater. People who cheat in law school are likely to cheat in the practice of law, hurting their clients and tarnishing a profession that is already held in low regard by many. The good news is that given the nature of law school exams, it's difficult to cheat effectively. The bad news is that this fact doesn't stop some people from trying. At every law school where I have taught, incidents of alleged cheating have occurred. Sadly, several students at different law schools have reported to me that cheating not only occurs, but is common, although I can't vouch for the accuracy of such indictments.

Of course, whether you decide to be a Cheater isn't going to be influenced by any advice I give you. Nor do you need a book like this to apprise you of the potentially severe consequences of cheating, which can include being suspended from law school or not being permitted to sit for the bar exam. You're the one who has to look in the mirror every day.

But here is some advice that may help honest souls. In some situations involving accusations of academic misconduct, I've come away convinced that the cheating was inadvertent or at least not motivated by a wicked intent. These incidents often involve students who, faced with a dilemma as to what is proper conduct, resolve the question in their favor without seeking guidance from the professor.

For example, cheating allegations arise disproportionately in first-year legal research and writing courses where gray areas may exist in the rules regarding matters such as collaboration and plagiarism. Instead of simply asking the professor for guidance when a question of right or wrong arises, the student makes a choice on his or her own—often unwisely giving him/herself the benefit of the doubt—that turns out to be the wrong choice. Even if the accused student is ultimately spared sanctions, the student endures the substantial emotional trauma of being investigated, put on trial, and suffering a tarnished reputation. In many cases involving alleged law school academic misconduct, the student could have avoided any problems simply by seeking clarification from the instructor. You cannot go wrong by following that course of action: when in doubt, *ask* the professor.

Related to overt academic cheating are violations of course policies. A common example is using personal computers to multitask on the internet during class. Most professors have explicit policies against this, which many students violate. I assume they do this because they think the rule is unimportant or simply cannot resist the compulsion to check their Facebook page. But students can't pick and choose which rules to follow. Professors not only take violations of course policies personally as a sign of disrespect, it diminishes their faith in the offender's capacity to be an ethical lawyer.

20. The Earnest Hard Worker. Last, but certainly not least, is the Earnest Hard Worker. Don't be misled by the negative types listed above. While the negative types tend to stand out more than the positive types, they are a distinct minority overall. The Earnest Hard Workers, I'm happy to report, represent a majority of law students. Some of them achieve high grades, some don't. But even Earnest Hard Workers who don't come out at the top of their class earn the respect of those around them, both students and professors. I happily write strong recommendation letters on behalf of Earnest Hard Workers even if they received less-than-stellar grades in my courses.

* * *

There you have them. Twenty law student types. Make a list of the types that appeal to you, the types that don't, and the in-between types. Think about the list, then put it away. Revisit your list during the first semester to see whether you're living up (or down) to your aspirations.

CHAPTER 5

THE FIRST-YEAR CURRICULUM: WHAT TO EXPECT

Here's a list of the courses I took as a 1L in 1978:

Civil Procedure

Contracts

Criminal Law

Legal Research and Writing

Property

Torts

Here's a list of the courses you are likely to take as a 1L:

Civil Procedure

Contracts

Criminal Law

Legal Research and Writing

Property

Torts

Hmm, can we detect a pattern here? Nowhere has resistance to change in American legal education been more apparent than in the static nature of law school curricula. Despite some changes and much more talk about the need to change, the first-year curriculum remains fundamentally unaltered at most schools.

The main purpose of this chapter is to give you a feel for the "Big Five" required doctrinal courses that virtually all full-time 1Ls will be immersed in, if not submerged under:

Civil Procedure, Contracts, Criminal Law, Property, and Torts.[23] "Doctrinal courses" are courses in which the primary purpose is to teach the body of substantive rules, or doctrine, in the particular area of law. They're distinguishable from so-called "skills courses" such as Legal Research and Writing.[24] Because Legal Research and Writing is such a different—and important—beast, it gets its own chapter (Chapter 18). Before we get into the Big Five courses, however, let's explore law school curricula a bit more in-depth.

Criticism of Law School Curricula: The Call for More Skills Courses

The curriculum at most law schools consists of a slate of required first-year courses and an upper-level course mix of electives and more required courses. The number of required (versus elective) upper-level courses varies widely by school.

Most law school courses, both first year and upper-level, are doctrinal courses as defined above. Three respected and influential reports—known generally as the *MacCrate Report*,[25] the *Carnegie Foundation Report*,[26] and *Best Practices for Legal Education* report[27]—have criticized the traditional law school curriculum as outdated and in need of major reform. In particular, the status quo has been attacked for paying too much attention to teaching legal doctrine and legal analysis and too little attention to practical skills and ethics and professionalism. Legal employers also have com-

---

23. Part-time students usually take only two of these doctrinal courses per semester, along with Legal Research and Writing.

24. There are five types of law school courses: (1) doctrinal courses, which comprise the majority of courses; (2) skills courses, which are designed to teach practical aspects of lawyering such as writing or advocacy; (3) seminars, which are small upper-level courses in which students usually write a scholarly paper and make a presentation; (4) externships, in which students earn credit while working outside the law school under the supervision of practicing lawyers; and (5) in-house "live client clinics," as they are called, where students work representing real clients under the supervision of law school instructors. While it is common to differentiate be-

tween doctrinal and skills courses, doctrinal professors teach important skills, such as legal analysis, and skills courses often also contain a doctrinal component.

25. A.B.A. SECTION OF LEGAL EDUC. & ADMISSIONS TO THE BAR, THE REPORT OF THE TASK FORCE ON LAW SCHOOLS AND THE PROFESSION: NARROWING THE GAP (1992) (called the "MacCrate Report" after the chair of the task force, Robert MacCrate).

26. *See* WILLIAM M. SULLIVAN ET AL., EDUCATING LAWYERS: PREPARATION FOR THE PROFESSION OF LAW (2007) (report of the Carnegie Foundation for the Advancement of Teaching) [hereinafter CARNEGIE FOUNDATION REPORT].

27. BEST PRACTICES FOR LEGAL EDUCATION, *supra*.

plained that law schools should be turning out graduates who are more "practice ready."

The standard law school curriculum is somewhat of an odd arrangement if one stops to ponder it for, say, two seconds. To prepare doctors to practice medicine, medical schools require, sensibly, years of clinical training involving hands-on patient care. Law schools traditionally have required nothing of that sort. At nearly all law schools, clinical courses and externships, in which students work with real clients, lawyers, and cases, are elective rather than required. Although changes are occurring, only 4.5 percent of law schools require clinical training or an external field placement.[28] I graduated law school without taking a single skills-related course other than my required first-year legal research and writing courses, a dubious feat that can be replicated today at most schools.

That being said, law schools are adding skills components to the curriculum at a faster rate, a change likely to accelerate in future years. In 2012, the ABA Section on Legal Education and Admissions to the Bar under the leadership of Professor Catherine Carpenter completed a comprehensive empirical study of curricular trends in U.S. legal education covering the period from 2002–2010.[29] Half of the 200 ABA-accredited schools reported offering ten or more skills courses, while 85 percent reported that they maintain one or more (with an average of three) live client in-house clinics.[30]

Sounds promising, but the figures present a glass half full/half empty picture. On average, law school course lists include 132 upper-level course titles, so "ten or more" skills courses still represents only a small percentage of total available courses. Also, half of law schools reported offering fewer than ten skills courses. As for live client clinics, they are by necessity small, usually limited to eight to ten students per clinic. Thus, with an average of three clinics per school, only a small percentage of law students are served by these courses. (Most schools would love to add additional clinics, but they are enormously expensive to operate on a per-student basis compared to regular courses.)

---

28. DAVID A. SANTACROCE & ROBERT R. KUEHN, CTR. FOR THE STUDY OF APPLIED LEGAL EDUC., THE 2010–11 SURVEY OF APPLIED LEGAL EDUCATION 9 (2011).

29. A.B.A. SECTION OF LEGAL EDUC. & ADMISSIONS TO THE BAR, A SURVEY OF LAW SCHOOL CURRICULA: 2002–2010 (Catherine Carpenter ed., 2012) [hereinafter A.B.A. CURRICULUM REPORT].

30. *See id.* at 16.

Nevertheless, change is occurring and, after many years of just being talked about, "experiential learning," as it is called, finally appears to have a strong wind at its back.

First-Year Curriculum Changes

While the traditional first-year curriculum continues to show impressive staying power, the 2012 ABA survey did detect a few changes. The most frequent change involves the ongoing juggling of the number of credit hours allocated to each first-year course. The total number of credit hours per year has remained largely stable over time, averaging 30–32 hours for full-time students and 20 hours for part-time students. Traditionally, four of the Big Five doctrinal first-year courses (all except Criminal Law) were taught in two semesters (e.g., Contracts I and Contracts II, Torts I and Torts II) with three credits per semester for a total of six credit hours per course.

A couple of decades ago, however, law schools developed a tremendous fondness for tinkering with the traditional model. The predominant change involves "semesterizing" all or some of the traditional two-semester first-year courses by compressing them into a single semester while also reducing the total credit hours for the course, usually from six to four.

One reason behind semesterization was to free up more hours for legal research and writing courses, a worthy goal given the importance of those courses and the fact that they traditionally have been under-credited (see Chapter 18). Another reason was to introduce more flexibility into the curriculum, allowing students to take more electives.

I've long argued against the semesterization of first-year courses, usually losing the argument. First-year courses are the critical building blocks of learning not only the fundamental principles of law in core subject areas, but even more important, the process of conducting legal analysis. You'll notice that daily reading assignments in first-year courses will be shorter than in upper-level courses. This is because first-year professors spend more class time training students in the art of critical-thinking. Also, the Multistate Bar Exam and many portions of state bar exams focus on first-year subjects. When first-year courses get cut by one-third, important material that is tested on the bar exam gets omitted with the result that many students are forced as a practical matter to take upper-level courses covering the deleted material, undermining the flexibility goal behind semesterization.

In addition to the continued juggling of course credit hours, modifications in first-year curricula noted in the ABA report included: increasing the credit hours for Legal Research and Writing (see Chapter 18); adding a course in skills, professionalism, or legislation/regulation;[31] and allowing 1Ls to take an elective course. In 2010, about 15 percent of ABA-accredited schools allowed first-year students to take an elective.[32]

The "Big Five" First–Year Doctrinal Courses

Below is a short summary of the first-year doctrinal courses that nearly every 1L will take. Having a rudimentary sense of what each course involves will help you know what to expect, as well as give you a better context for processing the rest of this book. At a minimum, when you see your course list for the first time, it won't feel like reading a menu in a foreign language.

Regarding the content of particular courses, law professors have a variety of casebooks to choose among for each first-year course. While casebooks for a subject generally cover the same basic material, some differences in coverage, and many more in organization, exist. Moreover, coverage may differ even between two professors using the same casebook because of the professors' individual preferences regarding which topics to emphasize.

Civil Procedure

All civil lawsuits are controlled by a set of procedural rules, cleverly titled "The Rules of Civil Procedure." The Rules of Civil Procedure tell the lawyers and the parties what they must do and may do in the pretrial and trial stages of a lawsuit, as well as how and when to do it. Criminal cases are controlled by a similar set of rules, but courses in criminal procedure usually are upper-level electives.

The Federal Rules of Civil Procedure, which are the focus of most 1L courses on the subject, govern lawsuits in the

---

31. One common criticism of the traditional first-year curriculum is that it is dominated by case law, understating the huge role in the U.S. legal system played by codified law in the form of statutes and government agency regulations.

32. A.B.A. CURRICULUM REPORT, *supra*, at 55.

federal courts. Each state has its own set of civil procedure rules to govern civil lawsuits in their respective state court systems, but those rules track the federal rules very closely for the most part. The Federal Rules of Civil Procedure contain eighty-six rules, but you will closely study only a small number of them.

You'll spend a lot of time studying cases (many of which predate the adoption of the Federal Rules of Civil Procedure) that developed the key concepts governing questions such as which court has jurisdiction to hear a particular case, whether a court has jurisdiction over the parties to a case, and which court system's rules of substantive law apply to a case.

Unlike your other first-year courses (except Constitutional Law if that is a first-year course at your school), many of the cases in Civil Procedure are U.S. Supreme Court cases. You will quickly learn that Supreme Court cases are different from and more difficult to digest than the state court cases that will predominate in your first year. They're usually longer, include more policy analysis, and often contain a maze of concurring and dissenting opinions that must be pieced together to discern the holding of the Court.

A substantial portion of "Civ Pro," as students call it, is devoted to the topic of "personal jurisdiction." A court has the power to hear a lawsuit only if it has jurisdiction over all the parties—i.e., the authority to make binding decisions on them. The basic concept is that each party to a lawsuit must have some connection to the court's geographic jurisdiction for the court to have personal jurisdiction over them.

Sound easy? It's not. Personal jurisdiction is one of the most difficult and heavily tested issues in Civil Procedure. (A good tip to remember across the board is that professors generally like to test on the most difficult material, not the easiest.) Depending on your professor, you might spend several grueling weeks studying the evolution of personal jurisdiction rules via a chronology of famous Supreme Court cases.

Each case modifies the one preceding it, leaving students wondering why they can't just study the last one, since it contains the most up-to-date treatment of the law. The answer is that a full understanding of complex legal doctrine sometimes can be achieved only by studying its historical evolution. It's probably a fair statement to say that in most

Civil Procedure courses, students cannot excel without a thorough understanding of the law of personal jurisdiction.

Every 1L course has at least one classic case that all law students remember studying. For Civil Procedure, that case is *Pennoyer v. Neff*,[33] a complicated artifact about personal jurisdiction with little modern relevance. Quoting Shakespeare's *Macbeth*, one law professor said about *Pennoyer*: "Confusion now hath made its masterpiece."[34] When I was a student, I'm not sure my understanding of *Pennoyer v. Neff* ever progressed beyond wondering why the case wasn't called *Mitchell v. Neff*, since the party who started the whole mess was not Pennoyer, but a colorful lawyer named J.H. Mitchell.

Other topics commonly covered include: "the *Erie* doctrine" (governing whether state or federal substantive law applies in a federal case), motions to dismiss, discovery, class actions, summary judgment (a mechanism for judges to dispose of a case without a trial), and the doctrines of res judicata and collateral estoppel (which determine whether a case or claim that has already been heard once can be relitigated).

As with all courses, student reactions toward Civil Procedure vary. One student consultant said it was one of her most "boring" courses, while another said it was "fun." Another student, who liked the course and loved the professor, said:

> This is not the most exciting class you will take. It is difficult to get excited about Rule 41, or 65, or any of the rules for that matter. They just aren't very "sexy." And honestly, I never heard any of my classmates come out of a Civil Procedure class and say, "Man, that was awesome. I can't wait to see how that Rule 18 issue is gonna turn out tomorrow!"

On one issue, near unanimity of student opinion exists: Civil Procedure is one of the most difficult first-year courses. This is attributable in part to the fact that the subject matter is unfamiliar ("not even covered on TV!" wrote a student consultant) and also because the rules are technical and not intuitive. Moreover, civil procedure rules usually have to be interpreted in the context of litigation involving other areas

---

33. 95 U.S. 714 (1877).

34. Wendy Collins Perdue, *Sin, Scandal and Substantive Due Process:* *Personal Jurisdiction and* Pennoyer *Reconsidered*, 62 WASH. L. REV. 479, 479 (1987).

of law (e.g., a contract, property, or tort dispute), which you'll be learning at the same time you're trying to learn civil procedure.

Contracts

Contracts focuses on the formation, performance, and breach of oral and written agreements. Much of the course focuses on the three essential ingredients to the formation of a binding contract: offer (a person has to make an offer to enter into a contract), acceptance (the other person has to accept the offer), and consideration (each party must give something of value to the other as part of the bargain). Infinite permutations exist regarding each of these requirements that make them much more complex than they might sound. One student advisor offered this capsule overview of the three requirements:

> This course is all about three words: offer, acceptance, and consideration. From the beginning of the course these three words are drilled into your head constantly. Chances are, if you're not paying attention in class one day and you end up getting called on, answering with one of the three "magic words" will at least get you in the ballpark of the correct answer. (Of course, I'm certainly not advocating drifting off in class.)

> This course began with a simple question, or at least what I thought was a simple question: What constitutes an offer? You will find that there are rarely any simple questions in law school. There's always something lurking under the surface of a seemingly simple question. We read and discussed LOTS of cases initially just trying to determine whether or not an offer was made. For me, this was interesting because as our professor correctly explained, we enter into contracts every day of our lives. From signing a credit card receipt to an apartment lease to accepting your first job offer after law school—we all have experience dealing with contracts even though we may not think about it.

> After addressing whether or not an offer was made, we examined what it means to accept an offer. Now, you might be thinking at this point, "Duh, I know

what an offer is and how to accept it. Can they just go ahead and give me my law degree already?'' That line of thinking would be a mistake. As you will learn, acceptance can be manifested in many ways, and one can be held to that manifestation even if they claim accepting the offer was not their intent. Be on the lookout for one of the most famous and interesting acceptance cases, *Lucy v. Zehmer*, which involved a negotiation between two intoxicated parties for a piece of farmland. One of the parties jokingly signed over his farmland on the back of a restaurant check thinking that the negotiation was done in jest. However, as he soon found out, this was considered a valid manifestation of acceptance and he had to sell his farm. (One moral of this case: don't drink and sell farmland. The two don't mix.)

The third piece of the Contracts puzzle is consideration. In my opinion, consideration was the most difficult of the three major concepts to understand. Whether or not a party gives consideration for an offer is a difficult question, and often court opinions will differ on seemingly similar cases with similar facts. Additionally, I found that most of our exam questions dealt with the issue of whether or not consideration was given to constitute a valid contract. [McClurg note: More support for what I told you about professors preferring to test on the most difficult material.] Don't feel too bad if you have no idea what I'm talking about now. Trust me, you will spend an inordinate amount of time discussing consideration during your Contracts class, and you'll likely be just as confused as I was afterwards. (Just kidding . . . I hope.)

In addition to offer, acceptance, and consideration, you'll learn about the scope of contractual obligations, remedies for breaches of contracts, excuses for performance such as impossibility, and something called the parol evidence rule, which relates to what, if any, extraneous evidence outside the contract can be considered in interpreting it. No point trying to explain it here. As a student consultant who finished number one in her class wrote: ''I still could not fully explain to you how the rule operates.''

Like Property below, the facts in Contracts cases can be detailed and complex, making the cases more time-consuming to read and brief than most cases in Torts or Criminal Law.

Criminal Law

Criminal Law is the study of criminal offenses and defenses, primarily the former. Because criminal cases are intensely covered by the media and are a favorite subject of law-related television series and movies, students arrive at law school thinking the subject area will be heavily emphasized. But Criminal Law is the only first-year course that takes students out of the realm of civil litigation and into the darker world of crime and how the legal system responds to it.

Like Torts, Criminal Law is highly "element"-based. All criminal offenses are composed of elements that must be proved by the prosecution beyond a reasonable doubt. If any element is missing, a completed crime has not occurred. A great deal of class time is devoted to understanding the two most fundamental elements of a crime: actus reus (the criminal act itself) and mens rea (the mental state required to be convicted of a particular crime). You'll study the elements of core crimes such as homicide, theft, and burglary, as well as the elements of "inchoate crimes" such as attempt, conspiracy, and solicitation. Inchoate crimes, which can be tricky to understand, are offenses for which a defendant can be convicted even where the object crime is never completed. If Amanda hires Bluto to kill Carl, that's a crime even if Carl is unharmed. Defenses to crimes also have elements that must be proved.

Making matters more difficult, because modern criminal law is mostly statutory, you probably will have to study and compare the common law (judge-made law) to statutory law (laws passed by legislatures). Learning to read, interpret, and parse statutes is a different skill from learning to read and interpret cases. Confusing matters even more, it's possible you'll be required to study and compare both the English *and* U.S. common law *and* both the Model Penal Code (a uniform code of criminal law often used as a model for criminal statutes) *and* the criminal statutes actually adopted in your state. This could mean that for one criminal offense, such as homicide, you might be required to learn the distinct elements under English common law, U.S. common law, the

Model Penal Code, and your state's criminal statutes. If your Criminal Law course is taught in this fashion, making graphs and charts can be an effective strategy for keeping all the elements straight.

But it might be taught in a *completely* different fashion. In Chapter 9, I discuss the difference between professors who teach from a primarily practical perspective and those who teach from a primarily theoretical perspective. These divergent approaches can occur in any course, but Criminal Law is a prime candidate for theoretical teaching among 1L courses. Instead of focusing on all the detailed rules and elements, your Criminal Law professor might choose to concentrate (as mine did) on big-picture policy issues, such as the societal policies and theories underlying criminal punishment and sentencing. The difference in these teaching approaches is like night and day for students.

One pitfall to watch out for is that some important doctrines of criminal law parallel similar doctrines under tort law. Criminal Law usually is a one-semester course taught in the second semester, while Torts is usually taught in the first semester or both the first and second semesters. As one student said, the overlap can be "both a blessing and a curse" because, while it's comforting to approach a topic with which you already are familiar, important differences exist in the details between criminal law and tort law. For example, "assault" under criminal law is a different concept from "assault" under tort law. Make it a point to keep the two subject areas separate in your mind.

One upside of Criminal Law is that, as in Torts, many of the cases have interesting, even juicy fact patterns. Where else are you going to find a case like *Regina v. Dudley?*[35] This classic from England is the chilling tale of some castaways who, after being stranded on a lifeboat for twenty days with nothing to eat but two cans of turnips and a turtle, cannibalized a seventeen-year-old cabin boy. Four days later they were rescued by a passing ship. Oops! Back in England, the three survivors faced a variety of criminal charges, including assault with a deadly molar and abdominal possession of a fibula. Also, murder. The crewmen defended on the ground of "justification." The defense of justification says you can commit a crime without penalty so long as it is committed in

---

35. 14 Q.B.D. 273 (Queen's Bench 1884).

the interest of avoiding a greater harm. The defendants argued it was better that one cabin boy die than all four of them starve to death, which isn't a bad argument. But oops again. The defendants never consulted the cabin boy for his thoughts on the matter before slitting his throat and feasting on him. The court rejected the defense.

A downside is that criminal law itself can be less than scintillating. Learning it often requires a lot of memorization of the different elements of different offenses. Students coming out of Criminal Law often experience polar-opposite reactions to the subject. Some students go into the course thinking they won't like it and come out wanting to practice criminal law. Others complete the course swearing they will never have anything to do with a criminal case.

Property

In Property, students study the principles of law governing the ownership and transfer of personal property (stuff not attached to land) and real property (land or structures attached to land). Your Property casebook, for example, is an item of personal property. The floor you slam it down on in frustration is part of real property. Most of Property—and most of what you will be tested on—will focus on the law of real property.

Your first assignments in Property may cover cases going back to the 1800s. Unlike the law of most other subjects, which has evolved over time, many of the rules governing property rights were frozen in place centuries ago. Thus, historical context is more important to understanding Property than some other 1L courses.

In approaching Property, keep in mind this big-picture point: a person does not "have" real property, but rather has an "interest" in real property. That interest can be purchased, found, gifted, inherited, sold, lost, given away, or devised. The interest can be absolute or conditional. It can be partial or whole. Much of the study of property is simply how the law treats various interests in real property.

Well, "simply" may be a bad word choice. Property is filled with alien concepts such as adverse possession, easements, restrictive covenants, the fee system, marketable title, and, of course, future interests. I recall Property being my hardest first-year course and it was all because of future interests. The law of future interests is a maze-like set of rules regulating the ability of one to control interests in land in the future, such as by way of a will or trust.

One famous future interests rule—the Rule Against Perpetuities—is so ridiculously complicated that the distinguished California Supreme Court once suggested it's impossible for a lawyer to commit malpractice for misunderstanding the rule.[36] You gotta love that, along with the fact that some of the satellite doctrines under the Rule Against Perpetuities have names that sound like old blues tunes. The "Bad as to One, Bad as to All" and "Unborn Widow" rules could have been classic hits for Muddy Waters. The only thing most lawyers remember about the Rule Against Perpetuities is that, for reasons never fully explained, "twenty-one years" is important to property law. It's all very confusing, so don't fret too much if your class notes on the Rule Against Perpetuities end up looking like this:

> **Professor's lecture:** No contingent future interest in a transferee is good unless it must vest or fail to vest within twenty-one years of the death of some life in being at the time of the creation of the interest.

> **Student's notes:** No astringent foosball interest?? . . . must vest OR FAIL TO VEST . . . twenty-one years . . . death . . . life in bean . . . creation? interest?

> **Professor:** The rationale for the rule is straightforward. It's designed to limit efforts by grantors to restrict the free alienation of property by burdening it with contingent future interests.

> **Student:** Rationale for rule straightforward—designed to limit grantees ORS . . . something, something, something—SLOW THE * * * * DOWN!—Alien Nation of Property? . . . BUY STUDY AID!

> **Professor:** The simple way to understand the rule is to remember that it all has to do with the vesting or failure to vest of a contingent future interest within the lifetime of a measuring life or twenty-one years after that person's death.

---

36. *See* Lucas v. Hamm, 364 P.2d 685, 690 (Cal. 1961) ("[F]ew, if any, areas of the law have been fraught with more confusion or concealed more traps for the unwary draftsman. . . . [A]n error of the type relied on by plaintiffs does not show negligence . . . .").

Student: Simple way to understand rule is to remember that it all has to do with ... TWENTY–ONE YEARS, TWENTY–ONE YEARS, TWENTY–ONE YEARS ...

Fortunately, precisely because it is so convoluted, the Rule Against Perpetuities usually isn't a major focus of a Property exam. But the rest of the law pertaining to future interests often is because, as mentioned, professors usually test more difficult material over simpler material. While future interest rules are technical and tricky, once you get a handle on them, they're easy to apply.

That's part of the good news about Property. Unlike the law in many subjects, like Torts, where shades of gray dominate, the rules in Property are more black and white. As a consequence, more definite "correct answers" exist to property law questions. As one student advisor wrote, "many property problems operate exactly like math problems." Once you master the rules, it's easier than in courses with more abstract rules to apply them with confidence.

Torts

You may think you have no idea what a tort is. Perhaps you think it's a dessert, but that's a "torte." In fact, Torts is a subject with which entering students have at least some familiarity, whether they realize it or not. Who, for example, hasn't heard about the infamous (albeit grossly distorted) McDonald's coffee spill lawsuit? That was a tort case. So are all the lawsuits for damages involving pharmaceutical products, asbestos, breast implants, and tobacco. Medical malpractice suits are tort cases. So are automobile accident suits. Basically, any time a person is physically or emotionally injured through the conduct of another, whether in a train derailment or through cyber-bullying, the potential for a tort suit arises. Tort law is also part of a controversial national political agenda known as the "tort reform movement" that receives substantial media attention.

A tort is a civil wrong other than a breach of contract (which is also a civil wrong) for which the law allows the plaintiff a right of action for money damages. Like Criminal Law, Torts is highly element-based. All torts consist of a set of elements, each of which must be proved by the plaintiff to make out a successful claim.

Most tort courses begin with a study of the seven basic intentional torts (i.e., claims arising from intentionally inflicted injuries): assault, battery, false imprisonment, intentional infliction of emotional distress, trespass to land, trespass to chattels, and conversion (the latter two relate to interferences with personal property). This is followed by a study of the basic privileges or defenses to the intentional torts: consent, self-defense, defense of others, defense of property, recovery of property, and necessity (such as eating the cabin boy in *Regina v. Dudley*).

Students usually enjoy learning about intentional torts because the case facts are interesting and the rules are straightforward and easy to organize. They are a good "learning bike" for new law students in the first few weeks of law school. For the same reasons, a lot of the examples used in this book will involve intentional torts.

The bulk of every Torts course is the topic of negligence. Negligence law is essentially the study of liability for "accidents." People are liable for damages under negligence law when they fail to exercise reasonable care and that failure causes injury. Negligence principles are mostly intuitive but can be difficult to get a firm grasp on because they are so amorphous.

What, for example, is "reasonable care"? And when can we say that an act is a responsible cause of an injury? If Bloodymess Productions makes and sells a violent video game to Alex, a minor, and Alex subsequently engages in violence against others after playing the game, did Bloodymess fail to act reasonably? Was Bloodymess a cause of the ensuing violence? These are the types of issues you will grapple with daily in trying to solve the puzzles of negligence law. The words "reasonable" and "unreasonable" will creep into your everyday vocabulary and contribute to your driving the non-law students around you out of their minds.

Depending on the number of credit hours allotted to Torts, topics of study apart from the intentional torts and negligence may include strict liability (of which products liability is the largest component), wrongful death, tort damages, and defamation and privacy.

Tort cases, like those in Criminal Law, can make for interesting reading because of the human element involved when people injure each other, either intentionally or negligently. Sex,[37] drugs,[38] and rock and roll[39]—Torts offers a little of everything. Torts is where students study one of the most famous and memorable cases in American jurisprudential history: *Palsgraf v. Long Island Railroad Co.*,[40] a wacky, confusing case with opinions from two heavyweight judges about an exploding package of fireworks that supposedly knocked a heavy scale on top of Helen Palsgraf at the Long Island train station in 1924. I always tell my students that *Palsgraf* may be the only law school case that *every* lawyer remembers. Several students have tested this assertion, always reporting back that the lawyers they ask about the case still remember it well. Try it.

Students sometimes mistakenly think Torts is "easier" than other first-year subjects and devote less time to studying it. It's true that many of the basic principles of tort law are not intellectually difficult, but like all subjects, Torts is full of little twists and nuances that make it more complicated than it first appears. And like all subjects, it has its own unusually difficult topics, with "proximate cause"—one of the elements of negligence—being the signature example. But even assuming one subject was somehow measurably easier than another, it would be a mistake to treat it any differently in terms of the amount of studying and preparation you put into it. You're not competing against the course. You're only competing against other students in the course. As I always remind my students: "There are just as many low grades in Torts as in other subjects."

* * *

Your level of interest in and enjoyment of any particular course will depend partly on your personality type and learning preferences. Students who are more comfortable with concrete rules may love Property. Students who prefer abstractions and possibilities may prefer Torts and, if offered in the first year, Constitutional Law. Your relative enjoyment of

---

37. *See, e.g.*, Doe v. Moe, 827 N.E.2d 240 (Mass. App. Ct. 2005) (suit against ex-girlfriend alleging that negligence during intercourse caused plaintiff to suffer a fractured penis).

38. *See, e.g.*, Hegel v. Langsam, 273 N.E.2d 351 (Ohio Ct. C.P. 1971) (suit by parents of college student against university alleging negligence in not pro-tecting their seventeen-year-old daughter from using drugs).

39. *See, e.g.*, McCollum v. CBS, Inc., 249 Cal. Rptr. 187 (Cal. Ct. App. 1988) (suit against rock singer Ozzy Osbourne on behalf of teenager who committed suicide after listening to Ozzy's song, *Suicide Solution*).

40. 162 N.E. 99 (N.Y. 1928).

particular courses also will be heavily influenced by the professors teaching them. Good teachers can make any subject come alive, while ineffective teachers can make even the most interesting material coma-inducing. Similarly, organized, well-prepared teachers with good communication skills can make even the most complex material accessible and understandable, while disorganized, unprepared teachers can render even simple material obtuse.

CHAPTER 6

THE FIRST DAYS: STARTING OUT RIGHT

The first days of law school are exciting, memorable, and usually quite stressful. Everything is a blur because it's all so new: new people, new physical surroundings, a whole new language, and a mysterious new teaching methodology. It's enough to make anyone nervous. Even professors get nervous on the first days.

The heartening news is that the comfort level in law school classrooms increases quickly. When I walk into Torts on the first day of class, even with eighty people in the room, it's so quiet one could hear a Xanax drop. But with each passing day, students get to know each other, their surroundings, and their professors a little better. They're relieved that the Socratic method is not nearly as torturous as rumored, that law professors are by and large nice folks who are good at what they do and care about their students, and that they can actually grasp the legal principles being taught. As in every other setting, familiarity breeds comfort and relaxes tension. Within just a couple of weeks, it sounds like I'm walking into a rowdy pub as I approach the classroom door. Instead of silence, I'm greeted with a cacophony of excited chatter and laughter.

You want to get off on the right foot in these first days. Missteps can result in embarrassment, risk branding you in a negative light, and create extra stress that can interfere with learning. The advice in this chapter is designed to help you come out of the blocks smoothly and cleanly as you begin the 1L race.

Getting the Most Out of Orientation

All law schools conduct an orientation for incoming students, usually in the week immediately preceding the commencement of classes. Orientations vary in length and scope, from two to as long as six days. Most orientation programs are two or three days, which is plenty long.

Students often find orientation frustrating and a waste of time. Who can blame them? Attending law school requires so much advance groundwork—from taking the LSAT to completing lengthy applications to arranging housing and financial aid to reading books like this one—that by the time law school actually rolls around, students walk through the doors champing at the bit to get going. But it doesn't work that way. First, it's orientation time.

A former student once drew an interesting analogy between law school orientation and having sex for the first time. These weren't the exact words, but they're close:

> You've waited all your life. You've dreamed about it, planned for it, obsessed over it, visualized it, practiced for it, and now the day finally arrives that you get to actually DO IT. You're totally psyched, when all of a sudden a bunch of people burst into the room and say: "Stop! You cannot have sex right now. Before you can have sex, you must to sit down and listen to us tell you for an entire week what it is *like* to have sex."

Students tend to take two diametrically opposed approaches to orientation: they either disregard it or immerse themselves in it with total devotion. Both approaches can be counterproductive. Blowing off orientation certainly is a poor way to get started on such a big new adventure in life. As discussed below, some orientation events will be of value to you. Equally important, not acting professionally during orientation reflects poorly on you.

The people responsible for organizing and running orientation are acutely tuned into negative attitudes, disparaging comments they overhear, and who doesn't attend required events. One of them is quite likely to pass the information on to one or more of your first-year professors, as in: "You have a student in your section—Mr./Ms. Blank—who skipped out on orientation." Or: "You're not going to believe what I overheard this kid in your section say during the reception."

Upper-level student orientation mentors and group leaders also sometimes relay information to faculty about the new students they encounter.

Here's a specific example of what I'm talking about. On the first day of orientation, a colleague came into my office, clearly irritated. He said he had just met with the entering class to do a case-briefing exercise. The new students, approximately 150 of them, were supposed to have registered for the legal writing TWEN course site (see below) and downloaded a case for the exercise. From data available on TWEN, my colleague was able to determine before going into the orientation session that eight of the new students had failed to download the case. What did he do? First and foremost, he formed a bad impression of the eight students. Second, he purposely called on them during the exercise to expose their unpreparedness to the entire entering class. Third, he informed me and perhaps other first-year professors about their lack of preparation. This is not the way you want to begin your new career: with a bad reputation before the first class has even been held.

On the other hand, depending on the rigor of the orientation, completely immersing yourself in orientation as if your life depended on it is not a great idea either. I taught at one law school that had a six-day orientation, which included a lengthy session on the Saturday before school started when the students would have been better off at home preparing for their first week of classes. Just reading the schedule of events, many of which went well into the night, was exhausting. Some of the events required substantial reading to prepare for them.

It was all well-intended and each individual event had value, but it was simply too much packaged together. I watched the students arrive eager and bright-eyed on Monday morning of orientation week and leave Saturday afternoon looking like they had just finished first-semester exams. When classes began the following Monday, many of the students looked worn out already.

I suggest a middle-ground attitude and approach to orientation in which your goal is to maximize the benefits while conserving your emotional and physical energy. Simply keeping in mind that orientation doesn't technically "count" for anything should help you keep your stress level in check and preserve some psychic energy. Take it seriously, but not gravely.

If the school assigns background reading material as part of orientation, by all means read it, but don't wear yourself out fretting over every line you don't understand. Pay particular attention to assignments pertaining to practical study skills, such as case-briefing or outlining. These crucial skills take time and practice to develop, so you want to take advantage of early opportunities to start learning about them. If the school holds a "sample class," which many schools do, make sure to prepare for it. They usually involve one assigned case to read. Personally, I've always thought these classes—which are intended to help "demystify" law school—are a waste of time. Because the students lack the background and context necessary to meaningfully process the case, they don't really resemble real classes. But since this is everyone's first group encounter with a professor and the Socratic method, you certainly don't want to be remembered as "that person" who showed up unprepared for the sample class.

Here are some things to focus on during orientation:

Get your first-week assignments.

You should receive your first assignments or be able to access them on the law school website well before Orientation, but if not, make sure to track them down. Nearly all professors post assignments in advance and dive into the material at the first class.

Buy your books and pick up other course materials.

If you haven't already bought books online, buy your required books at the law school or university bookstore as early during orientation as possible. Not infrequently, for a variety of reasons, snafus occur in book orders that result in the bookstore running out of books. Stress reduction, not enhancement, is the order of the day. You do not want to be scrambling around trying to locate an alternative source for the first week's course assignments because the bookstore ran out of books. See Chapter 2 for more information about what books to buy and what not to buy.

If for whatever reason you are unable to obtain a book before classes start, borrow a classmate's book and make a photocopy of the assignments for the entire first week. If you don't know any classmates, go to the professor and ask for help. She should be able to provide you with a copy of the assignment or lend you an extra copy of the book.

Some professors may also have handouts for you to pick up before classes start, so be sure to grab those. Again, early birds get the worm. I always put a sufficient number of handout packets for Torts in a box outside my office, but they somehow always run out. Students either take more than one package or students from the other section mistakenly grab one. This invariably results in some last-minute stragglers standing sheepishly at my door asking if I have extra copies or, worse, starting classes without having read parts of the initial assignment.

Register for your professors' online course sites.

Most professors use online course sites, either TWEN or LexisNexis Web Course sites. TWEN is an acronym for The West Education Network, operated by Westlaw. LexisNexis Web Course sites are built on the Blackboard platform. Westlaw and LexisNexis are the two major competitors in the arena of online legal research. Depending on the individual professor and type of site, online course sites may be used to access course materials (including syllabi, assignments, classroom policies, course calendars, etc.), participate in online discussions, receive and submit online assignments, work through quizzes, link to CALI (Computer–Assisted Legal Instruction) exercises, exchange email with your professors and classmates, and more.

Professors often use the email function of their online course sites to communicate with the class, including sending information about first assignments, class policies, and the like. Thus, register for these sites as soon as passwords are made available to you.

And be sure to check your law school email account once a day *at a minimum!* Some other law profs and I were recently discussing why it is that so many modern law students miss important email messages. It seems to be a trend. Perhaps it has something to do with the advent of smart phones. Whatever the reason, if a professor sends out an email on Tuesday changing the assignment for Wednesday, it's something you're going to need and want to know about.

Get a locker.

Most law schools offer student lockers for a nominal fee. At the beginning of law school, you might not be sure whether you'll need or use a locker. But unless you absolutely can't afford it, you're better off getting one if the opportunity is presented, especially if you're at a school where there are not enough lockers to go around. Even if you end up not using it every day, having a place to securely stash some of those heavy books will come in handy from time to time.

Listen to advice, but sort it carefully.

Everyone will be giving you advice on how to succeed in law school, especially upper-level students. Upper-level students love to give advice to incoming students. Sometimes it's good advice. When I started law school, an upper-level student told me to buy the *Gilbert* study aid for Criminal Law. He explained that while our professor would talk almost exclusively about theory in class, come exam time he would expect us to know and apply black-letter law (i.e., the actual legal rules). Sure enough, class discussions were geared almost exclusively toward theory. My class notes were a garbled mess.

I followed his advice. I bought and studied the *Gilbert* for Criminal Law. The moment I started reading the final exam, which was my first law school exam, I knew that study aid was the single best purchasing decision I had ever made. The exam questions were classic issue-spotting/problem-solving essays requiring mastery of the black-letter rules we never learned in class. I received my first A in law school in Criminal Law.

But upper-level students also give some really bad advice, much of which involves ways to cut corners, so be wary of what they tell you. Although it will be socially awkward, if an upper-level student starts piling on the shortcut advice, ask the person for his or her GPA or class rank. The most vocal advice-givers are sometimes the weakest students. You could phrase it like this: "Thanks for all the advice. Did it work for you? How did you come out in terms of class rank and GPA after the first year?"[41]

---

41. Be aware, however, that students have been known to prevaricate about their grades. At the end of an-swering a question about what advice they would give to a close loved one starting law school, one student added:

Law professors also give advice to incoming students. Law professor advice may be more reliable overall than student advice, but it might not be as practical or realistic. For example, I have a hard time picturing my Criminal Law prof explaining: "I'm not really going to teach you much actual law in this course, but I will expect you to know it all for the final exam, so I'd advise you to run, not walk, to the bookstore and get your hands on the *Gilbert* study aid for Criminal Law." Law professors may also go to the opposite extreme from giving shortcut advice, saying you will have to sacrifice every single second of your waking life to survive in law school, which is not accurate. If you follow the C.R.E.D.O. in Chapter 10, you can both succeed in law school and have time to enjoy life.

Both learning and teaching styles are idiosyncratic. You're likely to receive conflicting advice even from professors. Don't be overwhelmed by it all. Process all advice before acting on it.

Visit your classrooms.

A great trial lawyer taught me the value of always visiting a courtroom in advance of a trial or big hearing to check out the lay of the land and get a feel for it. Familiarity with a place or situation prompts brain neurons known as "place cells" to fire, making us feel comfortable and at home. Studies show, for example, that if a person is shown a geometric shape for just one-thousandth of a second, far too quickly to register in the conscious mind, the person will like that shape better the next time they see it.

Visiting all your classrooms during orientation week will not only raise your comfort level, it will eliminate the added stress you'll suffer if you have to hunt them down for the first time in the rush between classes during those first days. Knowing where the rooms are also will help you avoid the embarrassing predicament of arriving late to class, something you want to avoid (see below). Moreover, an early visit will allow you to contemplate in advance where you want to sit, since you will be stuck in that seat all semester and possibly all year (see below).

"Oh! And one more thang! Law students lie about their grades. They do. If seven people tell you they received an *A* in Civil Procedure or Property, some of them are lying."

Socialize.

Most orientations include one or more social events where students can meet and mingle with their classmates and some of the professors. Take advantage of these. Having a close network of supportive law school friends is invaluable to your success and well-being. Because all 1Ls are in the same overcrowded lifeboat, most people jump at the chance to make friends in these early days. When all is said and done, the friends you make in law school will be one of the best features of your entire experience.

If you spot someone at one of these events who you know is going to be one of your first-year professors (they'll usually be wearing name tags), go up and introduce yourself. This is hard for a lot of people to do, but as elaborated on in Chapter 9, there is value in getting to know and being known by your professors. The fact that they're attending the event (most profs don't) means that they're probably approachable people. Many law professors are shy, introverted types who are not good at "making the rounds," so don't wait for them to approach you. Don't worry. They're not going to ask you deep legal questions, but they may default to asking the classic introductory question, "What made you decide to come to law school?", which is the law professor socializing equivalent of "What's your sign?" or "What's your major?" So have an answer for that one.

Also make an effort to introduce yourself to the law school staff, such as librarians, faculty assistants, and employees in the registrar and admissions offices. These people can help you a lot. Treat them with respect, even deference. Some of them get treated shabbily by hierarchical professors and snotty students. They'll appreciate the courtesy and can do a lot to make your law school life easier and better.

Some law schools, although a diminishing number due in part to tort liability concerns, serve alcoholic beverages at these functions. Be careful about consuming alcohol as a way to calm your nerves. This is not a good time to get intoxicated.

Take a (Good) Seat

The Socratic method entails professors calling on students frequently. To do that effectively in such large classes, they use seating charts. Your professors will pass around a seating chart—sometimes with advance notice but sometimes on the first day—and you'll be stuck in that seat for the entire semester, perhaps even the entire year. Some students grow attached to their seats:

> Sometimes I feel as attached to my seat as my loved ones. I always get to exams early to sit in my same seat. Even in later semesters, I always try to get that same seat. It has become a comfort zone of normalcy and reliability in the midst of the chaos.

In the chapter on types of law students (Chapter 4), I differentiated the Backburners from the Front Row Crowd in general terms. Let's investigate in more detail why you should resist the natural temptation to sit in the back.

Non-law school educators have conducted a variety of studies on the relationship of seat choice to student personality-type and academic performance. They support one proposition quite clearly: students who choose to sit in the front of the room are generally better students. They have higher GPAs, participate more frequently in class, and receive better grades in the course.[42]

Several studies have linked this better performance to personality differences between students who choose to sit in front and those who choose the back. In other words, with regard to the cause and effect relationship between seat selection and academic performance, research suggests that students who sit in front by choice do better because better students choose to sit in front. Correlatively, students who sit in the back tend to have more negative attitudes about school and about participating in class. Many of these students want to be disengaged.[43]

Does sitting in back actually *cause* poorer performance? One interesting study found that it did. Conducted in a large physics course, the researchers randomly assigned seats to students and then measured their academic performance in the course. The study found that students in the back of the room were six times as likely to receive *F*s in the course as

---

42. *See* Mary Ellen Benedict & John Hoag, *Seating Location in Large Lectures: Are Seating Preferences or Location Related to Course Performance?*, 35 J. ECON. EDUC. 215 (2004).

43. *See* Herbert J. Walberg, *Physical and Psychological Distance in the Classroom*, 77 SCH. REV. 64 (1969).

students sitting in the front of the room.[44] While the overall research is inconclusive (a later study found no difference in exam performance[45]), common sense suggests several reasons seating choice could improve your law school experience.

Most important, you'll be able to hear much better nearer to the front. Under the Socratic method, much of the talking is done by students. While most law professors speak loudly enough for people in the back to hear them, most law students do not. Moreover, students usually are facing the front when speaking, naturally detracting from the ability of students behind them to hear what they're saying. On several occasions, I've sat in the back of law school classrooms observing other professors' classes dismayed at my inability to hear student comments, even in well-designed classrooms. Many law school classrooms are not well designed. They're acoustical black holes.

Of course, you'll also be able to see better. Many professors use technology, such as PowerPoint slides projected on a screen, as visual aids, but many others still write on the board. Generally, anything a law professor deems worthy of taking the time to write on a board or project on a screen is important. First-year classrooms are big, but law professors, even the ones who seem larger than life, have normal-sized hands and write in normal-sized lettering. From the back or sides of the room, you might not be able to read it.

You'll also have fewer focus-breakers to contend with. As discussed below, many students misuse their notebook computers to browse the web, etc., which can be distracting to the students around them. The farther toward the front you are, the fewer of these and other distractions you'll have to contend with.

Finally, it's well established by research that active learning is much more effective than passive learning and students closer to the front tend to be more actively engaged.

44. Katherine K. Perkins & Carl E. Wieman, *The Surprising Impact of Seat Location on Student Performance*, 43 PHYSICS TCHR. 30 (2005).

45. *See* Steven Kalinowksi & Mark L. Taper, *The Effect of Seat Location on Exam Grades and Student Perceptions in an Introductory Biology Class*, 36 J.C. SCI. TEACHING 54 (2007). The authors noted differences that might explain the conflicting results with the Perkins–Wieman study, including that the Perkins–Wieman study involved a larger group of students and larger lecture hall. First-year law school classes, as noted, average seventy to eighty students and are held in large rooms.

I'll share a closely guarded law professor secret with you. People in the very front get cold-called on less often than other students. One reason is that their physical closeness to the professor causes them to lower their voices even more than usual, as if they're engaged in a private one-on-one conversation, so they can't be heard by other students. Students in the front also may fall below the professor's sightline. Finally, there may be a wish, even if only an unconscious one, by professors to reward these brave souls.

Even assuming seating has no effect on academic performance, sitting in front will change the manner in which you experience law school. You'll be a participant in your class community, rather than simply an observer from a different zip code. Have you ever attended a play or concert and sat in the front? It's like attending a completely different event compared to sitting in the back. Law school classes are like that.

Classroom Etiquette

Law school classes are conducted more formally than most undergraduate classes, especially in the first year. Most first-year professors, for example, refer to students by their surnames, although younger profs are more likely to use first names. The expectations of student conduct and performance are substantially higher than in undergraduate programs, including the expectation that students conduct themselves like professionals. To avoid embarrassing yourself, offending your professors, and hurting your academic performance, follow these guidelines for classroom etiquette:

Be prepared.

As mentioned above, you will receive assignments *in advance* of the first class for each course. Don't get caught being anything less than fully prepared, particularly in the first days. An early unpleasant classroom incident could taint your view of law school, as well as how you are viewed by others.

Many law professors follow the approach of being much sterner at the beginning of a course and then gradually becoming more laid-back as the semester progresses. The goal is to set a tone in line with the expectations of a professional school. It's always easier for a professor to move from being strict to less strict, whereas it's nearly impossible for a professor to move effectively in the other direction; that is, from being easygoing or friendly to strict. This approach and mentality means that professors are more likely early on to "make examples" of students who commit classroom infractions.

For most professors, there is no legitimate excuse for being unprepared on the first day of law school. Here are some sample explanations from unprepared students and the likely mental reaction of the professor:

Student explanation: "I didn't know we had assignments for the first day."

Professor's thought process: "Everyone else figured it out. Therefore, you must either be lying or mentally defective."

Student explanation: "The bookstore ran out of books."

Professor's thought process: "You should have tracked down a book somewhere else, photocopied the assignment from a classmate's book, or come to me for help."

Student explanation: "I had a family emergency yesterday when I intended to prepare for class."

Professor's thought process: "You shouldn't have waited until yesterday."

What exactly does "being prepared" mean? As to each principal case assigned, you should know and have briefed: (1) the relevant facts of the case; (2) the procedural history that resulted in the case being heard by an appellate court (e.g., the trial court dismissed the complaint filed by the plaintiff and the plaintiff is appealing, or the trial court gave a legal instruction to the jury that the defendant asserts was incorrect and the defendant is appealing); (3) who won the case; (4) the substantive legal issue in the case; (5) the rule adopted by the court to resolve the substantive issue; and (6) why the court adopted the rule and resolved the case in the manner it did (i.e., the court's reasoning). We'll talk much more about these components in the case-briefing chapter.

Be on time.

Don't arrive late to class. Most law professors expect students to be punctual. It's distracting to everyone when students arrive late. Nevertheless, even when this expectation is made clear to students during orientation and in course materials, the beginning of every new school year is marked by uncomfortable incidents in which one or more students stroll casually into the room after class has begun, only to be publicly called out for it by the professor.

When students arrive late to my class, I give them what my students call, affectionately or not, "the evil eye." I stop everything and maximize discomfort by watching in silence as the student fumbles toward his seat. Why do I do it? Not to be cruel. I don't enjoy embarrassing students. I do it as a deterrent. I do it to let students know they have entered professional school, where learning is taken seriously. I do it because in the real legal world lawyers are expected to be on time.

My first job after law school was as a law clerk to U.S. District Court Judge Charles R. Scott, Middle District of Florida. Judge Scott taught me many valuable lessons about both life and law, including: don't ever show up late to court. Judge Scott was a kind man with a good sense of humor and mild judicial temperament, *except* when lawyers showed up late for hearings or trials. Each time this happened, I watched, wincing, as Judge Scott disdainfully scolded the lawyer—often in front of the lawyer's client and sometimes even in the presence of the jury—with comments like: "So, Mr. Smith, I suppose you think your time is more valuable than the court's time. More important than the time of these good jurors who came here to do their duty and serve their community. More important than the time of this court reporter who is being paid with taxpayer dollars." Looking at the jury, I sat there thinking, "There goes another lawyer's case down the drain." It's better to learn these kinds of lessons in law school than as a lawyer.

Of course, unexpected events arise that can cause even the most diligent students to arrive late. If that happens to you, simply apologize to the professor before (via email if you know you're going to be late) or after the class. Punctuality rules are aimed principally at the Chronically Late (see Chapter 4), those students who, without some kind of deterrent, will regularly barge into classes late.

I'll share two inside secrets with you about punctuality. First, your classmates may not tell you, but they don't appreciate the distraction of late-arriving students either. I hear from these students all the time. They're paying a lot of money to get the best education they can.

Second, many professors will not openly react to students who arrive late even though they care deeply about it. I remember a colleague at one school who stormed into my office seething about a particular student who routinely arrived late. I recall the term "sonofabitch" being liberally sprinkled throughout the conversation. I asked the professor why he didn't simply lay down the law on punctuality and he said he didn't like conflict and that it didn't fit his personality. Carrying a deep-seated grudge against the tardy, however, apparently did.

Having said all that, you will learn that some professors apparently really don't care about students being on time. A few profs even make a habit of arriving late themselves.

Mute electronic devices.

Yes, of course it's a no-brainer, but it still happens, so it's worth mentioning. One of my colleagues actually gives a "cell phone quiz" if a phone goes off—a real pop quiz that counts as part of the final grade.

Don't misuse your computer.

Don't use your computer in class to browse the web, play games, send email, or for any purpose other than taking notes. Trust me. This is a much bigger issue among law professors than you could imagine. I mentioned back in Chapter 2 that some law professors ban computers in class and listed their reasons. One of the biggest is that too many students misuse their computers to multitask in class. You would be shocked by how much attention law professors devote to this debate, in law journal articles, on listservs, blogs, any place they have a chance to rant about it. Many professors are truly torn between wanting to eliminate the problems computers can cause in classrooms while not taking away an important writing tool that most students depend on.

I'm a realist. I know from experience that this is one of those pieces of advice that many people will ignore. That's why I'm going to engage in a bit of what may seem like overkill in discussing the issue in the hope that your rational self-interest will prevail in deciding to follow this advice.

Good Reasons Not to Multitask On Your Computer in Class

You can't learn as effectively. The law is incredibly nuanced and complex. In most courses, a majority of what you will need to know for the exam will be derived from classroom elucidation of the reading assignments, not from the assignments themselves. It will require 100 percent of your mental processing power.

One response to the argument against extraneous computer use is that before computers, students played hangman, doodled, worked crossword puzzles, or simply daydreamed in class. True, but that was never a good academic success plan either. More important, there is a huge qualitative difference in the ubiquitous and pervasive distraction of a computer compared to old-fashioned classroom distractions. Yes, everyone has played tic-tac-toe in class at some point, but it's doubtful anyone ever spent a large portion of *every* class playing it. A study showed students underestimate the amount of time they spend off-task on their computers in class.[46] One student was found to be opening an average of 173 different active windows per lecture!

Some students scoff at the Luddites who would deny them these distractions, insisting they are so skilled at multitasking that they really can learn law and check sports scores at the same time. Is it true? No. Studies regarding the ability of the brain to engage in simultaneous tasks show unequivocally that the performance of one or both tasks directly suffers.

In one study, researchers divided a class into two groups. Prior to a lecture, one group was told to use their computers as usual, while the other was asked to close their computers. Afterwards, the researchers gave the students a surprise test. The students who used their laptops during the lecture performed significantly poorer on the test. Two months later the researchers replicated the test by switching the two groups of students, and got the same results.[47]

---

46. *See* James M. Kraushaar & David C. Novak, *Examining the Affects of Student Multitasking with Laptops During the Lecture*, 21 J. INFO. SYS. EDUC. 241, 249 (2010).

47. *See* Helene Hembrooke & Geri Gay, *The Laptop and the Lecture: The*

Another study suggested that even if multitasking does not necessarily decrease the overall ability to learn, it negatively affects the kind of learning used to acquire new concepts and information and to engage in deep analysis— learning abilities that are critical to law students. Researchers did MRI brain imaging of twenty-somethings engaged in dual-task learning. The brain imaging showed that multitaskers engaged in "habit learning" rather than "declarative learning." Habit learning relies on a portion of the brain used for repetitive skills, whereas declarative learning involves a portion of the brain used for storing and recalling information. The researchers concluded that even though people can learn while multitasking, they can't learn the material as well or be able to adapt it to changing conditions.[48]

Multitasking research also shows: that people lose considerable thinking-time each time they switch tasks; that multitaskers are more prone to commit cognitive errors while switching tasks; and, perhaps most worrisome, that habitual multitasking may permanently change the thinking process in ways that make it difficult for people to focus even when they want to.[49]

In short, the research verdict is unanimous. While some people are adept at doing several tasks simultaneously, they can't do all the tasks well because of the brain's limited processing ability. If your professor is defining the Rule Against Perpetuities at the same moment you're messaging your pal to see what time everyone is meeting up at the club, something has to give.

It's rude and disrespectful to your classmates. One complaint students have about computer bans in classes is that they are paternalistic. Basically, this amounts to an argument that they have an inalienable academic right to shoot themselves in the foot. Assuming arguendo that students possess this liberty interest, it overlooks that students who abuse computer privileges cause harm to the energy and

---

Effects of Multitasking in Learning Environments, 15 J. COMPUTING HIGHER EDUC. 46, 49 (2003).

48. *See* Karin Foerde et al., *Modulation of Competing Memory Systems by Distraction*, 103 PROC. NAT'L ACAD. SCI. 11778 (2006).

49. Anne Enquist, *Multitasking and Legal Writing*, 18 PERSP.: TEACHING LEGAL RES. & WRITING 7, 7–8 (2010) (discussing each of these items).

dynamics of the entire class when they mentally "check out." Closer to home (your seat), playing around on your computer is distracting to nearby classmates. As one student complained about instant messaging, "One IM sent during class has the possibility of distracting six people: two persons on each side of the recipient, the recipient, the sender, and perhaps two people behind the recipient. That's a lot of downtime in class for one little message."

Most professors have explicit policies against it. Violating any explicit class policy can constitute academic misconduct. Occasionally, computer misuse even crosses the boundary into the realm of overt cheating. Incidents have occurred where students instant message the answers to professors' questions to classmates being called on. Since classroom performance can be a basis for raising or lowering grades, such conduct could be grounds for Honor Code prosecutions.

Everyone can see what you're doing. Not only are you violating class policy and the professor's trust if you misuse your computer, you're doing it in front of a large group of eyewitnesses. Some students will lose respect for classmates who violate explicit law school or class rules. One of them might even tell the professor. The professor, in turn, whether or not he ever addresses the issue with you, may never trust you again.

The more frequently students misuse computers, the more justified professors feel in banning them, to everyone's detriment. I'm a supporter of computers and technology, but each time I sit in to observe another professor's class and see all the computer misuse going on, I move a step closer to banning computers in my classes.

If you're a well-intentioned student who wants to stay on task but fears you simply won't be able to resist the siren call of the internet during class, consider using—as some students do—one of the several programs available online that will help you resist the temptation, such as Freedom, Self-Control, and StayFocusd [sic]. The programs function similarly. Once you've downloaded the software onto your computer, you can block access to the internet or to particular websites or applications for set periods of time.

In general, in conducting yourself in class, keep in mind that your professors can see what's going on out there in the classroom. It always cracks me up that some students seem to think they're protected by a Harry Potter-type cloak of invisibility just because they're sitting in a group of people. Professors notice when students yawn, smirk, sigh heavily, roll their eyes, talk to their seat neighbors, or appear to be playing on their computers. Behave professionally in the classroom.

* * *

Following the suggestions in this chapter will help you get off to a good start in law school, particularly in your classes and with your professors. Just as important, it will put you on the right road to becoming a professional, which is what you are training to be. While most of the admonishments are common sense, some law students routinely ignore or violate them, often proclaiming ignorance. Don't be convinced you're too smart to fall prey to them. Conceit can make you blind to the obvious.

CHAPTER 7
THE SOCRATIC AND CASE METHODS: ORIGINS, PURPOSES, FACTS AND MYTHS

"Mr. Smith, what's a tort?"

Except for the student's name changing, those are often the first words I utter at my initial Torts class of a new academic year. No introduction, no "Let's get to know each other" chatting, no overview of the class or review of class policies, not even a "Hi, I'm McClurg." I enter the classroom, set my book and notes on the podium, look at the class roster, pick a name, and ask the question. I'm expecting the textbook answer—literally. When a student gives the right answer (it's not a difficult question—the definition is in the second sentence of the initial reading assignment), I start leading the student through a series of hypothetical fact patterns designed to explore what conduct might or might not qualify as a tort under the definition. And, in the words of legendary comedian Jackie Gleason, *awaaaaay we go.*

Likely within minutes, perhaps even seconds, of beginning your first official law school classes, you will be introduced to the Socratic method. Despite continuing criticism, the Socratic method has been, is, and will likely remain law school's "signature pedagogy."[50] The Socratic method involves professors calling on students, typically without prior notice, to recite and analyze cases (i.e., written judicial opinions) and

---

50. *See* CARNEGIE FOUNDATION REPORT, *supra*, at 23–24 (2007) (characterizing the Socratic method in these terms).

93

the legal principles raised therein. Most incoming law students are at least somewhat familiar with the Socratic method, usually through having heard exaggerated horror stories about it from people who went to law school or from fictionalized accounts in movies such as *The Paper Chase* and *Legally Blonde* or books such as Scott Turow's *One L.*

When I was a law student, my main question about the Socratic method was "why?" Why are the professors doing this to us? Why all the questions? Why no answers? Why don't they just tell us what the law is? Here's why:

How a Man Named Christopher Columbus Langdell Changed Your Life

The Socratic method is credited to and named after Socrates (470–399 BC), a Greek philosopher who engaged in continuous questioning of his students in a quest to discover moral and ethical truths. Along the way, he exposed their fallacies in reasoning, first, by getting the answerer to commit to certain assumptions and then asking questions designed to shine a light on the contradictions or other flaws in those assumptions. A hallmark of his method—one that continues to haunt law students more than two thousand years later—is that Socrates only asked questions. He rarely provided answers.

The origins of the Socratic method in law school teaching are traceable back to the 1870s and the inception of what is known as the "case method." To make any sense of the Socratic method, one must understand the case method. The two methods are inextricably intertwined.

In the old days, law was taught in U.S. law schools principally through a lecture method. Much like in many of your undergraduate courses, students would read explanations of the law in textbooks, professors would expand on that law in lectures, and students would be tested principally on their ability for rote memorization. But in the 1870s along came Christopher Columbus Langdell, the man credited with, or blamed for, irrevocably changing the way U.S. law students learn.

Langdell, a professor and later dean of Harvard Law School, believed that true mastery of the law could not be achieved by simply memorizing it. Rather, students had to develop a facility for *applying* legal principles to the varied fact patterns that lead to legal disputes, or what he called "the ever-tangled skein of human affairs."[51] By understanding how law is applied, Langdell believed students would be able to transfer what they learned in one context and apply it in other contexts. To implement his vision, he came up with the idea to replace explanatory textbooks with "casebooks" filled with appellate judicial opinions.

I still recall coming home from the bookstore before starting law school with my shiny new casebooks. I sat down and opened my Contracts book with excited anticipation. I was about to learn "law" for the first time! But I couldn't find any; well, not any I could make sense of. There was no explanation of contracts law, not even a definition of what constitutes a contract, just hundreds of pages of judicial opinions, many of them very old and opaquely written. I started reading the first case, but couldn't make heads or tails of it. I had no idea what the point was. If I had known then about Christopher Langdell, I probably would have cursed him. Casebooks haven't changed much. While most modern casebooks do contain some explanatory notes following the cases, the cases themselves remain the primary vehicle for learning law in U.S. law schools.

Under the case method, students do the heavy lifting. Instead of sitting passively listening to lectures, the case method requires students to think critically and discover the law on their own in response to questions posed by the professors.[52] The Socratic dialogue method of teaching developed as an instrument for implementing the case method. Think of it as the steering mechanism that guides the case method vehicle.

How It Works

The classic portrayal of the Socratic method in law school came from the 1973 movie, *The Paper Chase*, based on John Jay Osborn's book of the same name. Actor John Houseman won an Oscar for his portrayal of the curmudgeonly, imperious Professor Charles Kingsfield, a fictional Contracts profes-

---

51. Peggy Cooper Davis & Elizabeth Ehrenfest Steinglass, *A Dialogue About Socratic Teaching*, 23 N.Y.U. REV. L. & SOC. CHANGE 249, 263 (1997) (quoting Langdell).

52. *See generally id.* (exploring the history and present use of the Socratic method); David D. Garner, *The Continuing Vitality of the Case Method in the Twenty–First Century*, 2000 BYU EDUC. & L.J. 307 (2000) (providing history and summary of the case method).

sor at Harvard Law School, who torments first-year student
James T. Hart, played by Timothy Bottoms. The movie is a
classic that all law students should watch, but too few do. It's
fun. Rent it.

In the movie, Kingsfield is a terror, famously instructing
his Contracts students in that great John Houseman voice:
"You come in here with skulls full of mush and leave thinking like a lawyer." When poor Hart screws up in class,
Kingsfield tells him: "Mr. Hart, here is a dime. Take it, call
your mother, and tell her there is serious doubt about you
ever becoming a lawyer."

Is this a dated portrayal of legal education? Of course it is.
You can't make a phone call for a dime anymore. You can't
even find a phone booth. In today's wireless law schools, Hart
would simply minimize his Facebook page and get on Google
chat with his mom. Seriously, Houseman's performance was
exaggerated for dramatic effect, but it did capture the essen-
tials of how the Socratic method operates. The traditional
model incorporated these essential components:

- Cold-calling on a student from a seating chart.

- Asking the student to "state the case," which entails
  narrating the facts and other aspects about the case,
  such as its procedural history, issue, holding, and reasoning.

- Testing the student's understanding of the case with
  more questions, which usually include hypothetical fact
  patterns that require the student to interpret and apply
  the legal principle(s) from the case. This is the component of the Socratic method most closely connected with
  the oft-stated goal of the method to teach students to
  "think like a lawyer."

- Failing to offer concrete answers to the questions asked
  based on the assumption that the students, through the
  dialogue, should be able to figure out the answers on
  their own.

Depending on the skill and technique of the professor, for
students, the whole thing can come off as resembling a
bizarre treasure hunt in which neither the professor nor the
casebook provides the answers—at least not directly. In fact,
most of the answers are contained in or inferable from the

judicial opinions in the casebooks, but they're often hidden between the lines.

Rumors of the Death of the Socratic Method are Greatly Exaggerated

Some have proclaimed the demise of the Socratic method in law U.S. schools. One professor, an advocate of the method, wrote that "[p]opular myth has it that the Socratic method is pervasive in American law schools," adding that "nothing could be further from the truth."[53] But a different writer said "[t]he Socratic Method remains the primary method of law teaching today."[54]

Who's right? Both. The disagreement stems from problems in defining the Socratic method. In its original form as a dialectical "flight of the imagination through a world of allegories, parables and myths,"[55] the method is not only dead, it probably never lived in legal education in the first place because most law professors and students simply do not possess the skills and knowledge to carry it out.

In its modern law school image as a teaching method where the professor "hides the ball" and then humiliates students who can't find it, that too is clearly on the wane. Most professors, especially younger ones, practice what they call a "modified Socratic method," which is much less harsh than the traditional version. More on that in the Facts and Myths section below.

But broadly defined as a style of teaching in which professors call on students, usually without warning, expecting informed, intelligent answers as part of a back and forth exchange (as opposed to simply lecturing), the Socratic style does indeed remain the dominant teaching methodology in U.S. law schools, particularly in the first year.[56]

---

53. Donald G. Marshall, Socratic Method and the Irreducible Core of Legal Education, Presentation at Law Alumni Distinguished Teacher Inauguration (January 19, 1994), *in* 90 MINN. L. REV. 1, 2 (2005).

54. Cynthia G. Hawkins–Leon, *The Socratic Method–Problem Method Dichotomy: The Debate Over Teaching Method Continues,* 1998 BYU EDUC. & L.J. 1, 5 (1998).

55. Paul N. Savoy, *Toward A New Politics of Legal Education,* 79 YALE L.J. 444, 468 (1970).

56. Professor Stephen Friedland surveyed law professors back in the mid–1990s to determine how they teach. He sent out approximately 2,000 questionnaires, to which he received 574 completed responses. Ninety-seven percent of the respondents said they use the Socratic method at least some of the time in first-year courses, with 30 percent reporting they use it most of the

With So Much Criticism, Why Do Professors Still Use the Socratic and Case Methods?

The Socratic and case methods have faced resistance since their inception. Common criticisms include that the methods are intimidating, humiliating, alienating, bewildering, and inefficient, yet most first-year professors continue to use them. Why? Because we genuinely believe that the combination of the Socratic and case methods is the most effective way to train new law students to develop the critical-thinking skills they will need as lawyers.[57] Like most students, I hated the Socratic method back in law school. As a professor, however, I came to appreciate the great usefulness of dialectical questioning as a tool for teaching students to discover knowledge on their own. Plus, it's fun scaring the hell out of people.

Seriously, the Socratic and case methods, in the right hands, can be excellent tools for guiding students to "think like a lawyer," which simply means learning to reason well. As Langdell recognized, you could memorize all the legal rules in the world, but still be a lousy lawyer. Good lawyering is about problem-solving and the Socratic and case methods are intended to force students to learn by doing rather than simply by being told how it is done.

The difference in the way 1Ls think about legal problems at the beginning and end of the first year is dramatically apparent. Even the Socratic-haters would be hard-pressed to deny that they really did arrive at law school with "skulls full of mush," yet exited the Socratic arena as facile thinkers and astute legal problem-solvers. Look at this comment from a 1L two weeks away from finishing his first year:

> Just the other week I was eating lunch with some of my section friends and reading through a case for class. Without thinking, I said something like, "Don't you all think that we are so much better at reading

---

time, and 41 percent reporting they use it often. Comparatively, only 31 percent of the professors surveyed reported that they use a lecture method "some of the time" in first-year courses (a percentage that soared to 94 percent in upper-level courses). *See* Stephen I. Friedland, *How We Teach: A Survey of Teaching Techniques in American Law Schools*, 20 SEATTLE U. L. REV. 1 (1996).

57. After visiting sixteen law schools across the country, the authors of the 2007 Carnegie Foundation Report on legal education concluded that "nearly all the law faculty" with whom they spoke endorsed the case-dialogue method as the best way to train 1Ls in "the craft of legal reasoning." *See* CARNEGIE FOUNDATION REPORT, *supra*, at 66.

cases now?" They looked at me like I just stated the most obvious thing in the world. I had just never really thought of it like that. When you stop and think about the evolution of your abilities from the beginning of the year to the end, it is really astonishing.

Another student recognized, "When the professor is asking questions and things finally 'click' in my head, I'm much more likely to understand and remember what I learned than if the professor had just told me straight out."

The Socratic method has benefits in addition to fostering the development of legal reasoning skills. It helps train students to think on their feet and articulate their reasoning, vital abilities for any lawyer. It provides a strong incentive for students to be prepared, substantially enhancing the quality of the classroom experience for all involved. While the level of preparation varies among students, 1Ls rarely come to class unprepared, a big difference from most undergraduate classes. One big reason is that they don't want to be publicly embarrassed in front of their peers and professors if called on. The Socratic method also facilitates a much more interesting exploration of legal issues than pure lecturing, the principal realistic option in large classes.

Is it a perfect methodology? Far from it. First, the success of the method is heavily dependent on not only the preparation and intellectual levels of the students, but the skill of the professor. As one colleague commented in reading this chapter, "Some professors do it well, but I'm not sure that's the norm." Some professors simply ask questions to see who is prepared or ask random questions without using the answers as means to an end. As one student wrote: "It annoys me when professors use a Q & A just to see if we prepared a brief, rather than to engage in a genuine Socratic dialogue designed to expose fallacies and reveal truth."

Also, the large size of law school classes renders most students passive bystanders in the process at any given time. A true Socratic dialogue envisions one-on-one instruction or small group tutorials. Both the Socratic and case methods work better in small classes, but a lack of resources prevents most law schools from considering them for first-year courses. But even students who aren't directly participating learn from watching and listening to Socratic dialoguing. The Carnegie Foundation Report on legal education observed that one way in which the Socratic method enhances student intellectual development is through *modeling*; that is, the students learn by watching and modeling the cognitive skills of the professor displayed during case-dialoguing.[58]

Other shortcomings of the Socratic method are discussed in the Facts and Myths section below, but when all is said and done, I remain convinced that the Socratic method, while imperfect, beats the viable alternatives for training 1Ls to conduct legal analysis.

Sample Socratic Dialogue

With that introduction, let's see what the Socratic method looks like in action. Back when I taught at the University of Arkansas at Little Rock, I asked a research assistant to videotape several Torts classes in preparation for a presentation at the Institute for Law School Teaching. The following excerpted transcript from one of those tapes will give you an idea of how the Socratic method works.[59] This class occurred near the end of the first year.

The issue under discussion is defamation law (i.e., libel and slander), which is part of tort law. Specifically, we were exploring the famous 1964 U.S. Supreme Court case of *New York Times v. Sullivan*,[60] in which the Court held that the First Amendment limits the ability of states to award tort damages for defamation of public officials.

Without being overly specific, the Court imposed a high hurdle known as the "actual malice" test that public officials (later extended to include any public figure) are required to prove to recover damages for defamation. The test requires a public official to prove that the defendant knew the defamatory statement was false or published the statement in reckless disregard of whether it was true or false, which the

---

58. The Carnegie Foundation Report classified law school case-dialoguing as a type of "cognitive apprenticeship" in which student intellectual development occurs through faculty-student interaction. Observing professor-student Socratic exchanges at sixteen law schools, the report's authors observed professors employing four basic apprenticeship teaching methods identified by cognitive theorists: *modeling*, by demonstrating in class the type of cognitive skills the pro-

fessor seeks to instill in the students; *coaching*, by providing guidance and feedback; *scaffolding*, by providing support for students who haven't yet mastered critical-thinking skills; and *fading*, by encouraging students to go it alone when they've shown themselves prepared to do so. *See id.* at 60–61.

59. The transcription is not exact, but is very close to the original discussion.

60. 376 U.S. 254 (1964).

Court later interpreted to mean that the plaintiff must prove the defendant subjectively (i.e., internally in his own mind) entertained serious doubts as to the truth of the statement. Ever wonder why you don't read about more defamation suits brought by public officials or public figures? *New York Times v. Sullivan* is the reason.

On the videotape, the back and forth exchange set forth below, which explores the application of the *New York Times* test to a hypothetical, was lively, rapid-fire action. The tone of some of my questions, not apparent from the cold text, was sarcastic. But by this point, the students knew how to play the Socratic game. They didn't take my questioning personally, nor should they have. The discussion involves three students, whom I'll call Mr. Forbes, Ms. Davidson, and Ms. Carvel and label as S1, S2, and S3 in the transcript.

The discussion began with a good deal of lecture and dialoguing about the case itself. We pick it up just after, in good Socratic fashion, I got Mr. Forbes to commit himself to the desirability of the actual malice test as a means for protecting free speech:

> **Me:** Mr. Forbes, let me give you a hypothetical. Suppose we have a candidate running for public office. He's running for governor of the state. He's a man who has led an exemplary life. As far as we know, there are no blemishes on his record of any significance. Shortly before the election, an anonymous source calls the state's largest newspaper and says "I have personal information that this person has sexually abused children." The reporter tries to ask questions, but the caller says, "I'm sorry. It's just too personal. But the people need to know." Then hangs up. The newspaper publishes the allegation that the person running for governor is a child molester. It's false—completely false. Can he win? Can he prove actual malice under *New York Times v. Sullivan*?

> **S1:** Did the newspaper know that it was false?

> **Me:** All they knew is what I've told you. It was a tip from an anonymous source. They didn't check it out. They didn't investigate it.

> **S1:** I don't think the plaintiff can prove actual malice. He can show negligence. They obviously should have investigated. But that's not enough.

> **Me:** Why can't he prove actual malice?

> **S1:** It doesn't satisfy the test.

Me: Should they be able to get away with that? This person's life has been ruined. He lost the governorship. Would you vote for somebody if there were allegations out there that they had abused children?

S1: I don't know. I think probably not.

Me: We can certainly imagine a lot of people thinking that, "Even if it's *possibly* true, I don't think I want that person as governor."

S1: Public officials have to put up with a lot of things that are said about them that I think we know as a society, often times, are questionable whether they're true or not.

Me: Is that a fair price to expect a person seeking government office to pay? Should they have to put up with that? Ms. Davidson? [Raised hand to volunteer.]

S2: I'd just say that's an oversimplified hypothetical because people in the news business just aren't going to take one anonymous tip and publish something like that, something that's so defamatory and inappropriate. So they're going to follow up and—

Me: Let's suppose in this case they didn't follow up.

S2: But they are not going to do that because they know they're going to get sued and lose.

Me: But that's my question, are they going to lose? Mr. Forbes said they're not going to lose.

S2: Under the actual malice test? Well, I guess they wouldn't lose unless what the newspaper did was reckless disregard for the truth.

Me: Based on the facts I gave you, do we have any evidence that they knew it was false?

S2: No.

Me: Do we have any evidence that they in fact, and can we prove, that they entertained—in their heads—serious doubts as to whether it was true or false?

S2: No, I guess not.

Me: So that would mean that under the actual malice test, the newspaper would win.

S2: But I think that those instances are so rare that we need to protect it just as much as we need to protect the times when it's true.

Me: So you're a fan of the actual malice test?

S2: I think, well, I don't know, I'm not sure I really like the actual malice test, but I like protecting free speech at all costs.

Me: Well, then you love the actual malice test because that's basically what it does. It protects speech at almost all costs. Here, the cost is that an innocent person who has led an unblemished life has had his life completely ruined by a false, unsupported allegation and has no remedy.

S2: I think the court said in *New York Times v. Sullivan* that the value of free speech to society is worth more than one person's reputation. We have a greater good that we're concerned with and that's the public's right to free speech. It's a utilitarian view.

Me: That is what they did, but, of course, it's not going to be just one individual. It's going to be some number of individuals. The question is, where do we strike the balance between free speech and the states' interest in protecting the reputational rights of its citizens? Did the court strike the balance in the right place? In this case, you feel comfortable that this person's life has been ruined by a false allegation and he has no remedy whatsoever? He's just "one individual." One very sad individual.

S2: I think he'll have a remedy.

Me: What remedy?

S2: They have spin doctors who work for them. They'll fix it somehow.

Me: Oh yeah, it's easy to get around an allegation of being a child molester. It's no big deal, just spin it a little. "Oh well, I wasn't a child *molester*, I was a . . ."—how are we going to spin that one?

S2: If they can spin oral sex in the White House [referring to President Bill Clinton's sexual encounters with intern Monica Lewinsky], I think you can spin being a child molester.

Me: They didn't spin it all that well. [Laughter] But beyond that, it's still an allegation of—

S2: It's a shame, but it's the price we pay to protect free speech. So yeah, it's too bad, but I don't have a high opinion of public officials anyway.

Me: Ms. Carvel? [Raised hand to volunteer.]

S3: I was just going to say because they are public officials, they have an opportunity to speak to the public and defend themselves.

Me: Okay, that's true.

S3: Also, because they are unprotected, I think people will look at those statements and not take them as seriously because they are commonly done.

Me: Ms. Carvel, I've heard some of the most audacious stories about people right here at the law school. Have you heard any? About the students, the faculty. I'm thinking surely people couldn't possibly believe that. But then talking to students, I realize people do believe them—just because someone says it, people believe it. If you print it in the newspaper, don't you think a lot of people are going to believe it, even if it's completely preposterous?

S3: Yeah, but I go back to the person is probably going to be able to defend themselves. I agree there are a lot of negative aspects to it, but they are in a position to defend themselves compared to a person who is not a public figure.

Me: That's a very good point, and what we're going to see at the next class in *Gertz v. Welch* is that the Supreme Court has constructed different, more protective rules for private figure defamation plaintiffs. One of the main rationales they give is that public figures have greater avenues for self-help. Okay, so the guy comes out and says to a room full of cameras, "I am not a child molester," and that's just going to make it all go away?

S3: No, it's not.

Me: No. He's still going to probably lose the election, isn't he?

S3: I don't know. I hear so many different things in politics, and so many of them are false. Maybe in Brazil where I'm from, it's worse. I don't know. We just hear all kinds of things about politicians, and I don't believe them.

Me: You don't?

S3: I don't.

Me: So if you were going to vote for this person for governor, and it came out in the state's largest newspaper that someone has accused him of sexually abusing children, it wouldn't affect your decision? You'd just dismiss that.

S3: I don't know if I'd dismiss it.

Me: You'd still vote for him?

S3: Maybe.

So there you have it: your first real Socratic dialogue. It wasn't so bad, was it? If you could watch the videotape, you'd see that students seemed to be enjoying it. Of course, they were seasoned veterans by then who had long left their fears of the Socratic method behind. They'd been through almost an entire year of Socratic-dialoguing and learned that the terror tales they heard about it prior to coming to law school were myths.

Let's explore those and other myths, as well as some facts, about the present-day Socratic method and its intimate companion, the case method:

Ten Facts and Myths about the Socratic and Case Methods

1. The Socratic method strikes fear in the hearts and minds of 1Ls. FACT. There's nothing quite like being called on without prior notice in front of a large group of peers and expected to speak articulately and intelligently about a question you've never thought about before. It's enough to make anyone anxious. Imagine you're sitting there in class minding your own business. The professor is talking at a hundred miles an hour when all of a sudden your name rings out:

> *Mr. Smith!* A shoots at B, but misses and hits C, who loses control of her car and crashes into D, driving a school bus full of children—H, I, J, K, L, M, N, O and P—down a winding mountain road. The school bus careens into a gas pump at the exact second lightning hits the pump. In the explosion, E, a piece of glass, hits F, walking his dog, G, nearby. G gets loose and viciously attacks Q, a law student, carrying an armload of casebooks up a staircase. The books fall on R, causing massive head injuries. R is rushed to the ER by EMTs, gets CPR from an RN and an IV from an MD, but he's DOA. To make matters worse, his HMO refuses to pay for his MRI. Who wins? [Three second pause.] Quick, quick, Mr. Smith! We don't have all day.

There's no way around it. Even when wielded in a humane manner, the process is inherently intimidating. One of my favorite law school stories involves literally the very first person I ever called on as a Torts professor, way back in 1987. I asked a student to state the facts of a case. In a nervous, timid voice, she stated the facts quite suitably. Trying to give her affirmation, I said, "Yes, those are the facts in a nutshell." The student became visibly distraught. I later learned she thought I was accusing her of having not read the case and simply swiping the facts from the West *Nutshell Series* study aid for Torts. Those crazy law students.

One common fear students have about the Socratic method is that they will blank out when called on. Although rare, it does happen. In fact, it happened to me. My Constitutional Law professor was a Socratic traditionalist in the truest sense. I arrived at every class anxious about being called on. One day the professor called on me in that smug, challenging way some professors enjoy. I don't remember the question or even the subject matter. I only remember a cloud of anxiety enveloping my brain to the point where it stopped functioning. I heard the professor repeat "Mr. McClurg?" No response. After the passage of some time, probably just a few seconds but it seemed much longer, he moved on to another student. I never uttered a word. I share this story with my first-year students and they seem to find it comforting.

2. Professors use the Socratic method to intimidate and break down students. MYTH. In writing this book, I came across several articles by law professors talking about the degrading, alienating, and hostile wielding of the Socratic method, and wondered whom they were talking about. When I finished the manuscript, I thumbed through a law school prep book that compared the Socratic method to Darwin's theory of natural selection, warning that "only the strong will survive."

Trust me. While surviving the entirety of the first year is difficult, surviving the Socratic method is not. I've taught at several law schools and am acquainted with many law professors. While a few ruthless and sadistic law professors may still exist, I personally don't know a single professor who uses the Socratic method to *intentionally* bully or break down students. My experience is consistent with Professor Paul Brest's that "[t]he terrorist version of the Socratic method has almost disappeared."[61] Asked in a survey to name the biggest surprise about law school, a 1L wrote: "What is the big deal about the Socratic method? It is written about like it's some kind of torture. I have yet to see anyone really crucified."

61. Paul Brest, *Plus Ca Change*, 91 MICH. L. REV. 1945, 1948 (1993).

Professors use the Socratic method for the reasons described above—not for the purpose of intimidating students.

3. The Socratic and case methods are inefficient ways to convey information. FACT. One of the major complaints some students have about how law school classes are conducted is that the Socratic method and accompanying class discussion waste too much time with questions and student comments, time that could be used more efficiently if the professor would simply explain the material in a lecture format. It's true that the Socratic and case methods are not an efficient way to convey information. What students overlook, however, is that conveying information is only one goal of teaching law. As discussed above, training students to reason well and solve legal problems are the principal aspirations of both the Socratic and case methods.

As a student, it's hard to appreciate these goals because mastering legal reasoning is a gradual process and we live in an instant-gratification society. Compare studying law to working out at the gym to build and tone muscles. Many people who join health clubs give up too quickly because they don't see immediate results. But those who stay with it for a few months will be standing in front of a mirror one day saying, "Wow, check out those Calvin Klein abs!" It's sort of the same thing with law. After a few months, you can stand in front of the mirror and say, "Wow, check out those flabby abs, but at least I know how to apply the Model Penal Code to decide whether conduct constitutes a conspiracy!"

4. Under the Socratic method, law professors only ask, not answer, questions. MYTH. This may have been accurate in the past, but it is no longer true of most professors. Even most Socratic traditionalists lecture at least some of the time. Elizabeth Mertz conducted a study of first-year Contracts classes at eight law schools and found that the percentage of class time devoted to lecture ranged from 21 percent to 95 percent.[62]

In addition to doing at least some explaining via lecture, most professors will attempt to give concrete answers to student questions that have concrete answers (many questions don't), although it is common for law professors to try

---

62. *See* CARNEGIE FOUNDATION REPORT, *supra*, at 51–52 (discussing Mertz study).

to get students to figure out the answers to some questions first. "What do *you* think the answer is?" is a classic, frustration-inducing law professor response to student questions.

Professors don't do this to embarrass students or because they're too lazy to answer a question. Remember, the goal of the Socratic method is to force students to learn by doing. Accordingly, questions that relate to problem-solving are often met with the "What do you think?" response. For example, if we were discussing the defense to negligence known as "implied assumption of risk" and a student asked me to clarify a point of law involving the defense, I'd happily do it. But if the student asked, "Would it be implied assumption of risk for the plaintiff to get into a car with a drunk driver, knowing the driver is drunk?", my likely response would be "What do you think?" because I would want the student to try to reason through the puzzle applying the rules we learned.

5. In law, there are no right answers, only good arguments. MYTH. Some sources are fond of espousing this view to students, but it's simply not true. Many legal questions have clearly right or wrong answers. Not everything in the law is gray. If the professor asks whether the plaintiff prevailed in a particular case and you say "yes," that's a right answer if the plaintiff in fact prevailed but a wrong answer if the defendant won. If the professor asks you to state the elements of the tort of battery, you either know them and can state them (right answer) or you don't know them and can't state them (wrong answer). If the professor asks for the court's holding in a case where the court made the holding clear, again, you'll be giving a right answer if you can state the holding accurately and a wrong answer if you can't (although there is often room for interpretation as to what exactly was the holding of a case). In general, many of the questions posed in connection with Socratic case *recitation* are likely to have right and wrong answers.

On the other hand, much more so than in scientific disciplines, it is true that in law many questions do not have objectively right or wrong answers. Many legal standards are vague, purposely so because they must be applied to an infinite variety of factual permutations (that "tangled skein of human affairs" of which Langdell spoke). In Torts, for example, you'll see that much of the law of negligence, the principal topic covered in the course, concentrates on whether a person acted "reasonably under the circumstances." Certain answers to this question simply don't exist in many cases.

Note that any questions soliciting your opinion or other subjective assessment of a result, rule, or policy—of which there will be many—also lack objectively right or wrong answers. Or stated another way, such questions can have many right answers. This doesn't mean professors will not challenge your answers to such questions. They very well might, even if they agree with them.

Back in the beginning, I advised you to "embrace uncertainty" precisely because the law is so indeterminate. But don't buy into the absurd notion that there are no right or wrong answers in law school.

6. Professors penalize students who don't know the answer or who are unprepared for class. MYTH as to the first part and, depending on the professor, FACT as to the second part. Most professors show patience for prepared students who simply don't know the answer and empathy for prepared, but obviously nervous students, who fumble with their answers. Note the caveat *prepared*. While some professors allow students to simply take a "pass" when called on (sometimes limited to a certain number of passes per semester), most first-year professors expect students to be prepared for each class. Professor responses to unprepared students vary widely, but can include: no response, a scowl, placing a mark by the student's name on the seating chart, ranting at the student or the class as a whole, walking out of the room if several students are unprepared, or lowering the student's grade.

As with arriving late, you need to know that simply because a professor does not overtly react when a student is unprepared does not mean the professor doesn't care if students are prepared. The professor will most likely note and remember it. If nothing else, it will lower the esteem in which she holds the student.

7. The Socratic method entails cold-calling on students without prior notice. FACT, but undergoing change. Traditionally, this was a fact, and probably still is in most first-year classes. Part of what makes the Socratic method anxiety-provoking is the element of surprise. Most professors just call on students randomly from the seating chart, with no particular rhyme or reason to their selection process. Often I'll look at the seating chart before class, and jot down four or five names on a sticky note based on my recollection of not having heard from those students much or recently. Some professors use a more scientific method, such as keeping track of how many times they've called on students by making check-marks on the seating chart. Some professors randomly draw names from a stack of cards, as if they were awarding door prizes instead of interrogation. Some professors rely primarily on volunteers, usually more so as the year progresses.

Increasingly, professors have turned to what is called an "on panel," "on call," or "designated hitter" system of selecting students to be called on. Even many Socratic traditionalists use this method in upper-level courses, but until a few years ago, the panel system was uncommon in first-year courses. The panel system entails the professor identifying a group of students in advance (usually from four to six) to be in the Socratic hot seat on a particular day. The advantage of this method for the professor and the class is that, because the students know in advance they are going to be called on, they are better prepared, raising the level of classroom discussion and reducing the time wasted from engaging less than fully prepared students. The advantage for students is that they can relax and just concentrate on learning on the days when they are not "on panel," knowing they won't be called on. The downside of the panel system is that many students take advantage of it, using it as a license to not prepare on the days they are not on panel.

8.   Because the chances of getting randomly called on in a large first-year class are small, it's a worthwhile risk to not prepare and take your chances. MYTH. The first part is true. In a class of seventy to eighty students, the odds of getting called on in any particular class on any particular day are relatively small—but not lottery-odds small. A lot of it depends on the professor. Some professors call on only a few students, sticking with them for a long time. Others call on many students, asking only one question per student.

Let's use a conservative estimate and assume a professor calls on three students per class, placing your odds of getting called on at about one in twenty-five. Gamblers lose billions annually betting on worse odds than that. And this is setting aside subjective factors that may increase your chance of getting called on, such as: the professor thinks you're unprepared, the professor knows you're reliable, you're wearing a bright yellow shirt, you came up to talk to the prof before class and are fresh in her mind's eye, you arrived late to class, etc.

I can turn the low-odds argument around as a reason why you should *always* be prepared. Precisely because you *won't* get called on randomly very often in a large class, it's important that you don't screw up what may be your only opportunity to look good when you do get called on. A single incident of unpreparedness can define you in the eyes of your peers and professors. Unless you volunteer, you might not have an opportunity to redeem yourself.

Of course, the biggest risk of not preparing for classes is that you won't learn the material or do well in the course.

9. If you give a wrong answer during Socratic questioning, you'll be humiliated in front of the professor and all of your classmates. MYTH. No one likes to be publicly embarrassed. A central component of the angst generated by the Socratic method is the fear of "looking stupid" in front of the professor and one's peers. This is a needless worry, however, for several reasons. First, and regrettably, most students simply aren't listening that closely to what other students say in class, particularly as the year wears on. Those in the back can't hear a lot of student comments and many students who can hear aren't paying attention because they're interested only in what the professor has to say.

Second, if it's a hard question, most of the rest of the class won't know the right answer either. Thus, many students won't even recognize a wrong answer unless and until the professor points it out, at which point they'll be concentrating not on the wrong answer you gave, but on trying to get the right answer down in their notes and hoping the professor doesn't call on them in the meantime.

As for the professor, she's up there trying to orchestrate a large class and doesn't have time, even if she had the inclination, to stop and focus on wrong answers. Additionally, wrong answers don't trouble professors unless the professor believes the student is unprepared. When students approach me after a class profusely apologizing for giving a "dumb" answer during class, I often don't remember what they're talking about.

Coincidentally, the very day I was editing these paragraphs, I came out of Torts and found a student waiting for me at the bottom of the stairs. She said she wanted to apologize for her classroom performance. I had no idea what she was talking about. I remembered calling on her, but didn't notice any shortcomings. I told her so. She proceeded to reel off three perceived failings: "I said 'I don't know' to one question, but I did know. I had it in my notes. I just wasn't thinking right about it. Then I said 'I'm not sure' to another question. Finally, I was going to give the right answer on one question but you corrected me before I had time to finish." Bless her heart. I thought she did fine.

We all tend to be our own harshest critics. If you make a mistake during Socratic questioning, in most instances, you're likely to be the only one who notices or remembers it. Now, it's true that if a student says something that is *way* off-base, some students may snicker and even talk about it after class. But you just have to ignore those kinds of people and trust in karma. Their time will come.

Here's a little secret about the Socratic method that may also ease your mind about giving a wrong answer in class. In truth, at least for questions involving hypotheticals, the very last thing the professor wants to hear in many situations is a quick correct answer because it ruins the Socratic treasure hunt the professor was looking forward to engaging in. Often, when professors pose hypothetical fact situations, what they prefer is an answer that's just wrong enough to allow the professor to artfully nudge the student down the Socratic path toward insight, but not so wrong that the only path is directly to another student. An immediate correct answer can ruin everything. So take heart—some wrong answers are actually welcomed by the prof!

10. The Socratic method has a negative impact on women and minority students. Partly FACT as to practical effect. A substantial body of academic literature discusses the barriers women and minority students traditionally have faced in law school. One area where I see continued disparity—and I'm not suggesting it's the only area—is in classroom participation.

Several surveys have showed that female students voluntarily participate less frequently in law school classes than male students. The most recent data on the issue comes from a 2012 Yale Law School study.[63] The study, which involved monitoring 113 class sessions in twenty-one courses, indicated some progress in gender parity regarding class participation, but still found that men participated at higher rates than women, especially in large classes. Comparing the data to a 2002 Yale Law School study of the same issue, the report concluded that, ten years later, women were only 1.5 percent more likely to speak up.[64]

Reasons offered by scholars as to why the Socratic method negatively impacts women include increased feelings of alienation and fear, the adversarial and competitive nature of the method, sexist conduct by certain male professors, an interest in protecting the sanctity and integrity of one's beliefs, less willingness to engage in grandstanding, a lower interest in dominating class discussion, and—I love this one because it's so true—better recognition by women than men of the limits of one's knowledge. In short, male students, as a group, are more willing to engage in the adversarial, competitive "sport" of the Socratic method than women.

Studies also show that minority students volunteer in law school classes at lower rates.[65] The obstacles to participating may loom even larger for minority students because of the under-representation of persons of color at many law schools. Experience has shown me that the smaller the number of any group in a class, the less likely it is that individual members of the group are willing to inject themselves into class discussions. Minority students currently comprise 23 percent of law students nationwide, a substantial improvement from the past, but the percentage at many schools is significantly lower.

63. *Yale Law School Faculty & Students Speak Up About Gender: Ten Years Later*, YALE LAW WOMEN (Apr. 2012), http://www.law.yale.edu/documents/pdf/Student_Organizations/YLW_SpeakUpStudy.pdf.

64. *Id.* at 21–23.

65. *See* Carole J. Buckner, *Realizing Grutter v. Bollinger's "Compelling Educational Benefits of Diversity"—Transforming Aspirational Rhetoric into Experience*, 72 UMKC L. REV. 877, 887–88 (2004) (discussing the value of class participation and studies showing that minority students participate in law school classes at disproportionately lower rates than white students).

Because class participation carries several advantages (discussed in Chapter 8), the relative lack of classroom participation by women and minority students can have an adverse impact on them. We can't hope to reorder society here. The best I can do is offer my candid, practical advice to women and minority students, which is that an immediate solution lies solely in your power. To the extent men or non-minority students participate more in class, it's because they voluntarily ask more questions and offer comments in class discussions, undoubtedly for many of the reasons listed above.

Professors want to hear from all of their students. More important, your classmates need to hear from you. If you are a woman or minority student reading this, make a vow to yourself to raise your hand and contribute to class discussion. *Professors will call on people who raise their hands, regardless of gender, race, or other identity traits.* Band together with like students and commit to join the fray. There's strength in numbers. Even a small group of students can unify to build a stronger, mutually supportive whole.

* * *

So there you have it, the full story behind law school's unique teaching methodologies. Hopefully, this look under the hood of the Socratic and case methods has assuaged your anxieties about them at least somewhat, while also persuading you that there is indeed method behind the madness.

Before moving on, it should be noted that professors do use teaching approaches other than the Socratic and case methods in the first year. As mentioned, most professors do at least some lecturing. Some do a large amount of it. Some professors use a "problem method" in which students read cases and apply them to solve written problems, but the problem method usually entails Socratic-style questioning. Some doctrinal professors assign drafting or other exercises and some occasionally use small-group breakout discussions and projects. But ask any former or current law student what first-year law school classes are like and you won't be hearing much about those other methods. You'll hear about the Socratic method.

CHAPTER 8

REASONS TO PARTICIPATE IN CLASS AND TEN TIPS FOR DOING IT WELL

A law school class can and should be a vital and exciting learning environment. Many of the issues discussed in law school have enormous implications for society. Indeed, the most controversial issues of our time are rooted in the law: abortion, affirmative action, civil liberties, environmental policy, gun control, healthcare, presidential power, the rights of children, workers, and the disabled ... the list could go on and on.

If every student committed to being a participant in classroom discussion, even if only occasionally, law schools would be much more interesting places. When Socratic dialoguing and discussion are firing on all cylinders, the atmosphere in law school classrooms can be electric. The professor, however, is only one cylinder. No matter how much energy and effort he or she puts forth, stimulating classroom experiences cannot happen without the help of prepared, engaged students.

Unfortunately, too many 1Ls choose not to voluntarily participate in class, often because they're intimidated. Some students no doubt perform a cost-benefit analysis and decide it's easier and safer to just stay on the sidelines. I understand that decision. The problem is that students undervalue the return on participating in class, while, as discussed in the previous chapter, exaggerating the potential risks and costs.

This chapter explains the upside of being a class participator and offers ten tips for doing it successfully.

The Benefits of Class Participation

Class participation carries several benefits with it, both tangible and intangible. First, active student participation in class discussions adds to the energy level and sense of community in the classroom, making for a more lively and memorable experience for everyone. Class hours in courses where students actively participate in the discussion fly by compared to courses where lecture predominates. Lecturing may be less intimidating than active dialogue and discussion, but it's also approximately five million times more likely to induce drowsiness.

Second, you will better remember the classes in which you participate and feel more satisfaction about your law school experience. I sat through the first half of my 1L year in silence, except when I got called on. Part of me wanted to participate, but I was afraid. The second half I started to open up a bit, raising my hand here and there, and immediately felt better about myself and my law school career. Instead of sitting in class thinking, "I wish I could be one of those brave people who volunteer," I thought, "Hey, now *I'm* one of those brave people."

Third, participating will help sharpen your oral communication and group-speaking skills, essential abilities for lawyers of any stripe.

Fourth, your professors want to get to know you, but with so many students, we can't realistically accomplish that unless you speak up from time to time. As discussed in Chapter 9, getting to know and getting known by your professors carries its own potentially substantial benefits. Volunteering in class is one of the most effective ways to become known by your professors.

Fifth, it is an established fact of legal education that if you volunteer even once in a while, you will get called on less often when you are not volunteering. In fact, there's an inverse correlation between how often students raise their hands to speak and how often they get called on randomly, because professors want to hear from as many students as possible. Wouldn't you rather speak up at a time when you already have something to say than wait until the professor cold-calls on you?

Finally, class participation brings the possibility of the very tangible benefit of a grade raise, although this should be at the bottom of your list of reasons to participate. Many professors raise grades for class participation. In a typical first-year Torts class of seventy to eighty people, I usually raise from ten to twenty grades by one step (e.g., from a *B-* to a *B*) for consistent, quality class participation. In a system where class ranks can shift depending on hundredths of a grade point, even modest grade raises can have an effect.

Law school can be a scary place, but I encourage you to go to classes willing to discuss the material. Your thoughts and opinions are valuable and your contributions to class discussion will help make law school a more enjoyable, meaningful, and memorable experience for everyone.

Ten Tips for Shining in Class

Whether we're talking about voluntary or involuntary participation (i.e., getting called on), *any* student can shine in class by following these tips and reminders, which are aimed both at bolstering your performance and preventing you from making a bad impression:

1. Come to every class prepared. This is the threshold requirement for any successful participation. If you're prepared, you have nothing to fear from the Socratic method. Wrong answers from prepared students do not bother professors. But if you're not prepared, you're a sitting duck.

2. Commit to being a participator. Many students actually do want to participate, but leave their participation to the professor's decision to call on them. In other words, they don't volunteer. But given the large number of students and the small number who get called on randomly in a typical class, that's not a good participation plan.

Commit yourself to being a participant in class discussion. You don't have to participate every day to make a lasting, good impression in class. Just make a good faith effort to do it on a semi-regular basis. Here's my challenge to you: make a vow (and keep track of it) that at a minimum you will voluntarily participate at least *one time each week* during your first semester of law school. I'm not even talking about once a week in each class, although that would be great. Just once a week total, ideally mixing up your participation among different courses. The typical semester is fourteen weeks long, which means that following this vow will commit you to speak in class voluntarily only fourteen times during the entire semester. Even this modest level of participation will gain you many of the benefits of class participation.

Participation can assume three forms:

Ask a question. Asking questions is an easy way to participate. It's quite possible the professor could turn it around on you and ask, "What do you think?", but more often than not the professor will just answer the question. Thus, question-asking can be a painless form of class participation. Even if the professor turns the question back at you, chances are you'll do fine since it's something you've thought about at least a little bit or you wouldn't have asked the question.

Volunteer an answer. If a professor asks a question to which you think you know the answer, raise your hand! Professors ask some really hard questions, but they also ask a lot of easy ones. I was disturbed when a research assistant told me that many students won't volunteer to answer easy questions because they don't want to be seen as someone who only tries to answer easy questions. That's silly. The professor wants someone to answer them or she wouldn't be asking them. Moreover, what may seem easy to you probably isn't easy to everyone. You'll get just as much credit for volunteering to answer an easy question as a hard one, with better odds of giving a right answer.

Offer an opinion. The Socratic method often functions in two parts, beginning with one-on-one case-dialoguing and progressing into generalized, inclusive class discussions of the issues. At this stage, professors often seek answers about what students think the law should be, rather than simply what it is as espoused in the case. Since opinions cannot, by definition, be demonstrably right or wrong, you have little to lose by joining in such discussions. Of course, the professor may very well want to explore the basis for your opinion since gut feelings don't cut it as legal analysis, so be ready for follow-up questions that might require you to defend your opinion with reasons.

3. Know your professors' class preparation expectations. Law professors are unique individuals. Much of the advice in this book needs to be construed and applied within the context of your particular professors. We will revisit this crucial point. Here, we're talking only about class preparation expectations.

Some professors simply ask a student to state the facts of the case as a springboard for a broader class discussion, while others will stay with a student for a long time and expect him/her to be able to recite the case backwards and forward. Some professors will routinely ask about the procedural history of the case, while others will rarely or never ask about it. Figuring these things out will make it easier for you to prepare for class.

Asked to compare the second semester to the first, a student said that in some ways the second semester was easier because she and her classmates knew what to expect in terms of class preparation from each professor:

> We know that certain teachers will not call on you if they have called on you in a recent class, at least not usually twice in one week. For example, if I am called on to participate in class on Monday, I am usually safe for the rest of the week in that course. So I might not re-read the assignments right before class as I usually would to make sure I am extra-prepared. On the other side, some teachers really do call on people at random and therefore students know they always have to be ready because the teacher is unpredictable. This is just one example of how to learn and "work" the system.

Getting to know your professors' preparation expectations can take time, but you can speed up the process simply by making it a point to stop and think about it. Take notice of which components of cases Professor X asks or does not ask questions about on a regular basis.

4. Approach the Socratic method as a game or sport. A common criticism of the Socratic method is that it takes on the appearance of a game or sporting event. But so what? Most people enjoy games and sports. That should make it more, rather than less palatable. Instead of approaching the Socratic method with dread or terror, look at it as a potentially fun type of "brain game." Keep your wits about you. Free your brain from the shackles of fear. And remember, the goal of the game is not to win. The goal is the game itself.

Many professors still execute the Socratic method in the style, albeit not with the brilliance, of its creator: they seek to get the answerer to commit to a position, then, through questioning, attempt to expose the contradictions or fallacies in that position. They sometimes do this by leading students down a garden path, then cutting their legs off at the end of the path. Your goal is to make it to the end of the path with your limbs intact. Cues that you're on your way down the path can take the form of statements by the professor such as, "Well, let's change the facts just a little," or "Suppose instead of what happened in the actual case, the plaintiff. . . ."

The purpose of the game is to sharpen critical-thinking skills. Untrained legal minds think too narrowly about the consequences of adopting particular legal positions. One way to teach students to think beyond the immediate case is, once a student has committed to a position, alter the facts, have her apply her position to the new facts, and test whether she agrees with the results. (See the Socratic dialogue excerpt in the preceding chapter for an example.)

If a professor is leading you down the path, you'll be confronted with a recurring choice: (1) stick with your original position, which may now appear absurd in light of the altered application; (2) modify your position; or (3) distinguish the professor's new factual situation from your position.

If you believe in your position, don't feel compelled to change it simply by the nature of the questioning. As often as not, the professor will agree with you and will simply be playing devil's advocate. On the other hand, as Emerson said, "A foolish consistency is the hobgoblin of little minds." If the new result would be clearly ludicrous and cannot be distinguished from the original facts and position, there's nothing wrong with conceding your original view may need revising. Frequently, however, the best course is to try to distinguish the new situations posed by the professor from your original position. Again, trust your brain and reasoning instincts.

5. Give yourself permission to fail. Some students who are well-prepared and perfectly capable of discussing the issues in law school reading assignments freeze up in class because they put too much pressure on themselves to succeed. They have a hard time answering questions about a case even though they know the answers. If a friend came up to them before class to discuss the same case, they'd be able to do it with no problem. Why? Because they wouldn't be thinking, "Omigosh, everyone's watching me. I don't want to look stupid."

By giving yourself permission to fail, you'll stop trying so hard and actually perform better. This advice is commonly given to public performers. I first encountered it taking acting lessons. It works. I follow it when teaching. Law students aren't the only ones who feel exposed when talking in front of eighty or so people. Law professors get nervous too. One veteran colleague commented on reading a draft of this chapter: "I still can't eat before class!"

Don't worry about making a mistake in class. It happens to all of us and is no big deal. Give yourself permission to fail so you can stop trying so hard.

6. Don't be afraid to disagree with professors. A major point of the Socratic method is to stimulate a true dialogue—a back and forth colloquy between the professor and the student. But this can only work if the student is willing to partake in the back and forth. Most professors welcome and appreciate students who challenge them with contrasting legal arguments and policy positions. The problem is that most students are reluctant to dissent from their professors' views, either because they don't believe it's possible they could be right and the professor wrong or don't want to appear disrespectful.

Regarding the first point, viable arguments exist on both sides of most legal issues. If legal issues were clear-cut, they wouldn't be "issues." The *New York Times v. Sullivan* Socratic dialogue sample in Chapter 7 illustrates this point well. Reasonable minds can disagree as to where to strike the balance between protecting free speech and protecting the reputational rights of persons injured by defamation. It's a perfectly legitimate position, for example, to argue, as have some famous U.S. Supreme Court justices, that First Amendment freedom of speech should be absolute, precluding any tort actions for defamation.

As to the second point, it's true that some law professors are convinced they are right about everything, but most of us are in this business in part because we enjoy the stimulation of intelligent debate. Some of the best classroom moments occur when students are willing to mix it up. Looking back at the Socratic dialogue excerpt you can see that those students certainly were not afraid to disagree with me. The student I called Ms. Davidson even cut me off mid-sentence.

Generally, you want to limit outright disagreement with the professor in class to policy-based or other open-ended issues, rather than the fine points of black-letter law. Most experienced law teachers know their subjects well, so there's a much greater likelihood that you will indeed be "wrong" in contending with the professor on a point of pure law. Moreover, even if you're right—which certainly can happen because professors do make mistakes—it's a bad idea to call out the professor in class.

A colleague at another school told me of a brazen incident in which a prof made a legal point in class, and a student took it on himself to email the author of the casebook *during* class questioning the professor's interpretation of the law. The author apparently wrote back saying the student had it right and the professor was wrong. The student then used the email to show up the professor in class! Now, there's a case for banning computers.

If you think the professor is wrong on the law, approach the professor after class and raise your point in the form of a question, as in: "Professor, I wrote down that you said *a*, *b*, *c*, but this note in the casebook seems to say the law is *x*, *y*, *z*. I'm having a hard time reconciling them." Any professor not suffering a major insecurity complex (there are some of these, by the way) will readily admit their error, thank you for pointing it out, and insist on correcting it to the entire class at the next meeting.

7. Don't take it personally if a professor or another student challenges your position. Students come to law school with varying degrees of skin thickness. Some sensitive students will fall apart if you look at them the wrong way, while others would hardly notice if you zapped them with a Taser. Professors frequently challenge students to explain or defend their positions even when they agree with the position. This is part of the Socratic process. Don't take it personally. Don't get your feelings hurt.

A student told me a tale about a classmate who volunteered to answer a question in class during his first semester. According to the student reporting the event, the professor replied in a condescending tone, "Why would you think that?" Later, the student swore he'd never volunteer in class again. All I can say about this one is "Gimme a break!" Lawyers have to be able to defend and explain their positions. If you make an argument to a judge and she says, "Why would you think that?", you can't fall apart and swear never to go to court again.

I once represented a pro bono divorce client. We were in the judge's chambers for what I thought would be a simple five-minute motion hearing. The room was packed with other lawyers sitting in chairs lining the walls waiting for their cases to come up. To my shock and dismay, the judge decided to transform the mundane hearing into a debacle. He called my client "garbage" and refused to sign an order I prepared because it contained the phrase "among the parties." "As my eighth-grade English teacher taught me, Mr. McClurg," he said sarcastically, "when you're dealing with only two people, you say *between* the parties,' not *among* the parties.' " He berated me for what seemed like an eternity. I felt humiliated, but that's life in the real world. (A week later, the local newspaper reported the judge's spouse had sued him for divorce alleging physical abuse, just as my client was alleging against her husband.)

Folks, it ain't pretty out there practicing law. It makes law school look like summer camp. I'm sympathetic to the sensitivities of students and don't condone professors treating students rudely, but at some point you just have to suck it up and realize that responding to questions, even sarcastic ones, is simply part of being a lawyer.

Other students also may challenge your position in class discussions. I love it when this occurs and results in a good back and forth exchange. Hearty debate is what great law school class experiences are built upon. Unfortunately, it doesn't happen often enough. Older students are much more willing to challenge both their professors and classmates, which is one reason teaching in part-time evening programs (i.e., night school) can be stimulating.

8. If you're unprepared, have the good sense to keep your mouth shut. Not infrequently, students ask questions that are directly answered in the reading material, leading to the sound inference that they haven't read the assignment. This is a particular pet peeve of law professors. If you're not prepared, lie low and pray you don't get called on. Don't take it on yourself to announce to the class: "I'm not prepared and I'll prove it."

In a similar vein, don't come to class early to read the assignment five minutes before class starts. Professors get irritated when they arrive early and see students skimming the reading assignment in their unmarked books for what appears to be the first time. It's another case of announcing to the professor that you're not prepared. Some professors will purposely call on such students to expose them. I don't, because I know it will just waste time, but I do form negative opinions of such students.

9. Redeem yourself. If you get called on and come across as unprepared, whether you are or not, redeem yourself by volunteering at a later point. Most professors are forgiving souls who will respect the effort. If you're prepared and the professor asks you a question to which you don't know the answer, simply say "I don't know," but, if possible, toss in another relevant comment about the case to show you're prepared.

If you should happen to blank out when called on, approach the professor after class and explain what happened to avoid having the professor think you were unprepared. I once called on a woman who gave no answer at all. I concluded she was unprepared. Fortunately, two of her classmates came up after class and told me she was prepared but simply freaked out.

10. If at first you don't get called on, try, try again. Some students get discouraged from participating after they raise their hands once or twice and the professor doesn't call on them. They either think the professor is intentionally ignoring them or they just can't muster the courage for repeat attempts.

Don't take it personally if you raise your hand and the professor doesn't call on you. Managing discussion in a large class isn't as easy as it may look. The professor's mind is racing to stay ahead of the discussion at the same time he or she is asking or answering questions, many of which come from left field. In an active discussion, twenty hands may be raised at the same time.

Also, to keep from falling behind, the point comes in all class discussions, even the most stimulating ones, where the prof has to make the decision to cut things off and move on. So don't give up. No professor I know would intentionally ignore a volunteering student on a repeated basis except in the case of a notorious gunner who always wants to dominate the class discussion.

CHAPTER 9
LAW PROFESSORS

When I was a kid, I loved the television show, *Leave it to Beaver*. Through reruns, most young people are probably at least somewhat familiar with the misadventures of young Theodore Cleaver ("the Beav"). Beaver had a teacher named Miss Landers who began every class with a sunny, "Good morning, class." The class always responded in unison, "Good morning, Miss Landers."

In one episode, the Cleavers invited Miss Landers to their home for dinner. They dined on the back patio. Meanwhile, unknown to Beaver, his pal, Larry Mondello, had charged Gilbert and Whitey, two other regulars in the Beav's posse, twenty-five cents each to perch in a backyard tree to witness the event. When Miss Landers stood from the dinner table, the revelation that she wore sandals was met with shock and amazement:

Gilbert: Look! She's got toes!

Whitey: Where?!

Larry: There! Coming right out of her shoes!

Busted for spying, Larry explained why they did it: "Gee, Miss Landers, none of us ever saw a teacher eat before."[66]

New law students share a similar fascination about their professors. In part because the 1L universe is so small, your first-year professors will become the center of it, at least early on. Like the Beaver and his buddies, you and your classmates are likely to pay attention to and talk about not

66. *Leave it to Beaver: Teacher Comes to Dinner* (ABC television broad-cast Nov. 28, 1959).

126

only your professors' teaching styles, but their physical appearances and mannerisms.

While it diminishes fairly quickly, at the beginning law students often view their professors with something approaching veneration. At a social gathering during orientation many years ago, I was standing in the restroom at a urinal when a young man next to me exclaimed, "I can't believe it! I'm peeing next to Professor McClurg." I'm pretty sure he was serious.

So pervasive is the extent to which professors permeate the psyches of new law students that students commonly have dreams about them. A Torts student once reported a grisly nightmare in which I had him tied to a stake while peppering him with questions about the tort of battery. Each time he answered, I shouted, "Wrong!" and lopped off one of his limbs with an ax, saying "Is that a battery? Is that a battery?" Obviously, the dream was farfetched. I never would have asked such an easy question.

Who Are These People?

Whether cast in terms of "know your boss" or, as some students might say, "know your enemy," it's worth knowing a little about who becomes law profs and what makes them tick. Who are these people you can't escape even in your sleep, these maestros who will stand before you and orchestrate so much of your existence: your schedule, leisure time, success or failure, your very sense of self-worth?

Well, as it turns out, they're just that: just people, like Miss Landers. In the very first days of my career as a law professor, way back in the summer of 1986, the dean invited me to his house with a group of other professors to watch a football game on television. It was my first ever social encounter with a group of law professors. Except for the interviewing process to become a professor, my only brushes with law profs had been as a student. I was nervous—intimidated I might not be able to keep up with their deep thoughts and brilliant discourse.

When I arrived, I planted myself on the sofa in front of the television next to a dapperly dressed, gray-haired eminence who had been teaching law for decades. That's when something happened that forever changed my perspective of law professors. On the television screen, Alabama was playing an SEC rival, I forget which. Alabama had the ball. The quarterback took the snap and handed the ball off to a running back, who slipped through the middle of the line for a modest gain. The play prompted the oracle seated next to me to plunge his index finger into his cupped, orifice-imitating hand and cackle, "The old Ex–Lax play—right up the hole!" (Ex–Lax is a chewable laxative.) Hmm, a joke I might have made in the sixth grade. I relaxed and enjoyed the game. Just regular people.

Here's some information about law professors:

• Most of the nation's more than 11,000 full-time law professors are white males, although the number of women and minority professors has increased substantially in recent years. In the early 1970s, women and minorities together constituted only 8 percent of law school faculty members. Today, 37 percent of law professors are women and 15 percent are minorities, with some overlap between those two groups.[67] Given that most women and minority professors have entered the profession recently, they're more likely to be younger and untenured.

• Professors of Legal Research and Writing are disproportionately women. Due to the fact that these jobs traditionally have not been tenure-track positions (and pay lower salaries as a result), this subset of law faculty jobs is sometimes referred to by law professors as the "pink ghetto." Currently, 71 percent of full-time legal writing instructors are women.[68]

• Forty-two percent of law professors hold a Juris Doctor or an advanced law degree from just nine "elite" law schools, with 20 percent coming from Harvard and Yale alone. (My alma mater, the University of Florida, has generated eighty-nine current law profs for 1 percent of the total. Go Gators!)[69]

---

67. *See* ASS'N OF AM. LAW SCHS., STATISTICAL REPORT ON LAW FACULTY 2008–2009 (2009), *available at* http://www.aals.org/statistics/2009dlt/race.html [hereinafter STATISTICAL REPORT ON LAW FACULTY].

68. ASS'N OF LEGAL WRITING DIRS. & LEGAL WRITING INST., 2011 NATIONAL SURVEY RESULTS iv (2011) [hereinafter 2011 ALWD SURVEY].

69. STATISTICAL REPORT ON LAW FACULTY, *supra.* A report by an American Bar Association committee used strong language in questioning the wisdom of concentrating law professor hiring on such a small number of schools: "Were we biologists studying inbreeding, we might predict that successive generations of imbeciles would be produced by such a system." LAW SCHOOLS AND PROFESSIONAL EDUCATION: REPORT AND RECOMMENDATIONS OF THE SPECIAL COMMITTEE FOR A STUDY OF LEGAL EDUCATION OF THE AMERICAN BAR ASSOCIATION 82 (1980).

- Law review membership and other academic honors, such as Order of the Coif (top ten percent of the class), are common credentials for law professors.

- Many law professors hold advanced law degrees (i.e., an LL.M or S.J.D.) in addition to their J.D. degree, and a growing number also have Ph.Ds in other disciplines.

- Disproportionate numbers of professors have held one or more federal judicial clerkships, a prestigious kind of judicial assistant position.

- Most law professors have some previous practice experience in either the private or public sector.[70]

- Politically, more law professors probably lean left than right, although no recent data exist to support this assertion. As a general proposition (with many exceptions), law faculties at schools on either coast tend to be more liberal, while law faculties in the heartland tend to be more conservative.

I'm happy to report that the caliber of law faculties is extremely high, in all likelihood much higher than you encountered in undergraduate school or other graduate programs. This is true at all law schools because far more qualified candidates exist than available positions. Perhaps you've heard the adage, "Those who can *do*, those who can't *teach*." Applied to law profs, a more accurate statement of the second part would be, "those who are incredibly well-credentialed and extremely lucky teach." Law professor jobs are highly coveted and becoming one is a very competitive process.

Beginning law profs do lack one important credential: they generally have no classroom experience or training. To teach first-graders to spell "cat" or add 2 + 2, teachers are required to take courses in educational theory and do internships working in classrooms. Not so for law profs teaching complex material and analytical skills to adults. The only training new law professors receive is an optional two-day new teacher workshop sponsored by the Association of American Law Schools. It's a "learn while you earn" affair.

---

70. *See* Richard E. Redding, *"Where Did You Go to Law School?" Gatekeeping for the Professoriate and Its Implications for Legal Education*, 53 J. LEGAL EDUC. 594, 601 (2003) (study of all law professors hired between 1996 and 2000 showing that 87 percent had some practice experience).

When I was first hired as a law professor, the school assigned me to teach Family Law. Not only did I know little about Family Law, I knew nothing about how to teach it or any other subject. I defaulted to trying to imitate the professor who taught me Family Law back in law school. Big mistake. At my first class, after ten minutes of brain-death inducing lecture on the ecclesiastical history of domestic relations law dating from the twelfth century, I saw a woman in the back of the room roll her eyes and nudge the person next to her.

That image burned in my brain for the rest of my scintillating lecture. Fortunately, because I was so nervous, the students' pain was short-lived. Orating like Socrates on speed, I covered twenty pages of notes in about thirty minutes and ended twenty minutes early (by comparison, I now cover about seven pages of notes in fifty minutes). Starting at the next class I reverted to just being myself. That worked much better, although I still recall a comment on my initial set of student evaluations that said: "Is there a fund to send this guy back to Florida?"

A Kinder, Gentler Law School Nation

Prior to starting law school, you likely will hear horror stories about law professors. Some famous print and screen accounts of law school portray law professors as sadistic ogres. In modern times, these stories are more urban legend than reality. When I ask groups of new students to name their biggest surprise about law school, one of the most common answers relates to professors defying the stereotype of being cruel dictators bent on humiliating students. Here are a few sample answers:

- The biggest surprise has been the attitude of the professors. After reading Turow's *One L*, which was recommended by many friends as an accurate depiction of first-year life, I expected professors to create a clear barrier between themselves and the students. I anticipated a class environment based heavily in fear, with an undertone of student humiliation. I may have just been lucky in my draw of sections, but I have found that the professors actually enjoy what they do (or are great actors). In all classes, there is a relaxed feeling in the dialogue and discussion. This certainly has not taken away from the fear—but for me it has shifted the fear from a fear of public humiliation to a fear of disappointing. In discussions with my classmates, everyone seems to share the same view—that the desire to be prepared and understand the material is not to avoid being humiliated in class, but to live up to the expectations that we place on ourselves and that the professors place on us.

- The surprise would go back to a misguided belief in professors who are emotionally detached from their students. The professors seem to be genuinely concerned about the students understanding the material, raising their own opinions, asking questions, and not getting overwhelmed in the whole process. I think I would find it hard as a professor to remember names in a class of seventy to eighty students; however, I have already noticed that occurring in most of my classes.

- My biggest surprise has been the personality of the professors. While they have all made it very clear that we are to be prepared before class, I never felt as though they were trying to embarrass or belittle us. That being said, the professors are still quite intimidating.

Not every professor at every law school is kind and caring. A funny story handed down at my current institution involves a now-retired professor who a former student approached at a cocktail party. The student, several years removed from the professor's class, commented that he didn't seem to like law students. The professor replied that she was correct. She asked, "Then why do you choose to teach?" He replied: "The exterminator doesn't have to like termites."

But, overall, law professors are not mean-spirited people out to get students. To the contrary, law schools are getting "nicer" all the time. Many older professors would complain that legal education has become too nice, with profs going out of their way to be friendly to or even friends with students. Part of this attitudinal drift may be motivated by the desire to get good student evaluations, which both feed the ego and play a role in promotion and salary decisions. Also, with students paying high dollars for tuition and with so many law schools competing for the same pool of talented applicants, law school administrations feel pressure, which they pass on to the professors, to achieve customer satisfaction. In law school-speak, it's called being "student-centered." Some law schools have even resorted to advertising that their professors are nice.[71]

A larger explanation for the shift toward "feel good" legal education is attributable to the fact that the old school Socratic traditionalists are retiring and being replaced by a new breed of Gen–X and Gen–Y professors who grew up in a world environment emphasizing affirmation and self-esteem building. That young law professors have a different view of the Socratic method than their predecessors is routinely driven home to me at the annual Faculty Recruitment Conference. Most people become law professors by registering for and attending this conference, at which candidates can interview with several schools in one place.

At one recent conference, we interviewed twenty-five prospective law professors. One of our stock interview questions is: "What kind of teaching style do you see yourself adopting?" The answer from nearly every candidate was "soft Socratic" or "modified Socratic," uniformly followed by a clarifier to the effect that while the candidates would call on students, they wouldn't "put them on the spot," "embarrass them," or "intimidate them." Some of the candidates said they wanted to rely on volunteers, rather than cold-call on students. One candidate summed up the feel-good movement by saying: "Hey, let's all leave the classroom feeling good about ourselves!" That is an exact quotation I captured in my notes.

In one sense, I suppose this is good news for law students, but in another sense not so good. Tossing out softball questions to volunteers or letting unprepared students "pass" on questions is certainly less stress-provoking for students, but it's also much less intellectually rigorous, and, ultimately, more boring. The classes you will remember best will be those where your professors challenge you to figure out legal problems and defend your positions. Moreover, as mentioned in the previous chapter, the real world of practicing law is

---

71. *See* Michael Vitiello, *Professor Kingsfield: The Most Misunderstood Character in Literature*, 33 HOFSTRA L. REV. 955, 973 (2005) (quoting law school ads touting the schools' kinder, gentler atmosphere).

anything but kind and gentle. As Professor Michael Vitiello observed: "Treating our students gently is not kind. Instead, by abandoning the demanding form of the Socratic method, we fail to prepare our students for the rigors of practice."[72] But then, Vitiello is an old guy like me.

The Quirkiness Quotient

At their best, law professors are highly skilled, hardworking, creative intellectuals dedicated to perfecting their craft and concerned for the welfare of their students. At their worst, they can be arrogant, bitter, insecure, spoiled prima donnas who sometimes forget they have one of the best jobs in the world. In between those extremes, we're all a bit quirky. Not necessarily quirky in a bad way. We just tend to move to the beat of a different drummer, like maybe Keith Moon or John Bonham (deceased wild and crazy drummers from The Who and Led Zeppelin, respectively). This grand tradition started early on. Jurisprudential scholar Jerome Frank once described Christopher Langdell, the father of the case method, as "a brilliant neurotic."[73]

Why do so many law professors tend to be a bit . . . er, unusual? In part, it's because academia overall attracts highly intelligent people who don't fit comfortably into normal corporate or other business environments. It's not a matter of whether they *can* do it. They just don't want to. But the nature of the job also encourages people to let out what might otherwise remain hidden eccentricities in other settings. Most beginning law professors arrive at their first jobs behaving and appearing as pretty normal people. But unlike the rest of the working world, law professors are subject to very few workplace rules or restrictions.

There's the oft-repeated tale of the new law professor who arrived for the fall semester fresh from a corporate law firm wearing a dark blue suit, starched white shirt, silk rep tie, and shiny wingtips. By the time spring rolled around, he was walking around in a unitard and cape, head shaved, a tattoo of the great Judge Learned Hand covering his scalp, sticks of smoking incense in his ears, and insisting he be called Klaa-

---

72. *Id.* at 959; *see also* Robert M. Lloyd, *Hard Law Firms and Soft Law Schools*, 83 N.C. L. REV. 667, 667 (2005) (arguing that law schools have turned "soft" with the result "that law schools are doing a poor job of preparing students for [the hard world of] practice").

73. Jerome Frank, *A Plea for Lawyer–Schools*, 56 YALE L.J. 1303, 1303 (1947).

tu. Now here I am writing books about law school. Who would have thought?

Seriously, law professors can dress as they wish, say what they want to whomever they want, and come and go pretty much as they please. They enjoy more or less complete autonomy over their lives, a luxury enjoyed by few other workers. Once a law professor achieves tenure, he or she is virtually untouchable. Small wonder they let their inner-selves show through more than most other workers.

Lawhaha.com, my legal humor blog, collects, among other items, funny memories of law school. One category is "Those lovable, quirky law professors," which includes tales about a bald, white professor who raps in class, a professor who acts like nothing unusual has occurred when a tooth flies out of his mouth and bounces off a table during a lecture, a professor who begins teaching the wrong course from the wrong book, a legendary professor who walks smack into the door on the way in and proceeds to teach the entire class with blood streaming down his face, and a distinguished professor who stalks the classroom for an entire hour with toilet paper hanging out of his pants.[74]

As with all people, their uniqueness is part of what makes law professors interesting cats.

Theoretical vs. Practical Professors

Which would you find more appealing? Learning "rules of law" and how to apply them or studying the history, policies, and jurisprudential theories that shape those rules?

One difference among law teachers that affects students is whether they teach primarily from a practical or theoretical standpoint. Law can be taught from a variety of theoretical perspectives. Among the more popular are economic theory, feminist theory, and critical race theory. The difference between a subject taught through a theoretical or policy-oriented lens compared with a more practical and practice-oriented approach is so dramatic that it can seem like a completely different course.

As an inexact rule of thumb, the higher a law school's ranking, the more likely the professors will lean toward

---

74. You can read about these and other interesting law professors at Lawhaha.com, http://lawhaha.com/law-school-stories/those-lovable-quirky-professors/.

theoretical classroom teaching. Conversely, law professors at lower-ranked schools tend to be more practically oriented, focusing on teaching the substance and application of law. The perceived missions of law schools play a role in forging this rough dichotomy. Schools perceived to be "elite" see it as part of their mission to develop students into future legal scholars, policy-makers, and others who will shape the law. Lower-ranked schools, many of which are regional schools, are more likely to see their primary mission as training students to become competent practitioners. Of course, you'll get a mix of theoretical and practical teaching at all law schools and from most individual professors.

In my experience, most, although certainly not all, students, prefer practically oriented teaching.[75] Black-letter law and exposure to the "real world" of practicing law seem more meaningful and relevant to what they're trying to accomplish than legal theory. I felt similarly as a law student. Most of my professors were very theory-oriented. In some courses, my class notes for the entire term were fewer than ten pages. My classmates and I all appreciated the professors who taught us actual law. One reason adjunct law professors—practitioners hired to teach particular courses—tend to be popular among students, in addition to being notoriously easy graders, is that they approach their classes from a real world perspective, supplementing class presentations with large doses of "war stories."

In hindsight, I came to appreciate my theoretical professors. For most lawyers, law school will be the only time in their professional lives when they will be afforded the luxury of being able to think *about* the law. Practicing lawyers spend every day of their careers immersed in the practical application of law. For many, the real world they craved to learn about as law students gets old very quickly. Enjoy your law

---

75. One study identified three general types of law professor: the "Socratic Trainer," the "Caring Teacher," and the "Anti–Socratic Practitioner." The Anti–Socratic Practitioner was described as a teacher who "recognizes that the purpose of law school is to prepare students for the practice of law" and who emphasizes practical skills and "[h]ow-to knowledge." A group of seventy-seven law students at a midwestern law school was asked to rank their image of an ideal professor. First-year students ranked all three personae relatively equally. Third-year students, however, had a much different notion of the ideal professor, ranking the Anti–Socratic Practitioner a clear first. Fifty percent of third-year students chose the Anti–Socratic Practitioner as their ideal professor, 40 percent the Caring Teacher, and only 5 percent the Socratic Trainer. *See* Douglas D. McFarland, *Students and Practicing Lawyers Identify the Ideal Law Professor*, 36 J. LEGAL EDUC. 93, 96–98 (1986).

school opportunities to explore the origins, philosophies, and policies of law.

Important tip: Think back to my story in Chapter 6 about the *Gilbert* study aid that saved me in Criminal Law. If you have a professor who teaches principally from a theory standpoint, find out from the professor or upper-level students how the professor usually tests. Some professors will teach theory, but expect students to know and apply black-letter law on the exam.

Is It Important What Your Professors Think of You?

Here's something you need to know about law professors: they watch you, notice things about you, form opinions about you, and in many cases share those opinions with others. In other words, law professors behave about the same way toward students as students behave toward them. If there were a ratemystudents.com website similar to the popular ratemyprofessors.com, it might be heavily trafficked.

I suppose it would be nice if law professors, being professionals, could rise above forming opinions of their charges, but that's too much to ask. We're human beings. Just like professors make impressions on students, both good and bad, students make impressions on professors, both good and bad. Does it matter what your professors think of you? Well, yes and no.

Why it isn't important: anonymous grading.

Suppose you're convinced a professor does not like you. Maybe he happened to stroll by one day while you were indicting him in the hallway to your classmates as the worst professor in the history of legal education. (These things do happen, so be wary of what you broadcast within the small confines of a law school.) As if your stress level wasn't high enough, now you're saddled with the worry that the professor will take out his dislike for you in calculating your grade. Relax.

The main reason why it's *not* important what your professors think of you is that law school grading is anonymous. All law schools require students to use anonymous exam numbers, rather than names, on exams. The numbers are issued each semester by the registrar's office. I remember being suspicious as a law student as to whether professors had some way of matching exams with particular students, but they don't. The system really is anonymous.

What students don't realize is that professors don't want to know the identity of exam-writers. Students look at anonymous grading as protecting students, whereas professors look at it as protecting professors (against claims of favoritism, being punitive, discrimination, etc.). In truth, anonymous grading probably works more to the detriment of students than to their benefit. It's much easier to assign a low grade to a cold anonymous exam number than to a living, breathing person, particularly if it's a student the professor has come to like and respect. Human nature is such that professors might be inclined to give such students the benefit of the doubt when grading their exams. To the contrary, I can hardly imagine a professor intentionally grading an exam more harshly because the professor didn't like the student.

Two exceptions to anonymous grading exist that affect 1Ls: legal research and writing courses and grade bumps. According to the 2011 survey of legal research and writing program directors, 40 percent of legal writing programs do not grade any writing assignments anonymously, while 60 percent grade all or at least some writing assignments anonymously.[76] Maintaining anonymity in legal research and writing classes is difficult because students are sectioned into smaller groups than other first-year classes, submit more than one draft of the same writing assignment, and often meet with their professors individually to discuss those drafts.

The other exception has to do with grade bumps. Many professors raise or "bump" grades based on classroom participation/preparation/attendance. Some profs also lower grades for the same reasons. In most cases, such changes are limited to one grade step (e.g., from a B to a $B+$). Because evaluating the quality and consistency of class participation and preparation is a subjective undertaking, there is room for a professor's impressions of students to enter into the calculus, consciously or unconsciously. Grade bumps usually are submitted by the professor by student name along with the list of anonymous exam grades. The registrar then adds in the bumps before posting the final grade.

76. 2011 ALWD SURVEY, *supra*, at iv.

Why it is important: references, research assistant positions, and other helping hands.

While your grade will not be affected by your professor's opinion of you, professors can impact your life in other ways, often without you knowing it.

• **References.** In my second year of law school, I decided I wanted to become a law clerk to a federal judge on graduation. It became my single-minded goal. Federal clerkships involve working closely with a judge doing tasks such as researching and drafting court orders and opinions. They are highly sought-after positions. I was fortunate to land a clerkship with U.S. District Judge Charles R. Scott, Middle District of Florida.

Federal judges receive tons of applications from qualified people. My law school credentials were good, but most people who apply for federal clerkships have good credentials. How did I get the job? According to Judge Scott, a strong letter of recommendation written by Professor W.D. MacDonald, whom I worked for as a research assistant, tipped the balance in my favor. Four short paragraphs, just 110 words, literally changed my life. The letter opened the door to the clerkship and the clerkship opened the door to becoming a law professor.

Like all law professors, I write many recommendation letters for students. Whom do professors recommend? Any student they believe in. You don't have to be an *A* student to get a strong recommendation. Even students without high grades can obtain glowing recommendations if the professor likes and respects them and their work habits. I recently wrote a strong letter for a student who received a *D* in Torts that helped her land a summer job. Why? Because she impressed me with her work ethic and attitude.

Students don't realize how often professors' opinions of them are solicited without their knowledge. Professors commonly receive inquiries about students from judges, lawyers, and other professors who are considering hiring the student, even when the student didn't list the professor as a reference. Scholarship award committees may seek nominees or recommendations from professors. Admissions directors ask for professors' opinions when choosing students to serve as fall orientation leaders. Academic support deans seek input when hiring for tutoring positions. Bar examiners send forms to professors seeking their evaluation of former students. FBI agents conduct in-person interviews of professors for any student applying for a government job that requires a security clearance.[77] Accordingly, the impressions you make on your professors can impact your life without you even realizing it.

• **Research assistant positions.** Most law professors hire research assistants, which are good gigs. These are paying jobs, although they pay less than many law firm clerking jobs. They're flexible, allowing students to work on their own time. The assignments help sharpen research and writing skills. Research assistants receive one-on-one mentoring from experts. Sometimes the assignments they receive involve interesting, cutting-edge legal issues. A certain prestige factor is associated with the position.

And if you do a good job, you could end up with one of those killer recommendation letters like I got from Professor MacDonald. The best, most meaningful recommendations come from people who are closely familiar with a person's abilities and work habits. In law school, the professor-research assistant relationship is one of the primary avenues for a professor to gain that kind of insight about a student.

The work assignments vary widely depending on the professor and the professor's confidence in the particular research assistant. They often involve assisting the professor in preparing articles and books for publication (e.g., researching, drafting, cite-checking, proofreading). Numerous research assistants, for example, assisted me in writing the two editions of this book.

Unfortunately, like many other privileges in law school, research assistant positions usually go to students with high GPAs and class ranks, although this is not always true. If you're interested in working as a research assistant for a professor, be a proactive early bird. Approach professors around the midpoint of the second semester and ask whether

---

77. These interviews can be amusing because the agents are required to ask the same questions about everyone, even when they sound preposterous. An FBI agent recently showed up at my office to ask questions about a graduate who had landed a choice position in the U.S. Department of Justice. She was a top student, editor of the law review, and an all-around stellar person. It was hard to keep a straight face when the agent asked questions such as, "Has she ever participated in an attempt to overthrow the United States government?" I said, "I don't know much about her personal life, but that would really surprise me!" We both laughed.

they anticipate hiring any research assistants for the summer or the next year and, if so, whether you could apply.

• **Other helping hands.** Beyond references and research assistant positions, you never know when you might need a helping hand from a professor. Students frequently need law school advice, of course, but that's only the beginning. Sometimes they need legal advice. Sometimes they need life advice. Sometimes they just need a sympathetic ear. Many professors, used to playing dual roles as teacher and therapist, keep a box of tissue handy in a desk drawer.

Personal issues on which law students seek guidance and advice run the gamut. A few years ago, a third-year student I'll call Terrence asked to meet with me. When he came into my office and asked to close the door, I knew something was wrong. He sat down and unloaded a heavy burden he had been carrying around for three years. The bar application deadline was the following week. Everyone in his graduating class had completed and submitted their applications except him. He was terrified that an incident in his past would lead, at best, to a full-blown fitness hearing and, at worst, to the bar refusing him admittance. He even contemplated moving to another state before realizing he'd run into the same obstacle.

Terrence had impressed me more than once as being not only a good student but a good person. He received excellent grades and was a member of the law review. Most important, way back as a 1L, he demonstrated his integrity and good heart when he approached me after Torts class more than once troubled by legal doctrines that led to unjust results. I offered to help Terrence draft an explanation of the incident to submit with his bar application. I thought that, framed properly, the incident could be explained away. It worked. His bar application sailed through. Would I do the same thing for every student? No. I did it for Terrence because I believed in him.

The overarching point of this section is that your professors can be an important link in your legal education and development and future as a lawyer. Apart from tangible assistance, getting to know some of your professors will make you feel more a part of your law school community, which will make law school a more enjoyable and fulfilling experience overall.

Indeed, this might be the best reason of all to get to know your profs. It's a good, comforting feeling simply to walk down the hall and have a professor greet you by name. Researchers have suggested that the high student-teacher ratios in law school and the consequent disconnectedness between professors and students is a significant cause of distress and discontent in law students.

Five Easy Ways to Get to Know Your Professors

I was able to write the recommendation letter for the student who received the *D* in Torts and help draft the bar application for Terrence because I had come to: (1) know them; (2) like them; and (3) respect them. Most fundamentally, a professor can't help you if he or she doesn't know you. Professors often have to decline requests by students for letters of recommendation simply because they don't know the student.

Students can't remain completely anonymous—never participating in class, never asking questions after or out of class, etc.—and then expect profs to come up with glowing endorsements of them. What's to recommend? That their breathing never created a disturbance in class? That they appeared to be conscious when the professor looked in their direction? Many such students may actually deserve good recommendations, but professors can only go by what they know.

When I was in law school, I was too shy to get to know my professors except for the professor I worked for as a research assistant. I always envied my classmates who did get to know them. I'd see a group of them sitting with a prof at an outdoor picnic table at lunch and hear them in the profs' offices when I walked down the halls. At law school parties and other social events, they'd hang around the profs, chatting with them and yukking it up. If I re-did law school knowing what I know now, I would make it a point to get to know my profs.

Not all professors are easily accessible or approachable by students. Some professors, truth be told, want little to do with law students. Teaching as a visiting professor at one top-tier law school, I had lunch with another visiting professor. He made a comment that stuck with me: "Being a law professor would be the greatest job in the world if it wasn't for all the damn students." But most profs don't think that way.

Here are five easy ways to get to know your professors:

1. Introduce yourself as early as possible. Due to a psychological phenomenon known as "primacy effect," people tend to best remember the first things they see or hear in a list or series of events. Trial lawyers are well-acquainted with primacy effect and the corollary principle of "recency effect" (people also tend to better remember the last items in a series), and carefully structure their presentation of trial evidence based on these phenomena.

At the beginning of a school year, the profs don't know any of the students yet. If you make it a point to introduce yourself to your first-year professors at that time, they'll be more likely to remember you once school starts, when you will become just one of the madding crowd. Mixers during law school orientation provide a good opportunity to introduce yourself early. If you can't catch up with a prof during such an event, stop by the professor's office during the week before classes begin.

2. Volunteer in class. Professors take note of and appreciate the students who volunteer in class. As I've said, we need your help to make the whole Socratic thing work. Being known as a class participator also gives professors something concrete to say about a student seeking a recommendation. For 1Ls, except for their course grade, it's about the only specific thing professors can comment on because they have not yet had a chance to work with any students individually. As students progress through law school, professors get to know them in other contexts, such as by working with them as research assistants or in connection with law review, moot court, or other student organizations. Chapter 8 discussed the benefits of class participation. Getting known by your profs is one of the biggest ones.

3. Stop by your professors' offices to ask questions. Stop by your professors' offices from time to time with a question about the material being covered in class or any other question about law school.

Most professors post office hours during which they are available to meet with students, but surprisingly few students take advantage of them. If a professor hasn't posted office hours, don't hesitate to inquire about them. Many professors have an open-door policy, meaning that students are free to stop by any time the professor is in the office. If you feel intimidated about volunteering in class or going to visit professors in their offices, approach the professor after class and ask a question about the day's discussion. It's common for a few students to gather around the lectern after class to ask clarifying questions or continue discussion about the topic of the day.

Another way to ask questions and interact with your professors is through online course sites such as TWEN, which most professors maintain. TWEN sites feature a discussion forum in which students can post and answer questions about cases and other course content. Some professors participate in these online discussions, while others leave them for student use or don't activate them at all. Since usually only a small number of students use the forums, they're a good way to get your name in front of the professor and demonstrate your interest in and engagement with the course material.

4. Email the professor a topical news article pertaining to the course material. One easy, low-stress way to initiate contact with a professor, while also demonstrating that you have your eye on the ball, is to email the prof a topical news article relevant to a subject covered in class. You can send the article with a simple note such as, "I don't know if you saw this, but it reminded me of what we were discussing in class today."

5. Give the professor a compliment if it's sincere and deserved. Professors find it rewarding to be appreciated by their students. If your professor is doing a great job, let him or her know. Don't worry about being seen as a brownnoser. Profs can tell the difference between sincere appreciation and phony-baloney attempts to kiss up.

Five Easy Ways to Make Your Professors Wish You Had Chosen a Different Career Path

Whereas it can take a bit of extra effort to become known by your professors, it doesn't take any special effort to get them to like and respect you. It does, however, take a whole lot of regular effort. Professors like and respect good students. It's that simple. By good students, I don't mean students at the top of the class, although they usually will be included. I mean students who are diligent, committed, and hardworking. Good students come to class regularly, well-prepared, on time, and act like the professionals they are on the road to becoming. Referring back to Chapter 4, good students are best defined by the student types of Mr./Ms. Reliable and The Earnest, Hard Worker. If you're already in law school and suspect your professors of showing favoritism to some students, it might be true. But take an honest, objective look at those students. My guess is most of them will be "good students" as defined above.

But some students also act in ways that can make professors *not* like them. Here are five common ways students can get on professors' nerves:

1. Coming to class late, being unprepared, web-browsing during class, etc. Yes, I know these sound obvious and that we've already discussed them. Of course, professors don't like these things. But what students don't realize is that many professors *take it personally* when students show up late or unprepared or otherwise demonstrate a lack of commitment to the course. Caught up in their ivory-tower worlds, professors' courses occupy positions of supreme importance in their lives. Disrespect shown by a student toward a professor's course is sometimes internalized as disrespect for the professor, even if not intended that way.

More generally, if your conduct leads the professor to conclude that you are a Slacker (see student types in Chapter 4), there is a good chance you will be written off as a lost cause by that professor unless you do something to redeem yourself.

2. Acting belligerently or with a sense of entitlement. There's no quicker way to turn off a law professor than by approaching him or her about a law school issue displaying an air of belligerence or entitlement. Hard-nosed approaches will backfire faster than you can say res ipsa loquitur, if indeed you can say it at all.

You can't successfully bully a law professor. Usually, this is true even if the professor is out of bounds or dead wrong on the issue. As I've explained, law professors, especially tenured professors, operate with near-complete job autonomy. Even deans—their ostensible bosses—have a hard time making professors do something they don't want to do.

"You can catch more flies with honey than vinegar" are words to live by when dealing with law professors. You can influence people more effectively by acting respectfully and nicely than by being confrontational. This advice applies in all law school contexts, but a classic example involves students who want to meet with professors about an exam or writing assignment grade. Students who visit a professor to discuss a grade generally fall into one of four categories:

• Students who sincerely want to learn where they went wrong and how to do better next time.

• Desperate students who arrive with the hope they can somehow cajole the professor into changing the grade.

• Students who performed well on the exam or assignment, but who apparently want to bask in or relive their glory or make sure the professor knows they did well.

• Angry students who come to express outrage at the grave injustice that has been dealt them and to demand redress.

Of these four groups, professors have a genuine interest in talking only with the first group. Most professors are more than happy to try to help students who want to help themselves and the more sincere and nicer the student acts, the greater their willingness to lend a hand. Students in Group 2 are easily identified by the fact that they quickly lose interest in actually reviewing the exam or assignment once it's made clear there is no chance of a grade change. As for Group 3, professors are always happy to run into the students who did well, but don't really want to waste time engaging in unnecessary exam/assignment reviews with them. If you did well, just be happy about it and move on.

Then there's Group 4, whose methodology wins the award for "Most Likely to Cause a Law Professor to Shout 'Get the Hell Out of My Office!'" Approaching a professor with a mindset of entitlement, especially if tinged with belligerence, about an exam or any other law school issue is the worst approach one could take. It will practically guarantee your not getting what you want.

3. Whining and complaining. When professors give assignments or issue class policies about attendance, punctuality, etc., most students just do the assignments and follow the policies. But a few—some of whom qualify as Nattering

Nabobs of Negativism (see Chapter 4)—prefer to waste time whining and complaining about them. Most just whine or complain in the hallways, which is bad enough, but the worst offenders insist on wasting time doing it in class. In the words of the old Nike slogan, when a professor gives you an assignment or tells you to follow a particular rule, "Just do it!"

4. Making excuses. Everyone has problems. Most people accept and deal with them. Others use them as excuses for not fulfilling their commitments. Professors respect students who accept responsibility for their actions, instead of blaming someone or something else (e.g., the professor, law school administration, bookstore, traffic, their classmates, landlord, distant cousin, pet frog).

Having said that, some problems—health issues or death of a close loved one are good examples—do unavoidably interfere with law school commitments. The key is to address these types of issues with professors as they are occurring, not later. For example, don't go over your allowed absences in a course because of illness and then wait until the end of the semester when your grade gets lowered to raise the fact that you were ill earlier in the semester. Contact your professors while the issue is ongoing. A contemporary explanation of a problem will be more credible and, more important, could get you help when you need it, such as permission to record missed classes.

If you're late or get caught unprepared, apologize to the professor after class. Leave out the excuses. Just say you are sorry it happened and that it won't happen again.

5. Trashing your law school, classmates, or professors, especially publicly. Students who smear their law school or the people in it are not popular with professors or other students. Because whispers can become shouts in the claustrophobic halls of law schools, even privately intended denigration can end up reaching a wider audience. A few bitter students go much further, taking their attacks public by posting them on Facebook or other websites.

Growing numbers of law professors and law school staff are on Facebook and many accept friend requests from students. Overall, most law students show surprising maturity on Facebook, including awareness that it's a bad idea to post inappropriate remarks on the world's largest social media network. As you probably are aware, nothing posted on the internet can ever be truly deleted. But, occasionally, students will use Facebook as an outlet for trashing their school, classmates, or professors. News of these posts spreads quickly among the faculty, administration, staff, and students—even to people who aren't on Facebook—and taint the student in everyone's eyes.

Some students go beyond Facebook and attack their law school via other social media or websites, sometimes hiding behind anonymity. This is unwise for the same reason stated above (if the student gets exposed), but also because students have nothing to gain and much to lose by tarnishing the brand name of their law school, even if they hate the place. The value of your degree is directly tied to your school's brand reputation.

Learn Your Professors' Individual Styles and Expectations and Adapt to Them

I sent an email to my colleagues asking for input about the top traits of successful law students. Here's what one wrote back:

> Truth be told, my first reaction to [your] query was that the top trait of successful law students is that they do not waste their time or money on books telling them how to succeed in law school. I literally beg first-years to stay away from all manner of outside advice, and instead to follow what their teachers tell them to do in each of their courses.

Hmm, that can't be good for book sales, but she makes good points. I don't agree with the first part or I wouldn't have written the book, but I couldn't agree more with the second part. While most good law school advice applies across the board, the fact is that law professors, like students, are individuals. They have different teaching styles, preferences, and expectations. We touched on this earlier.

Ultimately, you want to do exactly what your individual professors tell you to do in their courses, even if it conflicts with other advice. Why? Because your professors will be the ones evaluating you—not the external advice-givers. So, for example, if your Civil Procedure professor instructs you to tell her everything you know about a subject area if it comes up on the exam, do it, even though this runs contrary to the standard exam advice to *not* engage in a general brain-dump.

The above is a real example. At one law school where I taught, a number of students came to me questioning my advice to stay focused on the issues in writing answers to essay questions and not to discuss law that is irrelevant to the specific issues raised. "Professor X," they said, "told us she wants us to write down everything we know about the subject." I told them that couldn't possibly be what she meant. Professors often say one thing while students hear another. But when I asked Professor X about it, she said they were right. She wants her students to tell her everything they know about a subject. Who's right? Well, she is for her exams because she's the one grading them. It doesn't matter what others think. Tailor all law school advice to your individual professors as necessary.

CHAPTER 10

THE TOP FIVE HABITS OF SUCCESSFUL STUDENTS: A C.R.E.D.O.

Assuming you're on the road to being a *successful* law student, you'll be spending the majority of your non-sleep, non-classroom hours during the first year studying and doing study-related activities. Accordingly, we'll spend a substantial portion of the book learning how to study and prepare for exams successfully. The mass of complex material, unique teaching methodologies, and unusual manner of student assessment (just one exam at the end of the semester) impose different and far more intense study demands than students are used to from previous educational experiences.

Later pages are packed with specific study and exam advice, with chapters devoted to case-briefing, note-taking, outlining, exam preparation, essay exam mistakes, and tips for tackling law school multiple-choice questions. This chapter approaches academic success from a wide-angle view. Every student begins law school at the same starting line. As the first year unfolds, some students pull ahead while others fall behind. By the end of the year, at law schools all across America, the class is divided into GPA and class rank strata that include a top, middle, and bottom. What factors determine which group students end up in?

Your LSAT Score Does Not Predetermine Your Fate

One obvious answer is innate ability. I'd be less than candid if I told you that everyone entered law school with the exact same chance of landing in the top of the class. Empiri-

cal studies show a correlation between LSAT scores and first-
year grades, between undergraduate GPAs and first-year
grades, between a combination of LSAT scores and undergraduate GPAs and first-year grades, and even between Scho-
lastic Aptitude Test (SAT) scores and first-year grades.

On the other hand, these correlations are not as strong as
most law students and law professors believe. As you perhaps
know, the predictor of success in law school receiving the
most weight in the admissions process is an applicant's LSAT
score. While validity studies do show a positive correlation
between LSAT scores and first-year grade performance, the
correlation is not as high as you might think.

Correlation is measured by a coefficient for which 1.00
represents a perfect correlation and zero shows no correlation
beyond one attributable to random chance. The Law School
Admission Council (LSAC), the good folks who administer the
LSAT, regularly conduct validity studies of the LSAT. The
most recent study, in 2010, collected data from 170 schools
for the 2007, 2008, and 2009 fall entering classes.[78] The mean
correlation between LSAT score and first-year grades was a
relatively weak .36. The correlation varied widely among
schools, from a low of .16 to a high of .56. Most sources agree
that a strong correlation is something above .50. Some
sources would not rate a correlation as high unless it reached
or exceeded .75. Of course, the context of what is being
considered is important in evaluating the strength of correlations.

LSAT scores are a better predictor of success than undergraduate GPA alone, but not by a wide margin. The correlation between undergraduate grades and first-year law school
grades in the 2010 validity study was a mean of .28, ranging
by school from .09 to .45. The correlations were highest when
LSAT scores were considered together with undergraduate
GPAs. The 2010 study found a mean correlation of .47 for
that comparison, ranging by school from .30 to .62.

While the LSAT correlates with success for many students, it does not reliably predict the success level of any
individual student. Do not start law school thinking that your
fate has been preordained by your LSAT score. I've witnessed

---

78. LISA ANTHONY STILWELL ET AL., LAW
SCH. ADMISSION COUNCIL, LSAT TECHNICAL
REPORT SERIES: PREDICTIVE VALIDITY OF THE
LSAT: A NATIONAL SUMMARY OF THE 2009
AND 2010 LSAT CORRELATION STUDIES
(2011).

students with extremely high LSAT scores flunk out of law school and I've known students with below-average LSAT scores (two students with 148 LSAT scores come to mind) who graduated in the top ten percent of their classes and were editors of the law review. When I asked a class of 1Ls who were close to finishing their first year what advice they would give to a close loved one starting law school, I received this reply from a fellow who wrote the top exam in Torts:

> Do not let below-average undergraduate GPA or LSAT scores discourage you from attending law school if you get accepted. Admittedly, I fell somewhere slightly below average in both, and I nearly decided that I shouldn't come to law school for fear that I wouldn't be able to pass. I spent the first month of law school in constant worry of not being able to compete with classmates who had great LSAT scores. I ended up in the top five of my class after the first semester. My friends love to give me a hard time about how worried I was. My advice would be that if you want to go to law school, use below-average entrance numbers as MOTI-VATION in proving your scores wrong, not as reasons you won't pass!

The LSAT measures a limited range of skills, primarily the abilities to read, comprehend, manage, and analyze complex text. While these abilities are critically important to succeeding in law school, other important ingredients to academic success in law school exist that are not measured by the LSAT.

The cheery news is that students have a greater degree of control over these other ingredients. Innate cognitive abilities and mental processing skills developed over a lifetime (e.g., reading comprehension skills) are what they are at the time a student begins law school. Over time, law school helps students advance these abilities and skills, but students who want to succeed at their highest level don't have time to waste in that regard.

A C.R.E.D.O. for Success

Keeping with the essential goal of this book to offer practical advice that can be implemented by any student on day one, I thought long and hard about the habits (as opposed to innate traits) that successful law students have in common. I observed the behaviors of my current top students. I considered outstanding students from years past whom I had come to know, particularly my many excellent research assistants. I thought back to my own law school experience. I consulted other law professors. From all of that, I came up with a list of five habits that most successful law students share. Top law students almost invariably are: (1) Consistent; (2) Rigorous; (3) Efficient; (4) Diligent; and (5) Organized. Put these habits together as an acronym and you have a C.R.E.D.O. for success in law school.

It's true that the C.R.E.D.O. habits are part of the intrinsic or at least ingrained personality of some people, but unlike mental processing ability, you have the power, with effort, to adopt and adhere to the C.R.E.D.O. habits even if they're not part of your default personality. *I urge you to do so.* Make a conscious decision at the beginning of law school to follow them and stick with it. Write the C.R.E.D.O. on sticky notes and post them on your refrigerator and study carrel.

As you read the descriptions of each habit below, consider whether the attribute is a natural part of who you are. Be honest with yourself. Your law school fate may depend on it. Identify your C.R.E.D.O. strengths and weaknesses. Take note that the habits overlap to a large extent. For example, students who are consistent are more likely to be organized. Those who are organized are more likely to be efficient, etc.

Consistent.

Time for a pop reading-comprehension quiz. Identify the recurring theme in the list below.

The most successful law students:

1. Read *every* assignment.

2. Attend *every* class.

3. Take good notes in *every* class and fill in gaps as soon as possible.

4. Brief *every* case.

5. Outline *every* course.

If you answered "consistency," congratulations! You can now brag to people that you aced your first law school test.

Successful law students are consistent and steady from beginning to end.

They don't skip a reading assignment because they were out late the night before. They don't miss a class unless they're seriously ill or have a true emergency. If they do miss a class, they still read the assignment and make sure to get good notes from classmates. If they have advance notice and the professor allows it, they arrange for the class to be recorded. They don't stop briefing their cases when they hit "The Wall" of the first semester, which occurs somewhere between the seventh and tenth weeks. They recognize that the material covered at the end of the semester is just as important and as likely to be tested as the material at the beginning of the semester (probably more so). They don't give up after the first semester because they're disappointed by their grades. They understand that law school is a marathon, not a sprint. Their consistency gives them a definite edge over their classmates who are less consistent, even classmates who are more gifted intellectually.

Of all the mistakes new law students make, being inconsistent in reading assignments, briefing cases, attending class, outlining, periodically reviewing the material, and conducting other study activities is one of the most fatal. Why? Because a law school exam—remember, there's only one per course—is only three or four hours long, yet covers an entire semester of material. For a three-credit class, that's forty-two class hours. For a four-credit class, it's fifty-six class hours. Do the math. How do professors work forty-two to fifty-six hours of material into a three- or four-hour exam? They don't. They can't.

Instead, they usually pick out a handful of issues—issues covered in just a handful of classes—and package them into the essay questions on which your outcome in that course will depend. It's true that many law professors also use multiple-choice questions, in part precisely because it allows them to spread the exam coverage more thoroughly and fairly, but multiple-choice questions, if included at all, usually make up only a portion of a first-year exam.

Here are two concrete examples to consider. I went back and studied my Torts I and Torts II exams from a recent year. I always split exams between essay questions and multiple-choice questions, with each section weighted to count for roughly 50 percent of the exam. In Torts I, the essay section was one lengthy, brain-busting issue-spotting/problem-solving question of the type found in the Appendix—yet it only addressed four major issues. I perused my class notes and calculated that the four issues covered in the question were directly covered in portions of only seven out of forty-two class hours. Thus, any student who missed one or more of those seven classes and didn't compensate for the gap was at risk of blowing a substantial portion of the exam.

In Torts II, I gave my students four shorter essay questions instead of one large one. I calculated that the material addressed in those questions was directly covered in only eight of forty-two class hours. Of course, with respect to both exams, background material necessary to comprehend the issues covered on the exams consumed more class hours, but that background material by itself would not enable students to perform well if they missed any of the classes covering the doctrines raised in the questions.

Take a quick look at the negligence essay question and model answer in the Appendix at the back of the book. Same thing. It's a ninety-minute complex issue-spotting question, but contains only four or five (depending on what one counts as a separate issue) basic issues.

This is the way it always works. While some professors may eke out somewhat broader coverage by using a larger number of short essay questions or by dividing longer questions into multiple parts, the bottom line is that missing law school classes or assignments is the legal education equivalent of playing Russian Roulette.

You could get lucky. In my courses, it's statistically possible that a student could miss several classes and still be present at every class where a major issue was covered that wound up on the essay portion of the exam. Even then, the student's performance would suffer for missing the preliminary coverage necessary to fully understand and analyze the issues. But it's also statistically possible that a student could prepare for and attend 80 percent of the classes in the semester, learning all of the material in those classes, yet still miss the direct coverage of *every single issue* tested on the essay portion of the exam. Of course, the most likely result is somewhere in the middle.

Here's an interesting factoid from the first edition. Out of curiosity, I went and dug out the grade and attendance records from a previous Torts class. I added up the absences of the students who received the top seven grades—that is, the top 10 percent—in the class (all *A* or *A-* grades) and those of the students who received the lowest seven grades—bottom 10 percent—in the class (all *C-* or *D+* grades). The results didn't surprise me. The top seven students had only one absence among them; that is, six had perfect attendance and one student missed one class. The lowest seven students had twenty-three absences among them.

I repeated the experiment with a recent class for this second edition. The results were eerily similar. The top seven students missed only one class among them, while the bottom seven students had twenty-four absences.

The inclusion of multiple-choice questions can broaden the course coverage of an exam, ameliorating somewhat the impact of missing a few classes, but students who miss classes or skip assignments still suffer comparatively because their *consistent* classmates will not miss *any* classes or coverage.

In short, to have a chance to succeed at the highest level, you must be consistent in your studying and preparation from the first day to the last day.

Rigorous.

Rigorous is a word with several definitions. Here, it's used to mean "scrupulously right" or "exacting." Legal language is precise. Loose language or vague definitions of legal tests don't cut it. Similarly, partial or incomplete statements of rules won't suffice. More broadly, partial or incomplete *understanding* of what you're learning isn't good enough.

A rigorous understanding of the law will come, in large part, from following the other C.R.E.D.O. components. Going back to consistency, if you miss one day of a two-day discussion of the tort doctrine of negligence per se, your understanding of that doctrine is going to be much less than rigorous. If negligence per se appears on the exam as an issue, you likely will not do well on it.

The starting point for rigorous understanding of the law is getting it down correctly in the first instance in your class notes and then course outlines. Without the "rigorously right" raw material, you'll have no chance to accurately state and apply the law on the final exams.

Part of being able to apply law effectively on exams comes from a natural analytical gift that some folks are fortunate to possess, but if you can train and police yourself to capture the law accurately and precisely in your notes and outlines, you can gain ground on many other students, even those with superior analytical skills. Note-taking is addressed in Chapter 12 and outlining in Chapter 13.

It's difficult to offer meaningful comparative illustrations of rigorously right and amorphously wrong statements of the law since many readers may not yet have started law school and, thus, lack a foundation to recognize the difference. But let's give it the old college try using a simple example from the law of intentional torts.

Suppose the professor is defining the tort of assault in class. She explains that "an assault is a volitional act intended to cause imminent apprehension of a harmful or offensive bodily contact to another person, and such apprehension results, directly or indirectly." This one sentence contains several important words and phrases constituting what we call "operative language." They include the elements of a "volitional act" (as opposed to an involuntary act), "intent" (specifically an intent to cause an imminent apprehension of a harmful or offensive bodily contact), and the requisite consequence (i.e., that imminent apprehension of a harmful or offensive bodily contact results, directly or indirectly). Within these elements, all of the following words have distinct legal significance: "imminent," "apprehension," "harmful," "offensive," and "directly or indirectly."

If one were attempting to state the definition of an assault on an exam, leaving out or mischaracterizing any of the above terminology would result in a non-rigorous—i.e., wrong—statement of the law. As an example, students often mistake "apprehension" for "fear," but technically they are not the same thing under the law. A person can apprehend a bodily contact from another without being in fear of it, in which case an assault would still occur. Suppose a 98–pound weakling came up to former basketball star Shaquille O'Neal on the street, shook his fist and said, "I'm going to sock you, Shaq!" Shaq is more than seven feet tall and weighs more than 300 pounds. It is unlikely he would be afraid of the 98–pound weakling, yet he could still apprehend that a harmful or offensive bodily contact was imminent. Thus, the elements of the tort of assault would be satisfied.

Here's another example, involving a non-rigorous *incomplete* statement of the law. When you take Torts, you'll learn that, as a general rule, landowners owe no duty to protect trespassers from dangerous conditions on their property. A major exception exists, however, with respect to child trespassers, to whom landowners owe higher duties. The dominant test nationwide for when a duty is owed to protect a child trespasser comes from section 339 of an influential treatise known as the *Restatement (Second) of Torts*, with which you will become very familiar in your Torts course. Section 339 provides:

§ 339. Artificial Conditions Highly Dangerous To Trespassing Children

A possessor of land is subject to liability for physical harm to children trespassing thereon caused by an artificial condition upon the land if

(a) the place where the condition exists is one upon which the possessor knows or has reason to know that children are likely to trespass, and

(b) the condition is one of which the possessor knows or has reason to know and which he realizes or should realize will involve an unreasonable risk of death or serious bodily harm to such children, and

(c) the children because of their youth do not discover the condition or realize the risk involved in intermeddling with it or in coming within the area made dangerous by it, and

(d) the utility to the possessor of maintaining the condition and the burden of eliminating the danger are slight as compared with the risk to children involved, and

(e) the possessor fails to exercise reasonable care to eliminate the danger or otherwise to protect the children.

Suppose you had a Torts essay exam question involving a child who was injured trespassing on the site of a chemical factory located three blocks from an elementary school when she went swimming in an unguarded and unfenced pool of sulfuric acid that looked like clear water. Which of the five factors from section 339 would you need to apply on the exam to analyze the problem fully and correctly? *All of them.*

Section 339 is what is known as a "multifactor legal test," which are common in the law. The five factors—(a) through (e)—are *all* part of the test. The determination of whether an occupier of land owes a duty to a child trespasser can be reached only by considering all five factors (note that they're joined by the conjunctive *and*, not the disjunctive *or* as is the case with many legal tests). Not just two or three factors, or even four. Why? *Because it's a five-factor test.* And the only way a student could possibly apply all five factors accurately would be if he or she had written them all down in her notes and/or outline and studied the complete test prior to the exam.

Sounds simple enough, you say. Well, yes and no. Even though section 339 appears in full in our casebook and even though we go over the test thoroughly—factor by factor— during a Torts class and even though I tell my students to make sure they get the complete test in their notes, and even though I let students bring in a "cheat sheet" to the exam on which they can write down all the legal rules and tests we covered, whenever I include a child trespasser issue on an exam, invariably more than half the class will fail to accurately set forth and discuss the entire five-factor test. Some discuss section 339 in general terms. Others discuss some but not all of the factors. Some students fail to mention section 339 at all. Because the individual factors are not terribly difficult to apply, the students who are able to state the test "rigorously right" in their exam answer can usually address the issue reasonably well.

(Note that it is unlikely all of the factors of section 339 or any other multifactor legal test will be *in issue* in an exam question or require equal discussion. In the hypothetical given, for example, factor (b) would not require extensive discussion because it's fairly obvious that an unguarded and unfenced pool of sulfuric acid that looks like clear water is a condition that a landowner should realize involves an unreasonable risk of death or serious bodily harm to trespassing children. Factor (b) could be addressed and dispensed with in perhaps a single sentence, but to be complete and rigorously right, it *would* have to be addressed, because it's part of the test.)

Another way to describe the quality of being rigorous is to say that good students recognize the importance of *paying attention to detail* in capturing the law. They're not just in the ballpark. Not just close enough for rock and roll. They get it precisely right.

Some law professors use partial or complete open-book exams. Depending on the professor, this may include allowing students to bring in their casebooks, relevant rule books (such as, in Civ Pro, the Federal Rules of Civil Procedure), notes, and outlines. Some professors, like me, allow students to bring in one or more sheets of paper which they can fill with whatever material they wish. Thus, it may not be necessary to memorize all of the rules with precision, but one would still have to know and understand them in advance to be able to readily access and accurately apply them. It's too late to begin figuring out the law or even where to find it during an exam. There's just not enough time. Most students like open-book exams, but they may actually diminish exam performance by giving students a false sense of security, with the result that students feel less pressure and, hence, incentive to rigorously understand the law prior to going into the exam.

Efficient.

So much to do, so little time in which to get it all done. Such is the nature of law school. With a typical load of four or five doctrinal courses and a time-consuming legal research and writing course, the plates of full-time students quickly fill up and begin overflowing. Part-time evening students have it even harder. They take fewer courses, but often have to juggle full-time careers and families along with law school.

As a consequence, it should come as no surprise that all successful law students possess or develop efficient time-management skills. They establish schedules for getting things done and adhere to them. They do all the things they need to do, but don't waste time on things they don't need to do. Being efficient can enable students to succeed at a higher level than inefficient students who labor harder and longer.

Think of efficiency as the ultimate and only officially approved "shortcut" method for law school success.

Efficiency in law school is a skill that takes some time to develop. At the beginning, everything is so new and confounding that students can't help being inefficient. The learning ladder, however, is climbed fairly quickly. Within a few weeks, you'll find yourself becoming much more adept at, for example, reading and briefing cases.

The E in C.R.E.D.O. is tied quite closely to the O. People who are more organized tend to be more efficient in how they allocate and apply their time. More on organizational skills below. Let's concentrate on some tips for improving your efficiency:

• **Don't waste time during the day.** Given that time is such a precious commodity, it's unfortunate that many students waste so much of it during the school day. First-year law students frequently complain that class schedules are not designed efficiently in that too many lengthy gaps exist between classes. They don't realize schedules are set up this way intentionally as a way to encourage (perhaps "compel" would be a better word) students to stay on campus during the day, rather than just attend their classes and flee the building. As a result, you're likely to have several free hours available each weekday. Use them productively rather than fritter them away.

Study habits and preferences vary by personality. I hated studying late into the night. I realized this at the very beginning of law school. When I studied late, I'd end up dreaming about law and working in my sleep all night. I awoke feeling tired and un-rested. After a few weeks of law school, I began developing an awareness of how many hours I wasted during the day. My friends and I began each morning playing ping pong in the student lounge. We'd shoot the breeze between classes, even when there were lengthy gaps between the end of one class and the start of another. At lunch, we'd hang out and talk some more. I don't recall the specifics, but I have no doubt that, in the grand tradition of all 1Ls, many of our lengthy discussions were wasted gossip and gripe sessions about courses, professors, and classmates. One day it occurred to me that if I became more efficient during the day, I'd have more free time at night.

So I changed course. I began using every spare minute of the day productively. Within a couple of weeks, I had refined my system to the point where, by the time I left to go home (i.e., when many of my classmates were just getting ready to begin their studying), I usually had every assignment for the next day read and briefed. I missed spending more time with my friends at school, but the payoff came each night. I found myself with plenty of time to work on my legal research and writing projects and still have time to just hang out and relax. Those long nights of working out legal problems in my sleep ended. I had found a time-management plan that fit me perfectly.

The point of this story isn't to persuade you to adopt my plan. It worked for me, but it might not work for others. Some people are "night people" who prefer to work and work better at night than during the day. My purpose is to encourage you to think about how to organize your days so as to be able to use your time more effectively. Each hour wasted during the day is one more hour that must be put in at night.

• **Don't let diligence work against you by taking on unnecessary tasks.** It's hard for a professor to tell enterprising students to stop "wasting" time in the pursuit of extra legal knowledge, but sometimes I do. Some superstudious and/or inquisitive types (see entry for Curious George/Georgettes in Chapter 4) go above and beyond the call of duty in ways that, while admirable, can actually be detrimental because time is such a limited resource.

A classic example is students who look up the note cases in their casebooks. Most casebooks have main cases called "principal cases," which are followed by notes that reference additional cases, sometimes dozens of them. After all these years, I'm still impressed when a student comes up after class and begins discussing details of one of the note cases that he or she has taken the time to look up and read in its full version. Impressed, but also a bit troubled.

If the professor hasn't instructed you to look up a note case, she's not going to expect you to know its content. Thus, although you might gain a bit of extra knowledge, it's essentially wasted knowledge. Or more apropos to the discussion, it's wasted time. It could even be harmful knowledge if your extra reading gets you looking at the legal problem in a way different from how the professor and principal cases covered it. Truth be told, I've used the same Torts casebook for more than twenty years and still haven't looked up all of the cases in the notes.

• **Prepare for *every* class, but don't over-prepare for *any* class.** As repeated endlessly throughout this book, consistent, diligent class preparation is essential in law school. But some well-intentioned students actually spend too much time preparing for class, especially in briefing cases. Students who focus obsessively on case briefs not only take away time that could be better spent, they sometimes lose sight of the big picture. They end up lost in a forest where they can only see the trees around them (i.e., unnecessary details of individual cases) rather than the forest itself (the essential rules from the cases and how they fit together in a broader framework).

It always saddens me when failing students bring me their thick packages of case briefs, as if to prove to me how hard they worked. I page through the stack, saying sincerely, "Wow, you really put a lot of work into these," but also thinking, "Wow, you really wasted a lot of time on these overly long and excessively detailed briefs, time that you probably could have used more profitably."

As discussed in Chapter 11, case briefs are *essential* for 1Ls, but the law of diminishing returns applies to them. A brief that takes an hour to write may not be significantly more helpful than one that takes twenty minutes. It could be less helpful if it contains too much irrelevant detail. Because cases vary in complexity, it's impossible to offer a specific time estimate as to how long you should spend writing a brief for any one case. As a general guideline, however, most cases can be adequately briefed in half a typewritten page.

An important time-saving tip for effective case-briefing is *know your professors*. We discussed this earlier. Professors approach classes and case analysis differently. By learning your individual professors' expectations for class preparation, you can save time on your case-briefing. In all courses, you want to be sure to get the rules out of the cases, but the importance of other details may vary by professor. Consider this comment offered by a recent editor-in-chief of the law review. He said he briefed every case all through law school. No surprise there. He didn't get to be editor-in-chief of the law review by accident. But he also emphasized:

Students should try to get a sense of what each professor is looking for from the class discussions, and modify their case-briefing style by professor accordingly. For example, Professor X would often want details on the parties, while Professor Y only cared about the rules. Professor Y *never* asked what the lower courts did, while other professors asked about that in *every* case. Figuring these things out was very helpful, not only as a 1L, but in upper-level courses with the same professors. I knew that when I had X for Evidence, I'd better know a lot more about the facts than I would for Y's Biz Org class. In short, students can save a lot of time preparing for class by getting to know their professors.

Do not misconstrue the above advice in this section: class preparation and case-briefing are crucially important. But so are lots of other tasks we perform in our daily lives that can be done more efficiently and, hence, effectively. It all comes back to the fact that time is a scarce, fixed resource that needs to be allocated and used wisely.

One reason some students give up on case-briefing is because they never learned to do it efficiently. So instead of compromising, they go directly from spending an hour per brief to not doing them at all. Brief all your cases, but don't spend disproportionate time on any one brief. Let this be your mantra: Prepare for *every* class, but don't over-prepare for *any* class.

• **Don't read far ahead.** Reading far ahead in your assignments seems like an effort that would earn you a grade of *A* under the "D for Diligent" part of the C.R.E.D.O., but that kudos would be offset by the *F* you would earn under the "E for Efficient" part. Reading far ahead is a waste of time because you will have to go back and reread everything before the classes to remember it, making the first reading wasted time and effort.

Some students, for example, try to read ahead for the entire week on weekends, but as you'll see from data cited in the note-taking chapter (Chapter 12), people forget 40–70 percent of what they learn by the second day. Generally speaking, you want to read only one or two days in advance of classes. Even then, you will have to refresh your memory before class, but it will require only a quick skim-through of the material as it will still be fresh. (A necessary exception to this advice exists for part-time evening students, most of whom work full-time day jobs. They often don't have any choice but to read ahead for the week on weekends.)

DO NOT carry this advice to the extreme and try to read your assignment for the first time right before class starts, as some students do. You won't have time to comprehend what you're reading or prepare case briefs and, in any event, you will be unlikely to finish the assignment in time. The first class you attend without having completed the reading will be your first step down the academic ladder.

• **Read and follow instructions on assignments.** Efficient law students read and follow the instructions for their assignments. Like the brick house-building pig in *The Three Little Pigs*, they spend a little more time up front and benefit from that investment later. Students who don't exercise the care to carefully read and follow instructions from their professors can end up squandering enormous amounts of time redoing assignments. Worse, often they won't even be granted the opportunity to correct their mistakes.

Legal research and writing courses offer the most opportunities during the semester for students to follow or not follow instructions, so I turned to a director of a legal writing program for help on this one. I emailed him the above paragraph and asked if he knew of any specific examples to demonstrate my point. Here are two attention-getters he sent back:

1. In the spring semester of the course, students must research and write an appellate brief. Students work on their brief for most of the semester, spending dozens of hours on it. The brief assignment covers two issues. I divide the class into two groups. One group works on Issue 1, the other on Issue 2. Students are told their issue and the issue list is posted on the TWEN course site. Despite this, at least one student a year researches and writes about the *wrong* issue. If they're "lucky" enough to figure this out before they turn in the final draft, all of their work will have been wasted. They have to start over and redo the entire brief. If they don't figure out the mistake before turning in the final draft, they get an *F* for the assignment no matter how good the brief is.

2. Each year, one or more students use the wrong ID number on their assignments. Students are assigned ID numbers at the beginning of the year and told to use the numbers in lieu of their names. Some simply make up their own number or use an incorrect number. Later, when I'm assigning final grades and can't find a grade for a pre-assigned ID, I simply mark it as an *F*. When grades are posted, offending students must then go through all the hoops to get the grade changed. They could have avoided all the distress and headaches associated with this time-consuming process simply by reading and following the instructions.

● **Limit your study aids.** Some students go overboard in trying to read too many study aids. Study aids can be extremely helpful, but one per course is, at most, all students need or can realistically handle time-wise. In addition to draining precious hours from your day, using more than one study aid for the same course can cause confusion since different study aids will present the material differently from one another, and all of them are likely to present it differently from how the professor presents it.

The key to using study aids efficiently and effectively is to identify the best study aid for each course before investing in any of them. Quite often, a "gold standard" study aid—one that is widely recognized by students as the best—exists for each course. As recommended in Chapter 2, find out either from the professor or upper-level students which one that is, get it, and stick with it.

Diligent.

I use "diligent" in the sense of being hardworking and staying on task from day one. The most frequently expressed reason I've heard from dismissed law students as to why they were unsuccessful is: "I didn't understand [choose one: how much work was involved/what I was up against/the demands of law school] until it was too late."

For any of the advice in this book to help—but particularly the study advice in the ensuing chapters—*you need to follow it from the very beginning*. The material is simply too vast in amount and too complex in content to try to play catch-up.

To be successful, commit yourself to being diligent before you ever cross the threshold of the law school front door. (More overlap: diligence overlaps with consistency, as well as rigorousness and efficiency.) While the first semester of law school may seem like an eternity when you're in the midst of it, you'll be shocked at how quickly it passes. You cannot afford to get even one class behind. If you don't follow any other advice in this book, believe this: If you fall behind, you are in trouble.

As mentioned at several points in this book, many 1Ls are cursed by their previous educational successes. They arrive at law school having performed well in high school and undergraduate school without having had to expend tremendous energy. They may have managed A averages with only a modicum of effort.

When first-semester law school grades are distributed, many students are shocked to find they are now only "average," or worse, hanging on to their status as students in good standing by the barest of decimal point margins. They're genuinely surprised. How could this be, they ask? In my experience, the answer in most instances is: they weren't sufficiently diligent.

Lots of students arrive at law school thinking, "Hey, I'm pretty darn great. In fact, I've always been pretty darn great. I'm sure I'll be pretty darn great at this as well." News flash: many are the "pretty darn great" students who get their butts kicked each year by law school. Consider this comment from a student asked whether the first year turned out better or worse than expected:

> Much worse, unfortunately. I honestly thought that law school would be a breeze, difficult, but not more difficult that what I had already accomplished. I was so wrong that in retrospect it's a little amusing. Law school was a hit upside the head for me. Having gone through high school, straight to college (where I graduated early), then straight to law school, I figured I was invincible.

Hard work can cure a lot of academic ills. I liked this comment from a student asked to list one thing she wished she had known when starting law school: "You don't have to come from a family of legal scholars to do well in law school. Hard work is truly the great equalizer."

Organized.

On the second day of law school in a fall semester, a student came to my office after Torts and said she missed class because she forgot it met on Wednesday. I smiled and said, "Make sure you get someone's notes because the stuff we covered was important." She assured me she had it covered, thanked me, and left.

I wanted to tell her that I doubted very much that she had it covered because the material was complex, especially for a beginning law student. I wanted to tell her that her Torts grade might already be in jeopardy because she missed the critical class at which we delved into the fundamental element of "intent" that underlies all of the intentional torts, a subject we would be studying for the next five weeks and which is invariably tested on the exam. I didn't say any of it because it was already too late. She had already missed the class. She missed it because she wasn't organized enough to keep track of her class schedule.

Last but certainly not least in the C.R.E.D.O. of successful law student habits is "Organized." Being organized is a fitting habit with which to conclude the C.R.E.D.O. because it's entwined with so many other habits of successful law students. Being organized makes it easier to be consistent, rigorous, efficient, and diligent because successful application of those habits depends on having an organized approach and plan. Being organized is an asset in the pursuit of any endeavor, whether it's planning a vacation or preparing your tax return. It's an especially critical habit in law school because of the volume of material and activities that need to be ordered and managed.

Other things being equal, law school is one place where being a bit "anal retentive" or "obsessive" can be a benefit, at least assuming students are obsessing about the right things. In Chapter 2, I talked about the Myers–Briggs Type Indicator (MBTI), a personality inventory grounded in Jungian psychological type theory that measures preferences for different personality indicia, specifically: Extraversion vs. Introversion, Sensing vs. Intuitive, Thinking vs. Feeling, and Judging vs. Perceiving. I explained that your "type" is a combination of four letters, one from each pairing. I suggested you take the MBTI and consider looking into Martha and

Don Peters' book, *Juris Types*, explaining how the MBTI applies to law student learning styles.

If you followed my advice or if you took the MBTI in a different context, track down your result sheet. Look at the last of the four letters in your personality type and see if you're a "J" or a "P." While Ps possess some advantages over Js in law school (Js need to work harder at accepting ambiguity, delaying decisions until all the evidence is in, and listening in class for more than "the answer"), Js have the advantage with regard to this critical trait of being organized. The natural preference of Js is to organize, plan, and order the world around them. In general, they are more methodical. To the contrary, Ps prefer flexibility and open-endedness to planning and deadlines. They often find themselves scrambling at the last minute to finish tasks.

These preferences frequently carry over to education and work environments, where Js benefit from their organizational and planning skills and attention to detail. If you are the type of person who often forgets or loses things, is frequently late, and is always finishing tasks at the last minute, the chances are excellent that you're a P. Be conscious of this preference and recognize that, while a P preference carries other benefits in educational settings, you'll have to work harder on organization, planning, and scheduling than your colleagues with a J preference.

Alright, enough with the psychoanalysis, especially since you're going to need a whole lot more of it after the first year. Kidding. Let's turn to two concrete organizational suggestions. I'll give you several others related to study techniques and exam preparation in later chapters. These are big picture organizational tips that are easy to follow if you commit yourself to doing so consistently. They not only will improve your chances of success in law school, but save you time, headaches, and unnecessary emotional trauma.

● **Keep track of your schedule religiously.** To even begin resembling an organized person, you need to keep detailed track of what's going on in your life. If keeping track of your schedule sounds like overly obvious advice, let me start by saying I've had students show up late for their one and only exam of the semester because they got the time wrong!

Your law school life will be much busier than your prior life. Added to all of your existing family, social, and (for part-time students) employment obligations, will be: class times (regular, rearranged, and make-up classes), reading assignments, room assignments, study group sessions, deadlines for legal research and writing assignments, speaker luncheons, review sessions, extracurricular meetings for law student organizations, professors' office hours, computer research training sessions, days you're "on panel" to be called on in class if your professor uses that method of class participation, application deadlines for scholarships and summer internships and jobs, academic support and writing workshops, and, of course, your exam schedule.

Beyond these specific events, it's helpful to manage your schedule by blocking out times for study activities (e.g., "work on Contracts outline," "read Property hornbook on future interests") and even recreational activities and errand-running (e.g., "lunch with Matt and Lisa," "go grocery shopping").

I never owned a day planner until attending law school, but used one religiously from the first week I got there. In preparing this book, I went to my attic and dug out the moldy day planner I used in my first term at the University of Florida College of Law. For the first three weeks I found, along with all of my reading assignments and regular class times, dated entries like these:

5 pm library tour

Buy Bluebook (Uniform System of Citation)

Buy supplement and highlighters

Study group meets at carrels 2 pm

Legal research lecture Rm 190, 4:10 pm

Get photos taken and fingers printed for FL bar application

Study group meets 7 pm

10:20 Lexis instruction

Dickey Betts concert 2 pm

9:00 pm poolside party at Viscaya

Torts–Contracts class switch

Exercise 1 due in legal research

Fla. Bar exec. dir. 1–3 pm auditorium

Torts meets for two hours—12:40 in Aud. 1:50 in 190C

No study group tonight. Call to confirm cancellation.

Poker game tonight

Extra K [Contracts] class 1:50 in 190A

Later in that first term, I found entries blocking off time for things like: "Study Property," "Work on memo," "Finish reading *Legalines*," "Review Civ Pro notes," and "Make case index for Con Law."

Maybe these calendar entries will cheer you up. I laughed out loud at the fact that I apparently was able to work in a pool party, rock concert, and poker game in those first three weeks of law school. So much for my stories about trudging twenty miles through the snow—in Florida!—to get to law school. But, hey, that's part of the beauty of being organized: it frees up more recreational time.

It's comforting to know that some things never change. In response to a request for organizational tips, here's what one of my research assistants, a top student, wrote. Notice the striking similarities in her approach to the one I adopted decades earlier:

My helpful hint for being organized with so much going on is to write everything down and block off time periods. My calendar breaks down each day of the week into hours so that I can block off class times and then also I'll block off each hour or so for a certain purpose (example: "update Civ Pro Outline" or "read *Glannon's* on res ipsa loquitur"). I even have workout time blocked off a few days a week. I realized I might be somewhat OCD after looking back at this. I found that having a plan of what I was going to study and when I was going to do it helped me get it done with much less stress. I did this especially on the weekends because I'm the kind of student who will sit down and work all day, but you have to take a break sometimes or you will quickly go insane. So with my list I would, on Saturday mornings and/or afternoons, do what I had planned, and then I would have the rest of the day to do something non-school related.

As I mentioned back in Chapter 2, I still use old-fashioned day planners with real paper, but it doesn't matter how you keep track of your schedule, just as long as you do it. If you prefer to use the calendaring functions on your phone or computer, that's fine. Whatever instrument you choose, just make sure you keep it with you at all times and keep it current.

- **Organize the materials you accumulate for each course.** Your course materials are the lifeblood of your survival and success. For each course, you'll have a mass of material to organize. For doctrinal courses, in addition to your casebook and other required books (e.g., statutory supplement books), course materials may include your syllabus, case briefs, class notes, outline, study aids, and extra materials distributed by the professor via handouts or electronically, such as through the professor's online course site.

Depending on the professor, these extra materials can add up. They may include additional cases, statutes, problems, law review articles, and treatise excerpts. For your legal research and writing course, you'll have assignments, exercises, research (e.g., cases, statutes, regulations), and drafts of your papers.

You need to keep everything organized, so you can put your hands on each item when you need it. Importantly, bring all necessary materials to each class. At least once a week, I experience a moment in Torts that provides me with enough information, if I stopped to gather it, to divide the class into two groups I could label *Most Likely to Succeed* and *Less Likely to Succeed.*

How is that possible? At the beginning of Torts I and Torts II, I distribute a package of paper materials to supplement our casebook readings called, not very creatively, the *Supplemental Materials for Torts I* (or Torts II). Each package comprises about fifty pages of state-specific tort statutes, key sections from the *Restatements* of the law of torts (influential treatises), extra cases, and a hodge-podge of other stuff.

At the beginning of the course, I tell students both orally and in writing to bring the Supplemental Materials to *every class* because they won't always know in advance when we'll be referring to them. I also caution them that everything contained in the Supplemental Materials is important and fair game for the exam.

Every few days, we'll come to a point during a class where I say, "Now get out your Supplemental Materials and turn to page *x*." The *organized* students—the students who are more likely to succeed—promptly pull out their Supplemental Materials or flip to them in their organized course notebooks. The *unorganized* students—those who are less likely to succeed—sit there looking around for the nearest organized student whose shoulder they can glance over, because they forgot to bring the Supplemental Materials. Frequently, this happens even when I've made specific advance assignments in the Supplemental Materials. Every semester, halfway through, a couple of students will come to me after we've covered something important in the Supplemental Materials and ask whether I have an extra copy because they lost theirs.

They're not bad people or even bad students. It's predictable that a separate item not used in every class will be inadvertently left behind in a locker, car, or at home. Regardless of whether their actions are foreseeable or understandable, unorganized students such as these are hurting themselves. When we're going over in class, for example, a complex statute that is contained only in the Supplemental Materials, there's simply no way for students who don't have the statute in front of them to follow the lecture.

Similarly, from time to time I'll distribute new, additional handouts in class with the instruction to read them and bring them to the next class. You'd be amazed how many students show up at that next class empty-handed.

Avoiding these omissions is a fairly simple matter: keep all of your course materials together in one place so that they go where you go. One efficient (ahh, see that overlap again) way to do it is by putting all your materials for each course into a three-ring binder notebook. In this one notebook, you can insert everything you could possibly need for the course, where it will be accessible at a moment's notice. Put the course syllabus and class policies at the front, followed by your case briefs, class notes, outline-in-progress, and extra "handout" materials such as those described above. Use tabbed dividers between the different materials. Keep the notebook current. If the prof distributes a handout, punch holes in it and insert it that day. Buy a three-hole punch to make it easier and more likely that you'll do it. Some students use an extra-large binder and put their materials for all courses in one notebook.

Of course, many modern students manage their course materials such as class notes, case briefs, and outlines on their computers. But even those students need to figure out a way to keep track of paper materials. Regardless of whether you manage your course materials in electronic or hard-copy form, the important points are to do it in an organized fashion and to bring all necessary course materials with you to class so you'll have them when you need them.

If you start out organized, it's a snap to stay that way. On the other hand, if you start out disorganized (e.g., briefs are in your locker, outline is in the back of your car, handouts are . . . hmm, not sure . . . maybe propping up the leg of that bar stool you were sitting on the night before), it will take considerable effort to collect everything when you need it. You might never be able to pull it all together and your performance will suffer accordingly.

* * *

As we prepare to launch into several chapters relating to study, exam-preparation, and exam-taking strategies, pause and take stock of the C.R.E.D.O. habits. Keep them in mind as you read the forthcoming specific advice for enhancing academic performance. Note how much of the advice ties in with the C.R.E.D.O. habits. Look up the definition of "credo" and you'll find something like "a statement of the beliefs or aims that guide someone's actions." Make the C.R.E.D.O. your credo.

CHAPTER 11

CASE–BRIEFING

Case-briefing is the grunt work of law school, one of the most tedious, time-consuming, unglamorous—and certainly most underappreciated—aspects of being a good law student. A "case brief" is a synopsis of a judicial opinion that captures the key elements. Most first-year professors will expect you to come to class having not only carefully read the assigned cases, but having prepared a written case brief for each of them. Some first-year professors demand that students prepare briefs, although such demands are difficult to enforce these days because of the wide availability of case briefs online.

Nearly all new students begin their law school careers as diligent case brief writers, but as the first semester wears on, some students stop briefing their cases. In the second semester, the number of students briefing all their cases dwindles further. The trend accelerates in upper-level courses.

Students who stop preparing case briefs try to compensate either by substituting online briefs or by "book-briefing," a technique in which students use underlining, highlighting, and marginal notes in the casebook to track the case in a brief-like form. I confess that I resorted to book-briefing cases in some upper-level courses when I was a student, but I prepared a written brief for every case in every course in my first year. You need to do the same. Here's why:

Why Case–Briefing is Essential to Success

Learning to read and analyze a case is crucial to understanding law and legal method. Indeed, it is the principal goal of the case method. By reading, I don't just mean decoding the words. That will be hard enough at the beginning given that law has a language of its own. In addition to all the new terminology you'll encounter, like "enfeoffment" and "summary judgment," you'll come upon familiar words that have different meanings in law than in their everyday usage. A new student reading a property law case might think "legal issue" means the procedural or substantive issue of law in the case, when, in fact, the term is legalese for "children."

But far more challenging than learning the meaning of legalese is *comprehending* what the case actually says and means: sentence by sentence, paragraph by paragraph, and, finally, as a whole. As you'll learn, a principal reason preparing for law school classes takes a long time is because cases require careful reading *and* rereading. But even reading a case several times is not by itself going to enable you, the novice legal reader, to fully comprehend and analyze it.

In evaluating the utility of case-briefing, students tend to focus on the usefulness of the final product—the briefs themselves—but the *process* of composing case briefs is more important. Case-briefing forces you to identify what's important, separate it from what's not important, extract it from the opinion, and assemble it into an organized framework. It requires you, as one writer on legal reading put it, to "talk back" to the opinion; that is, to go beyond simply underlining or highlighting the court's words and figure out what the case is really about by putting it in your own words. In short, case-briefing teaches you to analyze law. Additionally, the physical process of extracting this knowledge and writing it down in your own words will help you better assimilate and remember what you read.

You will not accomplish these goals as well through book-briefing, and certainly not by substituting online briefs (which, in addition to requiring no mental processing, are frequently inaccurate). This is no time to overestimate yourself. No matter how smart you are or think you are, beginning 1Ls simply are not capable of reading, deconstructing, and digesting complex law without composing case briefs.

Even law professors, who, unlike you, are expert legal readers, essentially brief all the cases they assign to students in their own class notes. They don't just read the cases, mosey into class and start talking about them. They extract all the essential ingredients from the case and put them into writing in their course notes in their own words.

The problem is that these benefits of case-briefing are intangible. That, combined with the time-sucking nature of preparing case briefs, leads many students to give up on case-briefing too soon. Trust me that the primary benefits of case-briefing, though unseen, are very real. In fact, you don't have to trust just me. Trust the students quoted below. I wrote to a group of top-gun students, the best of the best in their respective classes, and asked if they briefed all their cases as a 1L. Here are the responses from the three students ranked number one in their respective classes:

- I briefed all my cases in all my classes during my entire 1L (and most of my 2L) year. I know many people who relied upon "online briefs" but these were not typically the highest-ranked students. In my opinion, briefing cases during the 1L year cannot be overemphasized.—*Number 1 in 3L class*

- The first semester I personally did my own briefs for about 95 percent of the cases. The second semester I prepared my own briefs for about 75 percent of the cases. For the remaining cases, I would use online briefs to which I would add my own details.—*Number 1 in 2L class*

- I briefed every single case that I read as a 1L. That is not to say that I don't read online case briefs, or even incorporate some of the lines from those case briefs into my own. But I never *just* read an online case brief, nor do I copy-paste an online case brief into my own or print off an online case brief. I read the case, make notes in my textbook as I gather the reasoning that I believe is relevant, THEN read the online case brief, THEN make my own case brief. It sounds like a lot, but it doesn't take much time when you get efficient at it. While everyone is different, the three guys I study with, who pretty much followed the same process as me, all did well (top 10, 15, 25 percent).—*Number 1 in 1L class*

Note from the comments that even top students may consult online or other canned briefs as a way to supplement their understanding of cases and to bolster their own briefs.

There's nothing wrong with that, as long as you stick to supplementing, not substituting.

Students who brief their cases are demonstrating the essential C.R.E.D.O. qualities of Consistency and Diligence. Does this mean that all students who don't brief their cases are destined to flunk out of law school? No. I asked students who had read the first edition of *1L of a Ride* what changes they would make in a second edition. One student replied:

> I disagree with your emphasis on case-briefing. My GPA is not stellar, but I am certainly not on academic probation and my grades are above the 2.5 required to compete for law review. I think that less time spent case-briefing and more time spent working on hypos and old exams, and also reading study aids, is time better spent. I feel that the professor will tell me what they want to see on an exam during lecture and that by case-briefing I am merely reinventing the wheel. (Ironically, I see *1L of a Ride* advertised on case-briefs.com, which is where I go to get the majority of my case briefs for your class and all of my other ones.)

I loved having this guy as a student. He qualified as both a Lightning Rod and Class Joker under the student types outlined in Chapter 4, so it didn't surprise me that he would be a straight shooter. But his comment about professors telling him what he needs to know misses the point of case-briefing.

He's certainly correct that many students who don't brief their own cases succeed in law school, but while the student's 2.5 GPA is quite respectable, the top students quoted above all have GPAs in the 3.7–3.9 range. Briefing all your cases will not guarantee you will be a top student, but, with few exceptions, *not* briefing them will ensure that you won't be. Whether you intend to be a diligent, consistent case-briefer is one of those all-important decisions you need to make at the beginning in defining what "success" as a law student means to you.

In terms of more tangible benefits of case-briefing, the end-results—the actual briefs—are also useful. Briefs are helpful in class, especially if you get called on. They aren't a full-proof security blanket because your professors often will ask about parts of the opinion you didn't understand or didn't think were important enough to write down, but in most instances good briefs will allow you to get through the basics of Socratic questioning unscathed.

Briefs also are helpful in composing course outlines, although don't make the common mistake of simply incorporating your briefs as part of your outlines. This point is covered in Chapter 13, the outlining chapter.

Finally, briefs can be useful in exam preparation as a refresher for what was covered throughout the semester. However, because briefs are prepared before you attend the classes in which the cases are covered, you don't want to rely too heavily on them as an exam study aid unless you edit them during or after class to adjust them to the class presentation. Your professors invariably will emphasize different aspects of the case and/or present the material differently in class than the way you first conceptualized it.

Like most other skills in life, case-briefing is a skill that takes practice to develop. Your early briefs will be terrible. Expect it and don't let it alarm you. Your first briefs are likely to be too long and filled with unnecessary detritus while at the same time omitting important elements of the case. I still remember the first case brief I composed in law school. It was for Contracts. Our casebook contained no topic headings (which is unusual), so I was clueless even as to the general subject matter I was supposed to be looking for in the case. I studied the opinion carefully, then began writing longhand in a spiral notebook. My final product was anything but "brief," consisting of more than two single-spaced pages of rambling, unrelated fragments copied directly from the case. I knew it was junk, but had no idea how to improve it.

But within a few weeks, my case briefs began undergoing transformation. They became much more compact and accurate. Without realizing it at the time, I was learning how to analyze law. The case and Socratic methods were working. This will happen to you. Have faith.

Early inefficiency and overly long briefs are what tempt too many students to give up case-briefing. If you stick with it, your efficiency will improve dramatically. I still have my Torts I and Torts II class notes, which contain my case briefs. I looked at them recently and was surprised by how short my briefs were, yet they still managed to capture the essential nuggets of the cases. Tweaking one of the efficiency rules from the C.R.E.D.O. chapter, *brief every case, but do not over-brief any case.*

Casebook Structure and Organization

Before we get into how to prepare a brief, let's examine how casebooks are structured since they will be the source of all the raw material for your case briefs. Most casebooks are divided by topic, with broad topics divided further into more refined subsections. Thus, for example, most Torts casebooks will begin with a section on "Intentional Torts." That section, in turn, may be broken down as follows:

- A beginning subsection addressing "intent," the critical element common to all of the intentional torts;

- Separate subsections for each of the seven basic intentional torts (assault, battery, false imprisonment, intentional infliction of emotional distress, trespass to land, trespass to chattels, and conversion); and

- Separate subsections covering the main "privileges" or defenses to intentional torts (consent, self-defense, defense of others, defense of property, recovery of property, and necessity).

Within each subsection heading, the casebook will offer one or more principal judicial opinions that stand for and elucidate fundamental rules or principles regarding the topic. These opinions will have been heavily edited and redacted by the casebook authors. An appeal may require the court to resolve numerous legal issues in its opinion, but in law school casebooks the court's opinion usually is being considered only with regard to a single issue. Thus, portions of the opinion relating to extraneous issues will have been excised. Other extraneous content also may be trimmed or summarized, including case citations, analysis of case precedent, immaterial factual and procedural background, and dissenting and concurring opinions.

This is all good news for law students. It means that instead of having to read a fifty-page opinion, you may only have to read a five-page opinion. The extent of the editing depends both on the editing skill and philosophy of the casebook authors, as well as the nature of the course. U.S.

Supreme Court cases, for example, are usually longer, even after extensive editing, than other cases, in part because it's often necessary to include portions of concurring or dissenting opinions. Thus, in 1L courses where Supreme Court cases play a large role, such as Civil Procedure and Constitutional Law, the opinions in your casebook will tend to be longer.

Principal (or "main") cases usually are followed by notes, many of which discuss additional cases. Unless they tell you otherwise, it's safe to assume your professors do not expect you to brief or even look up the full versions of the note cases (also called "squib cases"), although you certainly will want to study any assigned notes carefully. Professors may devote significant class time to discussing selected notes. Also, the notes often contain clearer, more comprehensive explanation of the law than the principal case itself.

How to Read and Brief a Case

I can't give you a concrete formula for how to read a case. The ability to read and synthesize judicial opinions is developed through repetition and by modeling the case analysis conducted by your professors in class. I can give you some good tips though:

Place the case in context.

Before you begin reading a case, place it in the proper spot on your big-picture canvas of the course by paying attention to where the case falls within the casebook's table of contents and section headings. Every case is put in a casebook at a particular place for a reason. A tort case that falls under the broad table of contents heading of "Intentional Torts" and the subheading of "Intent" is inserted at that spot to teach you something about the crucial element of intent that is common to all intentional torts. Even if the case involves the tort of battery, it's not there to teach you about battery. Nor is it there to teach you about tort damages or negligence law or any other topic. How do we know? Because cases intended to teach you about those topics will be grouped under their own relevant headings and subheadings. Casebook authors place cases under particular topical subheadings because they want to use the case to teach you something important about that particular topic.

This tip may sound simple, but many students miss it completely. By failing to contextualize the case—i.e., figure out where it fits in the context of the particular reading assignment as well as the broader topics being covered—they are unable to make discriminating choices when reading the case about what is important and what isn't. Even a judicial opinion that has been substantially edited for a casebook can touch on several points. Contextualizing the case within the framework of the book will help you get your bearings before you begin reading, which in turn will make it easier for you to identify the correct issue when you come upon it. It also will help you tailor your briefs more efficiently.

Don't skim.

Judicial opinions can't be skimmed by novices. The material is too complicated. You need to read every word. As Legal Writing Professor Leslie Burton wrote me in an email:

> When you read, you can't just *read*. You have to read every word. You have to read every sentence. Then you have to reread and analyze to make sure you understand. I once had a class of students who clearly hadn't understood the statute that they had read for homework. When I explained in class how to interpret the statutory language, one student complained: "But that would mean that we would need to read every word." Yes, that's right.

The devil is in the details in law, so you need to pay attention to them. One problem for new students is they're not sure what details to focus on. While all details must be read, not all of them are important. Getting a feel for distinguishing which details are important (e.g., what was the court's holding?) and which ones aren't (e.g., what was the Court of Azzize and why did it have three Zs in its name?) takes practice.

Realistically, as you progress through law school, you'll learn that some portions of some judicial opinions in some courses can, in fact, be skimmed. Sometimes it depends on the length of the opinion and the manner in which it has (or hasn't) been edited. Sometimes it depends on the professor. You'll learn that some professors focus on the details of every assigned case, while some rely on the cases only to get the basic legal principles out of them. I still recall spending hours reading a sixty-page opinion in Corporations only to come to class and learn that the professor was interested only in the one-sentence holding that corporate officers owe a fiduciary duty to shareholders.

Some professors never even mention the cases they assign. My Secured Transactions professor assigned tons of reading from the casebook each class, but never breathed a word about any of the cases in class. After a couple of weeks, my mates and I decided it was pointless to continue reading the casebook assignments. Instead, we took furious notes, memorized Article 9 of the Uniform Commercial Code (which is the subject of Secured Transactions), and bought a study aid. But don't get your hopes up. It's unlikely you'll run into either that type of professor or course in the first year. Secured Transactions is what is known as a "code course," meaning the bulk of the law in the area is derived from a code, or book of statutes, rather than from cases. Most first-year doctrinal courses are heavily dependent on case law.

In any event, you won't be in a position to skim *any* portion of *any* case until *after* you've mastered the art of case-analysis.

Resolve confusion as you encounter it.

Research by Professor Leah Christensen on how law students read cases shows that higher performing students stop and clarify their confusion about portions of a case as they read it before moving on. To the contrary, lower performing students are more likely to just plow ahead, leaving their questions unanswered.[79] If you read a paragraph that doesn't make sense to you, go back and reread it before moving to the next one. As Christensen found in her study, students who don't stop and clear up their confusion when reading a case may make an incorrect assumption about the case that taints their entire view and comprehension of it.

Highlight.

Highlighting with markers is a helpful tool for law students. I highlighted my books extensively as a law student and still do it as a professor. I find that the process of highlighting helps me absorb and retain material better.

---

79. *See* Leah M. Christensen, *Legal Reading and Success in Law School: An*   *Empirical Study*, 30 SEATTLE U. L. REV. 603, 640 (2007).

Highlighting also facilitates quick review of the material, as when you're refreshing your memory of the reading right before class. If you're called on in class, highlighting makes it easier to track down the relevant excerpt of the case to answer the question.

Many students develop systems using different colored highlighters for different components of the case. For example: green for facts, yellow for procedure, purple for reasoning, and pink for the case holding. I stuck with basic yellow, but a multi-colored system is worthy of consideration.

Not long ago, I had a student who made no marks of any kind in her casebooks. When I asked why, she said she wanted to be able to recoup more money for the books when she resold them after the semester. Bad cost-benefit analysis. She was academically dismissed at the end of the first year. Your success, in which you're already investing many thousands of dollars, not to mention your blood, sweat, and tears, is worth far more than a few extra bucks come book resale time. Mark those books up!

Of course, highlighting is not a panacea. I'm not suggesting the academic difficulties of the student referred to above were attributable solely to a lack of highlighting. Some students think if they apply heavy-handed highlighting and underlining to a case, they've done an excellent job of studying the case, but that is not necessarily true. You can highlight every line of a case in a color pastiche worthy of being hung in a gallery, yet still come away without a real understanding of it. That's why you need to brief it!

Abbreviate.

With respect to both case briefs and outlines, developing a shorthand of abbreviations for oft-repeated words and terms will increase your efficiency. Traditionally, for example, law profs and students abbreviated "plaintiff" with a pi symbol (π) and "defendant" with a delta symbol (Δ). Why didn't we just use P and D? Because we didn't have computers and those two letters can end up looking like each other when handwritten. I still use π and Δ when writing by hand, but P and D are fine if you're using a computer. "Contract" is abbreviated "K," while "contracted" can be shortened to "K-ed." Similarly, "reasonable" can be shortened to "R" and "reasonably" to "R-ably." Terms can also be abbreviated.

"Fee simple absolute" can be "FSA," "intentional infliction of emotion distress" can be "IIED," and so on.

The Essential Components of a Case Brief

Different advice-givers offer different formats for case briefs, which can be confusing to law students. But don't worry. There is no single correct format to use for case-briefing. If you peruse different recommended templates for case-briefing, you'll see that while they may use different section headings or put them in a different order, they all seek to capture the same main points about a case. When you get to the case-briefing exercise below, for example, you'll see that the three students whose briefs are included as examples all used somewhat different formats in briefing the sample case.

Regardless of the specific format, when reading a case, especially when starting out, you want to identify and include in your brief these points about it:

The relevant facts.

Law means little except in relation to facts. A change in a single fact can change the outcome of the case. As the famous English jurisprudential scholar Blackstone said, for every case resolved on a point of law, one hundred will be resolved on the facts. I will never forget my professor in Business Organizations who drilled the importance of the facts into us in a most unforgettable manner. "It's the *blanking* facts! It's the *blanking* facts!" He would scream this at us several times per class hour, except he didn't say "blanking." He used the f-word. Even back then, it struck us as an unusual classroom technique. But we definitely got the point!

The trick is separating the relevant facts from the irrele-vant ones. Well-written judicial opinions will do much of the work for you in this regard. A skilled judge will focus on the relevant facts in setting forth the case in the written opinion. Further aid will come from the casebook authors, who may edit out unnecessary facts or even summarize the key facts for you.

Nevertheless, the cases in your casebooks (as well as questions on your exams) often will contain both material and immaterial facts. Thus, in compiling a case brief, one analytical challenge facing you will be to make this distinction and include only the material facts in your brief. This challenge, which is part of the broader challenge of learning to conduct legal analysis, will be especially difficult at the beginning of law school because you will lack any foundation for making the distinction. This is one reason case briefs are longer at the beginning of law school and get shorter as students progress. At the beginning you'll be more likely to include unnecessary facts in your briefs.

The number of relevant facts to include in a brief will vary by the course and individual case. For example, the relevant facts of many cases in Torts and Criminal Law may be simple and few in number as compared to the relevant facts of Contracts and Property cases, which often involve complicated business transactions. In tort cases, for example, the dates of events usually are not important, whereas they often are in contract cases. Of course, these are just general propositions. Everything depends on the particular case. In some tort cases the dates are crucial and in some contract cases they're not.

The procedural history/posture of the case.

The procedural history and posture of a case is the portion of the opinion explaining how the case ended up before the appellate court that wrote the opinion in the casebook. Under U.S. law, a party who desires to appeal an adverse ruling in a trial court must identify a particular error alleged to have occurred during the trial or pretrial proceedings. It's not a ground for appeal simply that the party lost the case and wants a second bite at the apple.

Understanding the procedural posture of a case is extremely difficult at the beginning of law school because students lack knowledge of the procedural mechanisms of the U.S. litigation system. The problem is exacerbated by the fact that the course designed to impart much of that knowledge— Civil Procedure—sometimes is not included as part of the first-semester curriculum and even when it is, the course is taken contemporaneously with the other first-year courses.

To give you a head start, below are the *Top Five Most Commonly Alleged Errors on Appeal* you will encounter in reading appellate court opinions in civil cases (as opposed to criminal cases), which will make up most of your first-year reading. Understanding these five errors will put you several steps ahead of your classmates in the early weeks of law school.

PRODUCT WARNING: If you have not started law school yet, studying the five errors may cause drowsiness. In extreme cases, eye-glazing can occur. If you experience these symptoms, stop reading, tab this page, and return to the five errors when you begin reading your initial casebook assignments.

Top Five Most Commonly Alleged Errors on Appeal

1. The trial court erred in granting the defendant's motion to dismiss (sometimes called a demurrer) before trial. All lawsuits are commenced with the filing of a complaint by the plaintiff. The complaint outlines the grounds for the lawsuit and essential facts supporting those grounds. The rules of civil procedure provide that if a complaint is defective on its face, the defendant can file a motion to dismiss the complaint (and, hence, the lawsuit).

A variety of grounds exist for dismissing a complaint. One of the most common is a generic assertion that the complaint fails to state a valid claim. If the defendant moves to dismiss the complaint and the court agrees that the complaint is deficient, the court will dismiss the complaint without a trial. Frequently, plaintiffs who have had their complaints dismissed will appeal on the basis that the trial judge committed error in granting the motion to dismiss.

2. The trial court erred in granting a motion for summary judgment before trial. Similar to a motion to dismiss, a motion for summary judgment is a mechanism for disposing of a case without a trial. The motion can only be granted when no major factual disputes exist and the moving party is entitled to judgment under the law. If material facts are in dispute, the case must go to trial so that the fact-finder (either the judge in a bench trial or the jury in a jury trial) can resolve the disputed facts based on all the evidence.

Unlike a motion to dismiss, which is based solely on the content of the complaint, a motion for summary judgment can be supplemented by external facts established by documents, affidavits, depositions, and answers to written questions called interrogatories. But again, those facts can't be in dispute. Alleged error in granting summary judgment is a common basis for an appeal.

3. *The trial court committed an error during a trial that led to an adverse jury verdict.* When the jury returns a verdict for one party, the losing party may appeal if the party can point to an error in the trial. While a variety of errors can occur during trials, two of the most common trial errors asserted as grounds for appeal are: first, that the evidence was insufficient to support the verdict; and, second, that the trial court erred in giving or failing to give a particular jury instruction.

The first ground—that the evidence was insufficient to support the verdict—is self-explanatory. The argument often arises in conjunction with the more specific assertion that the trial court erred in denying the losing party's motion for directed verdict made during the trial, which is discussed separately below.

The second ground—that the trial court erred in giving or failing to give a particular jury instruction—requires some elaboration. As it is often said, in a jury trial the "jury is the judge of the facts and the judge is the judge of the law." This means that the jury determines what actually happened based on the evidence it hears and the judge determines the appropriate law to govern the case. When all the evidence has been received, the trial judge instructs the jurors as to that law by reading them written "jury instructions." These instructions are often contentiously fought over by the parties. If the judge gives a jury instruction that a party believes is wrong under the law or refuses to give an instruction that a party believes is required by the law and that party loses, the party may assert that alleged error in an appeal.

4. *The trial court erred in granting or denying a motion for a directed verdict during trial.* A motion for a directed verdict is a motion made during a trial by either the plaintiff or defendant (usually the defendant) in which the moving party argues that, even viewing the evidence in the light most favorable to the other side, no reasonable jury could find in the non-moving party's favor. If the judge agrees, the judge will grant the motion, directing a verdict in favor of the moving party, hence, "taking the case" from the jury.

The party against whom the directed verdict was issued may appeal arguing that the granting of the motion was in error. Conversely, if the judge denies the motion and the jury returns a verdict adverse to the moving party, the moving party may appeal arguing error in refusing to grant the directed verdict.

5. *The trial court erred after trial in granting or denying a motion for new trial or judgment notwith- standing the verdict.* After a verdict has been rendered, it is common for the losing party to file a motion for a new trial or, less commonly, for a judgment notwithstanding the ver- dict (called "motions for j.n.o.v."). Such motions argue that the verdict was contrary to the evidence or that some other error occurred rendering the jury's decision defective. If the judge orders a new trial or enters a j.n.o.v., the non-moving party may appeal alleging error in that decision. Conversely, if the judge denies the motion, the moving party may appeal the denial as error.

Students face a dilemma in deciding how much procedural history to include in their case briefs. In some instances, the procedural history of a case may be complex, requiring a lengthy paragraph to explain it accurately. I recommend that you begin law school by including an accurate procedural posture for each case in your briefs, both to protect yourself in class in case the prof calls on you asking for such informa- tion, but also to start you on your way toward understanding litigation procedure.

This can be time-consuming, however, and often unneces- sary for class preparation purposes over the long term be- cause, as we've discussed, many professors are not interested in the procedural posture of cases when case-dialoguing. After you progress several weeks into the course, be more discriminating about how much procedural information you include in your briefs. If you have professors who rarely ask about the procedural history of a case, you can trim that section of your briefs in those courses.

The issue(s) in the case.

To have any chance of learning to analyze law properly, you will have to learn to "spot issues": in cases, on exams, and in the practice of law. Identifying the key issue in the case is the essential foundation on which any strong case brief is built. Some folks have an analytical knack for issue- spotting from the moment they start law school. Most others develop the skill over time. Regrettably, some students never master it.

"The issue" of a case is *the point* of the case, as in "What's the point?" For each case, ask yourself: Why is this case in this book in this section under this subsection? What are the casebook authors trying to teach me by including it? Thinking about these questions can help you pinpoint the issues.

Students frequently confuse the *procedural issue* in the case, such as those listed above, with the *issue of substantive law* they're supposed to be focusing on. Such mistakes are perfectly understandable and in one sense technically aren't even mistakes since courts often explicitly state the issue in procedural terms, as in: "The issue in this case is whether the trial court erred in granting the defendant's motion for directed verdict."

But that's not why the authors put the case in the book. That will be the technical procedural issue in a hundred cases you will read. The issue you're looking for is the underlying issue of *substantive law* that the court is taking time to explain and offer rules and reasoning regarding. It may be that your professor also will want you to know the procedural issue, but come exam time, you'll be tested on the substantive law.

How do you spot the issue of substantive law? Not infrequently, you'll be lucky and the court will expressly state: "The issue in this case is . . ." followed by the substantive legal issue. But more often the court will not expressly identify the issue, leaving it up to you to infer the issue from the court's discussion of the holding, rules, and reasoning.

Often you'll have to think beyond the narrow issue raised by the case facts and infer a larger issue from the holding. For example, in studying the tort of intentional infliction of emotional distress, you might read *Slocum v. Food Fair Stores of Florida, Inc.*,[80] in which a stock clerk told an elderly woman who asked for the price of an item, "If you want to know the price, you'll have to find out the best way you can . . . you stink to me." The woman allegedly suffered great emotional distress and a heart attack because of the statement.

---

80.   100 So. 2d 396 (Fla. 1958).

You will learn that to make out a claim of intentional infliction of emotional distress, the plaintiff must prove "extreme and outrageous conduct" by the defendant as one of the elements of the tort. The broad issue in *Slocum* was whether "mere insults" constitute extreme and outrageous conduct (the answer is that they generally do not), not the narrow question of whether it is legally permissible to inform a person that she smells bad. But, unfortunately, the *Slocum* court never came right out and said that was the issue, leaving it to students to infer the broader issue from the narrow facts.

Here's a great tip for issue-spotting. In addition to placing the case in the context of the subject headings as already suggested, study the notes following the case. Often these notes will identify the issue more clearly than the case itself. For example, the first note following the *Slocum* opinion as it appears in the famous Prosser, Wade & Schwartz torts casebook asks: "Why is the intentional infliction of mental disturbance by the *insult* not a tort in itself?"[81] This note question essentially identifies the issue for students. Thus, if you're struggling trying to figure out the issue in the case, skip to the notes to see if they identify the issue for you, then go back to the case.

The rule(s) adopted by the court regarding the issue(s).

Ultimately, you usually will be looking to find one or more legal rules in a case. These are the rules that you will be expected to know and apply on the exam. The rules are intimately tied to the issue. One way to think about it is that the issue is the *question* of the case and the rule as applied is the *answer* to the question.

Generally, each case in a casebook will stand for one particular rule or an exception to a rule. If the case stands for an exception to a broader rule and you haven't already studied the broader rule, be sure to capture both the broad rule *and* the exception in your brief. The case-briefing exercise below provides an example elucidating this point.

As with issue-spotting, sometimes identifying the rule is simple while other times the rule can be elusive. The rule of

---

81. Victor E. Schwartz et al., Prosser, Wade and Schwartz's Torts: Cases and   Materials 57 (12th ed. 2010) (emphasis added).

the case is often bound up with the court's "holding" in the case; and, indeed, many people label the rule section of their briefs as the holding section. The holding is the court's resolution of the issue, which often incorporates the rule. Thus, one tip for rule-spotting (as well as issue-spotting) is to look for sentences that begin with "We hold. . . ."

Here's an example from a case you will read if your Torts professor covers the topic of defamation. In *Gertz v. Welch*,[82] the U.S. Supreme Court, following up on *New York Times v. Sullivan*, the case we used for the Socratic dialogue sample, was faced with the question of whether the First Amendment dictates that the hard-to-hurdle "actual malice" test from *Sullivan* be applied to private figure defamation plaintiffs in addition to public figures. The Court, per Justice Powell, concluded it did not, stating:

> *We hold that*, so long as they do not impose liability without fault, the States may define for themselves the appropriate standard of liability for a publisher or broadcaster of defamatory falsehood injurious to a private individual.[83]

Well, that was easy. Thank you, Justice Powell. This is also a good example of how the holding often captures the main rule of the case. As a rule of thumb, the more modern the case, the more likely the court will clearly identify the holding.

Not all casebook cases will stand for specific rules. With some frequency, cases are included in casebooks to give general background about a particular subject area. These cases are harder to brief. In fact, some of them will not be brief-able under the traditional format.

The court's reasoning.

Life would be much easier for law students if courts labeled the different sections of their opinions like law students are advised to do in their case briefs. Certainly, this is true with regard to the court's reasoning, the last essential component of a good case brief. Identifying the court's reasoning can be particularly difficult because it may be scattered all over the opinion. Sometimes the reasoning will come before the holding, as a lead-in to it. Example: *"For these*

---

82. 418 U.S. 323 (1974).   **83.** *Id.* at 347 (emphasis added).

reasons, we hold that. . . ." But often the reasoning will come after the holding, as a justification for it. Sometimes, there may be reasoning both before and after the holding.

Also note that some of what could pass as reasoning is superfluous or nonessential. Because you're writing a brief and not a dissertation, you're looking for those nuggets of reasoning that *directly* support the court's resolution of the case. *Why* did the court take the position it did in resolving the issue the way it did? Answer that question before you begin trying to write down the court's reasoning. Don't just copy from the opinion. Think about it first and then put it in your own words. As one of my research assistants, a top student, commented on reading this section:

> I would emphasize the importance of *first* identifying and *second* putting in your own words the court's reasoning. The "why" of the case is what helped me the most in applying the law to different hypotheticals, both in class and on exams. Once I became effective at figuring out the "why" for the holding and/or rule of law, I found that briefing and understanding cases was easier.

A Case–Briefing Exercise

If you haven't started law school yet, here's an exciting chance to write your very first case brief using a real law school case: *Robinson v. Lindsay*, an opinion from the Supreme Court of Washington involving a lawsuit for negligence by a minor injured in a snowmobile accident against the driver of the snowmobile, who was also a minor. The case is included in the popular Prosser, Wade & Schwartz Torts casebook, used at more than 100 law schools. Here are the components of the exercise that you'll find below:

> **The case.** The opinion issued by the Supreme Court of Washington, with a short prefatory explanation of the legal doctrine on which the case rests.
>
> **A case-briefing form.** A template for writing your own brief of the case.
>
> **Sample briefs from real law students.** Three sample briefs of *Robinson* written by three top law students, followed by a comparative analysis.

The case: *Robinson v. Lindsay.*

To make the exercise meaningful, you'll need a tiny bit of background in the applicable legal doctrine. As explained back in Chapter 5, a tort is basically any civil wrong, other than a breach of contract, for which the law allows the recovery of money damages. Negligence law is the largest slice of the tort-law pie. Under negligence law, an actor is liable for injuries caused to another if the actor owed a duty of care to the injured person, breached that duty, and such breach caused injury to the plaintiff. When a duty of care is owed under negligence law, it is usually a duty to use the degree of care that a hypothetical "reasonable person" would have used under the same or similar circumstances. Most adults are held to this same "standard of care," as it is known.

As with everything in the law, exceptions exist. Thus, people with physical disabilities are expected to exercise the degree of care that a reasonable person with the same disability would exercise. Professionals, such as doctors and lawyers, are expected to act with the degree of care of other reasonably acting professionals in the same specialty. Children, as we learn below, also get their own standard of care, but with an exception (so we basically have an exception to an exception at work).

Robinson v. Lindsay appears in the Prosser, Wade and Schwartz casebook under the broad heading of "Negligence" and the subheading "The Standard of Care." Prior to reading the case, students know nothing about how children are treated under negligence law. Keep that in mind as you read the case and consider what the casebook authors and professor would expect a student to get out of the case. We'll also use this case for a course outline example in Chapter 13.

So here we go, beginning with the court's opinion:

ROBINSON v. LINDSAY

598 P.2d 392 (Wash. 1979)

UTTER, Chief Justice.

An action seeking damages for personal injuries was brought on behalf of Kelly Robinson who lost full use of a thumb in a snowmobile accident when she was 11 years of age. The petitioner, Billy Anderson, 13 years of age at the time of the accident, was the driver of the snowmobile. After a jury verdict in favor of Anderson, the trial court ordered a new trial.

The single issue on appeal is whether a minor operating a snowmobile is to be held to an adult standard of care. The trial court failed to instruct the jury as to that standard and ordered a new trial because it believed the jury should have been so instructed. We agree and affirm the order granting a new trial.

The trial court instructed the jury under WPI 10.05 that:

In considering the claimed negligence of a child, you are instructed that it is the duty of a child to exercise the same care that a reasonably careful child of the same age, intelligence, maturity, training and experience would exercise under the same or similar circumstances.

Respondent properly excepted to the giving of this instruction and to the court's failure to give an adult standard of care.

The question of what standard of care should apply to acts of children has a long historical background. Traditionally, a flexible standard of care has been used to determine if children's actions were negligent. Under some circumstances, however, courts have developed a rationale for applying an adult standard.

In the courts' search for a uniform standard of behavior to use in determining whether or not a person's conduct has fallen below minimal acceptable standards, the law has developed a fictitious person, the "reasonable man of ordinary prudence." That term was first used in Vaughan v. Menlove, 132 Eng.Rep. 490 (1837).

Exceptions to the reasonable person standard developed when the individual whose conduct was alleged to have been negligent suffered from some physical impairment, such as blindness, deafness, or lameness. Courts also found it necessary, as a practical matter, to depart considerably from the objective standard when dealing with children's behavior. Children are traditionally encouraged to pursue childhood activities without the same burdens and responsibilities with which adults must contend. (citation omitted) As a result, courts evolved a special standard of care to measure a child's negligence in a particular situation.

In Roth v. Union Depot Co., 13 Wash. 525, 43 P. 641 (1896), Washington joined "the overwhelming weight of authority" in distinguishing between the capacity of a child and that of an adult. As the court then stated (citation omitted):

[I]t would be a monstrous doctrine to hold that a child of inexperience—and experience can come only with years—should be held to the same degree of care in avoiding danger as a person of mature years and accumulated experience.

The court went on to hold (citation omitted):

The care or caution required is according to the capacity of the child, and this is to be determined, ordinarily, by the age of the child.... [A] child is held ... only to the exercise of such degree of care and discretion as is reasonably to be expected from children of his age.

The current law in this state is fairly reflected in WPI 10.05, given in this case. In the past we have always compared a child's conduct to that expected of a reasonably careful child of the same age, intelligence, maturity, training and experience. This case is the first to consider the question of a child's liability for injuries sustained as a result of his or her operation of a motorized vehicle or participation in an inherently dangerous activity.

Courts in other jurisdictions have created an exception to the special child standard because of the apparent injustice that would occur if a child who caused injury while engaged in certain dangerous activities were permitted to defend himself by saying that other children similarly situated would not have exercised a degree of care higher than his, and he is, therefore, not liable for his tort. Some courts have couched the exception in terms of children engaging in an activity which is normally one for adults only. *See, e.g.,* Dellwo v. Pearson, 259 Minn. 452, 107 N.W.2d 859 (1961) (operation of a motorboat). We believe a better rationale is that when the activity a child engages in is inherently dangerous, as is the operation of powerful mechanized vehicles, the child should be held to an adult standard of care.

Such a rule protects the need of children to be children but at the same time discourages immature individuals from engaging in inherently dangerous activities. Children will still be free to enjoy traditional childhood activities without being held to an adult standard of care. Although accidents sometimes occur as the result of such activities, they are not activities generally considered capable of resulting in "grave danger to others and to the minor himself if the care used in the course of the activity drops below that care which the reasonable and prudent adult would use. . . ." (citation omitted)

Other courts adopting the adult standard of care for children engaged in adult activities have emphasized the hazards to the public if the rule is otherwise. We agree with the Minnesota Supreme Court's language in its decision in Dellwo v. Pearson (citation omitted):

> Certainly in the circumstances of modern life, where vehicles moved by powerful motors are readily available and frequently operated by immature individuals, we should be skeptical of a rule that would allow motor vehicles to be operated to the hazard of the public with less than the normal minimum degree of care and competence.

Dellwo applied the adult standard to a 12–year–old defendant operating a motorboat. Other jurisdictions have applied the adult standard to minors engaged in analogous activities. Goodfellow v. Coggburn, 98 Idaho 202, 203–04, 560 P.2d 873 (1977) (minor operating tractor); Williams v. Esaw, 214 Kan. 658, 668, 522 P.2d 950 (1974) (minor operating motorcycle); Perricone v. DiBartolo, 14 Ill.App.3d 514, 520, 302 N.E.2d 637 (1973) (minor operating gasoline-powered minibike); Krahn v. LaMeres, 483 P.2d 522, 525–26 (Wyo.1971) (minor operating automobile). The holding of minors to an adult standard of care when they operate motorized vehicles is gaining approval from an increasing number of courts and commentators. (citations omitted)

The operation of a snowmobile likewise requires adult care and competence. Currently 2.2 million snowmobiles are in operation in the United States. (citation omitted) Studies show that collisions and other snowmobile accidents claim hundreds of casualties each year and that the incidence of accidents is particularly high among inexperienced operators. (citation omitted)

At the time of the accident, the 13–year–old petitioner had operated snowmobiles for about 2 years. When the injury occurred, petitioner was operating a 30–horsepower snowmobile at speeds of 10–20 miles per hour. The record indicates that the machine itself was capable of 65 miles per hour. Because petitioner was operating a powerful motorized vehicle, he should be held to the standard of care and conduct expected of an adult.

The order granting a new trial is affirmed.

Brief the case yourself.

Before you look ahead, take a little time and brief the case yourself. Here's a form you can use:

Robinson v. Lindsay (Wash. 1979)

Facts:

Procedural History:

Who won?:

Issue:

Holding/rule(s):

Reasoning:

Sample case briefs from three top law students.

To add authenticity to this case-briefing exercise, I solicited help from three top students. At the end of their first year, these students ranked number one, two, and three in an entering class of approximately 150 students. I asked the students to track down their case briefs for *Robinson*, which we had covered in the eighth week of their first semester.

Not surprisingly, being outstanding students (although they didn't know they would be at the time), *they had each briefed the case.* These are different students from those quoted at the beginning of the chapter, so we see reinforcement of the assertion that most top students brief all of their cases. By the eighth week of the semester, I'm sure quite a few of their classmates had stopped briefing all the cases.

The three students located their briefs, submitted them without alteration as requested, and gave me permission to share them with you. Their briefs illustrate the point I made earlier that case-brief formats can vary and still accomplish the same goals. The formats used are all somewhat different, yet each brief captured the essential elements of the case.

Student Brief No. 1

Facts. Billy Anderson (13 years old) was driving a snowmobile owned by Lindsay. Anderson had driven snowmobiles for about 2 years prior to the accident. He was pulling Kelly Robinson (11 years old) on an inner tube attached to the snowmobile. Robinson's thumb got caught in the tow rope and was severed. It was reattached but was not fully functional.

Procedural History. Trial produced a jury verdict for Anderson. A new trial was ordered because jury was not instructed to hold Anderson to the adult standard of care.

Issue. Whether a minor operating a snowmobile is to be held to the adult standard of care.

Holding. Yes.

Reasoning. Courts usually don't hold children to the adult standard of care. The standard is usually what is reasonably expected of children of the same age—a reasonably careful child of the same age, intelligence, maturity, training, and experience. But if the activity the child engages in is inherently dangerous (as it is here), the child should be held to the adult standard of care. This discourages immature individuals from engaging in such conduct/activities where the risk of harm is great.

Rule. When a child engages in an activity which is normally undertaken only by adults and requires adult qualifications, the child is held to the adult standard of care.

Student Brief No. 2

Facts. Snowmobile accident where plaintiff of 11 years of age was injured by a 13–year–old boy driving. The 13–year–old boy was driving a snowmobile, pulling the 11–year–old girl on an inner tube which was attached to the snowmobile with a tow rope. The girl's thumb got caught in the tow rope and was severed.

Alleged Error. The trial court instructed the jury to judge the 13–year–old boy's conduct against that of a reasonably careful child under the same or similar circumstances.

Legal Issue. What standard of care should the court use to judge the child's conduct?

Holding. Court overturns the trial court and holds that the 13–year–old boy should be held to the standard of care of an adult because he was partaking in an adult activity that was inherently dangerous (another chip in the "fault principle")—public policy must protect the general public over the interest of the children.

Rule. General standard of care applicable to children is that of a child their own age, experience, intelligence, maturity, training and experience would exercise under the same or similar circumstances. (Ultimately an objective standard, but not purely objective . . . based on certain similar attributes of the reasonable child.)

Rule. "Adult Activity Exception"—When children partake in inherently dangerous activities, normally undertaken by adults, children should be held to the standard of care of an adult.

Reasoning. The "adult activity exception" protects the need of children to be children but at the same time discourages immature individuals from engaging in inherently dangerous activities. There would be great hazards to the general public if children were not held to adult standards when undertaking in adult activities that are inherently dangerous.

Student Brief No. 3

Facts. Billy Anderson, 13, was driving a snowmobile, belonging to D, pulling P. P's thumb was severed when it was caught in tow rope.

Procedural History. Jury verdict in favor of Anderson, trial court ordered a new trial.

Legal Issue. Whether a minor operating a snowmobile can be held to an adult standard of care.

Alleged Error. Jury instruction to hold to adult standard.

Holding. Children involved in dangerous activities, usually reserved for adults, must be held to an adult standard of care.

Reasoning. Exception to the reasonable person standard when dealing with children's behavior. It would be a monstrous doctrine to hold a child to the same standard of an adult. The caution should be judged based on the capacity of the child. Held only to a standard of care of a reasonable child his age. However, when a child is engaged in an inherently dangerous activity, such as driving a motor vehicle, he should be held to an adult standard of care.

Rules.

Disposition. Affirm

Dissents/Concurrences.

Notes.

Comparing the student briefs.

All three sample briefs are of good quality, no surprise since they came from three top law students. Are they exquisite works of art? No, but case briefs don't have to be. In fact, the more perfect the case-brief composition, the more likely the student spent too much time on it. All three students got the job done.

Note one important quality all three briefs have in common: they're *brief* as case briefs should be. *Robinson* is a fairly simple case with simple facts. Not all briefs would be this short, but it bears reemphasizing that effective law students brief every case, but do so efficiently. They brief, but don't over-brief.

It's also worth mentioning, in part because it's the best brief of the three, that Brief 2 (as the writer told me) benefited from the fact that the student edited his briefs during or after class as part of his note-taking, as many students do. So, for example, when I made the point in class that the normal child standard of care is an *objective* standard (i.e., it compares the conduct of the child actor to how other similar "reasonable children" would have acted) even though it looks like a *subjective* standard (in that we tailor it to take into account the child's personal traits such as age and intelligence), the writer of Brief 2 inserted the point in his brief. Editing your briefs to fit the lecture is a wise strategy because it enhances their accuracy and completeness, making the briefs more useful as an exam prep tool.

Let's compare the student briefs, using my brief-formatting template:

Facts. The facts of this case, as is true of many tort cases, are fairly simple and straightforward. Brief 1 contains the most complete statement of the facts, but the two key facts— that the alleged negligent actor was a minor and was driving a motorized snowmobile—are set forth in all three briefs.

Procedural History. The procedural history of the case is stated most accurately in Brief 1. The procedural history in Brief 2 (designated as "Alleged Error") is incomplete and in Brief 3, even when the "Procedural History" and "Alleged Error" sections are combined, the result is incomplete and too vague.

The true procedural posture of the case is more complex than any of the students put in their briefs. The trial judge basically reversed himself, deciding he had erred during the trial in not giving the adult standard of care jury instruction that the plaintiff (called the "respondent" in the case) had requested. When the jury came back with a verdict for the defendant, the judge said he should have given the adult instruction and granted a new trial. This is unusual and somewhat convoluted, but note that the alleged error on appeal—the decision to grant a new trial—is included in my *Top Five Most Commonly Alleged Errors on Appeal* list, as is the underlying dispute over whether the jury instruction was in error.

I'm sure these smart students could have deciphered the full procedural history correctly if they had spent more time studying it, but I suspect they had already figured out that I rarely ask about procedural history after the first few weeks of the course. The students had learned the expectations of their professor—as I've recommended you try to do—and saved themselves time in preparing for class accordingly.

Who won? While not included in most case-brief templates or in any of the student briefs, it's a good idea to insert a separate section stating which party ultimately prevailed because it helps students see the forest through the trees. Very often in class, I'll ask "Who won?" during case-recitation dialoguing. You'd be surprised at the number of puzzled responses this simple question generates from even well-prepared students with full briefs.

Issue. All three of the students nailed the issue. Briefs 1 and 3 stated the narrow issue accurately and nearly identically; i.e., whether the minor snowmobile operator should be held to an adult standard of care. Brief 2 stated the issue more broadly in terms of what standard of care should be applied to children.

Holding/rule(s). Because the students had not yet learned the general standard of care applicable to children, it was important for them to get that general standard out of the case, as well as the exception to it that the court adopted and applied. Notably, all three briefs did include both the general standard of care applicable to children—even though it wasn't directly an issue in the case—and the exception for when children engage in inherently dangerous, adult-like activities.

Brief 2 did it best, stating the general standard of care applicable to children and the exception for inherently dangerous activities as two separate rules. Briefs 1 and 3 placed the general standard in their reasoning sections, but where they put it isn't as important as the fact that they got it in there.

Note that Briefs 1 and 2 basically quoted verbatim the court's definition of the child standard of care. That's good! Remember the R in the C.R.E.D.O. It's important to get legal rules rigorously right. The court defined the general standard of care applicable to children as "the same care that a reasonably careful child of the same age, intelligence, maturity, training and experience would exercise under the same or similar circumstances." Briefs 1 and 2 tracked that definition closely.

But not Brief 3. Compare the court's definition of the normal child standard of care to Brief 3, where the student stated the standard as: "The caution should be judged based on the capacity of the child. Held only to a standard of care of a reasonable child his age." That's too broad because it fails to include the several specific traits (age, intelligence, maturity, training, and experience) that judges and juries are to consider in evaluating how a similarly situated reasonable child would have acted. When I use child actors in negligence exam questions, I frequently will say something like, "Abby was an unusually bright child." I am looking for the students to pick up on the fact that Abby's conduct would be judged against that of a reasonable unusually bright child, not a child of average or below-average intelligence. In fact, if you look at the sample exam question and answer in the Appendix, you'll see that's exactly what I did on a recent exam.

Significantly, all three briefs accurately stated the court's holding/rule that when a child engages in an inherently dangerous, adult-like activity, the child will be held to an adult standard of care rather than the normal child standard of care.

Reasoning. Only Brief 2 captured the two essential reasons given by the court for its holding, which are that the exception to the child standard of care is intended to protect the public and to discourage immature individuals from pursuing dangerous activities. Brief 1 got one of the reasons. Brief 3 omitted both.

Sizing up your brief.

How does your brief stack up to the examples? Did it contain the essential components of the case as reflected in the sample briefs? Go through this checklist, looking at whether you:

1.   Included the two most relevant facts (that the defendant was a child and the accident occurred because of the defendant's carelessness in driving a powerful motorized vehicle).

2.   Took a shot at describing the procedural history. As explained, the procedural history in *Robinson* was tricky even for law students, so don't worry if you missed this. You wouldn't have much to go on in trying to figure it out.

3.   Stated the issue correctly, either broadly in terms of what standard of care should apply to children or narrowly in terms of whether children should be subject to an adult standard of care when they engage in inherently dangerous, adult-like activities.

4.   Included the general rule regarding the standard of care applicable to children.

5.   Included the exception to that rule for situations when children engage in inherently dangerous activities.

6.   Identified the court's two principal reasons for the holding: deterrence of children from engaging in dangerous activities and the need to protect the public when they do.

Also pay attention to anything you included in your brief that *doesn't* appear in the student briefs. Think about why you included the information. In retrospect, does it still seem important to you? If you got all or most of the points listed above, congratulations! If you missed some, don't fret. Like I said, case-briefing is a skill that takes time to develop. Consider this exercise your first baby step on the road to becoming an expert case analyzer.

CHAPTER 12
NOTE-TAKING

When students ask me to reveal the deep dark secrets of successful study strategies for law school, they're always surprised by the simplicity of my answer: read every assignment, brief every case, attend every class, *take good notes in every class*, and prepare course outlines. The C.R.E.D.O. chapter (Chapter 10) covered the importance of consistency in reading assignments and attending class. The previous chapter addressed case-briefing and the next one tackles outlining. Here we take up note-taking.

As shown by dozens of educational studies, taking notes furthers two important goals: encoding and storage of information. With regard to encoding, the process of taking notes enhances attention, idea-processing, organization, and retention of classroom material. In other words, writing down lecture content leads to better learning of the content than simply listening to it, even if one never reviews the notes. Thus, while students think it's a blessing when professors give them copies of their PowerPoint slides or notes, which some law professors do, they're missing out on one of the primary benefits of note-taking: the encoding function. One note-taking study showed that students who took and reviewed their own notes on a lecture performed better on a test than students who were given a copy of the *lecturer's* notes to review.[84]

Numerous studies also support the storage function of note-taking. Students who take notes and review them before tests perform better than those who don't. What a shock!

---

84. Judith L. Fisher & Mary B. Harris, *Effect of Note Taking and Review on Recall*, 65 J. Educ. Psychol. 321, 323 (1973).

Certainly, given the volume and complexity of material presented in a law school course and the long time lapse between its delivery and the exam—fifteen weeks from the first week's material until the exam—"storing" key classroom content is essential to success in law school. Using a computer analogy, your brain could be seen as the computer's temporary memory and your notes as the hard drive on which you're able to store the information permanently. Without good class notes, you'll have no hope of remembering what you will need to know to perform well on a law school exam.

As said earlier, casebooks are not designed to teach or explain the law per se. While cases selected for inclusion in casebooks usually stand for particular rules or principles, the rules won't necessarily be clearly identified or articulated, nor will the case cover all of the satellite doctrines or exceptions to the rule or show how the rule is or should be applied to fact patterns different from the one involved in the case. These are areas that will be, or at least should be, fleshed out in class.

Study aids can help fill these gaps, but are not sufficient standing alone. The same case can be viewed and interpreted through different lenses. Professor Fleener might approach a case from an historical perspective, while Professor Tweener may approach the same case from a law and economics standpoint. Even professors who approach the case from a plain vanilla, black-letter law approach will emphasize, define, and organize rules differently than the study aids.

The only approach that matters to you is the one taken by the professor who will be grading your exam and that professor's approach can only come from one source: class presentations. Accordingly, it's critical to work diligently at capturing with precision the law and its application as they emerge during class presentations. Carrying out this mission will be much easier to do in some courses than others as professors and their teaching styles vary greatly. The amount of effective notes a student is able to take in a course depends greatly on the particular professor.

Most law professors will attempt to present the material in a clear ("clear" being a relative term when it comes to law), organized fashion designed to facilitate student understanding and effective note-taking of the material. Some professors, however, look down on what they see as "spoon-feeding" the law to students, based on a belief that developing analytical skills requires students to bear more of the burden to figure out the law on their own. Recall that a hallmark of the traditional Socratic method was to ask questions without providing answers. Other professors may spend more time discussing the policies behind rules than the rules themselves. Attempting to take meaningful notes in courses taught by these professors can be frustrating.

And then there are those professors who are simply unclear or poor communicators. They deliver jumbled lectures and engage in confusing questioning and question-answering not for pedagogical reasons, but because they are inexperienced, unorganized, unprepared, or simply have brains that work that way. Needless to say, effective note-taking in classes taught by these professors also will be difficult. Students will be forced to fill in the blanks on their own through other means, primarily study aids.

Let's assume you're in a class conducive to effective note-taking. How do you become a successful note-taker? Effective note-taking consists of more than just trying to write things down. It's a four-step process that includes: (1) attentive listening and mental processing of the material; (2) capturing the key material while omitting unimportant material; (3) filling in gaps after class; and (4) conducting subsequent periodic review.

You Have to "Process" Material to Understand It

Your first challenge is to be a good listener. Obviously, you can't take effective notes if you're zoning out. This is easier said than done for a generation that has grown up with many more distractions than previous generations, including wireless internet service in the classroom. One professor has suggested that "Can you repeat the question?" has become part of a new law student lingo, blaming it on computer use.[85] I've already admonished you in Chapter 6 to avoid the temptations of wireless technology while in class, which is the biggest attention-distracter, so we won't rehash that here.

Listen to your classmates as well as your professors. Unlike other educational disciplines, in law school, due to the

---

85. Kevin Yamamoto, *Banning Laptops in the Classroom: Is it Worth the* *Hassles?*, 57 J. LEGAL EDUC. 477, 477 (2007).

Socratic method, notes-worthy comments often will come from your fellow students. If a professor asks a question and a student gives an answer to which the prof gives thumbs-up approval, that's essentially the same thing as the professor saying it. Some professors will stop to highlight correct student answers, but others will simply move on to the next point.

Also, class discussions are often one long complex chain, with professors chiming in clarifications and the like as it moves along. You can't effectively tune out and then tune back in without missing important links in the chain. To test this proposition, rent a movie with a complex plot. Stop listening at frequent intervals to check your Facebook page, buy a pair of shoes, and play a couple games of Words with Friends, then tune back in to see if you still know what's going on in the movie.

But you have to do more than listen: you have to process what you are hearing. Your brain can't just be a receptor during lectures. It must be constantly at work trying to figure things out, which brings us to step two.

Capture the Key Material and Leave Out the Rest

What do you write down? This, of course, is the million-dollar question with regard to effective note-taking. Due to the Socratic method, law school note-taking is hard to get a handle on at first. Instead of straight-forward lecture, most of your classes will be filled with back and forth colloquies between the professors and students. Which parts of them are important? As one student wrote when asked to name his biggest surprise about law school:

> The biggest surprise is the note-taking. It is not your usual note-taking, and I doubt that there is any real way to prepare for it. Law school classes are just not your usual lecture-based discussions, so you are left wondering whether you should write down the banter between teacher and student or just the hypotheticals, etc. People who are used to undergraduate lectures and things written on the board or shown on Power-Point are in for a rude awakening.

Some law students write down too little, while some students write down too much. It's easy to understand how capturing too little of the material could be a problem. If you don't record what you need to know in your notes, you'll forget it and won't have it available to study for the exam.

Students have a harder time understanding how they can write down too much. Isn't more always better? No. Students who try to write everything down in class spend too little time actually processing the information. You're not training to be a stenographer. You're trying to learn and understand law. You can't learn it without thinking about it. Note-taking research shows that when the presentation pace is quick and the informational density high, fast and furious note-taking competes with the mental resources needed to process the information.[86]

As previously mentioned, I started my legal career as a law clerk to a federal district court judge. In that role, I sat through many trials and got to know the court reporters who transcribed them. During one jury trial, I asked the court reporter what she thought about the testimony of a key witness. She said she didn't remember anything about it. Surprised, I said something like, "How could you not remember any of it? You took down every word verbatim!" She said she never thinks about what's being said because it would interfere with her recording it accurately.

Too many computer-equipped law students do the same thing in trying to transcribe every word spoken by the professor. This is one of the big drawbacks of using a computer to take notes, and a principal reason why some law professors object to computers in the classroom. Professors who ban computers assert that requiring students to take notes by hand increases their mental processing of the material, resulting in better notes and higher levels of class engagement.

Remember the student quoted in Chapter 2 who was ranked first in her class, the one who said she finds it much more effective to take class notes by hand? Lo and behold, another student ranked number one recently told me the same thing. She said: "It was really helpful to handwrite my notes because I actually thought about the material before writing anything down. I would just write down brief notes to jog my memory when I went back later to fill them in. When using a computer, it is tempting to type way too much."

86. *See* Gilles O. Einstein et al., *Note–Taking, Individual Differences,* *and Memory for Lecture Information,* 77 J. Educ. Psychol. 522, 522–23 (1985).

Not only does attempting to transcribe the class interfere with your actually hearing and processing the material, it results in you writing down tons of stuff that you don't need in your notes. This clutter, in turn, often gets transferred to course outlines (see next chapter), reducing their effectiveness.

Having said that, for most students, there's greater danger in writing down too little than too much. Note-taking research shows that college students take down fewer than 50 percent of principal lecture points.[87] Studies also show a correlation between the quantity of notes taken and better test performance. When in doubt, err on the side of recording a point rather than omitting it.

In terms of *how* you write it down, some non-law school research suggests that reframing the professor's words in one's own words can result in greater depth of information-processing.[88] That makes sense as a general proposition because it requires greater mental processing than simply recording words by rote. But the law, as we've discussed, is a precise business where every word can have significance. As just one example, in negligence law "should have known" has a completely different legal meaning from "had reason to know," even though they sound like the same thing. "Should have known" imposes a duty to investigate. "Had reason to know" means the actor had actual knowledge of facts that would cause a reasonable person to know a certain state of affairs.

Thus, with regard to legal rules, to ensure accuracy, you're better off trying to replicate the rules as closely as possible. If a legal test discussed in class is derived directly from a case, statute, rule book or *Restatement* treatise, get the operative language in your notes more or less verbatim from the original source. But do it after class. Don't waste your mental processing ability copying it into your notes during class.

With that introduction, let's look more specifically at what you should be looking to record in your notes. Generalizing is always fraught with danger when it comes to law professors,

---

87. *See* Alan C. Eggert & Robert L. Williams, *Notetaking in College Classes: Student Patterns and Instructional Strategies*, 51 J. GEN. EDUC. 173, 195 (2002).

88. *See id.* at 175 (discussing studies).

but for most first-year courses *your primary goal* will be to record anything resembling a legal rule, test, principle, or doctrine, including sub-rules, exceptions to rules and sub-rules, and exceptions to exceptions. Whenever a professor begins a sentence with "The rule is . . ." or "The test is . . ." or any words to that effect, write it down.

It's not sufficient to capture the general principles, which nearly all students will do successfully. The most successful students are those who capture—and understand—the more specific subordinate rules. A group of note-taking researchers categorized lecture points on four levels, with level–1 ideas being the most general and levels 2–4 representing subordinate ideas clarifying, defining, and describing the general ideas. They found that 91 percent of students listening to the lecture captured the level–1 ideas in their notes, but the percentages declined with each level of increased specificity. The students recorded only 60 percent of level–2 ideas, 35 percent of level–3 ideas, and 11 percent of level–4 ideas.[89]

Law school exams emphasize and reward specific analysis over general analysis. For example, if a Torts essay question involving intentional torts presents a fact pattern in which A shoots B, 100 percent of the class is going to recognize that act as a potential tortious battery. To give you some idea how much recognition and understanding of general issues and principles count as compared to specific issues and rules, when I give an issue-spotting/problem-solving intentional torts essay question worth 100 points, mere recognition of a simple battery in the question facts usually counts for only three points. More specific identification and analysis of subordinate issues, such as whether the tortfeasor had the requisite intent to commit a battery or a legal privilege to do so, count much more, usually in the neighborhood of 15–20 points. So don't just write down the "big rules." Record the small ones too: the distinctions, the exceptions, etc.

To enhance understanding of rules, include in your notes, if it's not already contained in your case briefs, the *core reasoning* underlying them. Understanding the "why" of a rule will make it easier to remember and apply it. As an example, you'll learn in Torts that a tortious battery can

---

89. *See* Kenneth A. Kiewra et al., *Qualitative Aspects of Notetaking and Their Relationship with Information–* *Processing Ability and Academic Achievement*, 14 J. INSTRUCTIONAL PSY-CHOL. 110, 113 (1987).

result from an intentional *offensive* touching of a person even if it doesn't cause physical harm. From one of our cases, my students learn, and we discuss in class, that the reason the law allows recovery for merely offensive batteries is to protect human dignity. In fact, offensive batteries are what we call a "dignitary tort." Understanding this reasoning allows students to solve legal problems they might otherwise not be able to resolve.

In class I pose a hypothetical in which Student A kisses Student B after she falls asleep while studying for an exam. Student B finds out about the kiss later and is extremely offended. Does B have a valid claim for battery even though she was asleep and had no contemporaneous awareness of the kiss? Students who understand the reasoning behind allowing recovery for offensive batteries can correctly answer that she would have a valid claim even though she was asleep because a person's dignity can be just as offended if they find out about an offensive bodily contact after the fact.

You should also strive to capture in your notes (either during or after class) the essence of the professor's hypothetical fact patterns posed in class. Remember that your goal is to learn to analyze and apply law, not simply memorize it. An extra benefit is that professors often base exam questions on hypotheticals they used in class or which are closely related to hypotheticals they used in class.

Finally, unless it's obviously immaterial, write down anything the professor takes the time to write on the board or project on a screen. In most instances, the professor wouldn't go through that trouble unless he or she believed the material was important.

What can you safely leave out of your notes? Frequently, in Socratic case-dialoguing a turning point occurs where the dialogue shifts from fleshing out the assigned case and corresponding rules to a more generalized policy discussion of the issues marked by "What do you think?"-type questions. At this point, you usually can relax and participate in and enjoy the discussion without worrying about having to write much down. Most professors expect 1Ls to analyze and solve legal problems on the exam, which usually does not require extensive policy discussion. But 1L profs do use policy questions, so, again, generalizing is always risky.

In addition to extended policy discussions, you're usually safe in omitting discussion of off-topic tangents, anecdotes by the professor, statistics offered by the prof to back up points, and cases and statutes the professor mentions offhandedly, but which are not part of the assigned reading.

Comparing Two Students' Notes

Before we move on to other note-related tips, let's take time out for a real example to highlight what we've covered so far. Below is a comparison of class notes taken in a Torts class by two students we'll call Jane and Roger regarding the privilege of self-defense to the tort of battery. The privilege of self-defense, where applicable, operates to negate what would otherwise be an actionable tortious battery (i.e., an intentional harmful or offensive bodily contact on a person).

I'll spare you further legal explanation because the class notes below, particularly Jane's, do a good job of explaining the doctrine. Jane's class notes are on the left and Roger's on the right. Jane did a good job capturing the salient information. Roger did an okay, but not a great job. I'm sure some other students took far worse notes, but Roger's notes suffer from omissions and errors. Jane finished second in her class of approximately 150 students after her first year, whereas Roger finished somewhere in the middle. In other words, the comparison below is between the notes of a "top student" and an "average student." My comments are bracketed and in bold on Roger's side of the ledger. I inserted spacing as necessary to make the same basic points line up side-by-side.

Jane's notes

Self-defense

Test of the Privilege of Self–Defense (another objective test):
  Were the circumstances such that a reasonable person would believe that they were threatened by a battery?
  Was the amount of force reasonable under the circumstances? Was it proportionate to the threat against you?

Hypo: A, a person who has martial arts training, is walking alone at night in a dangerous part of town. B comes up behind A and grabs A's shoulders from behind. A throws an elbow and shatters

Roger's notes

Self-defense

Reasonable Belief—If a reasonable person would believe that they were threatened with a battery or false imprisonment, they have a privilege regardless of a mistake. This is because the court believes in the "first law of nature is self-preservation."

[Roger got the basic rule down, but missed the "set-up" hypothetical (see Jane's notes on left) that formed the basis for most of the discussion. Getting the professor's

B's face. Turns out B is A's best friend playing a practical joke. B sues for battery. A claims self-defense.

What makes A's belief reasonable according to the facts? Under those circumstances—WHY?

Dangerous neighborhood
At night
Alone
B came up behind

Reasonable Belief: if a reasonable person under these particular circumstances would believe that they were threatened by a battery, they have the privilege of self-defense to protect themselves.

* Mistake: Self-defense is a privilege to prevent threatened battery and allows for a reasonable mistake.

Why? Self-preservation is the first law of nature
Why not make him wait and turn around? B/c it might be too late!

* You don't have to wait and determine that the force is absolutely necessary.

Hypo: suppose that A turns around and unloads a gun into B.

Unloading a gun into a person who grabs your shoulder would not be considered reasonable force.

Reasonable Force: if a reasonable person under the particular circumstances would believe that the amount of force used was proportional to the amount of force threatened.

You are allowed to use the amount of force proportionate to the force that is threatened against you.
Note: You might be privileged to threaten more force than is proportionate against you. You can threaten more force than you can actually use.

A turns around and threatens B with a gun would be reasonable force.

Deadly Force—Force that threatens death OR serious bodily injury

The only reason you can use deadly force is when a reasonable person would believe in your circumstances

hypotheticals down in your notes helps one understand how legal rules are *applied*. Note how the hypothetical that Jane captured involving A and B fleshes out the meaning of objective reasonableness (i.e., how would a reasonable person have acted under the same circumstances?), which is the test for a valid assertion of self-defense. The circumstances are what dictate whether conduct is reasonable, yet Roger—because he didn't take down the hypothetical—may have missed this crucial aspect, as we'll see below.]

[Critically, self-defense allows room for reasonable mistakes in the decision to use force against another. Roger mentioned "mistake" in his basic statement of the rule at the beginning, but did not explain what it meant. Jane, as we see on the left, elaborated on the mistake concept and the policies behind it.]

Reasonable amount of force—You are allowed to use the amount of force reasonably necessary to prevent the battery. You can use proportional amount of force to prevent the battery. You can however threaten to use more force than you are actually allowed to use.

[Again, we see that Roger got the basic rule down that not only must the *decision* to use force in self-defense be reasonable, the *amount* of force must also be reasonable. But we also see that Roger again omitted the hypothetical showing how this principle would be applied.]

Deadly force—threatens death or serious bodily injury. You must prove that he believed that he was threatened with deadly force.

that you are threatened with deadly force.

Because we want to restrict it, there is the old rule "the Retreat Rule." Now it's a minority rule. Doesn't have the relevance that it once did because of the modern use of guns.

[Oops. Roger misstated the rule regarding when it is permissible to use "deadly force" in self-defense in a manner that could prove fatal to his understanding of the entire doctrine. Note that he says that the actor must prove "he believed" he was threatened with deadly force. Because the privilege of self-defense is an objective rather than a subjective test, it's not enough for the actor to prove he personally believed deadly force was necessary. The test is whether a *reasonable person under the same circumstances* would have believed the use of deadly force was necessary. Since this same rule of objective reasonableness under the circumstances applies to the use of any force in self-defense, Roger's misstatement calls into question his understanding of the basic rule, even though he wrote it down correctly at the beginning of his notes. Roger's failure to capture the earlier hypothetical and explanation involving objectively reasonable mistakes may have led to this later error. Moreover, the absence of the earlier explanation in his notes would make it less likely that Roger would detect the contradiction and error when later reviewing his notes.]

Retreat Rule—if a person can safely retreat from the use of deadly force, they are required to do so to avoid defending with deadly force.
   Never from a dwelling
   Never if the retreat would be unsafe (and if you are threatened with a gun, you really can't retreat safely)
   Only applies to the use of deadly force

Traditionally we had the retreat rule, a person must retreat if they can before using deadly force. It is now seen as the minority rule. You are not required to retreat from your home ever.

[At common law, before a person could use deadly force in self-defense (except in his dwelling), he had to retreat *if he could do so safely*. Roger got the basic rule down, but left off the italicized qualifier. What would Roger do if the exam involved a person confronted on the street by an assailant with a gun? Would he know the actor had no duty to retreat, even in a jurisdiction following the retreat rule, before responding with deadly force? Jane would because she got the entire rule down.]

From this example, we see the difference between good notes and average notes. Jane went beyond the general rules and captured many of the subordinate rules. Roger tended to stop after he got the general rules. Jane recorded the class hypotheticals. Roger didn't. Jane stated the rules more rigorously right than Roger. Jane also got more of the core reasoning behind the rules than Roger.

Fill in Gaps Quickly

Note-taking is a two-part endeavor: taking initial notes in class and filling in the gaps shortly thereafter. For a variety of reasons—the density of the material, professors who talk too fast, daydreaming—you're likely to miss accurately capturing all important points in your notes during class even if you're a good note-taker. It's critical that you clarify any confusion and plug any holes in your notes shortly thereafter, preferably the same day.

Dr. R.L. Kaplan, a neurologist, points out that most college students mistakenly think that after learning new information, they gradually forget a little bit of it with each day that passes. Not so. Memory curves developed by psychologists more than 150 years ago show that the greatest memory loss occurs within hours—not weeks or even days—after learning the material. By the second day, people forget 40–70 percent of what they learned. For law students, this means that the material you learned in Property class on Monday is already being flushed from your memory by Tuesday. According to the memory curves, within thirty days after taking notes, students will have forgotten 95 percent of the material.

Thus, to the extent possible, you should update your notes daily. Make sure that any legal rules you took down were recorded completely and accurately. Fill in the professor's hypothetical fact patterns that you remember from class but weren't able to write down. Study groups can be useful for this purpose: the collective memory and understanding of the group exceeds that of any individual.

Resolve any points on which you were confused. Not only will it be easier to do this while the material is fresh in your mind, it's essential to do it because learning law is like building a brick house, with each brick being laid on top of the ones that precede it. The bricks on top are only as strong as the foundation below. As an example, most Torts courses begin with a study of the intentional torts. Intentional torts coverage usually starts with the crucial element of intent (the fault standard applicable to all of the intentional torts), followed by study of the individual intentional torts (e.g., assault, battery, false imprisonment). If you don't fully comprehend intent (which many students don't) before the professor moves on, you won't be able to fully comprehend the individual intentional torts. And if you leave points of confusion unresolved, there won't be time at the end of the semester to go back and begin clearing them up.

Means by which to clear up confusion include: (1) reading study aids; (2) working through CALI (Computer–Assisted Legal Instruction) exercises; (3) asking classmates for clarification, whether individually or through a study group; and (4) if confusion still persists, seeking help from the professor. Most professors are happy to help students who are struggling to understand material *provided* the students have already tried to help themselves.

If you have to miss class, make sure you get that material covered in your notes by borrowing a classmate's notes or arranging to tape the class if you know in advance you're going to be absent, but check with the professor first about his or her taping policies. As discussed in Chapter 10, you cannot afford *any* gaps in coverage.

Conduct Regular Periodic Review

Assuming you have managed to listen well, record good notes during class, and fill in any holes afterwards, you should sleep well at night, knowing that you're doing a good job of laying the major groundwork in your exam preparation. The final step in the note-taking process is periodic review. With only a few days between the end of classes and your first exams, you can't wait until the end of the semester to start reviewing the material. The importance of periodic review cannot be overstated.

At the beginning of their second semester, I asked a first-year class what they intended to do differently in the second semester than in the first semester. The responses were astonishingly consistent. A large number of students stated that they intended to engage in much more periodic review of their notes and, closely intertwined, start working earlier on their outlines and do a better job of updating them regularly. Composing course outlines is, in fact, one of the best forms of periodic review.

Consider Forming or Joining a Study Group

Student "study groups," in which a small number of students (usually from three to five) work collaboratively, are a popular law school study model. I include them in this chapter because one common study group strategy is for group members to get together and literally "compare notes." Regularly comparing and discussing class notes with others allows group members to reorganize, add to, and correct mistakes in their own notes, while also fulfilling the function of periodic review. Study groups also work collaboratively on outlines, exam preparation (such as working through old exams together), and function as social and emotional support networks.

Some students find study groups invaluable, while some don't. Whether you will benefit from a study group depends on two principal factors: your individual learning style and the "fit" among the group members. Extraverts, for example, may take to group study better than introverts. I joined a study group early in my first semester of law school because I thought it was the thing to do. I might have been influenced by the fact that study groups were featured so prominently in the movie, *The Paper Chase*, which we were all very much into at the time.

The group was made up of my buddy Mac, a woman named Lynn, and me. Three weeks in Lynn had the good judgment to quit. I don't recall her exact words, but the gist of her explanation was something like: "All you two ever do is debate everything. We never get anywhere." She was right. Mac and I wasted hours of precious time debating every point, in part just for the sake of the debate. In retrospect, my only surprise was that it took Lynn three weeks to jump off that train wreck. After that, I rarely participated in group study. I realized it was more effective for me to study on my own. You might be the same way. Or you might be completely different.

Many students give study groups an enthusiastic two thumbs-up. Look what this student said when asked to name the number one piece of advice she would give to a close loved one starting law school:

> Group study is key! I formed a study group (leading to great friendships) with two other classmates, and we surrounded ourselves with class discussion throughout

the day. To our surprise, all of our ranks after the first semester were inside the top ten. The odds of it being purely coincidental seem pretty minimal.

I have a feeling these particular students would have been successful even without group study, but the point is that whereas I found study groups to be of little use, she found her study group to be vital to both her success and well-being. Whether to join a study group is a classic example of a law school decision where you should let *your* personality and learning style guide you—not someone else's advice. Join a study group if it feels right to you. Don't if it doesn't.

Before forming or joining a study group, think hard about the people with whom you'll be collaborating. If it doesn't feel like a good match, it probably isn't. Discuss your objectives and strategies in advance. Make sure they are clearly articulated and that everyone in the group buys into them. When you meet, stay on task. Keep socializing separate from study sessions. Socializing is an add-on benefit of a study group, but business should be business when you gather to study. Plan separate social events for the group.

Consider Using a Computer Note–Taking Tool

Not only do most law students take class notes on computers, growing numbers of students have moved beyond basic word-processing programs and are capitalizing on specially designed computer note-taking programs. Many students swear by these programs.

Computer note-taking programs give students the ability to easily manage in one place all the information they will be collecting in their courses. Think of a note-taking program as one big digital three-ring binder notebook. Instead of using separate notebooks or computer folders for each course, you can use only one. Instead of paper dividers and tabs, you can set up computer tabs to organize your information. Instead of inserting pages of notes into your notebook after a class, you can insert notes directly into your digital notebook during class. You can organize your notes by the topic of discussion, date of the class, or any other way that suits your organizational style.

Microsoft OneNote, included in all versions of Office 2010, is the most popular computer note-taking program. OneNote works as a personal information collector, organizer, and manager, incorporating familiar Microsoft programs with familiar icons, keyboard shortcuts, formatting tools, and quick-find functions. I've never used OneNote, so I asked a couple of students who do to explain some of the advantages.

OneNote works a lot like Microsoft Word with the big difference that OneNote allows users to view and access all of their notes and files from any screen instead of having to access separate folders or sub-folders. Once a student labels a particular note or brief with a heading, the labels appear table of contents-style along the right side of the page where their content can be accessed with a click. So, for example, when your Property professor asks you to recite the facts of Case X, your brief for that case is one click away. No need to fumble around scrolling through virtual pages or flipping through papyrus pages in search of the brief. In addition, by opening a new window, you can view your case briefs and class notes side by side. Another advantage of OneNote is the facility to quickly move and reorganize text. You can also highlight text and drag and drop it into any part of the document.

The students also reported that OneNote is a good tool for outlining because the outlining function is not nearly as strict or structured as in regular Microsoft Word.

Another advantage of OneNote is the saving feature. OneNote automatically saves everything you type. You're never required to click the save button. If you open the program for a minute to type a quick note, then close it, the note will be automatically saved without having to take any other steps. If your computer freezes or shuts down, you don't have to worry about losing what you typed, which can be important on those days when you're running from one class to the next and forget to click save before shutting down your computer.

Dozens of other computer note-taking programs exist, some of them proprietary and some of them freeware. If you have an interest in OneNote or another note-taking program, you should become intimately familiar with the program prior to starting law school. You don't want to be trying to figure out a new computer program at the same time you're struggling to understand the concept of personal jurisdiction. Before you invest time or money in any computer note-taking program, familiarize yourself with your professors' computer-use policies. As noted, some law professors ban computers from classrooms.

Whatever computer information management system you use, make sure you regularly back everything up, including your case briefs, class notes, outlines, and drafts of assignments for your legal research and writing courses. This rule is so basic, yet every year I hear sad stories from students who lost all of their computerized notes, outlines, legal research papers, and other data when their computers crashed or were stolen.

Relying on cloud computing would avoid these disasters, but if your head is not yet in the cloud, buy a USB flash drive and back up all your computer work each day. Another option some students use is to set up a separate email account for the sole purpose of backing up their notes. Attach your documents to a message and email it to yourself at that account.

Three different manuscript readers, all of whom have witnessed the terrible consequences of student computer disasters, urged me to emphasize the need to frequently back up work more strongly, so let me repeat: **REGULARLY BACK UP ALL YOUR COMPUTER WORK!** Is that enough emphasis?

CHAPTER 13
OUTLINING

> I didn't listen. I didn't make outlines. I thought if I studied hard enough I wouldn't need them. That was a big mistake.
>
> —1L's lament about not outlining

One major factor distinguishing legal education from other disciplines is the sheer amount of material covered, which can become overwhelming in light of the fact that it is all tested in a single end-of-the-semester exam. Professors usually start out slowly, knowing that students need to become acclimated to the nomenclature and basic procedures of the law. The snail's pace at the beginning lulls some students into a false sense of security, prompting thinking along the lines of, "Hey, this isn't so bad. We're only covering one case per hour in each class!"

One week into a fall semester, a new 1L came to my office and said, "Professor, everyone kept telling me I'll be working day and night in law school, but this Saturday I was sitting there looking for something else to do. Am I missing something?" I told her to enjoy it while she could because the pace would start quickening soon.

Within a few weeks, the reading assignments get longer. The concepts get harder. Professors begin covering material at a faster pace. The demands of Legal Research and Writing kick in with a vengeance. It all comes at students relentlessly, without a break. Before they know it, students are mired up to their ankles, then knees, and finally necks in a quicksand of dense material.

Must I Really Make Outlines?—Yes!

Only one answer exists for administering this huge inventory of knowledge: preparing an outline for each course. Most law students do prepare course outlines. Certainly most successful students do. Many students prepare two outlines for each course, a comprehensive main outline and a secondary capsule outline that they use for review immediately before exams.

Some students attempt to rely solely on outlines prepared by students who took the course in earlier years. These are abundantly available. Some course- and professor-specific outlines are even available online. It sounds like a good plan on the surface. Why go through all the work to prepare an outline if someone else has already done it for the exact same course taught by the same professor? Especially if you can lay your hands on a really great outline composed by a top student, it seems like a no-brainer. And, in fact, you probably can obtain great outlines composed by top students. Every law school has its share of famous, ridiculously thorough student outlines for particular courses that get passed down from class to class year after year. Back at the University of Arkansas at Little Rock, for example, every 1L coveted a copy of "Bob's Bible," a student outline for the late legendary Professor Robert R. Wright's Property course that was so complete it even included Professor Wright's jokes.

But it's *not* a good plan to rely on outlines prepared by others. The reason the students who made the great outlines came out on top was because they *made* the great outlines, not because they *had* the great outlines.

As with case-briefing, the process of constructing outlines is more important than the final product. Making outlines is what forces you to organize, synthesize, and, hence, really learn the material. Assembling them will help you discover the framework for and big picture of all the tiny rules you've learned. Composing an outline and updating it throughout the semester also requires the periodic review of the material so essential to law school success. Moreover, because people have different learning styles and process information differently, even well-done outlines prepared by someone else are not likely to present the material in the manner or form in which you learned it.

Similarly, resist the temptation to rely exclusively on commercial outlines, even those keyed to particular case-books. Commercial study aid outlines are not adequate by themselves because they will not contain all of the material the professor covered and will include a lot of material the professor didn't cover. Just as important, they will not present the material in the same way—either substantively or structurally—the professor presented it and expects to hear it back on the exam. It is very easy when reading exams to spot the students who relied too heavily on external outlines. They cite cases that weren't covered in the course and state legal doctrines in formulations foreign to the professor. Professors do not react well to this. They want to hear things in their own brilliant words.

Having said all that, let me emphasize that both previously prepared student outlines and commercial outlines can be extremely helpful *supplements* in filling in gaps in your own outlines. But that should be their only use: as supplements.

If you're going to invest the time in doing outlines—and they take a lot of time—you might as well do them right. I've known several academically dismissed law students who produced prodigious outlines. I've seen 150–page outlines for my courses that were a waste of paper. Without the right content and schema, outlines are not only unhelpful, they can be a trap because students often mistakenly assume they're doing a good job if they're pouring tons of time into making long outlines.

Below are ten sound outlining suggestions. Effective outlining goes hand-in-hand with effective note-taking. Thus, several of the outlining tips overlap with suggestions given in the previous chapter on note-taking, and vice versa. Understand that, as with case-briefing and just about every other law school study strategy, there is no one single right way to do an outline. Content is more important than format. Following the tips are excerpts from the Torts outlines of three top students regarding *Robinson v. Lindsay*, the case from the case-briefing chapter.

Ten Tips for Preparing Outlines

1. Collect the raw material by briefing all your cases and taking good notes in class. A good outline can't be constructed without the raw material to put in it. For most courses, your outlines essentially will be an organized version of your class notes and portions of your case briefs (not the whole things—see below), beefed up in some places and streamlined in others. Think of outlines as the third step in exam preparation, with case-briefing and class notes being steps one and two. It's not feasible to skip or slack off on the first two steps and produce effective outlines. Use study aids, previous student outlines, and—if they work for you—study groups to help you fill in gaps.

2. Never try to outline a topic before you attend the class where the topic is covered. Usually, diligence pays dividends, but sometimes being overly diligent can work to your detriment. Some eager students go astray in trying to outline a topic before attending the classes where it will be covered. This cannot be done successfully. In outlining, pay attention to what the professor emphasizes in class about the reading material, not what you thought was important when you read it. A fellow Torts professor and I used to joke that we'd probably get *C*s if we took each other's exams because we emphasize different doctrines in class and present some of them differently.

Not only will professors be likely to present a case differently than you briefed it, they will add extra material you will need to know that was not covered in the case. An example, seen in the student outline excerpts below regarding *Robinson v. Lindsay* and the child standard of care, is the addition of the relevant rules from the *Restatements of Torts*. These were not contained in the case, but were included in the class discussion of the case.

3. Begin your outlines around the third or fourth week of the semester. You can't wait until the end of the semester to start an outline. There won't be enough time. The beauty of gradually assembling good outlines week by week is that by the time you get to the end of the semester, you will have already done most of your studying for the exam. At the same time, however, 1Ls can't effectively begin an outline at the very beginning of the first semester because they lack an understanding of the process of legal analysis, the material itself, and the course framework within which it fits. Start your outlines somewhere around the third or fourth week of classes.

At the beginning of their second semester, shortly after they had completed their first set of law school exams, I asked a class of Torts II students: "What, if anything, do you intend to do differently in the second semester than in the first semester?" The most common answer by far was starting outlining earlier and engaging in more periodic review. Here's a sampling of a much larger number of replies:

- Outlining as the classes progress! While I did not wait until the last minute for this, I felt that I did wait longer than I should have. The outlining process is very helpful for exams, but is very overwhelming when left for too long.

- Outline earlier in order to gain a more united rather than divided understanding of the material. It will also alleviate stress.

- I intend to use Fridays and Saturday to compile, clarify, organize, and consolidate the previous week's notes into a working outline. Waiting until six weeks before exams last semester to outline was a grave and very stressful mistake.

4. Keep your outline updated on a weekly basis. Some of the above comments touch directly on this point. You want to input material in your outline while it's fresh in your mind. As discussed in the previous chapter on note-taking, memory fades quickly. You also don't want to fall behind and leave yourself with too much ground to make up. If you follow the recommendation in the note-taking chapter to update your notes daily, you'll be in good shape to update your outlines on weekends.

5. Organize outlines by tracking the headings and subheadings in your casebooks or course syllabi. The organization (as distinguished from the formatting) of an outline is nearly as important as the content. Rules can only be fully understood within the proper context and framework. You could memorize every rule in an entire course area and still perform miserably on the exam if you didn't know where they properly fit in the overall scheme of things.

Organize your outline by *topics* (not cases) in the same chronological order as they are covered in the course. If your professor moves straight through the book starting at the beginning, simply track the table of contents and section headings in your casebook. Some casebooks are more clearly organized and include more helpful and detailed headings than others. If your casebook includes only broad topical headings, it will be up to you to develop more specific subheadings within them. Even with casebooks that have detailed tables of contents, you'll be required to add your own narrower subheadings.

Some professors prefer to skip around in the book, which can make outline organization more difficult. If a professor does that, you're better off outlining the topics in the order the professor covers them, rather than in the order the book covers them.

Many professors will provide a course syllabus with subject headings. Assuming the syllabus subject headings are reasonably specific (and that the professor does, in fact, follow the syllabus), you can use them as an organizational guide in structuring your outline.

Topic areas should be organized as an inverted pyramid beginning with the broadest topics on top and moving down toward increasingly narrower topics. Similarly, within topics, the broad rules go on top, moving down to narrower sub-rules and exceptions. See the *Robinson v. Lindsay* outline examples below.

Whatever you do, don't try to reinvent or redesign the law in your own organizational schema. Just about every year a student comes along who decides that he can reconceptualize the law in ways better than legal scholars (including his professors) have ever done before. I once had a student, for example, who decided that the entire course in Torts could be reduced to a flow chart. When he showed it to me, I didn't know whether to burst out laughing or refer him to psychological counseling. It looked like the schematic for the space shuttle, with hundreds of lines and arrows and circles and boxes going in every direction. The student flunked the course.

6. Emphasize rules, sub-rules, exceptions to rules and sub-rules, and exceptions to exceptions. Most law school exams will test your knowledge of specific legal rules and doctrines and ability to apply those rules and doctrines. See the Appendix for a sample negligence essay question and answer. While some professors include policy-type essay questions on first-year exams, they do not usually count as much as questions testing your understanding of and ability to apply black-letter law. As such, your outlines should focus on incorporating "the law" of the course with accuracy and precision in a sound organizational framework. This includes all rules, sub-rules, exceptions to rules and sub-rules, and exceptions to exceptions, as well as the core reasoning and policies behind them (i.e., the "why" of the rules).

7. Include case references, but not full case briefs in your outlines. Do not make the common mistake of simply incorporating your case briefs into your outlines. Extensive recitations of case facts and procedure not only are unnecessary, they'll clutter up your outline and distract you from the doctrine and rules on which you need to be concentrating. *Lead with the rules in your outlines, not the cases.*

Students frequently ask if they need to know the names of cases for the exam. With typical law school ambiguity, I tell them, "It depends." You definitely should know the names of the "big cases" that stand for big principles. To the extent legal doctrines are closely associated with well-known cases, integrate coverage of those cases into your outlines. If that doctrine is raised on the exam, you'll be able to discuss it more cogently and intelligently by knowing the case.

As an example, the sample negligence essay question in the Appendix raises a large issue involving res ipsa loquitur.[90] The facts in the question pertaining to this issue closely parallel those of a famous res ipsa loquitur case called *Ybarra v. Spangard* that we read and cover in class. Students who make that connection and analyze the issue in light of *Ybarra* do far better than those who discuss the issue in general terms. Take note of how many times *Ybarra* is mentioned in my model answer.

---

90. In addition to being a great legal term to toss around to impress your friends, res ispa loquitur is an interesting doctrine of tort law holding that the mere happening of some types of accidents proves negligence by the defendant even when no other evidence exists. Translated from Latin, the term means "the thing speaks for itself." In the seminal case of *Byrne v. Boadle*, (1863) 159 Eng. Rep. 299 (Exch.), the plaintiff was walking on a sidewalk when a barrel of flour rolled out the window of an adjacent flour business and conked him on the head. The plaintiff did not know and could not find out how or why the barrel flew out the window. Normally, a plaintiff will lose if he cannot prove a specific negligent act by the defendant, but the court recognized the doctrine of res ipsa loquitur and plaintiff won. As the court said succinctly, "A barrel could not roll out of a warehouse without some negligence." In other words, the thing spoke for itself.

Even with regard to non-famous cases you cover, it can be helpful, although usually not essential, to know the names. Tying specific rules to specific cases in your essay exam answers informs the professor you really know your stuff. To facilitate recall of case names and also to remind you of the context in which particular rules were covered, I recommend including in your outlines the names and very short descriptions of cases *following* the statement of the rules emanating from the cases. See *Robinson v. Lindsay* outline examples below.

8. Incorporate the professor's hypothetical fact patterns in your outlines. In Chapter 12, I recommended attempting to record in your class notes the hypothetical fact patterns your professors use in class. These hypotheticals should also be incorporated into your outlines alongside the pertinent rules. Exams are all about applying law, not simply reciting it. It is not uncommon for these same hypotheticals, or something very close to them, to show up on exams.

9. Err on the side of including too much, rather than too little, material. How long should a good outline be? No precise answer exists as many variables are involved, including the particular course, the way it is taught, and outline formatting choices such as line spacing, margins, and font sizes. One of my research assistants, a top student, said that when she started law school, she inherited a large batch of student outlines ranging from 18–127 pages in length. She said her own outlines averaged about seventy pages per course. Several Torts students have told me over the years that their outlines for each semester of the course range from 50–75 pages.

Outlines that are too short will lack essential details. Several years ago, I presented a workshop on course outlines with Professor Lillian Aponte Miranda, a colleague when I taught at the Florida International University College of Law. Professor Miranda had the good idea to use her law school outline from Constitutional Law as a sample for the students to look at. When she projected a page from the outline onto a screen, the students' jaws practically fell open. They couldn't believe how detailed it was. Good outlines are detailed because the law is detailed.

Of course, outlines that are too long cease to be useful outlines and become unwieldy treatises. But if you're not sure whether to include something in an outline, go ahead and stick it in there. Material can be deleted with ease. It's much more difficult to go back and add what you left out.

On a recent Torts II exam, I included a question concerning a famous products liability case called *Greenman v. Yuba Power Products, Inc.* The opinion, written by the great California Supreme Court Justice Roger Traynor, was the first to explicitly introduce strict liability (liability without fault) in tort for injuries caused by defective products. The opinion seemed radical at the time, but as Traynor explained in the opinion, he was merely properly relabeling what courts were already doing under a different legal theory, a contractual theory known as breach of the implied warranty of merchantability. The exam question asked students to explain Traynor's reasoning on that point. We spent a fair amount of time on it in class, even listing on the board all the reasons why strict liability in tort amounted to the same thing courts were already accomplishing under the contractual implied warranty theory. But a surprisingly large number of students—including a lot of good ones—missed the question completely. The explanation I heard several times was: "Darn, that didn't make the cut for my outline!" Over-include rather than under-include.

10. State rules completely and precisely. One reason good outlines tend to be lengthy is because they set forth legal doctrine completely and with precision. That is, they get the law rigorously right (see C.R.E.D.O. chapter). When you're taking notes or writing your outline, you might think a shorthand statement of a rule will suffice because the detailed version of the rule is still fresh in your memory. By the end of the semester, however, you're not going to remember the details you omitted.

Here's a comparative example involving the definition of the two types of tortious intent, an essential element of all of the intentional torts and a concept most law students encounter at the beginning of the first semester. Compare these two outline approaches to defining the terms, one complete and precise and the other incomplete and imprecise:

Complete and Precise Definition of Tortious Intent

Two kinds of intent. Two kinds of intent are recognized under tort law: "desire intent" and "belief intent."

Desire intent is where the person acts with the desire or purpose to inflict the requisite consequence of the tort (e.g., for a battery, a harmful or offensive bodily contact).

Belief intent is satisfied when the person acts believing to a "substantial certainty" that the consequence will follow, even if he doesn't desire the result to occur. (Hypo: throwing a rock into a crowd of people, but "not wanting to hit anyone.") It's not sufficient to constitute belief intent that the result would be foreseeable or even probable to a reasonable person. The actor must *subjectively* believe that the result is substantially certain to follow.

Incomplete and Imprecise Definition of Tortious Intent

Two kinds of intent: desire and belief.

Don't laugh. I've seen lots of outlines resembling this second example. Students who compose short and sweet outlines of this type may very well understand the two kinds of intent at the time they keyboard in the words. The problem, as stated, is that come exam time—many weeks and hundreds of rules later—they're not likely to remember the important details they need to know to apply the concepts.

Sample Outline Excerpts from Three Top Students

In soliciting suggestions on how to improve the second edition of this book, I received several comments asking for some outlining examples. It's difficult to give meaningful outlining examples to incoming law students for two reasons: (1) they don't know anything about the law, so the content of the examples may not make sense to them; and (2) because good student course outlines are lengthy, well-organized integrated wholes, short excerpts fail to convey the big picture. But let's try it anyway.

We'll stick with a topic you already know something about: *Robinson v. Lindsay*, the case used for the case-briefing exercise in Chapter 11, and the issue of standards of care for children under negligence law. Recall that negligence law imposes a duty on actors to use reasonable care in their conduct. When they fail to use such care and cause injury, they have breached their duty (an essential element of negligence) to the plaintiff. The nature and amount of care expected from an actor is called the "standard of care." For ordinary adults, the standard is "reasonable care under the circumstances."

You'll recall learning from *Robinson* that the law treats children differently from adults under negligence law by creating a special, lower standard of care for them. Thus, the child standard of care is an exception to the normal adult standard of care. But you also learned from *Robinson* that there is an exception to the exception when children engage in inherently dangerous, adult-like activities. In those situations, the child will be held the adult standard of care.

Organizationally, these rules would fit in a Torts outline under the following topic headings:[91]

Negligence >

    Breach of Duty >

        Standards of Care >

            Exceptions to Normal Standard of Care >

            Children>

See how the topics move downward from general to specific? Under the subheading for children, for my course, we should find something like the sample below in a good student outline. Note that my sample contains additional details not included in the *Robinson* opinion, such as variations of the exception to the child standard of care as contained in the *Restatements of Torts*. These are details that would be picked up in class and from the notes following the case.

Children—

General rule: Children are held to a different standard of care from adults. A child must "exercise the same care that a reasonably careful child of the same age, intelligence, maturity, training and experience would exercise under the same or similar circumstances." This is an objective standard (a "reasonably" careful child) even though it is tailored to the particu-

91. In a full outline, there would be   tween these headings.
additional subheadings and content be-

lar child's age, intelligence, etc. (a smart child will be held to a higher standard than a less intelligent one).

Exception for inherently dangerous or adult activities: An exception exists where the child is engaged in an "inherently dangerous activity" such as operating a motorized vehicle. (*Robinson v. Lindsay*—13–year–old defendant driving snowmobile injured another child.)

***Restatement* standards for exception:** *Restatement 2d* standard is activities "normally undertaken only by adults and for which adult qualifications are required"; new *Restatement 3d* standard is "dangerous activity that is characteristically undertaken by adults."

Reasons behind exception: To protect society and discourage children from engaging in dangerous activities.

Consistent with tip number 7 above, note how I led with the rules and only briefly mentioned the *Robinson* case, rather than, as many students mistakenly do, lead with the case and bury the rules within the case discussion. Come test time, most professors aren't going to give a whit about the specifics of *Robinson*. To test the rules from *Robinson* in an essay question, the professor most likely would use a fact pattern involving a child actor engaged in a dangerous activity. Note also that, consistent with my previous advice, I quoted the exact language of both the general child standard and also the variants of the exception from the *Robinson* case and the second and third *Restatements of Torts*.[92] This ensures that the rules in the outline are "rigorously right, the R in the C.R.E.D.O."

Okay, before setting forth my sample outline excerpt above I said that we "should find something like this in a good student outline." Will we? I contacted three top law students, one each from three different classes, and asked if they could send me the portion of their Torts I outline pertaining to the child standard of care. Because all three are

---

92. This is an example, of which there are many, where competing legal tests exist addressing the same issue. One jurisdiction might follow the *Robinson* standard while another might follow the *Restatement (Second) of Torts* standard. Yet another jurisdiction might follow the *Restatement (Third) of Torts* standard. When a professor covers multiple legal tests for resolving the same issue, you need to know all of them unless told otherwise.

top students, I didn't have to bother with the preliminary question of whether they had made an outline. I felt sure they had and was correct. The relevant excerpts are reprinted below. For the benefit of readers, I didn't use abbreviations in my sample, but a student normally would abbreviate many words and terms in an outline. I left the students' abbreviations intact below.

Student No. 1

I. CHILDREN

   a. (Exception) RULE: child must exercise the same care that a reasonably careful (objective) child of the same age, intelligence, maturity, training, and experience would exercise under the same or similar circumstances (subjective evaluation)—overall obj rule

   b. Different from adult standard because child standard specifically refines the reasonable person (child). The child actor is compared to a similar reasonable child (lower standard than adults). Child of high IQ would be held to higher standard

   c. **Exception to exception** for inherently dangerous activities, two approaches:

      i. Inherently dangerous approach: An exception exists when a child engages in an inherently dangerous activity, such as operation of mechanized vehicle, OR activity normally undertaken by an adult, the child should be held to an adult standard of care to protect society and discourage children from engaging in such activities

      ii. Restatement 2nd; Adult Activity approach: child rule should not apply when actor engages in an activity which is normally undertaken only by adults, and for which adult qualifications are required

         1. Case law has led to ruling that any motorized vehicle would hold child to adult standard of care

      iii. 3rd Restatement: would apply adult standard to children engaged in dangerous activity that is characteristically undertaken by adults (incl. firearms)

d. Reasons: discourages immature individuals from engaging in inherently dangerous activities AND protects the public from activities which are capable of causing grave danger to others and the minor

e. Robinson v Lindsay: 13 year old was pulling girl on tube behind snowmobile, lost thumb; ct reasoned that kid needed to be held to higher (adult) standard bec doing an inher. dangerous activity

Student No. 2

iv. Standard of care for children

1. Generally, it is the duty of a child to exercise the same care that a reasonably careful child of the same age, intelligence, maturity, training and experience would exercise under the same or similar circumstances.

a. Exception: when a child engages in inherently dangerous activities, he will be held to an adult standard of care. (*Robinson v. Lindsay*— child operating snowmobile held to adult standard)

i. This exception is in order to protect the public and to discourage children from engaging in dangerous activities.

b. Restatement 3d of Torts says—"dangerous activity normally undertaken by adults"; Restatement 2d says—"in an activity which is normally undertaken only by adults, and for which adult qualifications are required"

Student No. 3

i. **Robinson v. Lindsay**

1. 11–year–old girl's thumb cut off while riding behind snowmobile.

2. **Second Exception: Children's Normal Standard of Care:** "same care that a reasonably careful child of the same age, intelligence, maturity, training, and experience would exercise under the same or similar circumstances."

    a. It's objective because it is the "reasonable child."

    b. **Exceptions**

        i. RST—if it's an adult activity or inherently dangerous, adult standard.

Note how closely the first and second student samples track my own. They both include: (1) an accurate statement of the general standard of care applicable to children; (2) an accurate statement of the exception, including its variant forms from the second and third *Restatements of Torts*; and (3) the two reasons underlying the exception. The third student sample is a bit too skimpy, omitting some important details, but it's hard to quibble since the composer wrote the top exam in Torts I.

Also take note of an important quality that all three student outline samples have in common: they focus on the rules, including exceptions (which are also rules). Each of the students mentioned *Robinson v. Lindsay*, as I did in my sample, but only with a brief notation, just enough to give the rules a contextual anchor. The third student's excerpt, which begins with the case name, is contrary to my advice to lead with the rules rather than the cases, but only mildly so. Just as I recommend, the student devoted only a single tagline to the case. He didn't get enmeshed in the case details.

Three excellent students + three excellent outlines = three excellent grades in Torts.

* * *

Like so many skills in law school, composing effective course outlines is a technique perfected through practice. Don't just assume you're doing your outlines right. Get some input from your classmates or professors. I see nothing wrong with, after a couple of weeks working on the beginnings of an outline, asking your professors if they would be willing to take a look at your work to see if you're on the right track. Make it clear that you are not expecting the professor to do a line-by-line review to see if you have the law right. No professor is going to do that. Rather, explain that you just want to ensure that you're following an overall sound format and approach. Not all professors are willing to look at outlines, but many will do so if asked. Doing this early could save you hundreds of hours of wasted time if you're going down the wrong road.

CHAPTER 14

A SHORT COURSE IN LAW SCHOOL EXAMS: THE SINGLE–EXAM FORMAT, TYPES OF QUESTIONS, GRADING POLICIES, AND EXAM AUTOPSIES

> How fearful it is to go through the first semester with only one shot to make the grade. I just didn't realize how much that would freak me out.
>
> —1L's "biggest surprise" about law school

Like just about everything in law school, the exam and grading processes are unique among educational programs. Upcoming chapters give advice about preparing for and taking law school exams. This chapter goes behind the scenes for the inside dope about: (1) legal education's dreaded single-exam format; (2) the diabolical types of questions concocted by professors; (3) the severely misunderstood "mandatory curve" grading policy applied at most law schools; (4) and the avoidable, but inevitable self-torture students engage in by conducting post-exam autopsies.

The Single–Exam Format

As the opening quotation suggests, one of the most stressful aspects of law school is the single-exam format. New law students express both surprise and dismay when they learn that, except in their legal research and writing courses, their entire academic fate in a course usually rests on a single in-class examination at the end of the semester. Asked what they thought people should know and understand about legal education, several students targeted the single-exam format:

- The exam preparation period is probably the most difficult tribulation a law student will ever go through. Remember, each exam counts for 100 percent of the grade. In the second semester, I was literally sitting in a room for almost sixteen hours a day every day for about two weeks reading and studying. That's enough to drive anyone crazy. The exams themselves are an emotional and mental sledgehammer. Despite a whole semester's work trying your best to learn the law, and those final few grueling weeks studying every hour of waking life, the exams are such that they leave you feeling as if you know nothing and that all your efforts have been in vain. This is particularly true the first semester.

- Studying for exams is such an extreme process it almost defies explanation. It is an intense period—beginning months before the actual test—of condensing tons of hours worth of reading, thinking, and listening into digestible bits of information that can be instantly recalled in order to properly identify and competently analyze a number of complex issues. First-year students in particular struggle with even figuring out what it is they are supposed to learn.

- I always start my preparation four to six weeks before exams, depending on how many exams I have. Every semester, my husband makes fun of me for this. He never fails to tell me stories about how when he was as an undergrad at an "elite" university he studied the night before every exam and still did fine. I have tried to articulate to him the amount of information I need to comprehend and often memorize for each exam. I even try describing it to him using quantitative measurements, as in "I have X number of pages of outlines to memorize" or "I have X number of cases to grasp." It's impossible to convey this to someone who has never been through it.

In a survey in which law students were asked to rank the importance of twenty-four suggested changes to legal education, "more feedback on academic process" finished second only to smaller classes.[93] Of all the alleged deficiencies in legal education, the single-exam format is the one I have the hardest time defending. Law school is the only educational discipline in which students are evaluated based on a single end-of-the-semester exam. It's not done that way in medical school or business school or veterinary school or in any other field. Particularly because so much rides on grades in law school it seems unsound and unfair to evaluate a student's knowledge and understanding of fourteen intensive weeks of complex material based on a single exam.

The authors of the 2007 *Best Practices for Legal Education* report noted that effective student assessment tools must be *valid*, *reliable*, and *fair*, and concluded that law school's single-exam format fails all three of these criteria.[94] Flaws in the single-exam format include the time-crunch factor (the system favors students who can read, think, and write quickly), lack of comprehensive course coverage (one exam can't fairly cover 42–56 class hours of material, which are the number of classroom hours in a three- or four-credit course, respectively), and the absence of feedback to students during the semester (students have no way to gauge their progress until after the final examination, when it's too late).

While some schools require or at least encourage multiple testing instruments during a semester and some admirable first-year professors voluntarily supplement the final exam with graded midterm exams, papers, quizzes, or class projects, the vast majority of law schools and professors continue to adhere to the make-it-or-break-it single-exam tradition.

Why do law schools test this way? What are the justifications for not giving students more bites at the apple, including different-sized bites from different angles, during the semester? We've discussed in other contexts how legal education, rooted as it is in tradition, is slow to change and this is another good example.

---

93. Whitman et al., *supra*, at 56–57 (discussing this survey).

94. Best Practices for Legal Education, *supra*, at 239.

Part of the explanation for the single-exam format is historical. In the earliest days of American legal education, exams were administered weekly and even daily. The transition to the modern format came as a response to Christopher Langdell's case method back in the 1870s. As discussed, the goal of the case method is to train students to analyze and apply, rather than simply memorize, law.

To test these abilities, law professors developed the modern "issue-spotting/problem-solving" essay question, described below. The knowledge and training in legal analysis required to tackle this type of exam can be acquired only over time. New students simply aren't capable of effectively analyzing a legal problem until they've become acclimated to legal analysis. One has to learn to think like a lawyer before they can write like a lawyer. Of course, this doesn't explain why the single-exam format is used throughout all three years of law school.

Additional justifications include a legitimate concern that incorporating other exams, such as midterms, into the semester distracts students from their ongoing course work. It's true. When students have a midterm in one course, their attendance and class preparation suffer in other courses.

A practical explanation for why most law professors don't give exams during the semester, one that professors might be reluctant to concede, is that they simply don't want to take on the job of grading them. This is one more drawback of the large student-faculty ratios in law school classes. Grading law school exams, if done diligently, is a substantial burden. It can take several weeks to properly grade final examinations in a large class. A three-hour law school essay exam generates answers ranging from two to five thousand words, or seven to seventeen double-spaced typewritten pages. Multiply those numbers by the seventy to eighty students in the average first-year class section and we're talking about a thick mass of writing for the professor to analyze.

Unlike in other educational disciplines, law professors do not rely on teaching assistants to grade papers. And contrary to popular perception, most law professors (albeit not all) work hard. They put in long hours preparing for classes, doing administrative work such as serving on law school committees, and, especially, researching and writing. In legal academia, tremendous pressure exists to "publish or perish."

I know, go ahead and get out the world's smallest violin. Poor oppressed law professors. I'm not trying to justify the practice, just explain it. The bottom line is that it takes an unusual professor who is willing to devote a large chunk of time in the middle of a busy semester to grading a midterm exam or paper. If you have professors who do this, express your appreciation to them.

Perhaps the day will arrive in U.S. legal education where students get several attempts to prove their knowledge and ability in a law school course. Perhaps one day humans will travel to another galaxy or learn to make oil from water. In the meantime, be prepared to turn into a basket-case each time those all-or-nothing exams approach.

Types of Law School Exam Questions

Law school exams don't resemble any exam students have seen before. In other educational disciplines, a student who has studied hard and consistently can go into an exam feeling reasonably confident in her ability to perform well. That's not necessarily the case in law school. Consistent with the goals of legal education previously discussed, law school exams do not primarily reward memorization of the law, but the ability to engage in sound, organized analysis of it. While students obviously have to know the law in order to apply it, a student could know all the law in the world and still fare poorly on a law school exam.

Issue-spotting/problem-solving essay questions.

The classic type of law school exam question is the "issue-spotting/problem-solving question." I've included a sample from Torts as an Appendix to give you an idea of what you'll be dealing with.

These notoriously complicated and convoluted questions involve often elaborate hypothetical fact patterns in which various actors interact in ways that raise legal issues among them. As the name suggests, students must first spot the issues, then solve them through cogent legal analysis. Some issues might be easy to spot, but some might be very difficult to spot. Depending on the exam, a particularly tricky issue may be identified by only a handful of students in a large class. Obviously, if a student can't spot an issue, she has no possibility of analyzing it.

An issue-spotting question may contain many issues or only a few, but the instructions don't tell students how many issues they are supposed to be looking for.

If the exam isn't crafted well, which they often aren't, even well-prepared students may be left scratching their heads wondering what the professor wants them to discuss. Despite excelling in law school, I entered every exam with a lurking fear that I was going to read the exam and have no clue what the professor was looking for. Usually the fear was unfounded, but once, in a Corporations course, the exam content was so foreign that I actually went to the professor's office to make sure he handed out the correct exam.

Once students spot an issue, they must give a complete well-reasoned analysis of it by accurately stating the relevant legal rules and applying those rules to the facts of the question. In doing so, the student must address the relative strengths and weaknesses in each argument and offer a conclusion as to how each issue should be resolved.

Meanwhile, in the background, the clock is ticking away like a time-bomb. Although some professors give take-home exams, most exams are held within strict time limits, three hours being the norm. The professor usually writes the ending time on the board as the last step before the exam begins. Unfortunately, some professors craft exams that can't possibly be adequately completed within that time frame, adding even more pressure.

Just about every aspect of this most popular of all law school exam question-types seems designed to induce extra stress.

Short essay problem-solving questions.

Also common are short essay problem-solving questions. As the label suggests, such questions are literally shorter in length than issue-spotting/problem-solving questions. They're also narrower in scope, often focusing on a single issue. Accordingly, short essay questions are less daunting than issue-spotting/problem-solving questions. Often, the question will expressly identify the issue, eliminating altogether the challenge of issue-spotting. Even if the question doesn't expressly identify the issue, the issues are easier to recognize because fewer actors and actions are involved. For the same reason, answers to short essay questions present far fewer organizational challenges than questions raising multiple issues among multiple parties.

Policy questions.

Another oft-used type of essay question is known as a "policy question." Policy questions don't test students' ability to apply law to facts and solve legal problems. Depending on the question, they don't necessarily even test one's knowledge or understanding of specific principles of law. Rather, they focus on a student's ability to construct a thoughtful argument or analysis regarding a policy issue relevant to the course material. Here's a sample policy question that I once used on a Torts II exam:

> The U.S. rule regarding payment of attorneys' fees and litigation costs is that each side must bear its own fees and major costs, such as expert witness fees. Most other nations follow the "loser pays" rule, in which the losing party must pay the winning party's attorneys' fees and costs. Compare the two approaches as applied in personal injury cases and discuss their relative advantages and drawbacks to a legal system.

Be forewarned: Some professors will intentionally ask policy questions addressing issues never discussed in the course because they want to see how students apply what they learned to new situations. The story might be apocryphal, but I once heard of a policy question that asked simply: "What is law?" Most policy questions aren't that abstract, but by their nature, grading policy questions is subjective in the extreme. Will the professor reward you for thinking like he does about the policies? Punish you for thinking differently? Boost or lower your grade for taking an outlandish position? No way to know. Policy questions tend to benefit creative thinkers who are good writers over the students who worked the hardest and learned the most in the course.

Don't get me wrong. Policy questions have undeniable value. Lawyers often are at the forefront as lawmakers and legislative advocates, and the abilities to think beyond the rules and analyze, critique, and advance the policies behind law are vital. My problems with pure policy questions—which I no longer use—are that they don't measure or reward acquired knowledge and diligent learning and are not as susceptible to objective grading as non-policy essays, which themselves require a high degree of subjective evaluation. If your professor uses policy questions, it's perfectly appropriate to ask the professor what the grading criteria will be for them and for a sample question and answer to review. She might not provide them, but there is no harm in asking.

If this section has you worried about policy questions, don't be overly concerned. Although many law profs use them, they usually count for only a small portion of the exam.

Other types of essay questions.

Between the traditional "apply law to facts" essay questions and pure policy questions are a host of other essay questions—which can be long or short—limited in their content and format only by the ability of law professors to think creatively. In other words, there are no limits. A professor could ask you, for example, to draft a statute or answer a list of questions about a given fact pattern or put yourself in the role of the judge, or just about anything else. Such questions may be hybrids that combine legal problem-solving with policy discussion.

Multiple-choice questions.

Many, if not most, professors also use some multiple-choice questions. Good news for students, you would think, and in some ways it is. For one thing, multiple-choice questions facilitate broader coverage of the course material. But law school multiple-choice questions, like everything else in law school, are different from anything students have previously encountered. They often require the ability to read, manage, and analyze complex text, and like the law itself, may lack clear right answers.

Most law school multiple-choice questions are styled after the format used on the Multistate Bar Examination (MBE), given as part of most states' bar exams. One indicator of how hard these questions are is that, depending on the state, students can pass the MBE by getting as few as 125 of the 200 questions correct. That's only 63 percent of the total. Under standard grading scales, a 63 would be a *D*.

Chapter 17 more fully explains law school multiple-choice questions and offers strategies for addressing them.

Grading: The "Mandatory Curve"

Traditionally, few things in law school have been more detested by students than "mandatory curve" grading policies. But now, in an astounding turn of events, many modern students absolutely adore mandatory curves. Those would be the students who attend one of the growing number of law schools that have implemented inflated grading curves in an effort to make their students look more attractive in the job market. We'll talk about both sides of that coin, but first an explanation and a couple examples of what we're talking about.

In 2003, the Association of American Law Schools (AALS) undertook a survey of law school grading policies.[95] (It would be nice to have updated data, but this is the only comprehensive study of law school grading policies that has been conducted.) Of the 145 schools that responded, 79 percent had formal grading policies. Seventy percent of those policies were mandatory, while the remaining 30 percent were non-mandatory. The number of schools with mandatory grading policies has most likely increased since the study was done. A mandatory policy requires professors to follow the policy (meaning the professor's grades will not be issued until any deviation is fixed), while non-mandatory policies are not backed up by enforcement mechanisms other than peer pressure from colleagues or perhaps a "talking-to" from the dean.

Mandatory curves come in two basic forms: (1) Curves requiring that certain percentages of grades fall within specified grade categories; and (2) Curves requiring that the cumulative GPA for a course fall within a specified mean or median. Many schools have policies that combine both mandatory percentage distributions and mandatory means or medians. The specifics of the policies vary tremendously. It is also common to have different policies within the same school for first-year courses, upper-level courses, required vs. non-required courses, and seminars or other small courses.

Below are examples, plucked at random from the AALS report, of a percentage-based curve and a mean-based curve as applied to first-year courses:

95. Andy Mroch, *Law School Grading Curves*, Ass'n Am. Law Sch., 3 (Mar. 30, 2005), http://www.aals.org/deans memos/Attachment05–14.pdf. The report included the full text of the different policies, but did not identify the schools from which they came.

Example of a Percentage–Based Curve

Percentage of students expected to fall in each grading range for first-year courses:

3.6–4.0	3–15%
3.0–3.5	10–40%
2.5–2.9	15–55%
2.0–2.4	15–40%
Below 2.0	5–30%[96]

You can see that this policy gives professors substantial leeway by using wide percentage ranges as the mandatory parameters. Some percentage-based curves give professors less flexibility by using narrower ranges.

Example of a Mean–Based Curve

Mean grades for First Year courses should be between 2.5 and 2.7 (Fs excluded). The aggregate number of A+, A, and A-grades for First Year courses should not be fewer than 5% of the class nor more than 10% of the class.[97]

Apart from the new inflated grading curves being adopted by some schools (discussed below), law students tend to hate grade normalization policies because they believe such policies force professors to give lower grades to students who deserve higher grades. They theorize, "If we're all writing A exams, why should we be punished by an artificially imposed bell curve?" The fallacy in that thinking is that students are not all writing A exams. Not anywhere close. They're not all writing B exams either. Truth be told, many law students write exams that deserve far lower grades than the students end up receiving.

In virtually any large first-year law school class, honestly and diligently graded exams tend to naturally fall into a bell curve. The only artificial forcing of grades I see on a regular basis involves forcing *up* the grades on the low side of the curve. That's what many grade normalization policies, formal or informal, accomplish: they artificially increase grades that

---

96. *Id.* at 22.

97. *Id.* at 54. As you can see, this mean-based curve also includes a percentage-based limit for *A* grades.

if left to standard "percentage of the total points available" scoring would be much lower.

The most important benefit of grade normalization policies is that they ensure fair, consistent treatment of students. They guarantee that students in different classes and different sections of the same class get treated similarly. Absent a grade normalization policy, a single outlying professor, either an unusually high or low grader, can unfairly throw a wrench into the class rankings for a whole class. I taught at a school where my first-semester Torts grades fell right at the law school's institutional (but not formally imposed) first-year norm: a 2.67. The other first-year professors graded similarly, except for one. A professor teaching the other section of Torts awarded his students a cumulative GPA of 3.4. An analysis showed that this one professor unilaterally elevated the class rank of one section above the other at a statistically significant level. It can happen the other way as well. In a different year at the same school, a Civil Procedure professor gave his class a 2.2 cumulative GPA, unilaterally lowering the class standing of one section against the other.

As noted, more and more schools have recently inflated their grading curves. Law school grades have subtly drifted upwards over a period of decades, but here we're talking about officially sanctioned direct injections of GPA helium. One law school retroactively increased all students' grades going back several years by adding a third of a point (.333) to every grade issued. Other schools have raised their first-year grades simply by crossing out the old mandatory GPA mean in their grading policy and inserting a new, often significantly higher one. Instantly better students! It's like magic. Additionally, some law schools have created new top grades worth more than a 4.0. For example, one school invented a new grade of A+* worth 4.33 points. Rumor has it another school is considering a new grade of A+@$!, which will be worth 1,000 grade points, three months of free HBO, and a lollipop. Kidding about that one, but the A-plus-asterisk grade is real.

The explanation given for these actions is that the economic downturn that began in 2008 has created a tough legal job market and that higher grades will allow a school's students to compete better in that market. The first part is true, but the second part is questionable.

Most students, of course, welcome inflated grades, and who could blame them? But gross grade inflation demeans legal education, which has always been known for its rigor, and devalues the high grades of students who truly earn them (needless to say, those students do not like inflated grading curves). The less rigorous law schools become, the more they will fail to prepare students to pass the bar exam and for the much tougher world of real-life law practice. Practically speaking, legal employers aren't stupid. If every job applicant is suddenly a stellar student, no one's grades will mean much.

Give credit to the student below for seeing value in law school's traditionally more honest evaluation of student performance:

> Although the soul-crippling uncertainty of the first semester is just awful, when law school does provide feedback, you know it is sincere. ... Most of us were programmed to expect praise and reassurance for everything we did growing up, even if we couldn't actually draw, dance, catch a ball, or do any kind of math past long division. Now when I receive positive feedback, I know I actually deserve it. Law school does not always make us feel great about ourselves, but it helps us recognize our strengths while forcing us to address our weaknesses.

When the topic of grade normalization policies comes up with your new peers, as it inevitably will, use what you learned in this section to educate them.

Exam Autopsies and Waiting for Grades

When "Time's up!" is declared after each exam, the sense of relief is huge ... *until* the student walks out the door of the exam room and starts engaging in an exam autopsy with other students. Professors always tell students: "Don't talk about the exam when it's finished. There's nothing you can do about it. Just move on." But students never listen, and neither did we when we were students.

I still recall walking out of my first-year Criminal Law exam, feeling good, until I ran into a couple of classmates who started talking about a big conspiracy issue that I had missed. I stood there feeling like I had just wasted the three hardest months of my life, convinced I had flunked out of law school. In true law student fashion, I obsessed about this for

the remainder of the exam period. As it turned out, I got an
A on that exam. Once again, neurotic obsessiveness—a hallmark trait of law students—shows its limitations as a lifestyle.

What happened to me happens to most law students. One
of my research assistants read the above and wrote:

> My first (but not last—slow learner!) taste of the
> crushing emotional devastation caused by the inevit-
> able after-test chat was after my Contracts exam. We
> were all talking it up, asking each other how we
> answered this or that question, and someone asked me,
> "So was it a firm offer or an option contract? I wrote
> about both." We'd had an essay question on the sale of
> a racehorse with multiple issues, a major one being
> whether the seller had made a firm offer or whether it
> was an option contract, and I completely missed the
> distinction, writing instead about something else en-
> tirely. I literally spent the whole next day in bed under
> the covers thinking about *my* options, since it was
> obvious law school was not working out.

She got an A too. The moral of these stories is not that
students always get As on exams they think they botched,
but that students have no accurate idea how they fared on a
law school exam until the grades are released. Way more
often than you would imagine, the exam a student thinks she
did the best on will be her worst grade and the exam she
thought she bombed will be her best grade.

Despite the pain of post-mortem second-guessing, with
each passing exam, the weight on a student's shoulders
lightens considerably. But then the waiting kicks in, and as
rocker Tom Petty sang, "The wa-ai-ting is the hardest
part."[98] Okay, that's not true. Studying for and taking the
exams is the hardest part, but the waiting is still tough.

It takes several weeks for exam grades to be posted.
Sometimes students have to start their second semester without having yet received their first-semester grades. Talk
about cruel and unusual punishment. Needless to say, the
delay in posting grades is both perplexing and extremely
irritating to law students. "Why does it take so freaking
long?" they want to know. A few reasons. First, and most

---

98. Tom Petty & the Heartbreakers,
The Waiting (Backstreet/MCA 1981).

legitimately, it really does take a while to diligently grade a stack of lengthy essay exams for seventy to eighty students. Second, during the holiday break after the fall semester, law schools often close for a week or more, so there is no staff around to process grades even for professors who have finished grading and want to turn in their grades. Finally, and most inexcusably, some professors routinely turn in their grades late. At some schools, this holds up grades for everyone because of a policy to release all grades at the same time.

CHAPTER 15
EXAM PREPARATION

"At one-thirty, wild now with drugs and frustration, I rolled out and began to flail at the mattress: I was *trying* to destroy myself, I shouted; I was *insuring* failure." Drug rehab gone bad? Nah. Just another 1L freaking out the night before his first exam; in this case, Scott Turow, writing in his classic book, *One L.*[99]

Law school exams, especially the very first set, are likely to bring out an insane side in just about every student, but you can reduce your stress while increasing your chances of success in the final countdown days by following some easy practical tips outlined in this chapter.

But hold on a minute. Why is this chapter on exam preparation one of the shortest in the book when it seems like it should be one of the longest? Because—great news!—if you follow the advice in the preceding chapters, you already will have completed 90 percent of your exam prep by the time exams roll around. Indeed, Chapters 11 (case-briefing), 12 (note-taking), and 13 (outlining) could all accurately be denoted as "exam preparation" chapters. The C.R.E.D.O. chapter is the most important exam preparation chapter of them all. If you follow the C.R.E.D.O. from day one, you can feel confident that you will be very close to ready for your exams when the time comes.

This chapter is dedicated to that final home stretch: how to get ready for exams in the days immediately preceding and during exam week. Follow these suggestions:

---

99. Scott Turow, One L: The Turbulent True Story of a First Year at Harvard Law School 167 (Grand Central Publishing ed. 1997). Turow went on to become a bestselling author of legal thrillers such as *Presumed Innocent*, which was made into a 1990 blockbuster movie starring Harrison Ford.

Plot an Organized Study Schedule and Follow It

Nowhere are efficient time-management skills more important than during exam prep. You need to map out a schedule that allows you to arrive at each and every exam fully prepared. Usually (but not always), you'll be afforded at least a few days to study prior to the commencement of exams. This breathing space is called "reading week" or "dead week" ("dead" as in no classes), although it's not always a full week. Some schools don't afford any break between the end of classes and the start of exams. If you're at such a school, you'll need to begin your final exam preparation while classes are still in session.

Don't make the mistake—which many students do—of using all your free days during the reading week studying for the first exam. You need to spread your pre-exam study days among your different courses to account for the fact that some of your exams will be stacked back to back, with perhaps only one free day between them. One benefit of being a 1L is that law schools intentionally schedule first-year exams with at least one free day between exams. In your second and third years, you might have exams on consecutive days.

Begin by plotting all of your reading week and exam period days on a calendar grid so you'll be able to assess your available time from a big-picture point of view. You'll probably find that you need to begin studying for some of your later exams first. Below is a sample prep grid for a twelve-day combined reading week and exam period:

Day 1	Day 2	Day 3	Day 4	Day 5	Day 6
Study Civ. Pro.	Study Contracts	Study Torts	Study Torts	**Torts Exam 9:00 am** Study Civ. Pro.	Study Civ. Pro.
Day 7	**Day 8**	**Day 9**	**Day 10**	**Day 11**	**Day 12**
Civ. Pro Exam 9:00 am Break	Study Property	Study Property	**Property Exam 9:00 am** Study Contracts	Study Contracts	**Contracts Exam 9:00 am**

Note how the studying for the Civil Procedure and Contracts exams is front-loaded because of the one-day gap between those exams and the immediately preceding exams. This allowed me to allot a minimum of two full days to each exam. I built in a break after the Civil Procedure exam to take the afternoon and evening off to relax and recharge brain cells. Because of the gap in the preparation for Civil Procedure and Contracts, I included an extra half-day of study for those exams on the same day of the previous exams, but if you feel adequately prepared, you might want to consider taking breaks after the exam on all exam days. That's what I did back in law school. Whether you can afford yourself this luxury will depend on how prepared you are entering the exam cycle.

Divide your study time relatively equally among courses that weigh equally in credit hours. Sure, Property may seem harder than Torts, but if both courses are worth four credit hours, it makes sense to devote roughly equal study time to them. A *B* in Torts is worth the same as a *B* in Property. You also have no way of knowing how tough the exam or the grading will be in a particular course. Torts might seem easier than Property, but the exam could be harder. Similarly, your Torts prof might be a more rigorous grader than your Property prof.

Seeing the above grid should help drive home my point about most exam preparation being accomplished during the semester through consistent class preparation, note-taking, outlining, and periodic review. Two days per exam is barely enough time to review and absorb your notes and outlines. It definitely is not enough time to begin learning the material for the first time.

Within each study day on your grid, break your tasks down more specifically. For example, a "Study Torts" day might be broken down more specifically as follows:

Study Torts

1. Read case briefs once.

2. Read outline twice.

3. Review Torts flashcards with study group.

4. Work through one practice intentional torts and one negligence essay question.

There is no single correct way to allot your study time. I asked a research assistant, ranked number one in her class, to summarize her exam prep schedule from the first semester. Here's what she wrote:

I started about a month before the first exam and made a study schedule very similar to the one you included. I alternated one subject per day and studied anywhere from fifteen minutes to two hours depending on how much time I had. My studying consisted of reading over my class notes, rereading cases and other reading assignments, and doing practice questions. I looked at old exams, did problems in the textbooks, and did CALI exercises online. About a week before finals I increased my studying to two subjects per day (still alternating to give each equal weight). When dead week and exams started I upped my study time to about three hours per subject a day.

I continued to study two subjects per day except for the day before an exam, when I studied only the subject that was tested the next day. I always took the evening of an exam off and did something else (like go out with non-law school friends or watch a movie). Starting so early really helped to decrease my stress level when exams rolled around. Since I had so much of my exam prep already done, I had a lot more free time and was able to stay rested.

While there are differences in the details, notice the common thread in our approaches: *thoughtful advance organization and time distribution*.

Work Through Practice Exams

One of the best exam preparation strategies is working through practice exams. If you were training to be a motorcycle mechanic, you wouldn't just study books on how to do it. You'd get your hands dirty disassembling and reassembling motorcycle engines. It's like that with every skill in life. People training to be pilots don't just read books about it before climbing into the cockpit of a Boeing 747. They study, practice with flight simulators, and start with smaller aircraft. Since most law school courses don't offer this kind of practice, you have to do it on your own.

Students spend *soooo* much time memorizing the law and too little time studying and practicing the *process* of law school exam-taking. Many students know all the law there is to know, but still don't perform well on exams because they never learned how to take a law school exam. The best way to get a handle on that process is through practice exams.

Working through practice exams advances several goals. First, it helps you know what to expect, increasing your comfort zone. You don't want to show up for your first law school exams not having any clue what they're going to look like. Doing practice exams also helps train you to spot issues, the all-critical threshold step to good exam performance. Third, if you're working through old exams from your professors, you will get a feel for what to expect from that particular professor, since professors usually are consistent in their approach to fashioning exams.

You might even get lucky enough to stumble on a question that turns up on the real exam. Many professors recycle exams over the years. While most don't release exams they have any intention of recycling, a few do. I remember getting together with a group of classmates to go over old exams in preparation for my Civil Procedure exam the following day. We started later than I wanted and I've already told you I wasn't much of a group studier, so I barely glanced at the exams before calling it a night and going home to bed. As soon as the exam was distributed the next day, I wished I had stayed longer. The essay question was the *exact same question* I laid eyes on the night before.

Many law school study aid series contain practice essay questions. These can be helpful, but the best approach is to work with original source material: exams prepared by your professors. While there is marked similarity in the structure and format of most law school essay questions, professors have their own styles for writing exams. Returning to the analogy above, if you were training to be a Kawasaki motorcycle mechanic, you'd be better off practicing on Kawasakis than Hondas even though substantial similarities exist between the two brands.

Most law professors make copies of old exams available to students. Don't hesitate to ask your professors about this. Unfortunately, unlike the practice exams contained in study aids, most of these sample exams will not include answers.

Especially in your first semester, it's wise to actually "take" at least a couple of practice exams in a mock-testing situation. Treat it like the real deal. If possible, use the same rooms where real exams will be held. Time yourself. Try to replicate the entire experience. Remember: familiarity reduces stress.

I don't recommend writing lengthy answers to *every* old exam you come across because such a time-demanding approach will detract from your other exam preparation, *but do read* all sample exams made available by your professors to practice your issue-spotting skills. Each first-year course raises a limited number of issues suitable for essay testing, so you're likely to come across some of the same issues that will appear on the real exam even if they're packaged in different fact patterns.

In working through old exams from your professors, consider asking the professors if they would be willing to discuss your answers with you. Many professors will decline requests to individually review one student's practice exam answers because it is time-consuming and somewhat unfair to other students. But they might be willing to at least discuss the issues with you. No harm in asking.

If you're into group studying, reviewing practice exams can be a productive study group activity. A group of students is more likely to spot all the issues on a question than any individual student. Reviewing exams with a group can help you learn from your oversights. If someone points out an issue you missed, ask what portion of the question flagged the issue for him or her.

By all means, if your professors afford you opportunities to take one or more practice exams during the semester, which many professors do, take full advantage of them even if the exams are not graded. I distribute two practice essay questions in Torts, one addressing intentional torts and one addressing the tort of negligence, along with a full model answer to each question. I've witnessed students go from writing *F* or *D* answers on the practice exams to *B* or *A* answers on the real exam because they learned from their mistakes.

I've also watched far too many students unwisely squander the best opportunity they will have to learn how to take my exam by blowing off the practice exams because they were "too busy"—a classic case of penny-wise, pound-foolish. If a professor gives you a practice exam and answer, he's essentially telling you: "This is exactly how I want you to do it."

Get Exam Supplies

These days most law schools provide essential exam-taking materials to students at the exam. Your professors should tell you in advance what, if anything, you need to bring. If they don't, ask. For example, if you intend to write by hand, you don't want to show up without bluebooks if the school doesn't provide them. Most students take exams on computer, but if do you intend to write by hand, bring non-fine point black pens, which will make your writing easier on the eyes. Don't use pencils or pens with weird-colored ink. Some things may look pretty in pink, but law school essay-exam answers are not one of them. (Yes, I've really had students write exams in pink ink.)

Other supplies you might want to consider bringing to the exam are appropriate snacks (not loud, crunchy ones) and caffeinated drinks, pain-reliever such as Ibuprofen (in case your stress causes a headache, which is not uncommon), and soft-foam earplugs. I used the latter in every law school exam and also for the bar exam. Available at stores like Target and Walmart, they're inexpensive, comfortable, and do a good job filtering out background noise. They helped me concentrate. As for drinks, be careful about consuming too many fluids during an exam because restroom breaks will cut into your exam time and proctors may look askew at students who take more than one restroom break.

Register For and Download the Required Computer Security Software

The benefits of using a computer on exams were discussed in Chapter 2 and almost all modern students use them. To prevent cheating, law schools subscribe to one of a variety of exam-security software applications, such as ExamSoft. Students taking their exams on computer are required to register for, download, and use the software during the exam. The software blocks access to all folders, programs, and the internet during the exam.

Don't wait until the last minute to register for and download the security software. Glitches can and do occur. If they do, you don't want to be worrying about having to resolve them right before an exam. This happened recently. A student came to my office about forty-five minutes before her first law school exam was to begin. From our previous conversations, I knew she was already prone to stress and stress-related physical reactions. Flustered, she explained that she had just tried to download the exam security software, which had been available to students for at least a couple of weeks, and got an error message. Fixing it required a phone call from the law school's Information Technology (IT) guy to the software company. They finally got it working—she hoped—as she raced off to the exam.

Install the software as soon as it becomes available and give it a practice run-through. At most schools, IT staff will be on hand during exams to help with any technical issues that arise.

Rest and Relax

Even during exams, you need to allot yourself time to relax and recoup. This includes getting normal sleep every night and also scheduling breaks during the exam period for relaxation.

With regard to sleep, studies show that sleep-deprived students perform substantially worse than those with adequate sleep. These same studies show that "pulling an all-nighter" not only is ineffective at bolstering exam performance, it can impair performance. Lack of sleep negatively affects attention, concentration, and memory. Cramming is a particularly bad strategy for law school success because of the huge amount of material. If you're at the point where you feel the need to desperately cram all night for an exam, it may already be too late.

The flipside is that if you've worked consistently and diligently throughout the semester, you shouldn't have to cram all night. With the vast majority of your preparation completed before the exam period arrives, you should have time to study for your exams in an organized fashion that allows you to hit the sack at a normal time. Again, that is the critical point to appreciate: the bulk of exam preparation occurs long before exams begin, starting with the first week of classes.

Your best overall strategy for arriving at exams fully prepared is to follow the C.R.E.D.O. habits in Chapter 10 from the beginning of the semester until the end. If you read every assignment, brief every case, attend and take good notes in every class, compose outlines for every course, and engage in periodic review, you'll be rounding third base headed for home when exam week arrives.

CHAPTER 16

LAW SCHOOL ESSAY EXAMS: THE FIFTEEN MOST COMMON MISTAKES

Alright! Finally, the good stuff: the carefully guarded secrets to succeeding on law school exams. Well, kind of, sort of. Hate to be a buzz-kill, but the truth is that no secret formula or system for acing law school exams exists. If anyone offers to share such a formula or system with you, follow these steps: (1) restrain yourself from falling on the floor laughing; and (2) politely tell them thanks, but no thanks.

My best advice for excelling on law school exams, as I've already told you, is to apply the C.R.E.D.O. habits (Chapter 10) to all of the other advice in these pages. If you fail to consistently, rigorously, efficiently, and diligently pursue your studies in an organized fashion, no amount of exam advice in the world is going to put you on top.

But even following all that advice isn't sufficient to ensure your best performance. Lots of—no, make that *most*—diligent, hard-working students fail to maximize their potential on their first rounds of exams simply because they lack experience and understanding about what to do and what not to do.

Most law school exams consist of essay questions or a combination of essay and multiple-choice questions. This chapter focuses on essay questions, while the next chapter addresses multiple-choice questions. The chapters will both familiarize you with what to expect and offer strategies for maximizing your success. They are a perfect example of why you need to consider *1L of a Ride* to be a yearlong handbook, not just a book to be read before law school. These chapters will definitely be worth rereading as your first exams approach, including any midterm or practice exams you might receive.

I've graded thousands of law school essay exams. Year after year, at law school after law school, students make the *exact same mistakes*. So I decided an effective way to explain how to do things right in answering essay questions would be to explain what students commonly do wrong. I'm sure other professors could come up with additional mistakes or reframe entries on my list, but here are what I believe to be *The Fifteen Most Common Law School Essay Exam Mistakes*:

1. Failing to carefully read and follow instructions.

2. Starting to write before analyzing the question and organizing the answer.

3. Not managing time properly and efficiently.

4. Issue-spotting: Not paying attention to the facts.

5. Issue-spotting: Not recognizing "givens" and, as a result, analyzing non-issues.

6. Issue-spotting: Insisting on finding issues you just *know* must be in the exam.

7. Issue-spotting: Ignoring issues raised by the facts because the issue would ultimately fail on the merits.

8. Failing to structure exam answers in a rough IRAC (Issue, Rule, Analysis, Conclusion) framework.

9. Leaving out the *relevant* rules of law.

10. Failing to use precise, accurate language in stating legal rules and analysis.

11. Giving a general dissertation on the law rather than answering the question asked.

12. Omitting or skimping on the analysis.

13. Doing the "Monster [Issue] Mash."

14. Being sloppy.

15. Writing too little.

Think some of these errors sound obvious? Maybe, but smart law students regularly do themselves in by committing even the most bare-faced of them.

The traditional issue-spotting/problem-solving essay question remains a dominant tool for testing legal analysis in first-year courses, so we'll focus on that format in this chapter. But most of what is discussed also applies to short essay problem-solving questions and much of it applies to any type of essay question.

To give us a vehicle for illustrations, below is an intentional torts practice essay question. It's a simple question designed for students who are only four or five weeks into law school.

Intentional Torts Practice Question

It was the night of the gala company holiday party at the Holiday Inn lounge. Jane was an office receptionist hired by the company six weeks earlier. Dick was an office boor who was very attracted to Jane and tried to flirt with her every chance he got.

Throughout the evening, Dick followed Jane around, making eye contact with her whenever he had the opportunity. At one point, he decided to be daring. He approached her and, without saying a word, dangled a hotel room key in front of her. When she winked at him, he put his arm around her and pinched her. Unfortunately, Jane was not winking in response to Dick's advances, but because she had accidentally squirted the lime from her gin and tonic in her eye.

When Dick pinched her, Jane said, "Take your hands off of me, you jerk!" Hearing this, Moe, a coworker who was six-feet, four-inches tall and weighed 260 pounds, came to render assistance. Dick was just five-feet, seven-inches tall and weighed 120 pounds. Moe punched Dick in the face, breaking his nose. Moe drew back his fist to launch a second punch but before he could act, Dick pulled out a pocket knife and said, "Don't move even one inch or I'll cut you into linguini." Moe froze, staring at the knife.

Dick then saw Sikorsky, the company president, standing nearby with his back toward him. Figuring he could increase his leverage, Dick pointed the knife at Sikorsky and said, "Stay away or the boss gets it too." Sikorsky had a hearing impairment and was unaware any of this was going on. He kept talking to the person in front of him, chewing on a chicken bone. However, when he later found out about Dick's threat, he was outraged.

In his later deposition, Dick said: "I didn't mean any offense to Jane. I swear."

This is an intentional tort question. Do not discuss negligence. Fully discuss all potential claims and defenses arising from this unfortunate sequence of events.

We won't discuss all of them, but issues in the practice question include the element of intent, the torts of assault, battery, and false imprisonment, and the privileges of consent, self-defense, and defense of others. Don't make the mistake of thinking that all law school exam questions are this simple or short. For a contrast in complexity, read the negligence essay question and answer included in the Appendix, which we'll also refer to in this chapter a few times.

The Fifteen Most Common Law School Essay Exam Mistakes

1. Failing to carefully read and follow instructions. After twenty-five years teaching law students, I continue to be astonished at the number of students who self-destruct because they don't carefully read or follow the exam instructions. It happens in every course. It happened the first semester I taught; it happened the most recent semester I taught.

On law school exams, instructions show up in different places: (1) most exams begin with a set of instructions applicable to the exam as a whole; (2) each essay question will have its own instructions applicable to that question, usually at the end of the question; and (3) a multiple-choice (or other objective) section is likely to have its own instructions at the beginning of the section.

Knowing that it is impossible to be too clear when dealing with stressed-out law students who are overly anxious to begin writing, I go out of my way to include clear instructions. Nevertheless, year after year, a substantial number of students fail to follow parts of them.

Look at the last paragraph of the Dick and Jane practice question. The two basic divisions of tort law are intentional torts and negligence. While they are separate areas of law, there can be much overlap between them in many fact situations. To simplify students' lives and increase the coherency of their exam answers, I always keep them separate in my essay questions. Hence, we get the instruction: "This is an intentional tort question. Do not discuss negligence." If it were a negligence question, I would say the reverse. Would you believe that students have missed this instruction and spent their time writing, in whole or in part, about the wrong subject area? Believe it. It's happened.

Negligence is a much more complicated area than intentional torts, so I include more detailed instructions with negligence questions. To assist students in focusing on and addressing the issues I want them to discuss, I frequently include explicit directives not to discuss potential claims between certain parties and/or not to discuss particular issues.

You can see an example in the last paragraph of the sample negligence question in the Appendix. Note that one of the instructions states: "The question does not mention any statutes, so you should not discuss any." You'll learn in Torts that violating a statute can, in effect, automatically stamp the offender's conduct as negligent. It's called the doctrine of "negligence per se." The quoted instruction is basically the equivalent of shouting "THERE ARE NO ISSUES OF NEGLIGENCE PER SE ON THIS EXAM!" Nevertheless, in using the question on a recent exam, I only made it through three of seventy exams before coming to an answer that rocketed off course into a lengthy discussion of how Erwin Wizley and other actors in the question most likely violated some statutes and, therefore, were negligent per se. Other students made the same mistake.

Oversights like these are killers on several levels. First, time is a precious commodity when taking law school exams. Every minute spent writing about the wrong or non-issues is one less minute students have for writing about the issues that matter. Second, students receive zero credit for content addressing wrong or non-issues, no matter how brilliant their understanding of the law is on those issues. Law professors don't even read irrelevant analysis. We just flip pages searching for the point where the student (hopefully) gets back on track. Some professors mark down for incorrect analysis.

Finally, blunders from not following the instructions cast both the exam and exam-writer in a negative light. Picture your professor as a kind of forensic pathologist. Exam-writers are anonymous, but at every step of the way in reading an exam, the professor is picking up clues and drawing inferences about the writer, both positive and negative. Silly errors from misreading or not following instructions generate negative impressions that affect the grade the exam receives.

Why does it happen? Why do so many intelligent students fail to read and heed clear instructions? Often, it's because in the stress and rush of the moment they make the mistake of
. . .

2. Starting to write before analyzing the question and organizing the answer. Poor law students. Law professors give them incredibly difficult exams and, too often, not enough time to complete them adequately. It's no wonder students feel the urge to begin writing answers before giving sufficient thought to what they're writing about. The temptation is understandable, but you must resist it.

Failing to fully digest the question and organize your answer before you begin writing leads to a jumbled mess. It also substantially increases the likelihood of your overlooking key instructions (see above) and facts and issues (see below).

Take adequate time to carefully read and do a rough outline of the question before you begin writing. This can be very hard to do, especially when you hear some of your classmates pounding away at their keyboards while you're only halfway through studying the question. Hold course! Don't panic and abandon the plan when this happens.

How much time should you spend reading the question and outlining the answer before you start writing? It's impossible to say with exactitude because it depends on how much time has been allotted for the question and on the nature of the question itself. As a general guideline, I recommend devoting *at least* 20 percent of the time allotted for the particular question (e.g., twelve minutes for a sixty-minute question; eighteen minutes for a ninety-minute question).

Tips for Quick Organizing

Organization is critically important to writing a good exam. Here are three tips for organizing your answers on the fly:

Use a highlighter. Students are allowed to write on their exams. Use a highlighter to mark key facts as you read.

Make a rough outline as you read. On a piece of scratch paper, compose a rough outline as you read the question. Not a formal outline with Roman numerals, etc. Just jot down issues (including claims and defenses) as you spot them. Then take a few minutes to organize them. Address issues in the order they are raised by the question. It's always weird when students inexplicably take the issues up in reverse order.

In addition to improving the organization of your answer, outlining the issues will prevent you from forgetting about them. Many have been the students who, on reviewing their exams alongside the model answer, say, "Doh! I spotted that issue when I read the question, but then completely forgot about it."

Use subheadings to separate party disputes. If the question raises issues involving multiple parties, organize your answer under subheadings listing the parties, as in "A v. B." In addition to making your exam easier and more appealing to read, using subheadings will help force you to address all claims, defenses or other issues between A and B in an organized fashion before moving on to other parties.

Nothing wears out an exam-grading professor faster than the students who take the alternative stream of consciousness, mash-up approach. Thanks to amazing new brain imaging software installed on student computers, I was able to record the actual thoughts of an exam-taking student who failed to separate his party analysis in taking the Dick and Jane practice exam:

> Okay, first, I will discuss issues involving Jane v. Dick. [Writing] Alrighty, I'm done with Jane and Dick. Now I will move on to Dick v. Moe. [Writing] Sweet. I did an awesome job on those issues if I do say so myself. Time to move on to Sikorsky v. Dick, but, wait, I just thought of something I forgot to say about Jane and Dick. [Writing] You know, that makes me think of an

interesting point to add about Dick and Moe. [Writing]
... Phew, that was a grueling question. Time to wrap
things up ... but, first, I just had an *amazing* idea I
need to tack on about Jane and Dick! [Writing].

3. Not managing time properly and efficiently. Because time is scarce on most law school exams, it's crucial
that you efficiently allocate your time among the different
exam components and monitor it as you progress through the
exam.

Not infrequently, students will get so wrapped up in
answering one question, or addressing one issue in a multi-
issue question, that they run out of time before getting to the
others. This is a mistake that can have disastrous consequences. When students run out of time, it's usually not
because they spent their time profitably writing an exquisite
answer to one question or one issue at the expense of others,
but because they squandered time engaging in one of the:

Top Five Law School Essay Exam Time–Wasters

1.   Engaging in a generalized brain-dump rather than
focusing on the specific issues raised by the facts.

2.   Going off on wayward tangents analyzing non-
issues, including "givens."

3.   Writing lengthy introductions that simply restate
the facts of the question or lengthy conclusions restating what has already been stated.

4.   Restating legal rules that have already been stated
once.

5.   Spending disproportionate time on the first issue
simply because it's first.

Numbers 1 and 2 are parts of larger mistakes discussed
below. With regard to number 3, quickly cut to the chase
when writing answers to essay exams. You don't need an
introduction to your answer other than one sentence such as:
"This question raises several issues that I will address in the
order they appear." While you definitely want to discuss
relevant facts as part of your legal analysis (see below), don't
begin your answer by restating or summarizing the facts of
the question as you would for a law office memorandum in
your legal writing course. Similarly, while most professors
will want you to offer your predictive conclusions as to the

resolution of each issue raised in the exam, you do not need a concluding paragraph that summarizes or restates the conclusions you have already articulated in the body of your analysis.

Time-waster number 4 is similar to number 3 in that it involves avoiding repetition. Once you've stated a legal rule or test in an essay question, you do not need to restate it. For example, in the practice question, there is more than one battery claim. The first one would be Jane's claim for an offensive battery against Dick for pinching her. In discussing that, it would be proper to state the elements of the tort of battery. But when you get to Dick's battery claim against Moe for punching him, it's not necessary to restate them. Simply refer back to the previous statement of the elements. You might say, for example: "The elements of battery have already been stated above in connection with Jane's claim against Dick, so I won't repeat them." Then proceed to identify and analyze the specific issues raised by the facts as to Dick's battery claim against Moe.

As for time-waster number 5, it seems to be a phenomenon of human nature to devote a disproportionate amount of time and attention to the first item in a list of items for no reason other than it's first. I see this happen in faculty meetings. No matter how insignificant the first item on the agenda, the faculty will discuss it to death at the expense of items that appear later on the agenda, even if the latter items are more important. Thus, the law school's inclement weather policy (first item on the agenda) might get fifty-five minutes of discussion in a one-hour meeting, while a proposal to abolish grading (last item) gets five. Law students commonly do the same thing on exams. They'll spend far too much time belaboring the first issue at the expense of other important issues that come later.

Size up and apportion your time at the beginning of the exam and keep your eye on your watch or computer clock. Make sure they are set to the classroom clock, which is the clock the professor will go by. Some students calculate and write down specific starting and ending times next to each question before they begin. Some professors will include suggested time limits for essay questions and other components of the exam, but many will leave it to you to figure out on your own.

You want to allocate your time roughly in accordance with the points assigned to the various exam components. Most law school exams are three hours. If you have a three-hour all-essay exam with three equally weighted questions, you'd want to spend approximately one hour on each question. If the exam is half essay and half multiple-choice, split your time roughly equally.

If you do find yourself running out of time before you've had a chance to tackle a question or to address all the issues in a question, use your remaining time to hit the high points. Jot down as many issues as you can. Simply mentioning an issue, even without analysis, can get you some points. Some professors, particularly inexperienced ones, will load up a question with too many issues, making it impossible to analyze them all adequately. You're better off addressing all the questions and all issues within a question adequately than trying to address one question or one issue superbly at the expense of not getting to the others.

Finally, use all your available time on the exam. It kills me when I see people leaving exams early (even though I was guilty of doing so as a law student). Students devote hundreds of hours over a fourteen-week period to learning the subject matter of a course well enough to give themselves a fighting chance on a single three-hour exam. Why would anyone not take advantage of every available second? Are they in a hurry to grab lunch, take in a movie, start studying for the next exam?

If you finish early, it's almost always because you: (a) did not spot all the issues; or (b) did not fully analyze them. If you *think* you've finished early, use your leftover time to reread the questions and your answers. Maybe you'll spot an issue you overlooked. I remember walking out of a law school exam early and immediately realizing I missed a huge issue. If I had sat there a few more minutes, it might have come to me before it was too late. Or maybe you'll notice on rereading that you forgot to state the applicable rules in a question or that your analysis on a particular point needs beefing up. At a minimum, you'll be likely to notice missing punctuation, misspelled words, and other typos you can correct.

4. Issue-spotting: Not paying attention to the facts. Issue spotting is the all-important preliminary challenge for students on law school essay exams. If a student can't spot the correct issues, she has no chance of analyzing them. "How do I spot the issues?" is one of the most common questions law professors receive. Issue-spotting problems come in two forms: overlooking the issues that your professor wants you to analyze and finding or creating false issues that the professor is not looking for you to address. Unfortunately, there is no easy answer or magic formula to successful issue-spotting other than the broad generalization that the process is *always* rooted in the facts of the question. Mistakes 4–7 all relate to issue-spotting and can all be roughly grouped under the penumbra of not paying attention to the facts.

We'll start with failing to recognize the legal significance of key facts. Each fact in an essay exam question should be scrutinized from the perspective of, "Hmm, why would the professor insert that fact? It must be there for a reason." Reading the question in this manner will help you spot more issues. Most facts are included for a reason: either to raise issues or exclude them.

Refer back to the penultimate (second to last) paragraph of the practice question for an example. Dick's statement at his deposition that he "didn't mean any offense" to Jane is a fact of legal significance, but one which students frequently overlook, not even mentioning it in their answers. Dick's statement that he didn't mean any offense was included to raise the issue of whether Dick had the requisite tortious intent to commit an offensive battery against Jane. To have subjective tortious intent for an offensive battery, Dick technically must have either desired to inflict a contact that would offend or inflicted the contact believing to a substantial certainty that it would cause offense. The intent issue was worth more points on the practice exam than any other issue (generally, the more difficult the issue, the more it will be worth). It's a perfect example of how students could improve their issue-spotting by stopping to ponder each fact from the perspective of, "Why would the professor insert that fact? It must be there for a reason."

But not all facts in a question have legal significance. Unfortunately, there are no reliable rules here. Many professors will include introductory narrative simply to set the scene; that is, to set up the question for the legally significant events that follow. This is the situation in our practice question. None of the facts in the first paragraph has legal significance, but nearly all of the remaining facts do.

Sometimes, however, the very first sentence of the question may be vitally important, as is true of the sample negligence essay exam question in the Appendix. Other professors may sprinkle legally irrelevant facts throughout the question. Sometimes they do this with a pedagogical intent to challenge students to distinguish material from immaterial facts, but often immaterial facts will be included simply to facilitate the story-telling aspect of the question. Reading samples of previous exams by your professors will help you size up their question-writing style in advance.

Almost as common as overlooking the legal significance of facts, but much less understandable, is simply ignoring facts of obvious significance. When grading exams, I commonly scribble in the margin: "Read the question!" This comment is born of frustration in reading student analyses that are off-base simply because the student failed to take note of facts of patently obvious significance.

An example from a recent Torts exam involved a defamation question involving a lawsuit against a newspaper. There are two types of defamation: libel and slander. Students learn and understand the simple rule that libel is written defamation and slander is oral defamation. The defamation in the question was printed in a newspaper. It was libel. Nevertheless, I'd estimate as many as 15 percent of the students launched into a discussion of whether the defamatory words were "slander per se."

5. Issue-spotting: Not recognizing "givens" and, as a result, analyzing non-issues. As a subcategory of not paying attention to the facts, students often go off on tangents analyzing issues they don't need to be talking about because they aren't raised by the facts of the question. Often, this occurs with regard to what are called "givens." A given is an assumption either clearly stated in the question (an "express given") or one that is readily inferable from the facts (an "inferable given").

Often, express givens are inserted for the very purpose of preventing students from talking about the point. If an intentional tort question, for example, says that "A committed a battery against B," there is no need to analyze the elements of battery in connection with A and B because the question is already assuming they have been met. Similarly, if a negligence question states that "A negligently drove his car into B," you can assume A failed to exercise reasonable care while driving and do not need to discuss that point.

If something is a given, note it as such in your answer and move on to the real issues. For example, in the first illustration, an astute writer would say something like: "It is a given that A committed a battery against B, so there is no need to analyze that point."

Overlooking givens is problematic on several levels. It causes students to waste time writing about non-issues, tangles up the organization of their answers, and conveys to the professor that the student either didn't read the question carefully or doesn't understand what the heck they're doing.

Not all givens are expressly stated. Often they are inferences that can be readily drawn from the stated facts. For example, the elements of the tort of battery are: (1) a volitional act; (2) intended to cause a harmful or offensive bodily contact; and (3) such a contact results, directly or indirectly.

Suppose the question says "During an argument, A pulls a gun from his pocket, points it at B and pulls the trigger, shooting B in the abdomen."

Absent some privilege to shoot B raised by the facts (such as self-defense), this would be a battery. Unlike the example above, however, the battery is not an express given (the question doesn't actually say "this is a battery"), but satisfaction of the elements of a battery claim are easily inferable givens unless other facts call them into question. Accordingly, while you would want to state the elements of battery and briefly note that they are satisfied, you would not want or need to engage in long-winded discussions of whether A pulling out the gun and shooting B constituted a volitional act (it did), whether A intended the shooting (he did), and whether the contact element was satisfied when the bullet entered B's abdomen (it was).

Extensive discussion of any particular element of a legal claim is necessary only if the facts put the element in issue. Thus, for example, to make the volitional act element of battery an issue, we would need facts suggesting that what occurred didn't involve a voluntary act, as in:

A and B, two friends, got into a dispute at a bar one night over which songs to play on the jukebox. On the way home, A was still mad and told B, "I have half a mind to shoot you." B told A to shut up and sleep it off in the backseat while he drove. A agreed. While A was asleep, he rolled over on a handgun in his coat pocket, causing it to discharge, hitting B.

See the difference? Here we have specific facts raising the volitional act element (as well as the intent element) as an issue.

Here's another Torts example of an "inferable given" from the realm of negligence law, one that law students perennially mess up. One of the essential elements of a cause of action for negligence is that the defendant was a "but for" factual cause of the plaintiff's injury, meaning the injury would not have occurred absent the defendant's negligence. Because factual causation is an issue to which Torts profs devote substantial class time, students often search long and hard for the issue on an exam (see mistake 6 below). But as with all issues, causation is an issue only if the question facts raise it as an issue.

Suppose a negligence essay question states: "A, driving substantially in excess of the speed limit, loses control of his vehicle and collides into the back of B's car. B suffers a broken neck in the collision." Many students will erroneously launch into an elaborate discussion of whether A's negligence was a factual "but for" cause of B's injury. Why is it erroneous? Because, absent additional facts suggesting otherwise, it's a readily inferable given that A's negligence was a factual cause of B's broken neck. If A hadn't been speeding and lost control of his vehicle, B wouldn't have been injured because the accident would not have occurred. No facts suggest otherwise. While the question doesn't make factual causation an express given (it doesn't specifically say "A's negligence was a factual cause of B's injury"), causation is clearly inferable from the facts, meaning there's no need to discuss it. It is not an issue.

Bottom line tip: Look for facts that specifically raise particular issues. If no such facts exist, the professor did not intend it to be an issue (with the unhelpful caveat: unless it's a poorly written question).

One related point bears mentioning here. Essay questions sometimes require students to assume facts that are not specifically stated to fully analyze the issues. If the assumed facts are reasonably inferable from the stated facts, this is perfectly acceptable. For example, if the question states that a relevant event occurred at dusk and the amount of available light is important to resolving an issue (e.g., the possible negligence of a motorist driving without headlights), it is perfectly appropriate to say something like, "Assuming it was already dark . . ." or "Assuming it was still light enough to see at a distance . . ." Such assumptions are not only permissible, but necessary to completely and accurately analyze the issue. But you must *state* your assumptions. Don't just make assumptions in your head, even reasonable ones, without noting them in your answer.

Any assumed fact must be reasonably inferable from the given facts. I still remember the student from many years ago who was analyzing an intentional Torts question that said something like: "A shot at B, but the bullet missed him." The student came back with an analysis saying: "A shot at B, but missed him. However, assuming the bullet had hit B, it would be a battery." Then he plunged headfirst into an analysis of the law of battery. Assumptions that are *contrary* to the question facts are never reasonable.

6. Issue-spotting: Insisting on finding issues you just *know* must be in the exam. Also related to not paying attention to the facts, students often come into exams hellbent on finding particular issues in essay questions whether they exist or not. This occurs because every course has major issues to which the professors devote disproportionate class time. It's very smart to be on the lookout for those issues. If the professor is fair, it stands to reason that issues receiving substantial coverage during the semester will be more likely to show up on the exam than issues receiving less coverage.

But it's a mistake to go further and insist, as many students do, that regardless of the actual facts of the question, a particular issue *must* be present. Once when I was teaching at a West Coast law school, I discovered a student was operating a gambling ring in which he set odds and accepted bets from other students as to which issues would be tested on their upcoming exams, including Torts. I recall learning, for example, that the odds of the negligence defense known as "assumption of risk" turning up as a major issue on my Torts exam were 4–1. Presumably, these odds were tied to the fact that we had spent two full classes on the doctrine.

I bet heavily against the odds, omitted the issue, and cleaned up. Ha! That'll teach the little punk. Kidding, but I do think I omitted the issue from the exam. Again, it's wise to be on the lookout for issues on which the professor spent a lot of class time, but if the facts necessary to raise an issue aren't in the question, the issue isn't there and you shouldn't force in a discussion of it.

On the other hand, if you're unsure whether a question is intending to raise a particular issue, err on the side of discussing it rather than leaving it out. The principal harm from discussing a non-issue is wasted time. The harm from not discussing something intended by the professor to be an issue is much more severe: no credit.

7. Issue-spotting: Ignoring issues raised by the facts because the issue would ultimately fail on the merits. What if the question *does* contain facts that appear to raise an issue, but which you, with all your newly acquired legal knowledge, know is a red herring? Write about it! Don't think, "The professor's trying to trick me into thinking that's an issue, but I'm not falling for it." Do not confuse "exam issue" with "successful outcome on the merits."

Let's go back to the practice question for an illustration. Contrary to the popular understanding of the word, the tort of "assault" occurs when a person acts intending to create in another an *imminent apprehension* of a harmful or offensive bodily contact. No actual bodily contact is required. If a contact does occur, it's a battery.

In paragraph four, we find Dick trying to gain leverage in the dispute with Moe by threatening to stab the boss, Sikorsky. Sikorsky, however, has a hearing impairment and doesn't hear the threat. Because his back is turned, he also doesn't see the knife. Thus, because Sikorksy was not in imminent apprehension of a harmful contact, no assault occurred even though Dick was threatening him with a knife.

Some students read these facts and think, "Ah-ha! McClurg's trying to trick me into thinking this is an assault, but I'm not falling for it. No assault occurred because Sikorsky was never in imminent apprehension of the contact." So they omit discussing the potential assault claim. But I *am* looking for students to discuss it. That's why I put the facts in there. Assault is an issue in the question, even though the claim would ultimately fail on the merits. That's what I want students to explain in their answers. Don't outsmart yourself. If the facts raise an issue, it's an issue.

8. Failing to structure exam answers in a rough IRAC (Issue, Rule, Analysis, Conclusion) framework. In law school, you will learn about what's called the "IRAC" method for analyzing legal issues. IRAC is a mnemonic that stands for:

ISSUE

RULE

ANALYSIS[100]

CONCLUSION

IRAC is not a mechanical formula, but simply a common sense approach to analyzing a legal issue. Before a student can analyze a legal issue, of course, they have to know what the issue is. Thus, logically, step one in the IRAC methodology is to identify the issue (I). Step two is to state the relevant rule(s) of law that will apply in resolving the issue (R). Step three is to apply those rules to the facts of the question—that is, to "analyze" the issue (A). Step four is to offer a conclusion as to the most likely result (C). Exam answers to issue-spotting/problem-solving questions should be constructed keeping in mind a *rough* IRAC framework.

Here's an example using the practice question. When Dick pinched co-worker Jane at the party, Moe came to her assistance, punching Dick in the face and breaking his nose. Dick would sue Moe for battery (one issue) and Moe would assert as a defense the legal privilege of "defense of others" (another issue). Here's how the defense of others issue could be addressed in an IRAC format:

---

100. The "A" portion of IRAC is often stated as standing for "Application," but that's interchangeable with "Analy-sis." Legal analysis is applying the relevant legal rules to the relevant facts.

[ISSUE] Moe will assert the privilege of "defense of others" in response to Dick's battery claim, arguing that he had a privilege to use force to defend Jane from Dick's offensive battery. [RULE] The privilege of defense of others allows one to use reasonable force to protect another from a threatened battery. Reasonable force is measured by a proportionality standard. The force used in defense must be proportionate to the force being defended against. [ANALYSIS] Moe may have been privileged to use some mild force in defending Jane from a physically harmless pinch, such as pushing Dick away. But smashing Dick in the face and breaking his nose to ward off a pinch at an office party was disproportionate, unreasonable force. [CONCLU-SION] Because he used unreasonable force, the privilege will fail and Moe will be liable to Dick for battery.

Some students misconstrue the IRAC methodology as an inflexible formula, which it most definitely is not. Some even go so far as to set their answers up in the form of an outline with headings like "ISSUE: ...," "RULE: ...," etc. Don't do that! I inserted those words above only as a guide. An answer to an essay question should read like, well, an essay. IRAC is simply a structural way of thinking about legal analysis in a problem-solving context. It has no application to some types of essay questions, such as policy questions.

Moreover, even in problem-solving questions, IRAC cannot be applied with mechanical rigidity. It worked that way for the above issue because the issue was extremely simple. The more complicated the issue, the less likely you'll be able to fit your answer within a precise IRAC framework.

The issue may require more than one level of analysis. It may be necessary, for example, to first state the issue broadly, discuss and apply the general rules relevant to the issue, then move on to an exception to the general rules. Rules often must be intermingled with the application, rather than neatly separated from it. If a multi-pronged legal test is being applied, each prong or element may require a separate mini-analysis. Sometimes it might be more effective to state the conclusion before you give the analysis. See the sample negligence question and answer in the Appendix for an illustration of a more complex, multi-level IRAC analysis than the simple example above.

Nevertheless, even when IRAC cannot be mechanically applied, it is a useful framework for identifying the essential components of a sound legal analysis. In any complete evaluation of a legal issue, all of the IRAC components will be represented.

My goal here is to introduce you to IRAC and also to highlight below the two most common failings in executing it on essay exams, which are to omit the two middle parts: Rules and Analysis. Far too many students "IC" the exam, causing the professor to go "Ick!" when reading it; that is, they successfully identify the issue and offer a correct conclusion as to how it should be resolved, but leave out both the relevant legal rules and analysis.

Mistakes 9–12 below focus on those all-important middle parts. So let's hear a hearty rah, rah, rah for some helpful tips about the "RA" in IRAC.

9. Leaving out the *relevant* rules of law. It's unfortunate how many students, after spending a grueling semester learning hundreds of rules of law, neglect to include those rules in writing answers to essay questions on their final exams.

A student can't successfully perform legal analysis—applying law to facts—without articulating the relevant legal rules they are applying. What makes this omission so surprising, as well as a crying shame, is that so many students who fail to state the rules know them! They simply don't write them down. Frequently, when I point out to students during exam review sessions that they failed to include the relevant rules of law in their answers, the response is along the lines of: "Well, I assumed you knew the law, so I didn't think I needed to include it."

The cure for this deficiency, assuming the student does, in fact, know the rules, is simple. Even average students can bolster the quality of their answers just by remembering to perform the essential step of inserting the relevant rule(s) after identifying the issue and before proceeding to the analysis (or depending on the nature and complexity of the question, weaving rule statements into the analysis). Give yourself a memory prompt by making a note at the top your exam: "Don't forget the R in IRAC."

10. Failing to use precise, accurate language in stating legal rules and analysis. Many students understand the law, but lose ground on their exams by expressing legal rules and analysis in overly broad or layperson terms, rather than in precise, accurate legal terminology, which is what professors are looking for. Remember the R in the C.R.E.D.O. You want to get things rigorously right. *Specific always trumps general on law school exams.*

An example from the practice question will bolster the point. As discussed above, tort law recognizes as a defense to a battery claim a legal privilege to use reasonable force to protect other people. The privilege is known as the "defense of others." "Defense of others" is a term of art. It's the legal name attached to the privilege.

In the practice question, Dick harassingly pinched Jane at the office party. Jane cried out and chivalrous Moe came to her aid, punching Dick in the face. Because they are such easy issues, all students recognize Dick's potential battery claim against Moe and nearly all students successfully identify Moe's potential privilege to use force in defense of others. But compare the following two statements of the privilege issue from different students:

Student 1: Moe will raise the privilege of defense of others, asserting he had a privilege to use reasonable force to protect Jane from Dick's advances.

Student 2: Moe will argue that he is not liable because he was helping Jane.

Both students recognized the issue, but notice the difference—and it's a BIG difference—in how they framed it. Student 1 did it correctly, using rigorously right legal language. Student 2 did it incorrectly, framing the issue in vague, layperson language. "Helping Jane" is not a cognizable legal privilege. Thus, even though both students spotted the issue, Student 1 would considerably out-point Student 2 by paying attention to the language used.

11. Giving a general dissertation on the law rather than answering the question asked. Note the repeated emphasis above on *relevant* rules. The R in IRAC refers to the specific rule or rules that will govern resolution of the particular issue being discussed. It does not envision a treatise-like brain dump of everything one knows that is some-

how related to the general subject matter. This is an extremely common mistake. Professor Joseph Glannon estimates that
20 percent of his students fall prey to this error, which he
labels "abstract expressionism."[101] That figure may be low.

The only rules that should be mentioned in answering an
essay question are those needed to resolve the specific issues
raised in the question. This will rarely include broad-based
discussion of a large subject area. If a negligence question, for
example, raises an issue about factual causation, there's no
reason to discuss other elements of a claim for negligence
because they don't address the issue and, thus, don't "answer
the question." Indeed, there's no reason to discuss all of the
rules related to factual causation. The only rules that war-
rant mentioning are those necessary to resolve the specific
factual causation issue actually raised by the question. (Of
course, the question may also raise other elements of negligence as separate issues.)

Once again, specific always trumps general. Generalized
discussions of the law that don't answer the question asked
are a waste of time. Most professors won't even read them.

12. Omitting or skimping on the analysis. Many
students include the issue, relevant rules, and conclusion, but
leave out the analysis, thereby "IRC-ing" their exams and
irking the professors forced to read them.

Skimping on analysis may be the most common exam
deficiency of them all. Analysis is the meat of the answer that
separates the best answers from the rest. It's difficult to
explain in a vacuum how to analyze legal problems. Reading
the sample negligence essay exam question and answer in the
Appendix will give you an idea of what complete legal analysis looks like. Study the answer in light of these tips for
conducting legal analysis correctly:

*If you're not talking about the facts, you're doing it
wrong.* In its shortest definition, legal analysis is applying
law to facts. Highlight the relevant facts in the question and
make sure to weave them into your analysis. Facts dictate
results. Change one fact and you'll often get a different
result. Chances are good that if you're writing a lengthy
block of text without discussing the facts in the question,

---

101. JOSEPH W. GLANNON, THE LAW OF
TORTS: EXAMPLES AND EXPLANATIONS 632–35
(4th ed. 2010).

you've substituted brain-dumping in place of legal analysis. But you can't just *state* facts. You must explain their legal significance in connection with the rules. Again, study the model answer in the Appendix and take note of how it continually talks about the facts of the question.

Explain your reasoning process. A simple way to think of legal analysis is as an "explanation." You're trying to explain to someone what the legal issue is and how it should be resolved. The more complete the explanation, the better it will be. Too many students keep their reasoning to themselves. But professors, for all their powers, aren't mind readers. They can only evaluate what students actually explain.

Many students mistake conclusions for analysis. They're not the same thing. Analogize analyzing a legal issue to working through a math problem, such as: $2 \times 2 + 4 - 8 = 0$. Some students, presented with a fact pattern on a law school essay question, will begin and end their analysis with: "The answer is zero."

The professor needs to know what formula they used to get to zero, which includes both the rules and explanation of how the rules were applied to the facts. Other students will include some analysis, but leave out major portions, resulting in something resembling: $2 \times 2 = 0$. Because their analysis is incomplete, their work product is defective even when they reach the correct conclusion. As your elementary school math teacher taught you: "Show your work."

I just finished grading a batch of Torts II exams that involved a series of defamation questions. One of the issues was whether a libel plaintiff was a "public figure" versus a "private figure" (the rules are very different for the two groups). To assist in making this differentiation, students study and learn a five-factor test during the course. On the exam many students successfully listed the five factors, but never applied them. They simply skipped to the conclusion after listing the legal factors. Most of these students reached the correct conclusion that the plaintiff was a public figure. In other words, they applied the factors from the legal test in their heads, but never put the explanation on paper. The margins of their exams are filled with my scribbled comments such as: "You have to *apply* the factors—not just list them." They omitted the analysis and lost major points.

Avoid "he argues/she argues" analysis. Too many
students, having been told that they "should argue both sides
of an issue," fall prey to what I call "he argues/she argues"
analysis, which is not really analysis at all. He argues/she
argues answers track this format: "A will argue *w*. B will
argue *x*. A will argue *y*. B will argue *z*...." As Glannon
notes, while students who take this approach leave the exam
believing they have argued both sides, they, in fact, have not
argued either side. Arguing both sides requires not just
listing competing points of argument, but evaluating the
relative strengths and weaknesses of those arguments under
the applicable law.

Note also that not all legal issues require or are conducive
to arguing both sides. I think some professors get carried
away in espousing "you need to argue both sides," uninten-
tionally misleading students. More often than not, there will
be no opposing side to argue because the facts and law will
clearly point to only one resolution of an issue. "Arguing both
sides" becomes relevant only if there are facts in the question
that raise two sides.

Specific trumps general. I'm not senile. I promise. I
remember when I've already said something once. I remember when I've already said something once. Okay, well,
maybe not always. In this case, however, I realize I've already
told you this twice, but maybe third time's a charm: specific
analysis is always superior to general analysis.

*When you think you've finished your analysis, add
more.* Nearly all student exam analysis is too skimpy. Once
you think you've fully analyzed the issue, try to go one step
deeper. A single added cogent sentence can boost an exam
answer above others.

13. Doing the "Monster [Issue] Mash." In October
1962, Bobby "Boris" Pickett had a number one *Billboard* hit
with the novelty tune "Monster Mash." The perennial Hal-
loween favorite stars a mad scientist's monster that comes to
life in the lab late one night and starts a new dance craze.
The law school exam version of the Monster Mash is much
less fun.

Legal issues are discrete and should be analyzed as such,
even when they're interrelated. Discussion of each issue
should be compartmentalized with a topical sentence introducing the issue, followed by a full-blown IRAC attack on

that issue and that issue alone. Only when you have completed fully addressing that issue should you move on to another issue, which should also be compartmentalized, and so on.

Students often err by introducing several issues in a single paragraph, then trying to discuss them collectively. It can't be done. Instead of a coherent discussion of each issue, the result is one big monster mash of issues never destined to reach number one.

Here's a way to test yourself on this point. Look at your discussion of a particular issue. Visually cut it out with an imaginary pair of scissors. (Avoid real scissors. Hide all sharp objects during periods of exam stress.) The excised excerpt should be able to stand alone as a complete and coherent discussion of that issue without having to refer to other portions of your answer. If it doesn't, you may be dancing to the Monster [Issue] Mash.

Just as using subheadings to denote separate party disputes (e.g., A v. B) can force you to be more organized, using subheadings for each major issue can do the same. Take a look at the model answer to the sample question in the Appendix. Note that, in addition to party headings, I used issue headings, such as "Standard of Care," "Proximate Cause," and "Res Ipsa Loquitur." Using—and following—headings such as these will help you avoid the Monster [Issue] Mash, while also making your answer easier to read.

14. Being sloppy. This catch-all category includes a number of errors that can be grouped together as general sloppiness, including: using the wrong exam number or forgetting to include one, making repeated misspellings and grammatical errors, writing illegibly, not following procedural or formatting instructions, and resorting to too many abbreviations.

You want your exam to stand out for good reasons, not bad ones. You want to present your work in its most favorable light and that includes overall appearance. Sloppy errors, even small ones, affect the overall impression your paper makes on that forensic pathologist professor we were talking about, who is already displeased even under the best of circumstances about having to spend his or her holiday or summer break wading into a thick stack of exams. Avoid these common sloppy errors:

Using the wrong exam number or forgetting to include one. Most every class will include a couple of students who didn't obtain, lost, or forgot their anonymous exam number. When these students get to the exam, they just make up a number. When professors grade exams, the very first thing noticed may be the exam number because it appears in a large, bolded font on the cover page printed via the exam-security software, as well as at the top of every page of the answer, on both the left and right. If your number is nonconforming it will stick out like a sore thumb. Example:

Exam No. 321

Exam No. 324

Exam No. 8675309

Exam No. 341

Exam No. 344

This can create an instant bias against the nonconforming exam. Fair or not, the professor's thought process might be: "How could this student be so careless or stupid as to forget or lose his exam number?"

Using the wrong exam number also entails extra hassle for the professor and registrar, sometimes delaying the posting of grades for the entire class. Get your exam numbers right. It's one of the easiest challenges of law school.

Making repeated misspellings and grammatical errors. One of the most common questions students ask about exams relates to misspellings and grammatical errors. "Do they count?" I've heard that question a hundred times. Heck, yes, they count, but not in the way students worry about. Very few professors officially mark down exams for misspelled words and/or grammatical errors. But a paper littered with such errors obviously does not bolster the professor's estimation of the content or the writer. The occasional typo or misspelling is nothing to be concerned about, but some students misspell words pervasively—sometimes several words in a single sentence. Even if the content is good, it's hard to give high grades to such an exam. As mentioned early in the book, you won't be able to rely on your computer spell-check function because schools usually disable it on the exam-security software they use.

Be especially careful about correctly spelling legal terms of art. Because professors will be looking for these words, misspelling them will be particularly glaring. "Assault" looks really bad as "assalt." Spelling "Judge Hand"—the judge famous for his formula for negligence—as "Judge Hanks" can cause actual physical pain to a professor. (I know because it happened this past year.) Defendants in defamation cases may be liable for libel, but they are not being sued for "liable."

Spelling and grammar aren't things to obsess over during an exam, but they are things to pay attention to. If you finish an exam early, go back and reread your work product. Correct typos, insert omitted words, and make other corrections. Good writers spend more time editing and rewriting than composing the initial draft. You won't have that luxury during an exam, but you might have time to do a quick proofread.

Writing illegibly. Before computer-use on exams became widespread, deciphering illegible handwriting was one of the great scourges of being a law professor. Today, the problem has practically disappeared because almost all students take exams on computers. But if you plan on writing your exams by hand, you need to be certain that your handwriting is legible. Indecipherable handwriting will hurt you. A professor grading hundreds of pages of exam answers is going to be an unhappy camper if forced to spend three times longer grading your exam than the others because of illegible handwriting. Truth be told, many professors just skim past material they can't decipher.

Failing to follow procedural or formatting instructions. Above I talked about the essentiality of following substantive instructions. Here, I'm talking about less egregious but still important procedural or formatting instructions. Many exams contain specific instructions about "how to do things" in terms of formatting or turning in your exam. When students fail to follow these instructions, they stand out, in an irritating way.

Using too many or undefined abbreviations. In their rush, some students resort to sloppy and/or indecipherable shorthand and abbreviations. You want your answer to read like an essay, not an outline.

It's permissible to abbreviate the names of the actors you will be repeating in your answer, provided you spell out the names the first time and clearly note the abbreviations you will be using. Thus, if you're writing about Greta Garbonski and Henry Flankenhocker, it's okay to say "Greta Garbonski (GG) will sue Henry Flankenhocker (HF) for negligence" and then use GG and HF from that point on.

Similarly, it's permissible to abbreviate unwieldy legal terms that you will be repeating several times. Follow the same rules as for proper names. In Torts, for example, it would be acceptable to abbreviate "intentional infliction of emotional distress" as "IIED" or "res ipsa loquitur" as "RIL," provided that you wrote the terms out in full the first time, followed by the abbreviations in parentheses.

Do not use abbreviations learned in other walks of life. I've read exams written by doctors and nurses that were so full of shorthand symbols they looked like hieroglyphics.

15. Writing too little. This last mistake of writing too little subsumes some of the more specific errors already discussed. It's more of a general observation than a diagnosable stand-alone error. But it's worth pointing out and thinking about.

As noted, virtually all modern law students take their essay exams on computers. The exam-security software used by law schools spits out a cover page for each exam showing a word count for essay answers. Examining these word counts in relation to performance yields an important, if unsurprising, insight: students who write more tend to do better on law school essay exams. In the first edition, I mentioned an experiment in which I examined a batch of Torts exams and found that the average word count for the ten highest-scoring answers to a ninety-minute issue-spotting/problem-solving essay question was 1952, whereas the average word count for the ten lowest-scoring answers was 1163—a 40 percent difference.

For this second edition, I looked at a more recent set of Torts exams and found a similar result. The top ten students averaged 1933 words on the essay portion of the exam, while the bottom ten averaged only 1081 words—a 44 percent difference.

The moral of this story, of course, is not simply to write more. An essay answer with Tolstoy-esque bulk is worthless if the content isn't accurate and on point. The exam with the highest word count in the first run of my experiment, for example, wasn't in the top ten. On the other hand, the exam with the second highest word count was the top-scoring essay and the exam with the lowest word count was the lowest-scoring essay.

Tracing the connection between low word-counts and poor performance, one can almost always point the finger at one of two causes: (1) missing issues; or (2) IC-ing the exam; that is, leaving out or skimping on the rules and/or analysis portions of IRAC.

While no definitive conclusions can be drawn from my anecdotal investigation, there is no disputing that effective, complete analysis of complex legal essay questions entails more discussion than most students devote to it.

Hey, Maybe I *Can* Guarantee You *A*s After All . . . Nah

Hmm, after rereading all that, I'm thinking maybe I'll change my mind about not being able to guarantee you *A*s if you follow my advice. If you could truly avoid all of the above mistakes, you probably would get *A*s. Of course, you won't be able to avoid them all simply by reading this book. Several of them involve skills that need to be developed while you're in law school. At least now you know what to be on the lookout for.

On the other hand, several of the mistakes *can* be easily avoided. You *can* make yourself be more careful about reading instructions. That alone could alter your performance. You *can* make yourself spend at least 20 percent of the allotted time for an essay question studying the question and organizing your answer before starting to write. You *can* make yourself remember not to leave out the relevant rules of law (assuming you know them). You *can* pay attention to time and allocate it efficiently during the exam. You *can* stay for the entire exam time. You *can* be sure to get your exam number right.

Did you notice any common threads in the mistakes? Specifically, did you notice how the C.R.E.D.O. habits carry over even to actual exam-writing? The only one not implicated, because it's too late for it to apply, is being *Consistent*. But note that avoiding common essay exam mistakes requires one to be:

Rigorous in stating legal rules and analysis with precision and completeness;

Efficient in assessing and allocating the allotted time; specifically, in avoiding the *Top Five Law School Essay Exam Time–Wasters*;

Diligent in reading the question carefully, following the instructions, staying for the entire exam period, and proofreading your work; and

Organized in outlining your answer before you begin writing, using subheadings to denote party disputes and issues, following an IRAC framework, and compartmentalizing your issue discussions to avoid the Monster [Issue] Mash.

Now that you're familiar with common essay exam mistakes, if you haven't done it already, study the negligence sample essay question and model answer in the Appendix. If you haven't started law school yet or are in its early throes, studying the question and answer will be of limited value because the law addressed by the question will be unfamiliar to you. But it still will be helpful in giving you an accurate detailed picture of what you can expect to find on a law school exam. Think about each of the mistakes outlined in this chapter as you study the question and answer.

CHAPTER 17
TACKLING LAW SCHOOL MULTIPLE-CHOICE QUESTIONS

Back when I attended law school, exams comprised exclusively essay questions. Today, many, if not most, professors also include multiple-choice questions on exams. Some professors rely solely on multiple-choice questions. My own exams are split half and half between essay and multiple-choice questions.

A couple of good reasons exist for including a multiple-choice component on a law school exam. First, multiple-choice questions allow for broader course coverage. As already explained, law school essay questions by their nature usually can touch on only a handful of issues covered during the semester. Including multiple-choice questions allows the professor to test on a wider array of topics.

A practical benefit of multiple-choice questions is that they provide good practice for the bar exam, which is dominated by multiple-choice questions. The Multistate Bar Examination (MBE), administered in forty-nine states and the District of Columbia, is a six-hour monstrous marathon of 200 multiple-choice questions focusing almost exclusively on first-year subjects. The MBE covers Contracts, Constitutional Law, Criminal Law, Evidence, Real Property, and Torts. The state portion of the bar exam also often includes multiple-choice questions. In some states, as much as 75 percent of the total bar exam is made up of multiple-choice questions.

Multiple–Guess Mess: Questions
without Right Answers

Legal multiple-choice questions are unlike anything you've encountered in your prior educational experiences, primarily in that they're incredibly difficult and often don't have clear right answers. They test reading comprehension, reasoning ability, and memorization of the law. I've included a sample question at the end of the chapter.

Most, albeit not all, law school multiple-choice questions follow the MBE-style. They usually consist of a one- or two-paragraph fact pattern, similar to a mini-essay set of facts, in which events of legal significance transpire involving the named actors, followed by the "call of the question," followed by four or more answer choices. The "call of the question" is the part that tells you the issue you are to address. With some frequency, a series of two or three questions will be based on the same fact pattern. The succeeding questions in the series may add new facts or change the original facts. If they do, those new or changed facts apply only to that particular question unless otherwise specified.

The call of the question usually asks the reader to predict the most likely resolution of a legal issue raised by the facts. Thus, if the question facts describe actions and interactions between Bob and Jill on Bob's property, the call of the question might be something like "If Bob sues Jill for trespass, Bob will:"—followed by answer choices such as, "Win, because ..." or "Lose, because...." Another common format in the call of the question asks students to assess the relative strength of legal arguments, as in: "If Bob sues Jill for trespass, his best argument will be ....."

The problem for students is that the answer choices do not always include a clearly right answer. The essence of law school multiple-choice questions is perhaps best captured by an odd piece of advice I remember hearing for the first time many moons ago while taking a review course for the Florida bar exam: "Remember that on the MBE, you're not looking for the right answer. You're looking for the *best wrong answer*." While that might be a bit of an overstatement as applied to all law school multiple-choice questions, the basic point is sound: in law school multiple-choice questions that track the MBE-format, you're looking for the *best* answer among the choices given, even if you think a better "right" answer exists that's not included.

Ten Multiple–Choice Strategies

Here are ten strategies for tackling these beasts:[102]

1. Read the question carefully, evaluating every fact as potentially important and not assuming any facts not stated. The ability to comprehend and manage complex text is one of the most important skills of a law student and lawyer, which is why it is part of the skill-set tested on the LSAT, law school essay questions, and MBE-type multiple-choice questions. As with essay questions, read every sentence asking why it was included, while recognizing that multiple-choice questions can also contain immaterial facts. Overlooking a single word can change the meaning of the question, including small words like "and" or "or." Don't assume any facts that are not given.

2. Pay attention to the call of the question. Pay close attention to the call of the question (sometimes called the "stem"). The call of the question is the part that immediately precedes the answer choices. It's the part that tells test-takers what they're supposed to analyze. Sometimes the fact patterns of MBE-style multiple-choice questions will set forth a scenario seemingly setting up one legal issue, only to surprise test-takers by asking about a different issue in the call of the question.

For example, a question may raise what appears to be an intentional tort issue, such as battery, but then the call of the question will ask about a negligence claim, as in "If Bob sues Jill for negligence. . . ." Students will be reading along thinking *battery, battery, battery*, and wrongly pick an answer involving battery or intent (battery is an intentional tort), overlooking the call of the question. It's a good idea to glance at the call of the question before studying the entire question so you'll know what to look for as you read it.

3. Use a process of elimination. As on the LSAT, use a process of elimination to narrow down your answer choices. There always will be at least one and usually two answers

102. The most commonly cited law school multiple-choice strategies, including several of the suggestions in this chapter, are derived from MICHAEL JO- SEPHSON, LEARNING & EVALUATION IN LAW SCHOOL (Ass'n of American Law Schools Annual Meeting, 1984).

that are clearly wrong. Mark those out and focus on the ones remaining. Here are some tips to help in the elimination process:

- As you'll learn all too well in law school, very few legal questions have answers that are true all of the time or none of the time. Almost every rule has exceptions and many exceptions have families of baby exceptions. Thus, in answering multiple-choice questions, answers prefaced with words like "always" or "never" will usually be wrong.

- Answers relating to a different topic area than the question seems to be focused on usually will be wrong. In the sample question at the end of the chapter, both answers (a) and (e) are good examples of this. The doctrines of strict liability for harm caused by animals and implied primary assumption of risk are foreign to the question topic and issue and are clear wrong answers.

- If two opposite answers exist, one of them usually is right. For example, suppose a question included these two answers: "(a) Dinkle will lose because of the doctrine of modified comparative negligence; (b) Dinkle will win because of the doctrine of modified comparative negligence." These are opposite answers and there's a good chance one of them would be the correct answer.

- Some professors will toss in humorous answers to questions. These answers will almost always be wrong.

- A number of articles about multiple-choice strategies in general (not focused on law school) advise that the longest answer is often correct because the professor is trying to give a precise and accurate answer. This suggestion may have some validity in law school because right answers in the convoluted world of law often require qualifying phrases and other details to make them accurate. I haven't ever counted the words in the answers to my multiple-choice questions, but I do recall instances of writing longer answers to some questions to make them technically correct.

4. Don't answer by your gut reaction. Read all the choices carefully, eliminating the obvious wrong answers, before choosing a selection. It may be that one answer intuitively appeals to you the moment you read it before you've considered all the options, and that may be the answer you ultimately decide on, but don't choose any answer until carefully weighing all the options.

5. Divide your time equally among the questions. Unlike essay questions, which can vary in weight, multiple-choice questions will nearly always be worth the same number of points. Don't get bogged down on one question at the expense of others. Answer it and move on.

6. Don't skip questions. Even if you're not sure of the answer, you're better off picking an answer than skipping the question with the intention of coming back to it later. Skipping questions poses two risks. First, you might forget you skipped it and start bubbling in answers for the other questions in the wrong spaces on the answer sheet. Second, students frequently skip questions and forget to return to them. Every semester, a couple of students will leave some questions blank on my Torts exam. Since I don't penalize students for wrong answers, the only explanation is that they skipped the questions and forgot to go back and fill them in.

7. The devil is in the details. The students who do best on multiple-choice questions are those who know the law inside-out. I always tell my students that while I'm not trying to trick them, the multiple-choice questions are tricky in that students really must have mastered the fine points of the law (not just the general rules) in order to do well.

As an example, in the sample question at the end of this chapter, many students, relying on the general rule that there is no duty under negligence law to aid or protect other people, will pick answer (d), which is a wrong answer. The students who get the question right will have learned and retained a particularly narrow exception to the rule—that a person who, even innocently (i.e., non-negligently), creates an unreasonable risk has a duty to eliminate it—and will pick (b), the correct answer.

Thus, doing well on multiple-choice questions is directly tied to the case-briefing, note-taking, and outlining chapters. Many students assert "I've never done well on multiple-choice questions." To some extent, as we see in this chapter, it is true that test-taking strategies or "tricks" can improve performance on multiple-choice questions and it's probably also true that some people have an innate feel for them. But the biggest reason students don't do well on multiple-choice questions is that they don't know the law as well as the students who do.

8. Don't be afraid to change your initial answer. You've probably heard the conventional wisdom that you should not change your initial answers to multiple-choice questions because it's more likely you will change an answer from right to wrong than from wrong to right. I heard this advice my entire life, starting in elementary school.

Guess what? It's completely backward. Study after study, some of them dating back to the 1920s, consistently show that changing multiple-choice answers is more likely to increase, rather than decrease, test scores. As just one of many examples, a study of upper-level accounting students showed that 95 percent of the students changed answers on their multiple-choice examinations (changing a total of 5.6 percent of the answers). Fifty-six percent of the answers were changed from wrong to right, while only 21 percent were changed from right to wrong. The remaining 23 percent were changed from one wrong answer to another wrong answer.[103] These results are consistent with other studies.

9. Answer all the questions. If time is about to run out and you haven't finished, pencil in an answer for every question. Unless you've been told otherwise by your professor, points won't be deducted for wrong answers. You probably are better off choosing the same answer for all unfinished questions (e.g., all (b) answers or all (c) answers), rather than randomly alternating. That should assure you of at least some right answers. If you have enough time, skim the questions and eliminate any clearly wrong answers. Eliminating even one answer in a question will substantially improve your mathematical guessing odds.

In case you're wondering, I looked for, but didn't find any reliable research as to which answer to pick if you're completely guessing. Several assertions, supposedly based on "studies" that are never named or cited, can be found online saying it is better to pick one particular letter and best not to

---

103. *See* Marshall A. Geiger, *On the Benefit of Changing Multiple–Choice Answers: Student Perception and Performance,* 117 EDUC. 108 (1996).

pick another particular letter. I'm not going to repeat them here because they may be spurious myths. You can find the magic letters online if you poke around a little bit, but hopefully, you won't find yourself in the position of having to resort to complete guessing.

10. "How do you get to the Supreme Court? Practice!" This takeoff on the old joke about how one gets to Carnegie Hall captures one of the best strategies for succeeding on multiple-choice questions, which is to practice working through a large number of them. Unfortunately, your professors are unlikely to provide you with many, if any, multiple-choice questions as samples because, more so than essay questions, crafting valid, reliable, and fair multiple-choice questions is difficult and time-consuming. (Bad news: some professors draft really lousy multiple-choice questions and/or borrow questions from other sources without revising them to fit the material the professor covered or the way he or she taught it.)

Fortunately, sample multiple-choice questions are available from a number of other sources. CALI (Computer–Assisted Legal Instruction) exercises, which are accessible to law students without charge, are one excellent option. Several law school study aids feature practice multiple-choice questions. Books published for bar review courses, such as Kaplan PMBR and BarBri, contain loads of sample questions. You can sometimes acquire copies of these books from recent graduates who have completed the bar exam. The actual MBE itself is not released to the public on a regular basis, but a couple of older exams have been made available. Look for them in the law library.

Don't get bogged down in fretting about the specifics of practice questions unless they were handcrafted by your professors. Some practice questions you encounter may be poorly drafted or thought-out. Some questions will address the law differently than your professor did or address issues you didn't cover and won't be expected to know. Focus on the format and thought process involved.

Sample Multiple–Choice Question

To give you a taste of what to expect, here is a sample Torts multiple-choice question used on a recent exam, along with an analysis of the answer in case you're curious:

Caspid went out for a Sunday drive in his Bentley automobile. He decided to leave the city, crank up the music and just unwind for the afternoon. The farther out into the country he drove, the sparser the population became. Soon he was driving down a deserted winding road through the woods. He opened the sunroof and put in a nice relaxing jazz CD. Caspid was driving carefully around a curve when a 300–pound wild boar ran in front of his car. He hit the brakes, but could not stop in time. Caspid's car collided with the boar, killing the large animal and damaging the front of his automobile. Caspid got out of his car to survey the situation. He felt bad about killing the animal, but also felt bad about the crumpled front bumper on his Bentley. Shaking his head in disgust, he backed up, turned his car around, and headed back to the city. Ten minutes later, Dort was driving down the same road. He came around the curve and ran into the boar, which was lying in the road. This caused him to lose control of his car and crash into a tree. Dort sustained a head injury. If Dort sues Caspid, the most probable result will be:

(a) Judgment for Dort, because of strict liability for harm caused by animals.

(b) Judgment for Dort, because Caspid created an unreasonable risk that he had a duty to eliminate.

(c) Judgment for Caspid, because Caspid was not negligent in creating the risk.

(d) Judgment for Caspid, because Caspid owed no duty to Dort.

(e) Judgment for Dort based on implied primary assumption of risk.

Analysis. The correct answer is (b). Normally, under the law, one has no legal duty to act affirmatively to aid or protect others absent a special relationship with them. Such inaction is known as nonfeasance; i.e., a mere failure to act. For example, if Caspid overheard two men plotting to rob a convenience store and kill the clerk, he would have no legal duty to do anything to protect the clerk, not even a duty to dial 911. But the law is filled with exceptions and one exception to the ''no duty to aid or protect'' rule is that if an actor creates an unreasonable risk, even innocently, he has a duty to exercise reasonable care to eliminate the risk. Even though Caspid did nothing wrong in creating the risk (the question says he was driving carefully when the boar ran in front of his car), he had a duty to act reasonably to remove the boar from the road or warn approaching drivers.

* * *

Let's close with another practice multiple-choice question:

In reading this chapter, I learned that:

(a) Law school multiple-choice questions often don't include a clear right answer.

(b) Law school multiple-choice questions sometimes trip students up through the "call of the question."

(c) Law school multiple-choice questions usually contain one or two answers that are clearly wrong and can be easily eliminated.

(d) Law school multiple-choice questions are going to cause me to have nightmares for the next three years about being eaten alive by 200 of these little monsters on the Multistate Bar Exam.

(e) All of the above.

And, of course, the correct answer is (e).

CHAPTER 18

LEGAL RESEARCH AND WRITING: AN INTERVIEW WITH FIVE EXPERTS

The insane amount of work required for the two-hour course in legal research and writing. I knew that law school would require a lot of reading and studying, but I was not aware that, in addition to all our regular course reading every night, we also would be required to do the lengthy research assignments, memos, oral arguments, and briefs. It was almost comical to me when teachers were urging us to spend hours every weekend working on our outlines for class, when I was barely able to use that time to keep up with my legal research and writing assignments.

—1L's "biggest surprise" about law school

You heard it here first. Legal Research and Writing will consume you. You just don't know it yet. Legal Research and Writing is known as a "skills course." Your other 1L courses are known as "doctrinal courses." While first-year doctrinal courses differ in content, they are extremely similar in format. Each will involve similar daily reading assignments of judicial opinions from a casebook, some mix of Socratic Q and A and lecture about those cases in class, and the same single-exam evaluation method at the end of the semester. Whether it's Civil Procedure, Contracts, Criminal Law, Property or Torts, the quest for first-year success will follow a similar path and require similar tools and strategies. Thus, nearly all of the advice in this book applies equally to each of the traditional doctrinal courses in the first-year curriculum.

But Legal Research and Writing will be wildly different from your other first-year courses. Year after year, a disproportionate amount of the fretting and angst-letting I hear from 1Ls has to do with their legal research and writing courses. For every student gripe about their doctrinal courses, I hear five about Legal Research and Writing.

That the subject commands such out-of-balance attention from students alone makes it a candidate for its own chapter, but there's a more pressing reason for giving extended, separate treatment to legal research and writing courses: *they are the most important courses you will take in law school.* Five legal writing professors from different law schools will help explain why in more detail below, but the reasons are nicely summed up in this observation by Professor David Walter: "Because this is what lawyers do every hour, every day, every year of their careers—they speak and they write— and when they're not speaking and writing, they're listening and reading."

Legal research and writing courses are part of the mandatory first-year curriculum at all law schools. They usually extend through both semesters (as in Legal Research and Writing I and Legal Research and Writing II). Roughly a quarter of law schools require a third legal writing course in the fall semester of the second year. Legal research and writing course packages travel under a variety of names, including Legal Research and Writing, Lawyering, Legal Method, Legal Skills and Values, and Legal Writing and Analysis. From here on out I'll just refer to the courses generically as "legal writing," while recognizing that all legal writing courses also teach legal research skills and most have an oral advocacy component.

The fundamental goal of legal writing courses is to teach students how to research and analyze legal issues and effectively communicate their analyses in writing and orally. If the primary purpose of the other first-year courses is to teach students to "think like a lawyer," it could be said that the goal of legal writing is to train students to "write like a lawyer thinks." Legal writing isn't about how to construct sentences. It's about how to conduct and convey legal analysis in a written form.

As a teacher of doctrinal subjects, I know better than to give advice about an area that is so different from my own milieu. Hey, I didn't get to be a law professor for nothing. So I asked for help with this chapter from five experienced legal writing professors. The Q and A with these five experts is the highlight of this chapter. But before we get to it, here's an overview of some of the common components—and frustrations—of legal writing courses.

An Introduction to Legal Writing Courses
Legal research.

Typically, legal writing begins with a research component, which usually includes exercises designed to train students to find and use different types of legal resources in the law library (e.g., case reporters, digests, legal encyclopedias). Depending on the school, the person teaching you legal research may be a member of the legal writing faculty, a law librarian, a student teaching assistant, a Westlaw or LexisNexis representative, or some combination of these folks.

Every law student recalls traipsing around the library on treasure hunts for particular sources. As one student described it:

> I remember thinking to myself how stupid all us little 1Ls must have looked trekking through the library looking for all the old books while doing our physical research assignments and finding our way around. All the 2Ls and 3Ls were in there trying to study while we bumbled about muttering to each other or asking for their assistance. I remember looking forward to the day when I could watch all the neophytes do that as well.

Another student described legal research exercises more bluntly as "scavenger hunts straight from hell."

Law schools are still searching for the proper balance between old and new when it comes to teaching legal research skills. Should students continue to be forced to learn the old ways of doing book research in a technological world where legal research is increasingly performed online through computer databases such as Westlaw and LexisNexis? Schools differ in their answers. Some schools limit computer research until students have been taught book research, while others hand students the keys to the online world of legal research from the beginning.

It's important to first learn how to do legal research with real books, just like it's important that elementary school students learn how to do basic math before they are given calculators. Knowing how to do book research makes students better computer researchers because they better understand the sources with which they're working, which are the same whether the medium is papyrus or megabytes. Moreover, while law students enjoy the luxury of free access to legal research databases (in part to get them hooked), lawyers have to pay substantial fees for these same services. As a result, many lawyers still rely on old-fashioned book research.

"The memo."

You will be stunned to find that something as innocuous-sounding as a "memo" will be the bane of your existence in your first semester.

Shortly into the first semester of legal writing, students begin working on their first legal writing project: an internal law office memorandum from an associate (you) to a fictitious partner analyzing the law as applied to a given set of facts. These memos, common in real-life law practice, ask you to explain and analyze the legal issues in a client's case so the partner can make informed decisions about the case, which may include the decision whether to accept the case or pass on it.

It's common to assign two such memoranda in the first semester, often denoted as the "minor memo" (the first one) and the "major memo" (the second one). Often, the minor memo will be a "closed universe memo," meaning the professor will provide students with all the necessary research, while the major memo will be an "open universe memo," meaning you will be required to do the research yourself. Other first-semester writing assignments can include client letters (i.e., a letter from a lawyer to his or her client) or drafting a contract or pleading.

People around you will not be able to fathom your preoccupation with "the memo."[104] I asked students to explain why

---

104. When students talk about "the memo," they usually are referring to the major memo.

it is so all-consuming. One repeated answer was the tremendous amount of work it requires compared to the disproportionately low credit hours typically awarded in legal writing compared to the first-year doctrinal courses (see below). Also, as one student said, the memo is "the first opportunity we have to create something that is our own." Law school does not offer many outlets for creativity. It's not as if the law office memorandum throws the door open for prose stylists or performance artists. Strict rules regulate just about every aspect of the document, including structure, length, font size, and margin widths. But it is the first and often only opportunity students get in the first semester to create their own legal work product.

Along the same lines, the memo is a law student's "first turn-in homework." In other first-year courses, students simply read cases, day after day. Students prepare case briefs, but these are not turned in. Students also spend tons of time preparing course outlines, but same thing: they aren't turned in.

Last, but certainly not least, the memo not only gets turned in, "It's graded!" Because students receive so little evaluative feedback during the semester in their other courses due to the single-exam format, it is no wonder they over-obsess about their memo feedback.

Filleted by feedback.

"You write well, but made a substantive error of malpractice dimensions." Ouch! This comment, scribbled by my legal writing instructor on the last page of my major memo assignment introduced me to the harsh realities of law school grading. Like many law students, I was used to As and praise in my previous educational experiences. Now I had a professor telling me I screwed up so badly I could get sued for it.

One of the biggest practical differences between legal writing and other first-year courses is that students get performance feedback in legal writing, often including letter grades, as they go through the semester. That feedback is often negative and painful.

One can almost hear the self-esteem bubbles bursting when the first wave of legal writing feedback is distributed. Standing in class on those days looking out at rows of morose faces, I feel I should be delivering a eulogy instead of a Torts lecture. As one student put it: "As law students, the majority of us are used to receiving As and when you get that first draft of your first memorandum back with a C- on it (and believe me, this happens even to the students who finish at the top of the class), it can be discouraging." She should know. She finished the year ranked second in her class.

The credit-hour crunch.

The single most iterated 1L gripe—and that's saying a lot—is that the workload required for legal writing is disproportionately heavy compared to the credit hours allocated. Usually, the workload for a law school course corresponds to the number of credit hours for the course. But students would argue we reversed everything for legal writing, requiring more work for fewer credit hours (usually two). Students complain that this allocation is completely arbitrary, but they're wrong. It's all done according to a highly scientific, mathematical formula:

$$x/y = 2 \text{ credit hours}$$

with x being the number of hours required to complete legal writing assignments (rounded to the nearest thousand) and y being the number necessary to make the answer equal two credit hours.

Hey, just kidding. On the other hand, the real reasons for why legal writing courses get the short end of the credit-hour stick aren't much more satisfying. They include the fact that legal writing courses are, relatively speaking, newer additions to law school curricula. Some doctrinal professors, particularly older ones, think legal writing courses aren't as important as doctrinal courses. Related to that, territoriality and turf-protecting often come into play in faculty deliberations to increase credit hours for legal writing, which usually entail reducing credit hours for first-year doctrinal courses.

Most law schools have or are taking steps to alleviate the credit-hour disparity. Nevertheless, credit hours allocated to legal writing still lag behind those for doctrinal courses. In 2011, credit hours for legal writing averaged 2.38 hours in the fall and 2.31 hours in the spring, compared to three or four credit hours for most doctrinal courses.

Citation style.

Another component of legal writing courses that students find frustrating is learning legal citation style. "Citation style" refers to the form and format in which legal authorities (such as cases, law review articles, books) are referenced or documented.

The standard legal citation manual is *The Bluebook: A Uniform System of Citation* (19th ed. 2010). The *Bluebook* tells legal writers what citation information to include (e.g., volume, page number, date), what font to put it in (e.g., big and small caps, italics), when to use abbreviations and what they should look like, where to insert commas and periods, and many other details. It's somewhat similar to the MLA (Modern Language Association) style book you might have used in undergraduate school, except roughly one trillion times more detailed and complex. Look at the footnotes to this book for samples of *Bluebook* citation style.

The Bluebook is famously hyper-technical and obsessed with minutia. I had to laugh when reading a comment from a student consultant advising new students to pay attention to *The Bluebook* because an entire letter grade can be lost on a writing assignment "if you leave off just one comma!" The comment brought back memories of a humor column I wrote several years ago for the *American Bar Association Journal* satirizing a *Bluebook* rule that required a comma in a particular place under particular circumstances. An excerpt will give you a taste of what you're up against when dealing with *The Bluebook*. The setting for the column was a mock meeting of the board of *Bluebook* editors:

Irving: We need that ******* comma! Rule 15.2 means nothing without The Comma. I'll gladly die for it.

Frieda: *Accord.* [A *Bluebook* reference.]

Dan: *Accord.*

Wendy: Put down the gun, Irving. *The Bluebook* was meant to bring peace.

Irving: Not until I have proof of everyone's commitment to The Comma. I've decided to quit law school and become addicted to amphetamines so I can contemplate The Comma twenty-four hours a day.

Dan: I'm going to have Rule 15.2 tattooed on my thigh, right below the rules for Separately Bound Legislative Histories.

Frieda: I'll cut out my husband's entrails and form them into the shape of one huge comma.

Irving: What about you, Wendy?

Wendy: My parents died in a plane crash yesterday. I have to go to the funeral.

Irving: Doesn't The Comma mean anything to you?

Wendy: Alright, I'll send flowers.

While the *Bluebook* is the dominant legal citation manual, some law schools use the more recently developed *ALWD Citation Manual: A Professional System of Citation* (4th ed. 2010). When the *ALWD Citation Manual* was first published in 2000, its simplified approach to legal citation style earned acclaim and popularity in some circles. Which citation manual to adopt for legal writing courses has been a source of intense debate at many law schools. There was a time when it looked like the *ALWD Citation Manual* might give *The Bluebook* a run for its money, but the scale has tilted back to the old standard.[105]

Regardless of which manual is used, it's important to pay attention to learning citation style. Not only can bad citation skills lose you points on your assignments in legal writing and other courses with writing requirements, they can hurt you in the real legal world. If your school doesn't devote substantial attention to learning citation style in its legal writing program, make a point to study it on your own. If you are invited to join the law review, you won't have any choice but to master *The Bluebook*, but the opportunities to learn citation style are more limited for other students.

The second-semester appellate brief and oral argument.

In the second semester, legal writing usually includes a written and oral advocacy component. Typically, students are required to research and write an appellate brief and make

---

105. The Association of Legal Writing Directors 2011 survey showed: 131 law school legal writing programs (70 percent) use *The Bluebook* only, twenty-seven use the *ALWD Citation Manual* (down from fifty-six in 2005), twelve use both, and eleven leave the decision to the individual professor. 2011 ALWD SURVEY, *supra*, at 19.

an oral argument to a panel of mock judges. The brief, which may run thirty pages, is excruciatingly time-consuming and the subject of much complaining by second-semester students.

As for the oral argument, it's the most exciting, but also the most terrifying, event of the first year. It's exciting because the oral argument is often the first law school exercise in which students get to act and feel like "real lawyers" (meaning, in the minds of 1Ls, the lawyers they see on television, who, unlike real lawyers, are always in court). The terror aspect derives from a generalized fear of public speaking accentuated by the fact that oral arguments amount to public interrogations. They're not monologues. The judges drill students with lots of questions, sometimes starting before students have finished their first sentence.

It's normal to be nervous about public speaking. Surveys show that public speaking ranks higher than death on lists of people's greatest fears. These surveys, according to a great Seinfeld monologue line, mean that at a funeral the average person would rather be the one in the casket than the one delivering the eulogy. I was so nervous about my oral argument back in law school that I showed up on the wrong day! I arrived at school all spiffed-out in my suit, ready to go, and started freaking out when I couldn't find the correct room. Sweating buckets, I frantically searched the law school for my professor and judging panel only to finally figure out my argument wasn't until the next day. At least I was a day early instead of a day late. I got a good laugh out of it once I was released from the coronary unit.

Looking back, the oral argument still stands out as one of the most memorable, albeit most nerve-wracking, events of law school. A student consultant, quiet by nature, wrote that the "mere thought of having to stand in front of others and argue makes you nauseous." To help her get through the experience, she wrote the reminder to "BREATHE" at the top of her notes. She did fine though, as most students do, in part because they put so much time into the preparation. Sometimes the quietest students shine the brightest in the oral arguments. So don't underestimate yourself. A great oral advocate may be lurking beneath your shy exterior.

Balancing legal writing workloads with other courses.

Take legal writing seriously and give it your best, but not at the expense of neglecting your other courses. Keep in mind that from a cost-benefit analysis, your doctrinal courses usually will be worth more credit hours, meaning they will weigh more in your cumulative GPA.

And don't procrastinate. On days when assignments are due in legal writing, class attendance can drop off by a third or more. Professors find such major declines irritating and may take them personally. I know professors who intentionally test on material covered in class on days when there are large numbers of absences. At one school, in a faculty email exchange over this issue, a professor commented that the dismal attendance in his class on the due date of a legal writing assignment was "unfortunate" for the students because "[t]oday's materials will find their way onto my exam."

An Interview with Five Legal Writing Professors

Five experienced legal writing professors generously agreed to share their tips for success as to a variety of key issues common to all legal research and writing courses. Here's our all-star lineup, in alphabetical order:

Kimberly Boone is the director of the legal writing and moot court programs at the University of Alabama School of Law, where she graduated Order of the Coif and was a member of the law review. She worked several years in employment litigation before joining academia in 2000.

Chris Coughlin is the director of the legal analysis, writing, and research program at Wake Forest University School of Law. She also holds appointments in the Wake Forest University Graduate School of Arts and Sciences and the School of Medicine's Science Institute.

Joan Malmud Rocklin is a legal writing professor at the University of Oregon. Prior to joining academia, she clerked for a federal judge in California and worked in the litigation department at a corporate law firm in New York City.

Sandy Patrick is a legal writing professor at Lewis & Clark Law School in Portland, Oregon. Previously, she taught at Wake Forest University. Prior to entering academia, she served as a law clerk to a state appellate judge, an assistant state attorney general doing criminal appeals, and as a practicing attorney doing civil litigation.[106]

David D. Walter is the co-director of the legal skills program at Florida International University College of Law (FIU), with more than twenty years' experience teaching legal writing. Previously, he taught at Seattle University and Mercer University. He also teaches upper-level skills courses and directs the appellate advocacy program.

Our five experts answered ten questions about legal writing courses, including many that bear a direct connection to success or failure in those courses.

1. For students who recognize they have writing deficiencies, is there anything they can do to help themselves succeed in their first-year legal writing courses before they begin law school?

COUGHLIN: If a student knows he or she has a writing deficiency, I recommend the following—not only to succeed in their first-year legal writing courses, but to succeed in law school and the profession. First, consider investing in a program such as *Core Grammar for Lawyers*, http://www.core grammarforlawyers.com/, an online, self-directed tool to help students learn grammar and punctuation for legal writing. Accept that learning basic rules of grammar, punctuation, and parts of speech may not be exciting or fun. No "instant gratification" is involved. One student who took it on himself to upgrade his writing skills after his first year of law school analogized his summer remedial writing activities to repeatedly sticking a fork in his knee.

The nature of the deficiency, along with the nature of the individual learning style, must be assessed. Each student is unique and learns differently, and there is no magic pill or process to cure all deficiencies. If the deficiency involves

---

106. In addition to their other credentials, Professors Coughlin, Malmud Rocklin, and Patrick are co-authors of *A Lawyer Writes* (2008), a legal writing book for first-year students. Check out their book for expanded discussion of some of the points they make in this chapter.

simply a lack of knowledge, step one above might be sufficient. If the deficiency is more serious, the student should consider being tested for a learning difference or disability. If the deficiency rises to the level of a disability, such as dysgraphia (which is a neurological disorder characterized by writing disability), the school may be able to provide reasonable accommodations to help the student succeed. Obviously, any such disability would need to be documented by a medical provider and that information communicated to the law school as soon as possible.

Regardless, a student must understand how he or she learns best. To do this, the student should look back on her educational career, and determine whether there is a common denominator in the teachers, environments, situations, and subjects in which she responded most positively and successfully. Everybody learns differently and everybody writes differently.

ROCKLIN: Learning to write well is a lifelong process that should start well before law school begins and continue long after law school ends. There are no quick fixes.

That said, I recommend that all students read William Strunk and E.B. White's classic *The Elements of Style*. We should probably all read it once a year. Another great book on writing is Richard Wydick's *Plain English for Lawyers*. Both books cover the basics of clear, concise writing.

Once the student gets to law school, if she is still concerned, she should go to her legal writing professor to discuss her concerns. Her professor may have some helpful suggestions, especially if the student has submitted a writing assignment and the professor has had a chance to review the student's writing.

Finally, the student should become a critical reader. During law school, students see a lot of writing—mostly appellate opinions. Some appellate opinions are well written. Others are not. The distinction between work that is well written and work that is not is whether you can understand it. If you can't understand what the writer is trying to convey, the writer has failed. So when you cannot understand what you are reading, ask *why*. What could the writer have done differently? If you find yourself blissfully gliding through your reading, ask *why*. What has the writer done to make the ideas easy to absorb? By asking why some writing is effective and other writing is not, you will begin to develop better judgment about your own writing.

WALTER: Even students with serious writing deficiencies can improve their writing. The first step, of course, is often the most difficult—recognizing that you, the writer, have writing deficiencies. Sure, Cs and Ds in English classes and other courses with major writing requirements are a good clue, but I've seen several writers with serious problems who received Bs and even As in undergraduate courses with extensive writing requirements.

Once the need for assistance is recognized, several avenues are available for students who want to improve their writing. First, there are plenty of professors and tutors in English departments, other departments, and college "writing centers" who are willing to help students correct those writing deficiencies—find them ASAP and ask for their help! Ask them to read samples of your writing. Ask them to look for organizational issues—do your sentences and thoughts flow together in a logical manner? Ask them to check for mechanics issues—are your commas in the right place, is your word usage proper, and is your grammar correct? Ask them to examine the "readability" of your writing—is your writing clear, do you use words precisely, and are you concise in your writing?

Second, as suggested above, find a good "style" book and give it a careful review. That should give you a better idea about some of the topics you'll see in legal writing.

Third, review and critique a few of your writings and the writings of others to evaluate your deficiencies—if you can spot the problems in your past writings or the writings of others, you have taken one more step toward improving your writing in law school and beyond. The idea here is to learn how to read very carefully and with a critical eye.

Even excellent writers will benefit greatly from following the steps outlined above.

2. Is it common for students to enter law school entertaining mistaken assumptions about the nature of "legal writing"? What are those misconceptions?

BOONE: One of the most common misconceptions is that being a strong writer in other fields or being an English major necessarily translates to being good at legal writing.

This is not always the case. Different undergraduate majors both help and hinder you in legal writing. For example, English majors may love to write and know what it means to write in the active voice, but might have a terrible time learning to be more concise and direct. Math and engineering majors may sometimes forget to write in complete sentences, but they may pick up on legal analysis more quickly.

Students may also assume that they can use the same processes they used for college papers on their legal writing assignments. This will not work. The research is different, the citation style is different, and the analysis is new. Let's be brutally honest. Somewhere along the way, many of you wrote a paper shortly before (or even the night before) it was due. If you received a good grade, you may have made a habit of it.

Be forewarned that this will not work in legal writing for several reasons. First, good legal writing may look simple, but it usually requires long hours and multiple drafts to make complex ideas look simple. Second, you may not realize you are lost until you actually start writing. If you start assignments early, you'll have time to ask for help if you need it. And finally, as if you won't hear this enough, all of your law school classmates were at the top of their classes too. Your work will be judged in relation to other good students.

COUGHLIN: One misconception is that legal writing drains your creativity. The reason for this misconception is many legal writing professors require that students use a mnemonic (a specific order) to structure their legal arguments. For example, commonly used mnemonics in legal writing include "IRAC" (Issue, Rule, Application, Conclusion—pronounced similarly but not to be confused with IRAQ)—and "CREAC" (Conclusion, Rule, Explanation, Application, Conclusion).

In reality, using a mnemonic structure should not limit the creative process. Mnemonics are supposed to be flexible tools, not rigid formulas. They provide an effective starting point for drafting a legal analysis. The substance of your analysis—the way you frame your legal arguments and your unique application of the law—is necessarily creative.

To illustrate this point, think of the poetry form of haiku, a Japanese form of unrhymed poetry that is always three lines long, with five syllables in the first line, seven syllables in the second line, and five syllables in the third. While the haiku is written in a strict form, the writer has freedom within the substance of the poem to be creative. Likewise, while the legal writer may use a preset organizational structure, outstanding legal arguments build bridges between prior cases and new sets of facts, a skill that mandates creativity. As my colleague Professor Miki Felsenburg says to her students: "Bore me with your organization and thrill me with your analysis."

PATRICK: I agree with what Professor Boone said that one great misconception about legal writing is that researching and analyzing a legal problem will mirror the work students did for term papers in undergraduate school. This misconception arises in large part because new law students don't understand that legal writing is not just about "writing." It's about something much more complex—legal *thinking*. Committing sound analysis to paper requires far more skill than knowing the parts of a paragraph, how to use commas, or whether the period goes inside the quotation mark (it does). Legal writing requires students to find the law that governs a client's issue, discern the relevant parts of the law, weave those parts into a cohesive explanation, and apply it to a client's fact situation. Doing all of those things requires the student to mentally engage the material with critical reading, thinking, and questioning.

3. I commonly tell students that their legal research and writing courses may be the most important courses in law school and I'm sure you would agree. How would you explain to students why that is so?

ROCKLIN: Legal writing teaches the must-have skills to be a successful attorney. I promptly forgot most everything I learned in Contracts, Civil Procedure, and Constitutional Law within hours of taking the exams. On the job, though, that wasn't a problem. I worked for big fancy law firms and for government agencies but none of my employers expected me to remember much substantive law. My employers did expect me to know how to research the substantive law, synthesize it into a coherent explanation of the law that would apply to a client's problem, and then write my analysis in a clear and compelling way. I learned those skills primarily in my legal writing class.

PATRICK: From their first day of orientation, my students hear the proclamation that legal writing is the most important class they will have in law school. They initially hear those words from me (whom they might not believe), but soon hear them echoed by upper-division students, practicing attorneys, and prospective employers. Each year I invite guest speakers to class—upper-level students, law clerks, or attorneys. Invariably, without my solicitation, they confirm the notion that legal writing is the most important class in law school. Why? Because it teaches students the core skills for legal learning: how to assess law, think about law, and communicate law to someone else. Effective lawyering requires those skills. An attorney can know everything there is to know about tort law, but if he cannot assimilate law relevant to a client's issue and communicate his analysis, that attorney will not effectively represent his client.

WALTER: I do agree! I tell my 1Ls on the first day that legal writing courses are the most important courses in law school. Written and oral communication skills are so critical to everything lawyers do. In two American Bar Foundation studies, the lawyers polled overwhelmingly identified oral communication skills and written communication skills as the two skills/knowledge bases that are most important to lawyers. They ranked "knowledge of substantive law" as seventh in importance.[107]

The researchers also surveyed hiring partners to determine the most important skills students should learn in law school. The top three skills? Library legal research, oral communication, and written communication. Knowledge of substantive law came in a distant eleventh place.[108]

Why are oral and written communication skills more important than knowledge of the substantive law? Because this is what lawyers do every hour, every day, every year of their careers—they speak and they write—and when they're not speaking and writing, they're listening and reading.

4. The standard major assignment in most first-semester legal writing courses is the law office memorandum written from junior associate to senior part-

---

107. *See* Bryant G. Garth & Joanne Martin, *Law Schools and the Construction of Competence*, 43 J. LEGAL EDUC. 469, 473 tbl.1 (1993).

108. *Id.* at 490 tbl.11.

ner. Why is the office memorandum still seen as the most effective or important vehicle for teaching legal writing to 1Ls as opposed to, say, drafting pleadings or legislation or some other type of assignment? Related to that question, I'm sure 1Ls often wonder what drives the content of legal writing courses. Any insights on that point?

BOONE: The *process* required to write the memorandum is what makes it a good first-semester tool. The office memo, at least as we teach it, requires the students to research two legal issues and analyze them objectively. We ask the students to write an interoffice memo (from associate to partner within the same firm) to train students to fully and objectively evaluate legal issues, rather than argue for or against a certain result. For example, in a civil suit, we may ask the student to evaluate two issues to help determine whether the firm (the student's fictitious employer) should take the case. Even with an assignment structured this way, most first-year students struggle with the notion that we aren't seeking a single "right answer." In other words, I could usually care less whether the student concludes the firm should take the case. I'm much more concerned with whether the student has thoroughly researched and analyzed the issues and fully explained the reasons both for and against taking the case.

The content of our legal writing course is driven in part by a desire to prepare students well for their first summer jobs. An in-house memo is the type of assignment our students are most likely to be assigned in those jobs.

Learning to explain legal rules and apply them to a fact scenario also helps students develop the skills they will need to write effective exam answers.

COUGHLIN: While some students complain that the office memo is dated, it remains the optimal vehicle for beginning law students to develop the skills of legal analysis and argumentation. It is also important, of course, to learn to effectively draft pleadings and legislation, but those skills are more sophisticated, technical, and require knowledge of litigation and/or legislative processes. Such exercises are better taught after the students have completed Civil Procedure and/or a legislation or administrative law course or seminar.

Typically, most legal writing programs begin by assigning an office memorandum with a closed universe of research (that means that three or four cases are provided to the students and the analysis is limited to using those materials). The students must critically read and analyze the cases, extract the governing rules, and distinguish between relevant and irrelevant facts from the prior cases. These are fundamental skills all lawyers must develop.

Among other things, composing a law office memorandum teaches students two types of basic legal reasoning skills: (1) *rule-based reasoning*, where the student applies the language of a rule to a client's facts to predict an outcome; and (2) *analogical reasoning*, where the student shows that the client's case is sufficiently similar to, or different from, previous cases and that the outcomes in the previous cases either should or should not control the client's case.

PATRICK: Legal writing professors still use the legal memorandum as the primary vehicle for a writing assignment because it requires engaged analysis and exemplifies the type of assignments students will most likely be doing early in their legal careers.

Attorneys, particularly those in the private sector, will likely draft more legal memos than they can count during their first years of practice. In two years as an associate at a large law firm, I drafted three times more legal memos than I did pleadings, briefs, interrogatories, and other documents combined.

Legal memoranda are relevant to students for another reason: A memorandum assignment simulates what the students will be asked to do on most of their first-year exams. Most exams during the first year ask students to predict an outcome for a factual scenario and support their decision with the law they know. Although exams have certain differences from the office memo, both assignments ask students to assess a problem, discern and apply the relevant law, and communicate a cogent answer.

5. If you had to list just three hallmarks of an outstanding law office memorandum, what would be they be? Conversely, if you had to list three hallmarks of a poor law office memorandum, what would they be?

COUGHLIN: "The Outstanding Office Memorandum" is:

1. A direct and precise response to the question being asked. The writer tells the reader up front what the specific issue is being analyzed, as well as the predicted outcome. The body of the memorandum—the analysis—does not go off on tangents but builds bridges between each point to reach a conclusion.

2. A clear, concise response using plain English. As my colleague Professor Barbara Lentz puts it, if you wouldn't use the word when ordering at McDonald's, don't use it in your office memorandum. So just as you wouldn't say "Herewith my hamburger, french fries would be a most effective side dish and, accordingly, supersize me," when ordering at the drive-thru, do not use that type of language or sentence structure in your memorandum. For maximum clarity and effectiveness, use the KISS theory (Keep it Simple, Stupid).

3. A response that shows all steps of the analytical process. An outstanding office memorandum can be thought of as a math problem in elementary school. Simply getting to the correct solution or prediction is not enough. You must show your work.

Conversely, "The Not So Outstanding Office Memorandum" is:

1. A response that is overly formal in style. Students sometimes think that if they write formally their reader will not realize the writer did not take enough time or did not understand the analysis. When students are confused, they think that if they use eighteenth-century prose, the professor will not realize that they did not spend enough time to understand the links between the cases and/or build the necessary analytical bridges between the cases and their "client's" facts.

2. A response that is written in the passive voice. While there are strategic uses of the passive voice (i.e., "mistakes were made" rather than "the defendant made a mistake"), consistent use of the passive voice is a red flag that tells your legal writing professor one of the following: (1) I haven't spent enough time on this memo. One can think back to Samuel Clemens' (Mark Twain) famous quote "I apologize for the length of this letter, but I didn't have time to make it shorter."; or (2) I don't understand this analysis, but if I use really complex language maybe my legal writing professor will think I am really smart.

3. A response that is fraught with *Bluebook* errors, typographical errors, and formatting errors. Typically, there is a correlation between a lack of precision in analysis and a lack of precision in style. Errors with these "finer points" distract a reader from the analysis and limit the amount of confidence a reader has in the writer's prediction of the outcome.

PATRICK: I agree wholeheartedly with Professor Coughlin's comments regarding the hallmarks of a good memo, so let me concentrate on the hallmarks of a bad one. Local attorneys at large law firms in our city recently asked our Legal Writing and Analysis department to conduct a seminar instructing young associate attorneys on how to improve their writing. The partners articulated a fairly consistent list of problems with which associates struggle. Those problems mirror the hallmarks of a poorly written law office memorandum:

1. Poor organization. Often neither the overall presentation of issues nor the component substantive parts within each issue are presented in a logical, clear order that the reader can follow, absorb, and understand.

2. The legal substance of the memo is not clearly communicated to the reader. The paragraphs fail to signal their points, leaving the reader lost as to what each paragraph will prove. The law may not be fully explained. Additionally, the memo may be organized around cases instead of legal points, with the writer failing to show how the cases fit together. The application of the law to the client's facts often has leaps in logic, leaving the reader unclear about how legal precedent requires a particular outcome for the client's case.

3. The product is not professional. Often, because of time constraints so prevalent in law practice, memos are rife with errors—typographical errors, poor grammatical choices, inappropriate punctuation, and poor citation. The overall effect of the errors paints the attorney as either lax or incompetent.

Ironically, writing an outstanding memorandum does not take that much more time than writing a poor one. A little extra time spent organizing the research, mapping out the most logical flow of arguments, and polishing the final draft can transform a mediocre memorandum into a great one.

WALTER: First, the most important hallmark of an outstanding office memo is its selection and development of the law (i.e., relevant cases, statutes, regulations, and so forth). Accuracy is critically important because the writer is flying solo—no one else will be researching and analyzing the issues—so the writer must get it right the first time. If the writer fails to find or discuss a key case, or if the writer explains the case or the legal rule poorly, the attorney relying on the memo may give the client inaccurate legal advice. Thus, the writer's most important task is to find the appropriate law and explain it accurately.

The second hallmark of an outstanding memo is its organization. The large-scale organization of an outstanding memo will be perfect from beginning to end: from the memo heading, to the framing of the legal questions presented, to the brief answers to those questions, to the statement of the facts, to the discussion, and finally to the conclusion. The mid-scale organization of an outstanding memo also will be near perfect. For example, the discussion section will be organized into appropriate subsections, each one starting with a conclusion, followed by explanation of the law, application of the law to the facts, and ending with a mini-conclusion. Finally, the small-scale organization of an outstanding memo will be excellent, with nearly every sentence and idea leading to the next idea in a logical manner, like climbing a staircase step by step to reach the logical conclusion on the landing at the top of the stairs.

The third hallmark of an outstanding memo is superb application of the law to the facts; that is, clear explanation of the legal arguments.

6. Some students mistake functional writing (e.g., coherent sentences, good grammar, etc.) with good legal writing. They don't realize how important the analysis is or even what analysis is. How would you define "analysis" in a way that law students can understand what it means?

BOONE: Everyone can read the rules (cases, statutes, etc.) and most students can learn the rules well enough to predict accurate answers to many legal questions. But analysis goes further than that. Analysis is not about the answer. It's about the process of reaching that answer. Some have analogized it to long division: if you don't show all your work, you get no credit. For example, if you are asked to "analyze" what time it is, you would first explain to the reader the "rules" of time zones, identify the important facts about the time zone you are in, and apply the time zone rules to those facts to reach an answer.

COUGHLIN: Analysis is the process of evaluating the law on a particular topic. In a legal analysis, the writer will show how an established rule of law will function given a new set of facts (i.e., rule-based reasoning) or explain why a client's case is like or unlike a previous case and how those comparisons work to yield a particular result (i.e., analogical reasoning). In other words, it is deducing a likely outcome considering prior law and new facts. Analysis is where a student's creativity and brain power truly come to light.

Analysis is like the fixings in a sandwich. While two pieces of bread may be homemade and quite good, it isn't enough unless you add the meat, veggies, cheese, and condiments. Before all the fixings are added, there is no sandwich. There are simply two pieces of bread. Likewise, in your memorandum, the analysis is the fixings—it is the most important component of the memorandum.

ROCKLIN: In the typical fall-semester memo, there are three analytical components that distinguish functional writing from really good, insightful legal writing. The first analytical component involves separating the whole into its parts. Every legal analysis will begin with a governing rule. Almost all legal rules are made up of component parts known as "elements" or "factors." For example, the tort of negligence has four elements (duty, breach of duty, causation, and injury). Part of analysis is breaking down broader rules and principles into their constituent elements or factors and examining each of them one by one.

The second important analytical component is the explanation of the law. For each element or factor that is at issue to a client's problem, law students must coherently explain the relevant law. Doing so is difficult because students must pull together the law from numerous, disparate sources. But that's the analytical challenge: assembling a group of relevant disparate legal snippets into a seamless whole. This component of legal writing is analytical in that it requires students to understand both the whole and the parts and explain their relationship to the reader.

Finally, students must apply the law to a particular fact pattern in order to predict an outcome in the client's case. This part of the argument is analytical in the sense that students must think precisely about why the law will lead to one outcome and not the other and then articulate their thinking in a compelling way. Law professors commonly refer only to this last part—applying law to facts—as "the analysis." But please know that the first two parts are also analytical in their own way.

7. If we divide the process of composing a law office memorandum or other legal writing assignment into three parts—researching, writing the initial draft, and rewriting/editing the final product—which part commonly gets the short end of the stick from students? In other words, which of the three steps do less successful students regularly not devote enough time and attention to?

ROCKLIN: Editing—it's key to a professional work product. A study by Anne Enquist of Seattle University showed that successful legal writing students spend approximately three-fifths of their writing time revising and proofreading, while less successful students divide their time more equally between writing the first draft and revising and proofreading it.

But to say "edit more" is unhelpful. One has to know *how* to edit. Effective editing requires first a big-picture understanding: What's my goal? If you understand your goal, you can step back from your project and ask yourself, does this work achieve my goal? For example, if you are writing an objective memo, the goal is to educate and inform. Understanding that goal allows you to step back and ask yourself, have I educated the attorney receiving this memo about all the relevant law? Have I done so clearly? Have I informed the attorney about the areas where the law favors our client and the areas where our client will struggle to make her case? Have I clearly explained why those strengths and weaknesses exist?

Second, effective editing requires you to understand the problems that typically get in the way of achieving your goal and actively look for those problems. Essentially, you have to create a checklist out of your legal writing class. Let's say in class you've discussed that a well-organized legal argument states a conclusion, explains the law, applies the law, and then concludes again. Well, have you done that? Be sure to go back and check. Let's say your professor has pointed out that your sentences tend to be wordy. Well, that needs to be added to your checklist, and with each memo you write, you'll need to check your sentences for wordiness.

Because editing often seems like such drudgery, I'd like to put in a personal plug for editing. Editing is about creating a synchronized, lucid solution to a complex problem. The reward and "fun" comes from seeing the improvement.

Let's say I want to build a machine that will squirt just the perfect amount of mustard onto a hotdog. The parts lay before me. I start trying to fit them together. I discover at the end of my first attempt that I've done pretty well, but the machine has a leftward tilt, so that all the mustard winds up on the conveyor belt to the left of the hotdog. I tinker until the mustard is hitting dead-on, but there's too much of it. I tinker a little bit more so that just the right amount of mustard is hitting the hotdog. Finally, for a flourish, I adjust the machine so that instead of the mustard running in a straight line, it has an S-shaped flow down the hotdog's spine. I did it! I created the perfect mustard-hotdog combination. To me, that's the pleasure in editing. It's the time when I sync up all the parts to create exactly the product I want to deliver. There's beauty in that.

PATRICK: Without a doubt, students spend the least amount of time revising and polishing the final product. Realizing that the revising and polishing steps can often take longer than the research and drafting steps is a secret to success.

The research phase is often the most enjoyable because students can wander mindlessly, breezily, through library stacks or online databases—working, yes, but minimally engaging difficult material. Research can be a delightful black hole, allowing students to save the thinking for later.

Once some thinking has occurred and the student has slogged through statutes and cases and mapped out some kind of tangible structure, students are willing to devote some time to hashing out that draft—what they hope will be the *only* draft. That draft is like painting the walls of a room; we all paint expecting immediate gratification and hoping that two coats will not be necessary. And maybe even that we can skip doing all that difficult trim work! Likewise, some students hope one slapdash draft will be enough.

When students finally finish the first two laborious stages (research and writing the first draft), they are spent—from both a time and a mental standpoint. They rationalize that the first draft is good enough, and submit it.

Early in my legal writing career, colleagues introduced me to Anne Lamott's book on writing, *Bird by Bird*. Lamott's ideas on fiction writing transfer quite easily to legal writing. In one chapter she accurately captures the three stages of composing a written document. The first draft is the "down draft," where the goal is just to get the words down on paper. The second draft is the "up draft"—you fix it up and "try to say what you have to say more accurately." The final draft is the "dental draft," where you check "every tooth to see if it's loose or cramped or decayed, or even, God help us, healthy."[109] My students love this analogy, although sometimes they add their opinion that the final draft is called a dental draft because getting it done is worse than having a root canal.

Students who are willing to complete that third step—revising and polishing until they get a dental draft—usually are very successful.

WALTER: While all three aspects of the research and writing process often get the "short end of the stick," I think the legal research process gets "shorted" most often, causing great damage to students (and their clients) in the long run.

Here's what frequently happens. After the students are given the facts for the open memo problem (i.e., a memo where students have to do the research themselves), most of them begin their legal research. Some perform in stellar fashion, devoting the necessary hours in the books and on-line, carefully researching the issues, closely reading the cases, and finding nearly all of the relevant law. Many students, however, underestimate how long it will take to locate the relevant law, and some underestimate how frustrating it can be to find the law. In both instances, these students do not complete the research task. Unfortunately, and as surprising as it might sound, there are also a few

---

109. *See* ANNE LAMOTT, BIRD BY BIRD: 25–26 (First Anchor Books 1995).
SOME INSTRUCTIONS ON WRITING AND LIFE

students who never start their research, figuring instead that they'll simply rely on another student, or the professor, to tell them which statutes and cases are important.

Once the research phase ends and the drafting phase begins, the students typically discuss the law both in and out of class, and most students will then learn which cases and statutes should be included in the memo. Even if a student did not do a great job during the research phase, the student *might* be able to earn a good grade on the draft and final project by "borrowing" the research and ideas of others, without going back and completing the research on their own.

Students know they have to turn in high-quality drafts and final versions of the memo to do decently in the course, so built-in incentives exist for these phases. In the long run, however, students who shirk quality research will earn lower grades in legal writing courses, as well as future courses, such as seminars, that require research. And because they never develop efficient research skills, they'll actually spend more time earning those lower grades than their classmates. But the bigger harm will befall the clients of these students, as less effective and less efficient researchers pass the short end of the stick to their clients.

8. One would assume a correlation exists between the amount of time spent on a major legal writing assignment and the result. But we all know students who fruitlessly pour in tons of time inefficiently. What are some of the ways time devoted to a major legal writing assignment is not time well spent?

BOONE: I don't think this should count as time devoted to the assignment, but apparently an amazing amount of time is spent worrying about the assignment and complaining about how hard (or how simple) it is to one's classmates. I would not want students to completely miss this chance to bond with their fellow 1Ls, but they should try not to waste too much time commiserating. Inefficient research and the quest for a perfect outline also take up untold hours. If students have been lost for hours or days in the research or the writing process, they should stop and ask for help. Finally, searching relentlessly for a very clever turn of phrase is probably not the best use of your time.

COUGHLIN: Many law students are competitive. Because many law schools grade on a curve, this population of students want to make sure they are on the top end of that curve. For many students, instead of focusing on answering the question asked by the assignment, they try to go above and beyond the facts and relevant authorities to find alternate areas and authorities to explore so as to make legal arguments that other students are not making. While students may spend inordinate amounts of time researching to come up with unique arguments that no one else may make, it is time that would have been better spent proofing and editing their papers or relaxing with a cup of coffee and newspaper.

While researching all arguments thoroughly is commendable, and spending time thinking about alternative arguments is helpful, students tend to go down tangents and waste a lot of time for minimal or no return. An analogy is going to the doctor and telling her that you have a runny nose, cough, and are achy. You would expect the doctor to say you have a cold and that you need rest and lots of fluids—not to send you in for a full-body MRI in search of any possible ailment.

In legal writing, to maximize time and effort, spend sufficient time researching, writing, editing and proofreading so that you feel comfortable that you have done the best you can. The rest will take care of itself. Even if all the students use the same authorities, every student's thought process is unique. So, be strategic with your time. While you want to consider all viable arguments, don't create arguments that really aren't there.

PATRICK: Students become the most inefficient at two points in time: when they postpone thinking until *after* the research process and, similarly, when they start writing before they've developed a map of how the pieces of the legal argument should be arranged.

Research can seem like a productive time, but it can actually be a waste of time when students avoid critically reading and thinking about the sources *before* wasting time and resources printing them. Thinking during research makes the task a little more difficult, but understanding early on how each source will (or will not) contribute to the answer will certainly save the student a lot of time later in the process. I encourage students to use charts or diagrams along the way to see how the legal authorities relate to each other and how the authorities together answer the legal question.

Once the authorities are compiled, students too frequently want to jump into the writing without first organizing the law around the points they need to explain. Many students have never outlined assignments before writing them, and they utterly resist this step. Outlining or mapping the structure of the arguments saves the writer time and aggravation. Students normally find that once they understand the document's overall organizational structure and the organizational structure within each issue, the writing is not so difficult. To the contrary, students who try to figure out the organization as they write hit a lot of dead ends and usually must discard a lot of what they wrote along the way.

The most successful students quickly learn that producing a solid piece of legal analysis is a multi-step process. Skipping steps inevitably backfires and makes the student's effort less efficient.

9. Related to the previous question, research obviously is a key ingredient of successful legal writing, but ineffective or inefficient research can go on with no end in sight and little to show for it. Any tips for how students can improve the efficiency of their research? How does a student know when he or she has done enough research?

BOONE: To effectively research a legal issue, students must understand two things. First, if there were an easy answer to the question, they probably would not have been asked to research and write about that issue. Second, students must make sure they understand the question. For example, if I ask my students to predict how a California state court will rule on a particular issue, a student who answers only with law from other states has not answered my question effectively. The most relevant law would, of course, be California law. If you are thinking that this student simply failed to follow my instructions, you are partially right. My students don't intentionally disregard the instructions, but they often end up with poor research results because they got lost somewhere in the process. This tends to happen when the students are trying too hard to come up with the "perfect" case to answer my question. When there isn't one, they tend to start changing the question. They are, after all, going to be lawyers, right?

Seriously though, students can research much more efficiently if they keep in mind that there is usually no "golden egg" in the treasure hunt. Students often spend days looking for the "perfect" case to resolve their issue. They quickly discard cases that are fairly similar and provide good rules in the relevant jurisdiction, because they just know that there is a better case out there if they just keep looking. Surely, some court somewhere has addressed this exact issue before! These are great students, and they just know they can find THE answer—even if I have told them there is not one. Once they are completely exhausted and the deadline for the assignment is fast approaching, they realize that those cases they discarded might have been exactly what they needed. That leads us to another suggestion. Students should carefully track their research paths. This allows the exhausted student to avoid further frustration because he can at least go back and find those sources he discarded earlier.

A student has probably done enough initial research when he begins to see the same sources over and over again. When a student starts noticing that all of her sources seem to be citing each other, rather than citing sources the student has not yet seen, she is probably done with this round of research.

COUGHLIN: Take advantage of all training opportunities from Westlaw and Lexis. Not only will you enhance your research skills, you'll have the opportunity to win prizes and eat lots of free pizza.

But do not rely on computerized legal research as your only option. An understanding of print resources will provide you with a better idea of the scope of information you are researching. In addition, computerized legal research has the drawback of being only as good as your search terms. If your search term does not precisely appear in the document, you may miss a big case. You are more likely to get a wider breadth of relevant materials when you combine computerized and print research.

It is difficult to be efficient in legal research at first. Initially, the best way to begin is to use a flow chart and make sure that you document each step or source that you find for easy retrieval in the future. There are many such flow charts or decision trees for basic case law and statutory research skills that will be available in the legal research materials you receive in class or on the web.

As far as knowing when you are finished, a good rule of thumb, as Professor Boone said, is to continue with your initial research until you start seeing the same sources appear over and over again and the cases or sources begin to cite each other.

PATRICK: Efficient and thorough research requires a student to do four things: know the question being asked, follow a methodical process of reviewing sources, keep a trail of where you have been, and above all, think as you go.

Students, and even young lawyers, can be horribly inefficient at research because they do not adhere to those four mandates. Research can be deliciously mindless as one prints off stacks of cases to read later or as one follows tangential queries down a cyberspace rabbit hole. But once that illusion of productivity wears off and that young student or attorney realizes he is no closer to answering the legal question than he was hours or days ago, frustration and panic erupt.

Using a methodical process for research can foster efficient and thorough research. First, always know the exact legal question you are being asked to answer. Usually clients pose narrow legal questions; understanding the question before you delve into myriad sources can save time and energy.

Next, establish a logical method for going through the various sources of authority. Most research texts students will see in law school set out some sort of step-like process to use in research. Understand that process and use it consistently.

Keeping a trail of where you have been and the sources you have checked can be crucial for a successful research project, particularly in real-life practice. Whether in school or practice, finishing a research project at one sitting will not likely happen. In reality, a research project may take several days or weeks and may be interrupted by competing tasks. Keeping a detailed list of search terms, sources, queries, will prevent duplicative research efforts later in the project.

Finally, think as you go. Never print a stack of "possibly relevant" cases to read later when you have time. No one, not even an experienced attorney, can read and assimilate two dozen cases at once. I warn my students to print a source *only* after they know what part of the legal puzzle that source solves. Thinking as you go through the research process is more difficult (and sometimes not as much fun), but saving time and finding the answer efficiently is well worth the effort.

I also echo that research is finished when either your search efforts start to yield the same legal authorities time and again or you run out of time on the project.

10. I'm always all over my seminar students about typos, *Bluebook* errors, formatting mistakes, and other fine points. They think I'm just being an unreasonable nitpicker. You've touched on this, but could you elaborate about how important these finer points are when it comes to evaluating either a student's or lawyer's writing product?

COUGHLIN: The finer points mentioned in the question are essential. While my students may consider my strict attitude toward citation, formatting, etc. frustrating, they generally come to appreciate that precision and attention to detail make the difference in being invited onto the moot court board or law review, or getting a job offer.

Specifically, many times I take a point off the student's final grade for any *Bluebook* error. My philosophy is that these finer points represent the area of your writing product over which the student has the most control. You do not have control over your client's facts, and you do not have control over the state of the law. You cannot control what your professor, judge or senior partner will think of your legal argument because of personal bias or prior life experiences or simply because the law may be against you. You can control, however, citation, formatting, and proofreading.

If you are sloppy with these finer points, your reader will think that your analysis is likewise imprecise. If you are not precise with your typing, your proofreading, your citation, your punctuation, how then will your reader have confidence in your work? For example, when I was in practice, a colleague sent out a letter that was supposed to read "return receipt requested" but instead read "rectum receipt requested." One can imagine recipients having a difficult time placing confidence in the substance of a letter when the heading makes an illicit proposition.

ROCKLIN: You are being a nitpicker, and your students should thank you for it. Let's fast-forward to the question of how important these finer points are in the real world. Imagine you are a lawyer interviewing two job candidates. One candidate walks in wearing a suit and presents you with a crisp, clean resume. The other walks in wearing jeans, flip-flops, and presents you with the same resume content-wise, but full of typos. Which one would you hire? Whether we like it or not, those reading our work make judgments about our capabilities based on its appearance, just as people make judgments about us based on our appearance. Sloppy citations, punctuation, grammar, or formatting will make your reader skeptical about the quality of your analysis.

Because attention to these details matters in the real world, we pay attention to them in legal writing classes. Although legal writing grades are always more dependent on the legal analysis than on mechanics, they will ultimately be lower if the student doesn't pay attention to the "finer points" of grammar, typos, punctuation, and citation errors.

WALTER: The "fine points"—punctuation, usage, grammar, spelling, citation, and formatting—are very important to the overall grade on a legal writing memo and may be even more important in the real world. In my legal writing classes, I give a specific point value for the errors listed above, a value that is typically about 10–15 percent of the overall assignment grade. Committing too many of these errors will cost a student about one-third letter grade, dropping a *B*+ to a *B*, for example.

For legal writing professors who use a more "holistic" grading system rather than a specific point system, I think that the grading penalty for such errors is likely to be even more severe. Why? Because of something called "heuristics." The concept of heuristics is pretty straightforward: when decision-makers are short on time or information, they often make judgments based on more observable factors, even if those factors don't necessarily lead to a purely rational decision. In other words, heuristics are a decision-making shortcut often based on appearances.

In practice, it might operate like this: A trial judge, looking over a three-foot tall stack of court documents so that she can make decisions on dozens of pending motions, begins reading the plaintiff's memo. It's full of typos, the cases are cited incorrectly, and some of the sentences don't make sense because of grammar and usage problems. Frustrated, the judge picks up the defendant's memo. It's perfect. There are no misspellings or typos, the cases are properly cited, and the memo is well written. The defendant could very likely prevail on the motion even if the law actually favors the plaintiff.

It works the same way in legal writing courses. Poor mechanics may cause the grader to undervalue the substance of the writing, giving a lower grade than the substance might otherwise dictate.

* * *

Despite all of the talk in this chapter about the importance of Legal Research and Writing courses, you may end up as one of the many students who don't appreciate the courses until they obtain their first legal job. Legal writing professors hear from these students all the time: "Professor, I really hated—er, well, sorry, not *hated* ... I really *unloved* my legal writing courses while I was taking them,[110] but as soon as I got to my law firm job this summer, I realized what you said is true: they're the most important courses in law school. That's all I did all summer long: research and write!"

---

110. Most law students are sharp enough to recognize the lack of wisdom in telling a professor they hated the professor's course.

CHAPTER 19
THE BLEAK SIDE OF
LAW SCHOOL: ANXIETY,
DEPRESSION, AND
SELF-DOUBT

Can't put it off any longer. I said in the beginning I'd be honest about the good, bad, and ugly of law school, so it's time to share the news that law students typically are not a happy, contented group, at least not according to multiple studies. One law professor offered this grim assessment:

> Law students get sick more frequently than others: headaches, stomachaches, colds, allergies. They have problems in their relationships with friends or family. They worry more than they work. They are continually agitated or lethargic. They gain or lose weight. They take up or increase their chemical crutches, such as caffeine, nicotine, alcohol, or cocaine. They often become angry and bitter—especially at their teachers, sometimes at their colleagues or at the profession—or they withdraw, dropping out, skipping classes, or simply avoiding getting to know their classmates. When called upon in specific stressful situations to use reserves of courage and confidence, they may be debilitated; and they often have no reserves to call upon.[111]

111. B.A. Glesner, *Fear and Loathing in the Law Schools*, 23 CONN. L. REV. 627, 631 (1991).

Well, that doesn't sound good. Let's see what she's talking about.

* * *

Just months before I started law school in 1978, a new book came out: Scott Turow's *One L*. It's the classic book about law school. *One L* tells the story of Turow's experience as a first-year law student at Harvard Law School. The book scared the heck out of me at the time. I didn't really remember why until recently rereading it, when I realized that a dominant theme of the book was negative affect. I counted specific references to: anxiety, fear, stress, panic, vulnerability, self-doubt, shame and grief, wounded self-esteem, unhappiness, paranoia, embarrassment, oppression, and insanity. Turow's 1L story turned out to be my 1L story and the story of many law students since.[112]

This chapter explores the negative psychological impact of law school on students. However, it's important to emphasize up front (ab initio, as we say in the law) that not all law students are overly anxious or depressed. In fact, outwardly, most law students appear to be quite happy. Appearances can be deceiving, but it is true that some students appear to be genuinely unaffected by the aspects of law school that cause other students high anxiety.

If you're a laid-back, happy person by nature and continue that way in law school, be thankful for it. Also be aware, however, that some "no sweat it" law students are laid-back simply because they do not care enough about law school or succeeding in it (or don't understand what it takes to succeed) to undertake the workload with the same motivation as some of their "peace of mind"-challenged classmates. "Sad but true," as James Hetfield of Metallica would sing,[113] many of the most successful law students are obsessive-compulsive worriers. So if you find yourself lying in a fetal position in the corner of the closet clutching your memo in despair, cheer up! It might actually be a good thing.

With that introduction, prepare yourself for some disquieting information about law students.

---

112. *See* Andrew Jay McClurg, *Neurotic, Paranoid Wimps—Nothing Has Changed*, 78 UMKC L. Rev. 1049 (2010) (recounting my rollercoaster 1L experience).

113. METALLICA, SAD BUT TRUE (Elektra 1993).

Anxiety and Generalized Psychological Distress

That a competitive, demanding professional degree program like law school would cause students to be anxious is no big surprise. But the situation is worse than that. Studies have found that psychological distress in law students significantly outpaces not only the general population, but other graduate student populations, including medical students.

As early as 1957 a study comparing law students and medical students found that law students scored higher on an anxiety scale, both in the first year and also at graduation.[114] A 1980s study of law and medical students at the University of Arizona found that the law students scored significantly higher than both the general population and the medical students in nearly every category of psychological dysfunction measured, including anxiety, depression, feelings of inadequacy and inferiority, hostility, and obsessive-compulsiveness.[115] A study of lawyers in Arizona and Washington found that 30 percent of male lawyers and 20 percent of female lawyers exceeded the clinical cut-off for measuring generalized anxiety disorder, compared to 4 percent of the general population.[116]

While law school attracts some people already inclined toward anxiety (such as over-achieving obsessive-compulsive types), evidence suggests a causal relationship between law school and psychological dysfunction. A later study of University of Arizona law students found that law students begin school with psychopathological symptoms similar to the general population, but that those symptoms become substantially elevated during law school and stay that way after graduation. Researchers administered a battery of psychological tests to groups of law students before, during, and after their legal education. Depending on the particular symptom, 20–40 percent of the students reported significantly elevated symptoms above the normal population after starting law school for anxiety, obsessive-compulsiveness, hostility, interpersonal

114. Leonard D. Eron & Robert S. Redmount, *The Effect of Legal Education on Attitudes*, 9 J. LEGAL EDUC. 431 (1957).

115. *See* Stephen B. Shanfield & G. Andrew H. Benjamin, *Psychiatric Distress in Law Students*, 35 J. LEGAL EDUC. 65 (1985).

116. Connie J.A. Beck et al., *Lawyer Distress: Alcohol–Related Problems and Other Psychological Concerns Among a Sample of Practicing Lawyers*, 10 J.L. & HEALTH 1, 49–50 (1995).

sensitivity, paranoid ideation, and psychoticism (social alienation and isolation).[117]

A 2004 study reached similar conclusions about 1Ls.[118] Researchers administered a battery of tests to entering law students at Florida State University to measure their state of happiness, life satisfaction, physical symptoms, and depression. Their scores were compared to a set of advanced undergraduate students at the University of Missouri who took similar tests. The comparison showed that the law students began law school as a contented, normal group, with higher positive affect and life satisfaction scores than the undergraduates. By the end of the first year, however, the law students showed significant reductions in positive affect, life satisfaction, and overall well-being, and increases in negative affect, depression, and physical symptoms.

Several studies suggest that women law students suffer greater anxiety and depression and are more apt to drop out of law school than men, but other studies have found no significant gender differences. A 2000 study of law students at the University of Denver, for example, found that beginning students suffered higher negative affect and depression as they progressed through the first semester, but found no gender differences. The same study found that a month before the end of the first semester, 24 percent of the students agreed or strongly agreed that they considered dropping out of law school, but again, with no gender differences.[119] (One study found that 60 percent of all law students consider quitting.[120])

Anxiety, ranging from mild to extreme, affects nearly all law students. The effects can be both psychological and physiological. Anxiety comes in too many forms for us to try to explore here. The American Psychiatric Association breaks anxiety down into several different disorders in the Diagnostic and Statistical Manual of Mental Disorders (usually called

117. G. Andrew H. Benjamin et al., *The Role of Legal Education in Producing Psychological Distress Among Law Students and Lawyers*, 11 AM. B. FOUND. RES. J. 225, 236 (1986).

118. *See* Kennon M. Sheldon & Lawrence S. Krieger, *Does Legal Education have Undermining Effects on Law Students? Evaluating Changes in Motivation, Values, and Well–Being*, 22 BEHAV.

SCI. & L. 261 (2004) [hereinafter Sheldon & Krieger, *Does Legal Education have Undermining Effects on Law Students?*].

119. Mary E. Pritchard & Daniel N. McIntosh, *What Predicts Adjustment Among Law Students? A Longitudinal Panel Study*, 143 J. SOC. PSYCHOL. 727, 735 (2003).

120. Heins et al., *supra*, at 520.

DSM–IV),[121] including panic disorders, obsessive-compulsive disorders, phobic disorders, and the catch-all generalized anxiety disorder.

Be self-aware. Keep a lookout for worrying that is *excessive and prolonged* and that appears to be *impairing* your ability to function. I once had a first-year student rush out of class thinking she was having a heart attack. I ran out after her and found her sitting on a bench clutching her chest. Her face was flushed and she was sweating and trembling. But it wasn't a heart attack. It was a panic attack.

An overly sensitive Nervous Nellie/Ned? Not at all. She went on to be not only an outstanding law student, but a star at moot court, where she regularly stood before panels of judges who grilled her with tough questions. Law school anxiety does not prey only on the weak. The point of the story is she had no idea she was under such duress. Not only are people good at hiding their distress from others; we often expertly hide it even from ourselves.

Depression

Law students also suffer disproportionately higher rates of depression than the general population and other graduate students. On depression scales, 17–40 percent of law students in the second University of Arizona study mentioned above were found to suffer from depression,[122] much higher rates than exist among the general population.[123]

A 2000 study of University of Michigan law students found that more than half of law students showed symptoms suggestive of clinical depression by the end of their first year and that these high levels remained throughout their law school careers.[124] Comparing the law students' scores on the Center for Epidemiologic Studies Depression Scale to scores for other groups subject to extreme stress yielded somewhat startling results. The 50 percent of law students who scored

---

121. *See generally* AM. PSYCHIATRIC ASS'N, DIAGNOSTIC AND STATISTICAL MANUAL OF MENTAL DISORDERS (4th ed. 2000) [hereinafter DSM–IV].

122. Benjamin et al., *supra*, at 247.

123. According to a 2010 survey by the U.S. Centers for Disease Control, 9 percent of the U.S. adult population experience some depression symptoms, while 3.4 percent meet the definition for clinical depression. Ctr. for Disease Control & Prevention, *Current Depression Among Adults—United States, 2006 and 2008*, 59 MORBIDITY & MORTALITY WKLY. REP. 1229, 1231 (Oct. 1, 2010), http://www.cdc.gov/mmwr/pdf/wk/mm5938.pdf.

124. Alan Reifman et al., *Depression and Affect Among Law Students During Law School: A Longitudinal Study*, 2 J. EMOTIONAL ABUSE 93, 101 (2000).

above the depression cutoff compared to rates of 30–45 percent for unemployed people, 30–45 percent for people testing HIV-positive two weeks after they received notice, 50 percent for people experiencing the death of a spouse or marital separation in the past year, 50–60 percent for persons being treated for substance abuse, and 50–70 percent for homeless people.[125] This isn't to suggest, of course, that being a law student is as bad as the listed traumatic events, but law school can strongly push the brain's depression buttons.

As with anxiety, the gloominess pattern continues after graduation. A Johns Hopkins University study found that lawyers ranked fifth in the overall prevalence of depression out of 105 occupations.[126] When the data were adjusted to focus on the association between depression and the particular occupation by taking into account non-occupational factors contributing to depression, lawyers moved into first place.[127] The study of Arizona and Washington lawyers mentioned above found that 21 percent of male lawyers and 16 percent of female lawyers exceeded the clinical cut-off measure for depression, significantly higher than depression rates found in the general population.[128]

Symptoms of depression to watch out for include:

- Loss of interest or pleasure in activities normally enjoyed

- Social withdrawal

- Reduced (or sometimes increased) appetite

- Decreased energy

- Feelings of worthlessness or guilt

- Persistent irritability or anger

- Feeling "blah"

- Brooding

- Obsessive rumination about minor failings

- Difficulty concentrating

- Memory difficulties

125. *Id.*

126. *See* William W. Eaton et al., *Occupations and the Prevalence of Major Depressive Disorder*, 32 J. OCCUPATIONAL MED. 1079, 1082 tbl. 1 (1990).

127. *Id.* at 1085 tbl. 3.

128. Beck et al., *supra*, at 49–50.

- Insomnia or other changes in sleep patterns
- Loss of interest/desire in sex
- Recurrent thoughts of death or suicidal ideation[129]

If you're suffering from anxiety or depression, or think you might be, seek help. Most universities have counseling departments where students can obtain free, confidential counseling services. Call and make an appointment. Don't delay. Don't accept depression as a normal consequence of law school. Take to heart the comments of this student who when asked what single piece of advice she would give to a close friend or relative starting law school said:

> Stay psychologically sound and watch for warning signs. I already had a graduate degree when I came here and was still overwhelmed by the culture of fear they promote and the massive inferiority I felt as a result. I only survived the first semester because I sought psychological counseling from the amazing university counseling center. The day I finally went, it was beautiful outside, and I wasn't feeling as bad. "You don't need help," I told myself. But I knew when I woke up the next morning at 4:30 (I could no longer control my sleep habits) with nervous anxiety, it would be no different. The anxiety gave way to major depression, and I started taking anti-depressants shortly before finals. I was a new person.

There's no shame in experiencing psychological distress or seeking counseling for it. Simply unloading one's pent-up feelings to a neutral listener can be therapeutic. I talk to my students in class about depression and, each time, a couple of them contact me confidentially afterwards to say thank you, explaining that simply having someone acknowledge the issue helped them feel less alone.

Self–Doubt

Law school is the undisputed champion of causing talented people, people who have achieved at a high level their entire lives, to almost instantly begin questioning their self-worth. As one student put it, "It seems that law school is *designed* to make the student feel unsure of himself and inadequate." Other students amplified the point:

---

129. *See* DSM–IV, *supra*, at 349–52.

- Law school is where smart people go to feel dumb. It is difficult having gone through life being at the top of the academic heap to deal with the stress involved in having to lower one's expectations for perform-ance.

- I feel like I came here being a really good public speaker and writer. I've won awards for both. Some-how, law school has managed to turn that on its head. I'm apparently a bad public speaker and a mediocre writer at best.

- My biggest change in personality is a complete loss of self-confidence and feeling of self-worth.

"Cognitive distortion" is a psychological term used to describe a condition that occurs when a person internalizes neutral or mildly negative external stimuli as signs of severe personal failure.[130] Law school establishes optimal conditions for this to occur. Everything a student does is judged and it never seems good enough. Every word uttered in law school classes is critically scrutinized. Professors often critique stu-dent classroom comments even when they wholeheartedly agree with them. It's the nature of the Socratic beast. Some students shrug it off, but many take it personally and let it diminish their self-image. As Beck and Burns said:

> As part of his internal recurring, cognitive pattern, [the student] globalizes and catastrophizes. He views any evidence of substandard performance as ... cata-clysmic to himself, his friends and family. For instance, the student may evaluate his classroom performance as poor. When reciting in class, he fumbles, blanks out or is told by his professor that he is wrong. He views his inadequate performance as conclusive evidence that all his classmates are superior to him (globalizing). He is convinced if he continues in school, he will humiliate himself, his friends and family (catastrophizing). He will be dropped or placed at the bottom of his class.[131]

A large part of the problem is that most law students have never before felt matched or over-matched by their class-

---

130. Phyllis W. Beck & David Burns, *Anxiety and Depression in Law Stu-dents: Cognitive Intervention*, 30 J. LE-GAL EDUC. 270, 273 (1979–1980).

131. *Id.* at 274.

mates. Their previous educational experiences taught them they were the best. Now comes law school, filled with smart people and administered in a way that puts one's work habits and thinking-skills on public display every day.

If you find yourself struggling, it's important to stop and recognize that most other students are feeling the same way, even the ones who appear to have it all together. Despite receiving high grades, law school shook my confidence so deeply that it took until midway through the first year before I voluntarily raised my hand in class for the first time. Our Property professor was everyone's favorite, an excellent teacher with a great sense of humor. One day he asked a simple question. "What is the legal relationship of bank to bank depositor?" Several hands went up. "Bailor-bailee?" "Wrong." "Assignor-assignee?" "Wrong." "Mortagor-mortagee?" "Wrong." This kept going until the class had tossed out every possible combination of two words ending with "or" and "ee." All but one. I thought I knew the answer.

This was it. My moment of glory. I took a deep breath and stabbed my hand in the air.

"Mr. McClurg?"

"Lendor-lendee?"

"Wrong!"

Dang. The correct answer was debtor-creditor. Double "or"-words! Who would have thought? Another law school trick on the mind. O for 1. In *One L*, Scott Turow described a similar experience and crisis of confidence when he gave a wrong answer in Criminal Law. He said it made him feel "horribly embarrassed—worse than that, corrosively ashamed."[132]

* * *

It might not be too late to get your law school deposit back. Just kidding. Pretty grim chapter, I know, but don't worry. Law school isn't all gloom and doom. The research just makes it look that way. No one has ever studied the positive aspects of law school, of which there are many. Here's a happy statistic that might surprise you in light of

---

132. TUROW, *supra*, at 103.

what you just read: 83 percent of the 33,000 students who responded to the 2011 Law School Survey of Student Engagement rated their law school experience as either good or excellent.[133]

Sure, law school is a challenge, but it's supposed to be. It obviously is doable though, or we wouldn't have 1.1 million lawyers in America. I like this comment from a student asked whether her first year was better or worse than expected:

> I love law school. I love the material, the professors, my classmates, and especially those few close friends I've connected with and grown close to. Law school is definitely more challenging in so many ways than I ever could have anticipated, but that's what makes it great. If it was easy, I can say in all honesty that I would be disappointed. It's supposed to be hard because it means something. The challenges are what help us grow and learn and open our minds and I wouldn't have it any other way.

Recognize that the studies showing higher rates of psychological dysfunction in law students do not predict an outcome for any individual student and also take comfort in the fact that law school inflicts its most visceral impact on students in the first year. There is truth in the old law school adage: "In the first year they scare you to death, in the second year they work you to death, and in the third year they bore you to death."

While research shows that law student psychological dysfunction continues into the third year and even past graduation, the most intense whirly rides of anxiety and emotion occur in the first year, especially the first semester, when there is so much uncertainty. After that, things settle down and life falls into a more or less normal pattern. Stressors undergo a fundamental reprioritizing. Panic over the Socratic method and exams is replaced by external worries about finding a job and paying back student loans. These external pressures are significant, but in terms of day-to-day law school, most 3Ls do, in fact, seem more bored than afraid.

---

133. LAW SCH. SURVEY OF STUDENT ENGAGEMENT, 2011 ANNUAL SURVEY RESULTS: NAVIGATING LAW SCHOOL: PATHS IN LEGAL EDUCATION 8 (2011) [hereinafter 2011 LAW SCH. SURVEY OF STUDENT ENGAGEMENT].

My first year was marked by heavy stress, but by the third year, I was loving law school so much I didn't want to leave. Loved it so much that I decided to come back and stay forever. As you're counting the days until you become a 3L, let's consider some strategies for managing stress and maintaining well-being.

CHAPTER 20
MAINTAINING WELL-BEING

To the extent law school is responsible for causing emotional distress in law students, one doesn't have to look far for plausible explanations: the heavy emphasis on grades and corresponding worries about failure, the competitive environment, high student-teacher ratios, intimidating instructional methods, professors who are sometimes imperious and distant, brutal workloads, lack of performance feedback, the adversarial nature of the legal system in which law students are constantly immersed, the emphasis on objective analytical thinking over personal values and emotions, strains on personal relationships, doubts about whether law school is the right career path, burdensome debt-loads, worries about getting a job, and, of course, for 1Ls, general fear and uncertainty about what to expect.

Stress isn't inherently bad. In proper doses, it can be a good source of motivation. As a law student, for example, I felt tremendous pressure to not sound stupid in class in front of my peers. That made me work harder in preparing for class—not a bad thing. Some degree of law school stress is inevitable and unavoidable, just as "military stress" is unavoidable for service members, "relationship stress" for couples, and "parenting stress" for mothers and fathers.

Law school takes a heavier psychological toll on some students than others, some of which is attributable to personality makeup. Happiness research shows that from 40–80 percent of a person's happiness level is determined by genetics.[134] But *all* law students have a substantial degree of

---

134. NANCY LEVIT & DOUGLAS O. LINDER, THE HAPPY LAWYER: MAKING A GOOD LIFE IN THE LAW 33 (2010) (discussing research of genetic contributions to happiness levels).

control over their well-being by the choices—lifestyle and otherwise—they make. This chapter discusses a dozen strategies to reduce your stress, keep your spirits up, and generally maintain a higher level of well-being.

Get and Stay in Good Physical Shape

The first year of law school is part academic test and part endurance test. It will tax your mind and body to the limits. As one commentator said, "Physical and psychological exhaustion are, I think, programmed into the first year."[135] As the first semester progresses past the halfway mark, classrooms start sounding like tuberculosis wards as more and more students begin showing up sick. The reasonable apprehension about missing class and, hence, important material that could be on the exam, keeps students coming to class—and spreading germs—when they'd be better off at home in bed.

One student consultant shared this tale, which is at once funny, disconcerting, and a revealing statement about law school:

> During the second semester, it seemed like everyone in our class was coming down with the flu. When I felt that familiar achy, feverish feeling one morning, I cried. Literally, I cried because I knew there was no way I could skip class or slow down. So I struggled through that day and the next and finally went to the health clinic on campus. When the nurse practitioner asked if I had been exposed to anyone who had the flu, I said, "Well, three people who sit next to me have it." She asked if they had been coming to class and I said, "Yeah. I mean, we are in law school. You can't miss class." She got this very frustrated look on her face and said emphatically, "Well, if that's the case then maybe we should make the entire law school get flu shots next year so you don't infect the whole campus!"

I felt guilty reading her story because I'm part of the problem in repeatedly emphasizing how important it is to not miss class. In any event, although you can't control the sick people next to you, you can help yourself by arriving at law school in

135. Stephen C. Halpern, *On the Politics and Pathology of Legal Education*, 32 J. LEGAL EDUC. 383, 388 (1982).

good physical shape and paying attention to keeping it that way.

Exercise is a proven stress reliever and promoter of physical and mental well-being. Indeed, a list of the benefits from regular exercise resembles a cure-all prescription for many of the ailments suffered by law students. Exercise reduces depression and anxiety and increases energy, strength, and stamina. It improves mental acuity, enhances the immune system, promotes better sleep, and raises self-esteem.

Join the university's fitness center. Memberships usually are available at low cost to students or included as part of student fees. Use the stairs instead of the elevator at law school. Do bicep curls with your Contracts and Property casebooks. Just find a way to work exercise into your routine. Also concentrate on maintaining a healthy diet (it's *very* easy to fall into a fast-food habit in law school), go to bed at a reasonable time, and at least *try* to avoid germs. Most illnesses are spread through hand-to-mouth contact. Wash your hands frequently. Carry and use an anti-bacterial hand sanitizer.

Staying healthy will enable you to stay consistent, and staying consistent will help prevent you from falling behind, one of the major causes of stress in law students.

Beware of Alcohol and Other Substance Abuse

Lawyers like to drink. Alcohol flows freely whenever and wherever they gather socially. Several studies have documented alcohol problems in the legal profession. A survey of North Carolina lawyers found that nearly 17 percent reported consuming three to five drinks a day. A study of Washington lawyers concluded from a random sample that 18 percent of practicing lawyers were "problem drinkers." One researcher of alcoholism among lawyers estimated that at least 15 percent of lawyers are alcoholics, compared to 7–8 percent of the general population.[136] Although the data are less extensive, statistics also show that abuse of other chemical substances is prevalent among lawyers.

Alcohol and other substance abuse reportedly are involved in 50–70 percent of all disciplinary actions against attor-

---

136. Patrick J. Schiltz, *On Being a Happy, Healthy, and Ethical Member of an Unhappy, Unhealthy, and Unethical* *Profession*, 52 Vand. L. Rev. 871, 876–77 (1999) (collecting and reporting on these studies).

neys.[137] Small wonder that every state bar organization maintains a lawyer assistance program for substance abuse and other mental health problems.

Law students enjoy alcohol as well. In one survey, more than one-third of law students answered affirmatively to the question: "Do you think you drink too much?"[138] And those were the ones who recognized they had an alcohol issue. Many people don't. A George Mason University study found that 11 percent of law students experienced eight or more hangovers during the previous semester, while 36 percent experienced one to three hangovers.[139] The 2010–2011 report of the Illinois Lawyers Assistance Program, launched in 1980 as one of the first such programs in the country, stated that "the most noticeable change" in the data regarding persons seeking help was an increase in the number of law students, up from 5 percent in 2008–2009 to 16 percent of the total in 2010–2011.[140]

Law schools may contribute to the problem by maintaining and fostering structures and activities that emphasize the consumption of alcohol. In addition to teaching students "to think like a lawyer," law school culture could be accused of teaching students "to drink like a lawyer." At some schools, student organizations sponsor weekly social events for students at local bars that amount to little more than drinking-fests.

Following a Torts class discussing the potential liability of individuals and businesses for providing alcohol to persons who then drive drunk and cause injury, a student asked if he could speak with me privately. Because first-semester grades had just come out, I was expecting a sad story about his Torts grade. Instead, he said: "Professor, I didn't want to bring this up in the class discussion because I didn't want the class to turn against me, but I don't understand how or why law schools encourage so much drinking."

---

137. Carol Langford, *Depression, Substance Abuse, and Intellectual Property Lawyers*, 53 U. KAN. L. REV. 875, 902 (2005) (stating that an ABA survey of California and New York lawyers "determined that 50 to 70 percent of all disciplinary cases involved alcoholism").

138. Heins et al., *supra*, at 521.

139. *See* Gerald W. Boston, *Chemical Dependency in Legal Education: Problems and Strategies*, 76 MICH. B.J. 298, 299 (1997) (discussing this study).

140. LAWYERS' ASSISTANCE PROGRAM, ANNUAL REPORT 2010–2011, at 8.

He described a social event promoted by the student government organization in which the local bar association offered free drinks at a bar during a happy hour. "Everyone just came for the free drinks," he said. "Because they were free, people were pouring them down as fast as they could. When the free drinks ended, everyone just got in their cars and drove somewhere else." He went on to describe ugly scenes at other law school social events where some students get "falling-down drunk." "You'd never recognize them from class, Professor," he said.

Substance abuse is an issue at all law schools, just as it is at all undergraduate institutions, not surprising since most law students are only shortly removed from undergraduate school. But the stakes are higher in law school. Students learning to become professionals have to face the fact that, whether they like it or not, they can't continue behaving like undergraduate party animals.

Not all substance abuse is for partying. I hear repeated tales from law students about the widespread use, particularly around exam time, of Adderall and other stimulants commonly prescribed for attention deficit disorder. According to one source, so common is its use that students excitedly announce, "I found someone to sell me the 15 mgs for four bucks instead of five. Only seven bucks for the 20 mgs!" In addition to obvious health concerns, taking prescription drugs without a prescription is illegal.

Excessive drinking or other substance abuse is problematic for law students on several fronts. First, alcohol is a depressant, so while it might provide short-term relief for stress, it actually feeds depression. A close association between depression and heavy alcohol use is well-established by research. Second, the adverse consequences of an arrest for drunk-driving or other substance-related illegalities are substantially enhanced for law students, who have a much stronger interest in maintaining a good reputation and clean record than they did as undergraduate students. State bar organizations conduct thorough background checks of applicants. Misconduct in law school that might have been excused as youthful indiscretion had it occurred in undergraduate school will be more carefully scrutinized and harshly judged.

Drinking too much in public carries its own pitfalls. Not uncommonly, intoxicated students embarrass themselves in front of their colleagues, unwisely pose for party pics that get posted online,[141] and even become victims or perpetrators of sexual assaults. You can count on the fact that any untoward behavior at a law school social gathering will be quickly and widely circulated among your peers.

Don't Fall Behind

This piece of advice sounds *so* familiar to me, but I just can't place where I've heard it before. Oh yeah, I remember. It was in Chapter 2 ... and Chapter 10 ... and Chapter 13 ...

One of the surest ways to ratchet up your anxiety level, and one of the most dangerous pitfalls to avoid in law school, is falling behind. Not only are consistent students who stay current more academically successful, they can justifiably feel more confident and less stressed-out because they don't have to go to bed every night worrying about how far behind they are.

Believe what I and law students tell you throughout this book: once you fall behind in law school, it is literally impossible to catch up. There are no restful gaps in law school semesters that one can use to get up to speed. Every day brings new cases, new concepts, and new rules in each course. Weekends are usually needed for outlining, periodic review, or working on legal writing assignments. Dismal as it might sound, my greatest joy of the Thanksgiving holiday in my first year of law school was that I had two full extra days to study. The risk of falling behind is exponentially higher for part-time evening students. Chapter 22 addresses the unique challenges that they face.

Previous chapters have emphasized the importance of being a consistent, organized law student—i.e., one who doesn't fall behind—and offered specific suggestions on how to stay that way.

Find and Maintain a Healthy Support Network of Positive-Minded Classmates

We all need the support of loved ones when we're going through an ordeal and law school is quite the ordeal. It's

---

141. Here's a useful tip: Before allowing anyone to take a picture of you in a social setting, set aside any alcohol containers so they do not appear in the picture.

well-established in academic literature that social support promotes well-being. Being involved in a happy intimate relationship, for example, has been shown to have positive effects on overall well-being—all the more reason to pay attention to and take care of your preexisting relationships when you arrive at law school. (Chapter 23 covers outside relationship issues.)

Unfortunately, your non-law school loved ones aren't going to be able to help with some of your law school travails because they won't understand what you're going through. To the contrary, they might be or seem overtly unsupportive because they feel neglected and jealous of the time you're devoting to your new endeavor. Thus, in addition to your non-law school champions, you'll need a social support network within law school.

Fortunately, making friends in law school is easy because of the psychological bonding effects of group terror. In a famous social psychology experiment, researchers put a group of monkeys in the same cage with a group of lions. Monkeys and lions usually don't socialize because the lions eat the monkeys, which causes hard feelings. Early in the experiment, it appeared events would follow this customary pattern as the lions began chasing the monkeys and the monkeys began bonking the lions on the heads with coconuts.

At this point, the researchers inserted a Contracts professor into the cage who began conducting a Socratic dialogue about the doctrine of promissory estoppel. An amazing transformation occurred. The lions and monkeys immediately locked paws and began singing pub songs. Within a few minutes, the lions were giving the monkeys foot massages and the monkeys were encouraging the lions to get in touch with their inner cubs.

Okay, that wasn't a real experiment, but I'm confident it would work out that way. That's what happened to me. Normally, I'm quite shy, but on the first day of law school orientation I was anxious and desperate to make a friend. We were packed like matchsticks into an auditorium, sitting in alphabetical order. Speaker after speaker took the podium, but the only thing I remember them emphasizing was the lack of bathroom facilities in the law school. I'm sure they talked about other things, but that's what stood out. The way people went on and on about it, adequate restroom facilities seemed to be the most important issue in legal education.

After the speeches, we were divided into groups, still in alphabetical order. A 3L took us on a tour of the law school. We traipsed in single file down hallways, through classrooms and finally into the library, where in a narrow aisle between the stacks a large puddle on the floor blocked our passage. Everyone, including our 3L tour guide, stood stymied staring at the puddle until the guy behind me deadpanned, "I guess they weren't joking about the bathrooms." In the stress of the circumstances, this struck me as hilarious. I turned and introduced myself to James H. "Mac" McCarty, Jr. Mac and I went on to form a study group together and even became roommates. We spent many law school days and nights working and playing together.

To this day, good old Mac is one of my favorite people in the world. Every student will find their own "Mac" in law school. I guarantee that the friendships you develop will be one of the best features of your legal education. Some of them will last a lifetime.

Your law school friends can be a lifeline to maintaining your well-being. They will give you someone to vent to (don't overdo it), borrow notes from, ask clarifying questions of, laugh, cry, mourn, and celebrate with. Hold on to them for dear life and treat them well. You'll need them and they'll need you.

In forming your inner circle, seek people who are generally optimistic about life, even if cynically so. Nattering Nabobs of Negativism, described in Chapter 4, should be avoided lest they pull you down into their pit of pessimism and despair. A 1L recently shared this tale of an encounter she had with a Nattering Nabob:

> The other day I made the mistake of muttering "Good Morning" to one of my peers. Apparently, this is all the carrot one must dangle for a Nattering Nabob of Negativism to launch into a soul-sucking tirade, against legal writing instructors, Emanuel Outlines, exams ... I was cornered for ten minutes by this person, with whom I'd never spoken before, while she drained the lifeblood out of me with her incessant complaining.

If you get trapped by a Nattering Nabob of Negativism, tell them you've enjoyed talking with them and wish you could stay longer, but are running late for a root canal you've been looking forward to, then sprint in the other direction.

Don't Take On Stressful Situations That Can Be Avoided or Postponed

With law school supplying plenty of stress already, avoid situations that will predictably add even more psychological distress. The classic example that comes to mind is starting or ending intimate relationships. Starting a new romantic relationship can be exhilarating, of course, but it's also a huge distraction. Who can concentrate on *Pennoyer v. Neff* when they're worrying about things like, "Does she like me or does she LIKE me, like me?" There's a reason why Little Anthony and the Imperials' 1964 hit, *Goin' Out of My Head* has sold more than four million copies.

Ending bad relationships can be a blessing in the long term, but causes pain, longing, and distraction in the short term even when the dissolution is in everyone's best interests. So long as the relationship is tolerable (i.e., blah rather than harmful), you might be better off sticking it out at least until you're between semesters. Way back in Chapter 2, I recommended terminating relationships that are already on life support *before* you arrive at law school.

Then, of course, there are law school intimate relationships. Insert a large group of bright, interesting, and attractive men and women in a closed setting and, well, you know what's going to happen. Some of them are going to hook up. Often this can be a good thing, as I've known many students who met in law school and went on to get married. But for every fairy tale law school romance that ends in wedded bliss, messy entanglements occur that never should have seen the light of day.

Romantic relationships between first-year law students are particularly problematic because unlike most other intimate relationships, when they fail, you can't escape from the person. In a normal breakup, parting sentiments such as "I never want to see your ugly face again!" can be enforced. Not so in law school. Even if you end up detesting your former paramour, you'll be trapped in the same room with him or her every day for at least one year and in the same building for three years. When I asked a group of 1Ls nearing the completion of their first year what advice they would give to new law students, one student wrote:

> I have some ideas of what not to do. This lesson I found very important. I got sucked into the social scene of school too much the first semester. It is reflected in my grades. I started off strong but after a couple of weeks I chased a girl around and we had a relationship. But when it was over and exams rolled around I found that I couldn't concentrate on my studies. If I had to do it over I would focus on school and not worry too much with going out during the week (or weekend). Though hanging out with class-mates is a good thing, too much can be very bad. It clouds the mind.

Relationships are just one example. Other major distractions can include family, financial, health, and work situations. Some of them can't be avoided, of course, but avoid the ones you can.

Use Study Aids to Bolster Confidence

As discussed back in Chapter 3, one of the greatest law student fears is that they won't understand the material. It's scary to feel like you're in the dark about what you're supposed to be learning. In a normal higher-education environment, students can rely on the course textbook and the professor, together, to teach them what they need to know. But, of course, we've seen that law school is not a normal learning environment. The case method and nature of case-books preclude your textbook from being a reliable place to turn for answers and the Socratic method of teaching can interfere with your professors being an in-class source of understanding.

These are key reasons why supplemental study aids are so popular in law school. In undergraduate school, you didn't have to buy extra books to explain the book assigned for the course. In law school, you'll probably have to, at least for some courses. In addition to helping you learn the law for exam purposes, study aids can bolster your confidence and sense of self-efficacy by flipping on light bulbs in your murky confusion.

Study aids are particularly helpful for reducing anxiety (and enhancing performance) in classes taught by professors who either rely exclusively on Socratic questioning or who simply are poor or disorganized communicators. Most law professors supplement Socratic dialogue with explanatory lecture, but not all professorial presentations are models of clarity. Whether due to their own non-linear thinking patterns, lack of preparation, or an intentional design to "hide the ball," some professors are masters of obfuscation. Even clear, well-organized professors won't be able to explain everything in class thoroughly, in part because imparting information is not the sole goal of first-year classes and in part because there's just not enough class time. Or they'll explain things too quickly to absorb or write down.

One student consultant recommended reading the relevant sections of reliable study aids *prior* to attending classes on the theory that it allows one to enter the room with more confidence, already possessing a mental framework for processing the material covered that day. The downside of such an approach is that students may enter the classroom with preconceived notions of what they should be getting out of the day's presentation, which might conflict with the professor's goals. But if it helps to substantially promote confidence and well-being, as she swears it did for her, that risk might be an acceptable trade-off.

One type of study aid warrants specific mention: "canned briefs," either from a hardcopy study aid or an online source. Law professors hate canned briefs because too many students rely on them in lieu of preparing their own briefs. They also can be inaccurate or include extra facts not included in the edited casebook version of the case—i.e., the case the professor and everyone else read. Law professors have been known to take great delight in exposing students they think are relying on canned briefs. Canned briefs can serve a useful purpose though. As we saw back in the case-briefing chapter, even top students often use canned briefs as a *supplement* to their own conscientious reading and briefing of the cases. They can be helpful in clueing you in on what to look for in a case and for summarizing complex fact patterns.

Establish Contact with a Faculty Member You Like and Respect

In their study documenting elevated psychological distress in law students, Benjamin and colleagues noted that one cause may be the high student-teacher ratios that exist at most law schools. They speculated that the resulting distant relationship between law students and faculty is "related significantly" to student dissatisfaction.[142] More than one-third of law students in a national education survey reported that they "felt substantial or severe stress because they were unable to establish rapport with faculty."[143]

Back in 1975, 84 percent of law students responding to a survey said they had no faculty member who took an interest in their academic progress and 71 percent said they had no faculty member to turn to for personal advice.[144] Recent evidence suggests a welcome trend in a positive direction. Data collected for the 2012 Law School Survey of Student Engagement showed that 82 percent of responding 1Ls had discussed career plans with a faculty member[145] and 55 percent rated their relationships with faculty highly with respect to availability, helpfulness, and being sympathetic.[146]

Having a faculty contact can make you feel more comfortable, connected to, and at home in your law school environment, as well as give you a person to turn to for advice and other help. Chapter 9 gives specific suggestions about how to get to know your professors.

Live Frugally to Minimize Debt

Early on, as part of your pre-arrival trip planning, I urged you to pay particular attention to developing a plan for how you intend to finance your legal education. Piling up debt is a major source of anxiety—justifiably so—for law students, especially in uncertain economic times.

Unfortunately, it has become increasingly difficult for students to avoid substantial loan debt due to rising tuition costs. Between 1985 and 2009, the average tuition at private law schools soared 375 percent compared to a 97 percent cost-of-living increase.[147] In the same period, the average annual

142. Benjamin et al., *supra*, at 249.

143. WHITMAN ET AL., *supra*, at 58 (discussing this survey).

144. Carl A. Auerbach, *Legal Education and Some of Its Discontents*, 34 J. LEGAL EDUC. 43, 57 (1984).

145. *Frequency Distributions, 1L Students, in* 2012 LAW SCH. SURVEY OF STUDENT ENGAGEMENT, *supra*.

146. *Id.*

147. Philip G. Schrag & Charles W. Pruett, *Coordinating Loan Repayment Assistance Programs With New Federal Legislation*, 60 J. LEGAL EDUC. 583, 585 (2011).

tuition at public law schools rose from $5,000 to more than $30,000.[148]

I was fortunate to escape law school with minimal debt, in large part because tuition was cheap, but also because my law school mates and I lived at a very low standard of living. Five of us shared a ramshackle house, so rent was cheap. We didn't use the air conditioning even though it's hot as Hades in Gainesville, Florida for much of the year. We never ate out, so food was cheap. For lunch, I took a can of tuna and piece of bread to school on most days. We picked our entertainment based on cost. Our big nights out were parties in the backyard or a couple pitchers of cheap beer during happy hours. We didn't take vacations. Our cars were falling apart. We didn't buy clothes. This isn't a sob story. To the contrary, we were probably happier then than we've ever been.

I'm convinced that even in this era of rising tuition law students could shave a substantial percentage off their loan debt by living more frugally. Compare my Spartan law school lifestyle to many of today's debt-ridden law students: they live alone without roommates, drive nice cars, eat out frequently, own smart phones and pay for monthly data plans, drink $5 cups of coffee like water (which they also buy instead of turning on the tap), enjoy $15 martinis, take vacations, belong to health clubs, etc.

Witnessing the lack of money consciousness of some debt-burdened students reminds me of a time when my daughter was a small child. We were driving and she was barraging me with one of her gazillion requests to buy her something. It might have been "Baby Uh–Oh," a doll that soiled its diaper. I remember that being a must-have item among the toddling set at the time. Whatever it was, I said in my best Ward Cleaver voice: "Honey, that costs money. We don't have money to buy everything you want." She said innocently, "Daddy, just go to the machine that gives out the money," referring to an ATM machine. With student loan money so easily available, it seems like some students view the student loan spigot the same way my kid viewed the ATM machine: as if it's free money.

Being frugal requires short-term sacrifices, but they will be worth it. The debt you accrue will weigh you down for

---

148. *Id.*

many years and, justifiably, can add tremendous stress to your law school experience.

Students can—and should—scrimp in all areas of consumption, but the easiest way to cut expenses *substantially* is through shared living. Students sometimes mention their woes to me, and they often involve finances. One student recently complained about the size of her student debt. I asked if she lived by herself or with roommates, mentioning she could save a lot of money by living with roommates. She said, "Oh, I don't really like living with roommates." A couple weeks later another student told me his debt fears were tearing him apart, causing him to not be able to sleep at night and making him think about dropping out of law school. "Do you live by yourself or with roommates?" I asked. "Myself. I don't like living with roommates."

Most people don't like living with roommates! I didn't. I'm an introvert. But living communally is the single most effective way to cut student debt-load. Students can't control the direct costs of education (tuition, books, fees). They can only control their consumption expenses, and housing is the largest consumption expense of them all.

If you're moving to a new city to attend school and are in search of roommates, check with your law school admissions office. They sometimes provide formal or informal roommate matching services. Also, many law schools establish Facebook pages for new students on which students post roommate solicitations.

Here's another possibility to consider on the dwelling front: attending law school where your parents live and requesting if you can move back in with them. You may be shrieking at the thought. Your parents might shriek even louder. Poor things. Just when they thought they could get a little privacy and be rid of your dirty dishes and loud music. But what if you could save fifty thousand dollars in room and board—and debt—over three years? It's definitely worth considering.

A substantial amount of information about budgeting and managing student debt is readily available, both in book form and online, including specific information for grad students dealing with loan debt. A good place to start looking is the Law School Admission Council (LSAC) website, which provides a load of information and related links on financing law

school: http://www.lsac.org/jd/finance/financial-aid-repay
ment.asp.

Make a point of getting up to speed on federal legislation
designed to reduce the burden of student loan debt. Congress
enacted four laws between 2005 and 2010, culminating (as of
this writing) with the Education Reconciliation Act of 2010.
Together, these laws contain significant provisions easing
educational debt repayment, including a reduction in monthly payment requirements and a shortened loan forgiveness
date. Monthly loan repayment plans are based on income.
Previously, student loan payments could not exceed 15 percent of income. Under current law, that percentage is 10
percent. The laws also cut the loan forgiveness date from
twenty-five years to twenty years.

The best news is for students interested in pursuing a
career in public interest law. Many students come to law
school wanting to help people. They want to practice public
interest law, such as working for a government agency or a
non-profit organization, but their high student debt prevents
them from pursuing these internally rewarding, but lower-
paying jobs. For graduates who go into public service, federal
legislation cuts the loan forgiveness period in half, from
twenty to ten years. The federal legislation defines public
service broadly as any full-time employment by any federal,
state, local, or tribal entity or any non-profit organization.[149]
Hopefully, these laws will remain intact, but with budget-
cutting high on the national agenda, that's not a sure bet.

In addition to the federal legislation, sixteen states and
the District of Columbia sponsor loan repayment assistance
programs, or "LRAPs," for law graduates who take public
interest jobs, while more than 100 law schools offer their own
LRAPs for such students.[150] If you're interested in public
service law, be sure to investigate these programs. The details vary significantly from school to school.[151]

All is not bleak in the financial picture. Take heart that,
over time, most lawyers will earn salaries sufficient to live
comfortable lives, although it may take several years. According to 2011 U.S. Bureau of Labor data, the average income

149. *Id.* at 592.

150. LEVIT & LINDER, *supra* at 137
(discussing loan repayment assistance
programs).

151. *See* Schrag & Pruett, *supra*
(thoroughly explaining both the federal
legislation and law school LRAPs).

for lawyers is \$130,000, fifth among all professions (doctors top the list).[152]

Don't Give Up Your Primary Hobby/Interest

All law students need a healthy non-law school related outlet for their energy, something they find fun and that requires focus in a way that preempts obsessive thinking and worrying about law school. One of the neat things about law students is how multi-faceted they are. On my entering-student questionnaire, I ask students to list their outside interests. Reading about their interesting hobbies and hidden talents always leaves me impressed. As a conversation point, when I run into students outside of class, I'll sometimes ask, based on their questionnaires: "So do you still like to [play Frisbee golf/write poetry/collect lunch boxes/build cabinets, etc.]?" More often than not, the answer is something like, "No, I had to give that up when I started law school. There wasn't enough time."

Wrong answer! There *is* enough time to continue a fun, non-law related recreational pursuit if you develop and implement effective time-management skills. Maybe not to the same degree you engaged in it prior to law school, but enough time to enjoy the benefits of it. If it's an activity you're good at, so much the better. Because law school can inflict such a beating on one's sense of self-worth, it's comforting, confidence-boosting, and relaxing to partake in a hobby you know you're better at than your classmates and even your professors.

Nearly every day for my entire three years of law school, I carved out an hour or so in the evening to just sit around playing my acoustic guitar. It helped me stay sane and took my mind off my troubles. Whether your passion is a musical instrument, chess, rugby, or bird-watching, make a deal with yourself before you start law school that you will not give it up.

Treat Yourself to a Day Off

Related to the above, all work and no play makes Jack and Jill Law Student not only dull boys and girls, but candidates

---

152. Press Release, Bureau of Labor Statistics, Occupational Employment and Wages—May 2011 12 tbl. 1 (Mar. 27, 2012), http://www.bls.gov/news.release/pdf/ocwage.pdf.

for early mental health intervention. Set aside at least one day and night a week to relax and unwind. If you have a significant other, this is vital not only to you, but to your partner and to you both as a couple. Don't feel guilty about it or look at a night off as wasted time. Look at it as recharging your batteries so you'll be more effective when you get back to work the next day.

Make it a point to leave law school behind during these R & R breaks. This is much easier said than done, particularly if your time off involves socializing with law students. If you end up sitting around talking or complaining about law school the entire time—as many students do during social activities—you're not really spending time away from law school, which partly defeats the purpose.

Turn it into a contest: every time a person mentions anything about law school, they have to pay a penalty of some type. I held an end-of-the-year party at my house for my Torts students. One of the student party organizers came up with a game in which each student was issued three clothespins on arrival. If a student mentioned anything about law school, anyone who overheard the statement could take one of their clothespins. The students with the most clothes-pins at the end of the party received prizes.

Being intense and competitive, the students really got into the contest. Nevertheless, even the most determined players regularly slipped up. All afternoon, I heard cries of "Gotcha!" and "Darn!" as students snatched clothespins back and forth. (Particularly amusing were the lengthy legal debates as to whether certain comments were or weren't actually about law school.) Watching that game unfold reminded me of the extent to which law school permeates the souls of poor 1Ls.

Never Forget: The Number of Excellent Students Far Exceeds 10 Percent

Most students, even if they deny it, arrive at law school hoping they can be one of the top students in the class. Professor Lawrence Krieger, who researches law student well-being, asked his first-year class how many of them wanted to be in the top 10 percent of the class. Ninety-percent of the students raised their hands. As Krieger noted, herein lies a major obstacle to law student well-being. If the "want" to be on top is perceived as a "need," most everyone in the class is going to end up perceiving themselves as a failure.[153]

Just because you're not in the top 10 percent doesn't mean you're not a good law student or won't be a great lawyer. Compare law student class rankings with the annual rankings of law schools themselves by the *U.S. News & World Report*. The rankings, on which many students rely in choosing a law school, are a source of tremendous stress and pressure on law schools. All schools would like to be nearer to the top, and many think they deserve to be in the top 10 percent. Law schools devote enormous effort and resources to improving their *U.S. News* rankings, but in the end, only twenty law schools out of the 200 or so ABA-accredited schools can finish in the top 10 percent.

Does that mean the other schools are "failures"? That they're not any good? Of course not. To the contrary, all accredited law schools are of very high quality. The problem is that the rankings don't take into account and reflect many of the attributes that make a law school good. Same thing with law school grades. Law school exams measure only a limited set of skills. They don't measure oral facility, resourcefulness, dedication, heart, grit, integrity, or even necessarily the amount of knowledge a student has acquired.

Back in 2006, a majority of law school deans signed an open letter to LSAT-takers warning them not to put too much stock in the *U.S. News* rankings (even as they worked hard to bolster the ranking of their own schools). The letter said: "The idea that all law schools can be measured by the same yardstick ignores the qualities that make ... law schools unique...." Substitute "law students" for "law schools" and the statement rings just as true. Hmm, maybe it's time for law schools to reevaluate how we evaluate students.

This isn't to suggest you shouldn't care about your grades. Grades are important. To say otherwise would be a lie. High grades open more doors to more opportunities than lower grades, especially early on. But recognizing that grades are important and that it's worth doing your best to improve them is different from letting grades define who you are as a

---

153. *See* Lawrence S. Krieger, *What We're Not Telling Law Students—And Lawyers—That They Really Need to* *Know: Some Thoughts–In–Action Toward Revitalizing the Profession from Its Roots,* 13 J.L. & HEALTH 1, 11 (1999).

person. People come to law school to get a professional degree and a license to practice law. No one sits down and says, "I think I'll go to law school to see if I can rack up three more years of good grades!"

Law schools and legal employers are the major culprits in making grades so important because most of the glittery prizes—such as law review, research assistant positions, scholarships, awards, and many of the best external jobs—go to students with high grades. But students also are complicit in fostering grade competition and anxiety by obsessively comparing their grades and talking about the grades of others. Grades are awarded anonymously. If all law students kept their grades—good, bad or medium—to themselves, it would lessen their environmental impact. If you tell your grades to even one classmate, many others are likely to hear about them as well.

Compete only against yourself. If you work diligently and consistently, your grades will improve. Hard-working, reliable students will earn the respect of their classmates and professors regardless of their class rank.

Cling Tightly To Your Personal Values

On the questionnaire I give to incoming students, I ask why they came to law school. A substantial percentage of students give sincere answers about wanting to help people, often targeting specific groups such as children, the elderly, or the disabled. Very few students, however, end up pursuing those original goals once they become lawyers. What happens to them?

Research by Kennon Sheldon and Lawrence Krieger suggests a plausible explanation.[154] Sheldon and Krieger conducted a study of law students at two law schools to test a number of hypotheses about declines in law student well-being. They grounded their research in self-determination theory. Self-determination theorists study the connection between human motivations and optimal well-being. In short, self-determination theory hypothesizes that people are happier when they are motivated by autonomous, rather than externally coerced, goals and values.

---

154. *See generally* Sheldon & Krieger, *Does Legal Education have Under-* *mining Effects on Law Students?*, *supra.*

As applied to law students, Sheldon and Krieger hypothesized that 1Ls experience a decline in autonomous motivations and an increase in externally controlled motivations, and that this change is accompanied by a shift from internal to external values. They further hypothesized that these changes lead to lower levels of happiness and life satisfaction. Their study results supported their hypotheses.

Here's a plain-language example to illustrate their points: Sarah arrives at law school with the goals of enjoying the learning process, getting a degree, and becoming a lawyer who will help people with mental disabilities. Sheldon and Krieger's hypotheses predict that the coercive environment of law school, with its emphasis on external rewards, will cause Sarah's motivations and values to change. Her autonomous motivation to simply enjoy learning will decline, replaced by external motivations such as achieving high grades. Her personal value to serve people with mental disabilities will be replaced by extrinsic values such as enhancing her image and obtaining a lucrative job. Significantly, the more successful Sarah is in law school, the larger the threat that law school will reconstruct her values. As Krieger explained, these shifts can lead to an overall lowering of well-being:

> Scientific research for the past 15 years has consistently shown that a primary focus on external rewards and results, including affluence, fame, and power, is unfulfilling. These values are seductive—they create a nice picture of life but they are actually correlated with relative unhappiness. Instead, people who have a more "intrinsic," personal/interpersonal focus—on personal growth, close relationships, helping others, or improving their community—turn out to be significantly happier and more satisfied with their lives.[155]

Sheldon and Krieger's hypotheses bear spooky similarities to my own experience. I attended law school with dreams of becoming a great civil rights lawyer. My hero was Clarence Darrow, the Chicago criminal defense lawyer known for championing unpopular causes. He was my hero because he was my mother's hero and she told me stories about him when I was growing up. Before I even knew what a lawyer

---

155. LAWRENCE S. KRIEGER, THE HIDDEN SOURCES OF LAW SCHOOL STRESS: AVOIDING THE MISTAKES THAT CREATE UNHAPPY AND UNPROFESSIONAL LAWYERS 4 (2005).

was, I knew that there was this great man out there, this *lawyer*, who always stood up and fought for the underdog.

Somewhere along my law school journey, I took a wrong turn and got lost. I either forgot or sublimated my dream. I allowed the culture of law school to inculcate a new value system in me, one in which prestige, high salaries, expense accounts, and other perks became the most valuable prizes of becoming a lawyer. Success as a law student, just as Sheldon and Krieger predicted, made matters worse. With high grades and law review membership, all signs pointed in one direction. On finishing a judicial clerkship, I found myself interviewing only at prestigious, high-paying firms. I didn't contact or interview with a single civil rights firm. On receiving an offer from a highly regarded commercial litigation firm, I accepted the job even though I didn't enjoy the interview or think I wanted to work there.

Everything turned out fine in the end, as I love being a law prof. But I still regret never having made an attempt to be that civil rights lawyer I dreamed about. Words to live by from Shakespeare: "To thine own self be true."

Complicating this advice is that, much more commonly than in other graduate programs, far too many law students come to law school for the wrong reasons, such as "What else am I going to do with an undergraduate degree in Things that Happened in England in 1208 A.D.?" or "I figured it would be a decent way to make a living." They aren't equipped to be true to their selves because they haven't figured out who they are or what they want in life. The well-being of these students is more at risk than people who pursue a legal education because they really want to be there. It's one thing to tolerate the workload and stress of law school if you have a good reason and strong motivation for being there, but quite another if you have no clue why you are there or arrived with only a vague goal of improving your career options. Anecdotal evidence suggests that the happiest lawyers are those who genuinely wanted to be lawyers before they got to law school.

Good Advice, But Will You Follow It?

Hearing advice and following it are two different things. That's a particular problem with the recommendations in this chapter, some of which constitute "lifestyle advice" as applied to law students. Admittedly, some of my tips for maintaining well-being fall under the "I didn't need to buy a book to tell me that" category. Will couch-potato readers start an exercise regimen because it's suggested above? Will law students with drinking issues become teetotalers because of the alarming statistics cited regarding law student/lawyer alcohol abuse? Will 1Ls keep up with their hobbies because a law professor said it's a good idea? Maybe, but I'm not counting on it. My goal in this chapter is more modest: to alert you to recurring issues that contribute to higher stress and lower well-being among students and offer you some ideas for dealing with them. It's up to you, of course, to manage your life.

CHAPTER 21
WELCOME *BACK* TO THE JUNGLE: THE PERILOUS SECOND SEMESTER

> In a way I kind of feel as though the first semester was like me going into a burning building to pull somebody out of the fire. I wanted to go and was happy to do it, and after coming out I was glad I did it, but felt like I wouldn't want to do it again. Now for the next semester I feel as though there is somebody else in the house and the fire has gotten worse. I groan and make myself go in again, and part of me wants to go back in, but in the back of my mind I'm aware of how tired I am from the first time and am a little more worried about whether or not I will get out of the building alive this time.
>
> —1L's comment about starting the second semester

Virtually all of the advice in this book up to this point applies equally to the first and second semesters, including advice about study and exam techniques. This chapter focuses on the particular issues and obstacles the second semester raises for students. Knowing and understanding those obstacles will lessen the blow of smacking into them face-first, and also make it easier to navigate around them.

The second semester, particularly in the opening days and weeks, is one of the most daunting challenges in all of law school. How students respond to it is a crucial determinant of their long-term success. This is the juncture where, for reasons described below, students make judgments and decisions about themselves and law school that play a large role in determining and defining their ultimate "law school selves."

The Second Semester Has Upsides

It may seem counterintuitive that many law students find the second semester more difficult and dispiriting than the first. With three months experience under their belts, one might think the second semester would be a "been there, done that" relative breeze for students. In the first semester, students are lost in a maze of uncertainty and bear the weight of the fear and stress that stumbling blindly carries with it. Beginning law students must acclimate themselves to an entirely new educational world. They spend forever preparing for class only to arrive feeling unprepared because the professors are asking questions they hadn't thought about. Some live in paralyzing fear of the Socratic method. A new vocabulary converts reading a single paragraph of a case into a marathon love-making exercise with *Black's Law Dictionary*. The first semester is when students, many of whom arrive at law school in search of "the right answer" to every question, are dragged kicking and screaming toward the realization that legal doctrine is frustratingly ambiguous. All of this must be accomplished in strange surroundings full of strangers. Aggravating matters, students have no clue if they're doing anything right because everything transpires in a vacuum of feedback.

These conditions are vastly improved come the second semester. Students know how to prepare for class. They're much more efficient at reading and briefing cases. The Socratic method is less intimidating. To their pleasant surprise, students saw that no one got tortured or executed for giving a wrong answer. The physical environs are familiar. Many of those strangers from the first semester are now good friends and at least some of the professors are known quantities. Students know what to expect on law school exams. After receiving their first-semester grades, they finally have the feedback they craved so desperately. They've made it through the first crucible of law school. Full-time students are one-sixth of the way to becoming lawyers. Part-time students are one-eighth of the way home.

Nevertheless, Student State of Mind Is Mixed

So what's not to like about the second semester? Plenty. It's true that all of the reasons listed above work to alleviate some major causes of stress and anxiety in students. But the second semester brings its own set of new problems. Before considering them, let's take a glimpse at the state of mind of 1Ls returning after the holiday break for their second semester. For a couple of years, I polled my Torts students at the start of the second semester with this question:

What is your dominant feeling as you begin the second semester?

- Excited
- Tired
- Bored
- Depressed
- Rested and ready

Very few students select "Excited" or "Rested and Ready." The most common answers by far are "Tired" and "Depressed." A couple of students even pick "Bored"—definitely not a good sign with two or three years of law school to go, followed by a lifetime of being a lawyer.

I decided to probe more deeply into student sentiments about starting the second semester. Just before classes began, I asked a section of Torts students to comment on, among other things, their: (1) state of mind; (2) motivation level; and (3) happiness level in comparison to the first semester. The responses showed that, while some students feel better off in the second semester, a significant segment are less happy and less motivated. In between is a large group of students who are ambivalent about their feelings.

Students expressing positive feelings about their state of mind, motivation level, and happiness level emphasized many of the improved conditions listed above: more efficient study skills, a larger comfort zone from knowing what to expect, new friendships, increased confidence from having made it through the first semester, and excitement about being on their way to becoming lawyers. Here are some sample positive responses:

- Overall, I am happier than at the start of the first semester. I am one-sixth of the way through! If the second semester goes as fast as the first, the three years should fly by. I feel engaged by all of my professors and am genuinely happy to be *learning*. (Cheesy, I know, but it's true.)

- I am definitely happier! I know now that I made the right decision in coming to law school. I have met many great friends and am very impressed with the law school and the professors. I learned that law school wasn't as horrifying as I was told it would be, and after a semester of it, my confidence is really boosted.

- I might actually be a little more motivated now that I know what to expect. I was so nervous at the beginning that I couldn't concentrate on anything else. Now that I know what to expect from the finals, I feel like I have more of an opportunity to improve my study skills and just my performance in general.

Unfortunately, these feel-good vibes were more than offset by a strong current of discontent among many students. Note the similarity in the responses of the three students below to my questions regarding, respectively, state of mind, motivation level, and happiness level:

Student 1:

1. My general state of mind as I start this semester is unmotivated.

2. I am definitely less motivated at the start of this semester than I was at the beginning.

3. I am also unhappier than I was during the first semester.

(The student added a post script: "Though this sounds depressing, I'm not depressed. Just struggling a little at the moment.")

Student 2:

1. Unhappy and sullen.

2. Much less motivated—I'm already convinced I failed out of school, so the last thing I want to do is continue to work hard.

3.   The same amount of light unhappiness, but it's for different reasons. In the beginning it was fear and anxiety. Now I just feel defeated.

Student 3:

1.   I generally feel depressed to be quite honest.

2.   I am less motivated now than when I started the first semester.

3.   I am a bit unhappier than when I began.

Potential Pitfalls of the Second Semester

Difficulties in the second semester that contribute to feelings like those described above are largely overlooked in giving advice to first-year students. I make an effort to give my students relevant advice as they progress through law school, but until composing this book had never thought deeply about the special challenges of the second semester. Let's take a look at them:

Ignorance can be bliss.

The uncertainty of the first semester is a substantial cause of strain on 1Ls, but removing the veil from law school can be problematic as well. In the second semester uncertainty about law school is replaced by a disquieting *certainty* that it can be exhausting, onerous drudgery. In his 1709 *An Essay on Criticism*, eighteenth-century English poet Alexander Pope coined the phrase "A little learning is a dangerous thing." Law students might modify it to say a little learning can be a depressing thing. Look at how some 1Ls weighed in on their newfound awareness in response to the questions about starting the second semester:

- Now I know exactly what I'm walking into. First semester there was a bit of excited anticipation, etc. Now I know I'll be in the library for the next four months.

- In some ways I'm happier because I really enjoy the process of learning and have really enjoyed school, but in other ways I am unhappier because I now know how hard I will have to work this semester.

- The hardest thing to me about starting the second semester is knowing that I have to go through the whole exam process at the end again, and not only one more time, but five more times.

The thrill is gone.

The realization that law school is going to be a long haul is worsened by the fact that the excitement and adrenaline that fueled students through the first semester have evaporated. Students arrive at law school brimming with anticipation and energy. Seeing and feeling it is one of the great pleasures of being a 1L law teacher. But like romances that lose their dizzying effects when the newness wears off, law school becomes more of a chore than an adventure after the ebullience of the first semester subsides.

Students start the second semester with a hangover effect of physical and emotional exhaustion from the first semester. The holiday break is just long enough to remind students what it's like to live like a free person, but not quite long enough for students to fully recharge their batteries. As bluesman B.B. King would put it, "the thrill is gone."

Be prepared for this letdown at the beginning of the second semester. Know that it's completely normal, natural, and, happily, transitory. Within a week or two, most students bounce back to their old selves. While they never quite regain that exhilaration that comes with newness, they do get their second wind and perk back up substantially.

The double-edged grade blade.

Depending how they turn out, first-semester grades can be either a major boost or impediment to starting the second semester. You've heard the aphorism, "Be careful what you wish for." It applies to law school feedback big-time. We've discussed how most students begin law school with at least some hope of finishing near the top of their class, but we've also discussed the mathematical reality that only a small percentage of students can fulfill that dream.

For those who performed well, first-semester grades can infuse new energy and confidence. It shows up in class. Every year, in the early days of the second semester, students who never raised their hands the first semester start volunteering in class. When they do, I smile inside as I call on them, thinking: "Ah, good for you. You must have done better than you expected."

But for every student whose confidence gets a jolt from grades, three or four others get their egos electrocuted. High expectations, previous educational success, mandatory grading curves, and an abundance of talented people create a perfect storm for dashed hopes. The storm is unleashed the moment first-semester grades are released. Suddenly, students who rarely have seen a grade below an *A* in sixteen-plus years of education would be willing to trade 100,000 shares of Apple stock for a *B* or even a *B-*. Anything without the dreaded *C* in front of it.

Making lower-than-hoped-for grades is particularly demoralizing for the students who worked their tails off in the first semester, which includes most students. It undermines spirit and confidence to work harder than one has ever worked before and come up short, at least (or perhaps especially) in one's own eyes. Many students just don't see a connection between their hard work and the results. One student comment to my happiness question touched thoughtfully on this point. He included a note saying he wrote it mostly for his own benefit:

> You are told when you come to law school that, more likely than not, you will not be the best of the best. That's fine. From my personal experience, everyone lies if they tell you they do not wish in their heart that when grades are posted they will be perched towards the top of their class. Reality dictates that many of us will be disappointed—seriously disappointed in some cases. Personally, I did "fine" this semester. I had grades that I am proud of and one in particular that I am not happy with. I am, at the moment, your everyday Average Joe law student. Middle of the pack or a notch or two above.
>
> I have many deep and close friends here, and I know that I worked very hard the previous semester. I know that I worked harder than some of my dearest friends. I know that several of them did better than me—some did tremendously well. It's difficult to describe the frustration that causes. You are happy for the individuals who did well, yet you are mystified and deeply frustrated that the hundreds (thousands?) of hours that you worked did not provide the reward you sought.

How students respond to first-semester grades is crucial to their remaining law school existence, as well as their post-law school lives. Far too many students define themselves by their first-semester grades. If they received Cs, they tell themselves: "Well, I guess I'm only a C student." Then many of them proceed to behave like C students by not working as hard from that point on.

It bears repeating: Law school is a marathon, not a sprint. Suppose you really were a serious marathon runner. A marathon is roughly 26 miles. The one-sixth mark—that is, the equivalent mark of finishing one of the six semesters of law school for a full-time student—would be 4.3 miles. Suppose you came to that point of the race and realized you were in the middle of the pack (i.e., the C student of marathon runners). Would you give up? Of course not. With so much ground remaining and so much time and terrain to gain on the competition, you wouldn't tell yourself, "Well, I guess I'm no good as a marathon runner. I might as well slow down."

It's *way* too early to give up after just one semester. For people who continue working hard, grades generally go up. For people who start working less, grades generally go down. I've seen it happen a hundred times. Think back to the student mentioned in Chapter 9 for whom I wrote the strong recommendation letter even though she received a D in Torts I. One reason I was willing to endorse her was because after she received the D she came to me and said she intended to work even harder in the second semester. She got a B- in Torts II, a five-step increase. And I'll never forget the student who broke down crying in my colleague's office after receiving a D on his Contracts midterm exam—his very first law school exam. He went on to graduate number one in his class and serve as editor-in-chief of the law review.

Law school exam-taking is a learning process for most students. It's true that a few people in each class have a natural knack for it right off the bat. It's also true that a small number of students never get the hang of it. But for most students, as with any new skill, it's a matter of improving through repetition. You're only at the one-sixth mark of the race at the beginning of the second semester. Don't slow down. Turn it up a notch.

Getting back in the groove.

A universal challenge of starting the second semester is simply getting back into the routine of daily classes and class preparation. After going and going like the battery bunny on meth for three months, students finish that last exam of the first semester and everything suddenly stops. Many students don't know what to do with themselves during the holiday break. They're not used to having so much free time. Many report that they can't enjoy the break at the beginning because they feel guilty about not studying. Then, just about the time they readjust to an unstructured lifestyle full of leisure time, it's time to get back to the grind.

Included in my "starting the second semester" survey was this question: "The hardest thing for me about starting the second semester is [fill in the blank]." The dominant response was getting refocused to do it all over again. Look at the commonality—indeed, near identicalness—of the following responses, and there were many more just like them:

- The hardest thing for me about starting the second semester is getting refocused to do it all over again. The first semester felt so draining both emotionally and physically. It is hard to adjust to getting back and getting refocused.

- The hardest thing for me about starting the second semester is getting back into the mindset (you have to get into a certain mindset, I think, to get into the habit of briefing, etc.).

- The hardest thing for me about starting the second semester is feeling like I'm back at the beginning. I felt so good about finishing that first semester, and even though I was unsure about my grades I was still pretty proud of myself for making it. Now I feel like I have to start all over again. But I'm sure once I'm back in the swing of things, the semester will begin to fly by just like the first semester did.

And in that last sentence we find the saving grace of this challenge. This too shall pass. Student *do* get back into the swing of things and, once they do, the second semester flies by just like the first one did and like the third, fourth, fifth, and sixth ones (and seventh and eighth for part-time students) will.

Key to your success is forcing yourself back into the groove *at the very beginning*. Don't squander the opening weeks of the second semester moping or dawdling. If you'll forgive the mixed metaphor, you'll get back in the swing of things quicker if you come out swinging. The C.R.E.D.O. (Consistent, Rigorous, Efficient, Diligent, Organized) from Chapter 10 applies to each semester of law school. It's important to be consistent from the get-go in the second semester, just as in the first semester. Warm-up class sessions are even less likely to occur than in the first semester. Profs generally come in and start teaching new law in the opening minutes of the first class. Hit the ground running or you can lose ground quickly.

Increased competitiveness.

Even if they don't admit it (perhaps even to themselves) most law students are competitive. And even if they aren't competitive by nature, law school forces them to become that way because the entire process is structured around competition. The competition for high grades and class rank is intense. Many schools have a first-year oral argument competition. To get on law review requires successful participation in a summer write-on competition. Students compete to land limited interview slots for on-campus interviews by potential employers. Just about every undertaking in law school, including writing the best exam in each course, carries the potential for an individual award.

Before you start law school, you're likely to hear stories about how competitive law students are, to the point where many are alleged to be "cutthroat." The classic repeated story is a variation on students hiding the case reporter volume containing the key case that everyone needs to complete their memos for Legal Research and Writing—or even more egregiously, tearing the case out of the book. The latter actually happened to me in law school. I tracked down the reporter volume in the library containing the essential case for my memo, but when I turned to the case, it was missing. Someone had actually ripped out the pages!

In general, my experience as a professor has been that law students are quite supportive of one another. Of course, like all human experiences, the level of competition in law school varies depending on the particular group and individuals. I frequently observe students going out of their way to help and support their classmates, sometimes to astonishing degrees, but also hear occasional ugly stories of ruthless competitiveness.

To the extent competitiveness is an issue with which to be concerned, it gets worse in the second semester. Much of it relates back to that first set of grades having been issued. In the first semester, everyone is in the same boat, struggling to stay afloat. The shared experience creates a communal bond. But once first-semester grades have been issued, there may be a feeling—both among some high achievers and some lower-than-hoped-for achievers—of "Hey, you're in *that* boat and I'm in *this* boat." Reading this assertion, a research assistant commented:

> This is definitely true. One thing that surprised me in law school was its clique-ish nature. Very early on groups of people became friends and always hung around each other. This became even more pronounced in the second semester after grades came out. It seemed that students in each clique generally received similar grades, thus reinforcing their companionship— seemed like everyone was in their own boats now.

Some students with high grades may consider themselves superior to their classmates and project, or be perceived to project, that image to others. In turn, some lower-performing students may resent the students at the top, particularly if they flaunt their success. As one disappointed student wrote:

> When first-semester grades came out, I literally watched my classmates high-five and fist-pump each other and say their grades out loud. It reinforced a feeling of inadequacy that I had to talk myself out of. I vowed that if/when I get the grades for which I am striving, I will never tell a single soul at the law school.

Meanwhile, students who may not have appreciated the importance of class rank and GPA in the first semester become all too aware of it as the second semester progresses and they see the top-ranked students landing the good summer law firm jobs, research assistant positions, etc.

To say this is unfortunate would be an understatement. The fact is you and your 1L mates are all in the same boat. There's not much meaningful practical advice I can give you on this issue other than to put you on notice that over-competitiveness is not an attractive quality. If you do well your first semester, follow the vow of the student above. Keep it to yourself. People will respect you all the more for it. If you brag about your high grades, people will hate you, and probably should. A colleague at another law school told me about a student who received an *A* on her memo assignment in Legal Research and Writing, then proceeded to carry the memo around on top of her stack of books, with the *A* clearly showing, for three weeks until my professor-friend had a "chat" with her about it. "Her classmates were about to crucify her," she reported.

Enhanced workload.

Depending on the law school, a major cause of second-semester stress is an increased workload. Some schools add an extra course in the second semester. Professors may move at a quicker pace, which means more material and longer reading assignments.

And then there's the appellate brief and oral argument, one of the heaviest burdens of 1L existence. As discussed in Chapter 18, most students' second semester load in Legal Research and Writing will include having to write an appellate brief and engage in an oral argument before a mock appellate court. No reason to rehash the subject, except to note that these requirements add substantially to second-semester workloads. It takes more time and effort to research and write an appellate brief than to compose the law office memoranda assigned in the first semester. Additionally, the oral argument consumes tremendous emotional energy. Some schools make it into a formal competition, adding to the pressure and workload.

One plus, however, is that increased efficiency in class preparation resulting from lessons learned in the first semester helps to counterbalance the extra workload.

Second-guessing life as a lawyer.

One obstacle some students face in the second semester is the global issue of wondering whether one made the right choice in sacrificing everything (e.g., time, effort, financial resources, relationships, other opportunities) to come to law school. Should I be here? Is this what I really want to do with my life? In the first semester, students are struggling just to keep up, giving them little time to ponder the long-term wisdom of their career choice. In the second semester, nagging doubts kept at bay in the first semester may start to creep into consciousness.

Most students come to law school with very little understanding of what lawyers actually do. For many, their exposure to the law has been limited to glamorized media accounts. Some students are disappointed to find themselves consumed with studying un-scintillating, often archaic rules and doctrines.

Marketable title? Collateral estoppel? Who cares about those? When do we get to conduct those awesome television "gotcha" cross-examinations that extract confessions from murderers just in time for the last commercial break? And what's up with all these very un-John Grisham-like cases? Where's the intrigue, the suspense, the romance?

In the second semester, if not sooner, students are hit with the realization that being a lawyer, while potentially rewarding on many levels, is anything but glamorous. Instead of inspiring students about practicing law, professors may actually dampen student enthusiasm, although not intentionally. While I try to enthuse my students about the institution of law, I feel an obligation to be candid about the sometimes hard reality of actually practicing it. My four years as a practicing lawyer were marked by long hours, high stress, lack of fulfillment, and an intense dislike of billable hours, which require a lawyer to keep track of and document every moment of the day.

While law professors hold the legal profession in high regard, they may have less fondness for the actual practice of law, especially private practice. Many law professors fled the practice of law for what they saw as a better life in academia. Consequently, we might be the wrong people to be talking to our students about the pros and cons of private practice.

The good news is that numerous studies of the legal profession show that most lawyers are satisfied with their career choice. One prominent example is the *After the JD* project, which comprehensively tracked the careers of 5,000 lawyers over a period of ten years. The researchers released their data in two waves. The first wave, reporting survey data collected two to three years after graduation, showed that 80 percent of the lawyers were either "moderately" or "extremely" satisfied with their decision to become a lawyer. The report found no evidence of pervasive unhappiness in the legal profession. The second wave, surveying the lawyers as they closed in on a decade of practice, found similar results, with 76.2 percent of the lawyers indicating they were moderately or extremely satisfied.[156]

If you have doubts about your career choice, stop and ask why. First, understand that it's normal and appropriate to reevaluate such a life-changing decision as going to law school. Unfortunately, an informed evaluation isn't possible prior to actually attending. The second semester is a good time to pause and size things up. Some students decide they simply don't like law school, the law, or the prospect of being a lawyer—or all three—and withdraw. There's nothing wrong with such a decision if it's made for the right reasons.

If you feel quite certain you don't want to be a lawyer, it's better to cut your losses by figuring that out sooner rather than later. I'll never forget the student who showed up at my office the Monday after her law school graduation and asked if I would write a letter of recommendation for her to enroll in a graduate program in social work. Surprised, I asked what prompted her decision. She said she knew from the beginning of law school that she didn't want to be a lawyer, but felt pressure to complete her legal education so she wouldn't be seen as "a quitter" by her family and in her own eyes.

The key in making this assessment is to be sure you're looking at the long-term prospects for happiness in the legal profession, rather than at the frustrations or stress of the moment. Law school itself will pass, more quickly than you realize. In my first year, I did not enjoy law school, but I did like the law itself. I loved that every case was different. I was awed by the power of law to affect people's lives. I found the mental challenge of solving the puzzles of the law to be thrilling. My love for and appreciation of "the law" kept me going during tough times. When students come to me second-guessing whether they want to be a lawyer, the first question I ask is: "Do you enjoy the law itself?" If the answer is a

---

156. *See generally* Jerome M. Organ, *What Do We Know About the Satisfaction/Dissatisfaction of Lawyers? A Meta–Analysis of Research on Lawyer Satisfaction and Well–Being*, 8 U. St. Thomas L.J. 225 (2011) (reporting the results of the *After the JD* project and also discussing several other studies of lawyer satisfaction).

clear no, I suggest that maybe law isn't the field for them. But if the answer is yes, I usually encourage them to hang in there.

Take heart in the fact that many students absolutely *love* law school and many lawyers *love* the practice of law. Here are some glowing endorsements of law school and the prospect of becoming a lawyer that I received from second-semester students in response to a question about their career choice:

- I'm excited! I know this is what I was meant to be!

- I love the career. I do love the law. I'm surprised with how much I actually enjoy reading the cases, even the cases that I'm reading for the appellate brief.

- I have always wanted to be a lawyer, since I was in sixth grade. I cannot see myself in any other profession, so I feel like this is the right career choice for me. Also, I really enjoy talking about the law and politics, and I enjoy being in law school where I don't have to feel like a dork if I get excited to talk about something related to the law, like the difference between assault and battery. I feel that being a lawyer is a respected profession, and even though as you know, we are always made fun of, when someone finds out I am in law school, there is definitely a respect there.

Related to questions about whether they want to be lawyers, some second-semester 1Ls begin stressing over *what kind* of lawyer they want to be. They get worried when they don't know the answer. In response to my career-choice question, one student wrote he was happy he came to law school, but added: "I just wish that when everyone asked what kind of lawyer I want to be I had an answer. When I answer with 'I don't know,' they look at me like I have been wasting my time. That is really getting annoying."

Certainly, it's a good question to start considering, but it's nothing to get agitated about. There's no reason 1Ls should know what kind of lawyers they want to be because they haven't been exposed either to enough law or to the real world sufficiently to develop informed opinions. Many lawyers' career paths end up being determined purely by fortuitous circumstances, such as where they happen to land a job. My older brother was one of the most prominent bankruptcy attorneys in the country, listed in that field in the *Best Lawyers in America* book. I once asked him how he ended up as a bankruptcy lawyer. He said that when he took his first job at a large law firm, he was assigned an office that just happened to contain the law firm's set of *Collier on Bankruptcy*, a multi-volume treatise that is the bible of bankruptcy law. Other lawyers started coming into his office asking him bankruptcy questions simply because he had the set of *Collier's* in there. He said he started looking up answers to the questions and the next thing he knew he was a bankruptcy lawyer!

Don't feel rushed to pick a specific career path. I didn't figure mine out until six years after graduating from law school. Finding the right fit—both in terms of the field of law and the particular place and people you work with—is one of most important decisions you will ever make in terms of your long-term happiness. You'll spend more time working than doing any other activity in your life, even sleeping. Better to make the decision correctly than quickly, while also recognizing that you might not get it right the first time. That's not a problem as long as you're willing to change course later.

Unless you came to law school to be a specific type of lawyer, keep your mind open to all options and trust that you will find your way. In the meantime, when someone asks what kind of lawyer you want to be, just say, "A great one! But I need to do more exploring before deciding on a particular type of practice."

Summer job anxiety.

Students feel pressure in their second semester to land summer legal jobs at law firms, often called "summer associate" positions. In many cases, this pressure arises from pressing financial needs, but it also stems from an expectation that getting a summer legal job is something that all 1Ls absolutely must do.

Certainly, there are benefits to obtaining a summer legal job. Income is an obvious one. Big law firms pay summer associates handsomely, but these jobs are reserved for top-performing students or students from elite law schools and have dwindled in response to the economic downturn that began in 2008. Small firms pay less, but are a good way to get some experience and get your foot in the door. Many firms hire associate attorneys from the ranks of former clerks who performed well, but it's certainly not an absolute rule.

I tell my 1Ls not to worry too much if they can't land a paying summer legal job. For one thing, they don't have a great deal of control over the situation. The job market is tighter than it used to be. Also, many law firms simply don't hire students after their first year because they haven't learned enough yet to be of value.

If you need money, consider non-legal jobs as a way to get a hiatus from law school. Many students can earn more waiting tables than by clerking at a law firm, while also getting a refreshing break from the law. If you don't need the money, summer school is a good option. Getting a couple of courses out of the way in the summer will lighten your burden during the regular academic year. It's even possible to graduate a semester early if that's your goal.

Volunteering in a legal capacity as an intern for a public agency or non-profit organization is a good way to network and get some experience. One thing I personally would *not* do is work for free at a law firm. I have had several students recently report to me that in applying for summer jobs, some firms have offered to let them work without pay. What a great deal . . . for the law firm. It strikes me as exploitative and, in fact, such "intern" arrangements may violate the Fair Labor Standards Act. According to the U.S. Department of Labor, "if the interns are engaged in the operations of the employer or are performing productive work . . ., then the fact that they may be receiving some benefits in the form of a new skill or improved work habits will not exclude them from" being classified as employees subject to the minimum wage and overtime requirements of federal law.[157]

If you have the resources (don't do it on borrowed money), consider a summer abroad program. Law schools sponsor summer abroad programs in every corner of the world. I've never had a student attend one who didn't come back saying it was one of the greatest experiences of his or her life.

---

157. U.S. Dep't of Labor, *Fact Sheet #71: Internship Programs Under the Fair Labor Standards Act*, WAGE AND HOUR DIV. FACT SHEET INDEX (Apr. 2010), http://www.dol.gov/whd/regs/compliance/whdfs71.pdf.

In the meantime, concentrate on doing the best you can in law school and trust that things have a way of taking care of themselves.

* * *

I want to close with a reminder of why you should keep this book handy throughout the year rather than just reading it before law school and setting it aside. A student, one of my favorites, who worked very hard but did not get the grades she hoped for, sent me this message shortly after the start of her second semester:

> Your book has come through for me again! I just read the chapter on the second semester and it was just what I needed to read. My grades are not where I want them, and I am not one of those people who complain about *B*s, if you know what I mean. I was gravely disappointed, but I own those grades 100 percent. The chapter was particularly helpful in encouraging me not to waste energy on past grades about which I can do nothing and to focus on this semester—something I do have control over. It really captured the emotions I wasn't expecting to feel when I started this journey, but every good journey requires overcoming adversity to get what you want, right?

Good for her! She wrote me again at the end of the year to report that her Torts grade increased from a C- to a B, a four-step rise. Be sure to come back and reread this chapter after the first semester.

CHAPTER 22

THE SPECIAL PLIGHT OF NONTRADITIONAL STUDENTS, ESPECIALLY "NIGHT" STUDENTS

Too often overlooked in law school preparatory books are nontraditional students, especially the dwellers of the night. Most law students attend law school full-time during the day and graduate in three years, but approximately 25,000 students—17 percent of the total—are enrolled in one of the nation's eighty-five ABA-accredited part-time evening programs and graduate in four years.[158]

This chapter focuses on these "night students," as we'll call them for convenience, but a good portion of it applies to all nontraditional law students, full- or part-time, day or night. "Nontraditional student" can carry different meanings, but one of the primary ones and the way the label is used here is to describe students who are older and have not gone straight from college to law school. Most day students are "traditional" students in their early twenties. Most night students—the largest subset of nontraditional students—are significantly older. The 2011 Law School Student Engagement Survey found that 47 percent of part-time student respondents were over the age of thirty compared to 17 percent of full-time students.[159]

Night law students face the same rigors as day students, but with some huge extra challenges thrown in. They take

---

158. In addition to evening-division students, approximately 4 percent of day students have part-time status.

159. 2011 LAW SCH. SURVEY OF STUDENT ENGAGEMENT, *supra*, at 10.

the same curriculum taught by the same professors. They use the same casebooks, read the same cases, and do the same legal research and writing assignments as the day students. The only difference is they take fewer credit hours per semester, 10–11 hours compared to 15–16. Their classes typically are held three or four nights a week, three or four hours per night.

Some part-time evening students start law school concerned they will get a lesser legal education because it's "night school." Not true at all. The 2011 Law School Survey of Student Engagement found that part-time students were just as satisfied with their legal education as full-time students.[160] In fact, classroom experiences at night are often more energized and exciting than day classes. The main reason is that, unlike many traditional students, night students, being older, are less afraid to express their opinions and mix it up a bit in class discussions. They don't worry about being labeled as "gunners," as do many younger students. If they have something to say, they raise their hands and say it. The other reason for the high-energy level is that night students typically consume copious amounts of caffeine prior to class.

The extra challenges for night students center around the fact that, as one student put it, they are "spinning more plates in the air." Most of them work outside of law school, a majority in full-time day jobs. Because they are older, night students also are more likely than day students to have spouses and kids. This is true of nontraditional day students as well.

When most day students have left campus for the day, night students are just arriving. Many of them have been up since the crack of dawn getting kids ready for school, rushing off to full-time jobs, then hurrying to law school. It's a grueling schedule. As one student described it: "I didn't see my house in the daylight for almost three and a half years. Getting up at 4:45 a.m. to go to work, leaving work and going straight to school, and getting home at 11:00 p.m. was brutal on my mind, body, and my wife." Not all night students have hours quite that bad, but it's an around-the-clock challenge

---

160. *Id.* at 10, 11 (containing charts comparing relative satisfaction of part-time and full-time students with various law school services and self-reported student gains in skills and professional development).

trying to keep those spinning plates in the air. And we haven't even mentioned the studying part yet. Oops, where is that supposed to fit in?

I've taught well over a thousand night law students at three law schools and, like many professors, have a special fondness and respect for them. Night students come from all walks of life: social workers, police officers, doctors, nurses, teachers, business executives, homemakers, you name it. The life experiences they bring with them add tremendously to the classroom experience. Their ability to manage so many different roles—employee, parent, and law student—never ceases to amaze me.

For help with this chapter, I called on former night students from three diverse law schools (in Little Rock, Miami, and San Francisco) for their insights about this unique slice of legal education. Their comments, in response to survey questions, illuminate both the extra challenges faced by night students (and nontraditional students in general), but also the benefits. That's right. There are definitely some "cons" to being a night student, but there are also some significant "pros." We'll start with the downsides, so we can end on an up-note.

The Ultimate Time–Bandits

The single biggest obstacle faced by night law students is finding enough hours to successfully attend law school while still managing the rest of their busy lives. Night students are particularly at risk of falling behind in their studies—the law school kiss of academic death. That they have good explanations for letting that happen isn't going to help them, so we'll focus on some strategies for maximizing time management and efficiency.

Figure out and resolve employment conflicts in advance. Employment conflicts are the most common reason for part-time students failing law school. I've sat through countless readmissions committee meetings listening to part-time students explain how their job didn't allow enough time for them to succeed, along with their "new plan" for reducing employment hours, etc. The "new plan" needs to be worked out before you set foot in the door.

Talk to your employer. Don't try to hide that you're going to law school. Work out an arrangement that will allow you get out of work in time to get to class without having to drive like a potential tortfeasor before you even learn what that is. If at all possible, shorten your work hours. Cutting them from forty to thirty hours per week, for example, can make a big difference.

Be sure to plan ahead for exams and try as hard as you can to arrange vacation days during that period. You will need blocks of time both to study for exams and give your best performance on them. Working all day before taking a mind-numbingly complex law school exam the same night is a recipe for disaster. You must approach each exam with a fresh, rested brain, in part because you will be competing against other students who are not working or only working part-time.

Develop a specific scheduling plan and stick to it. Nowhere is an efficient, organized scheduling plan more important than when you are a night law student. Learn from the student below, who finished number one in her class overall—not just among the night students. It's a long comment, but I wanted to include it in full, so you could take note of the high level of specificity in her well-organized scheduling plan:

At our school, we were in class Monday, Tuesday, and Thursday nights when we were 1Ls. Monday night was Legal Writing and Research, and Tuesdays/Thursdays were Contracts and Torts (an hour and a half of each on each night). So dividing time was simple. I'd spend Saturday and Sunday preparing for Monday and Tuesday classes, and Wednesday preparing for Thursday's classes. Legal writing assignments were reserved mostly for Friday night and Saturdays.

Here's how the breakdown worked:

Monday night: Go to Legal Research and Writing. After class, skim whatever assignment we got in that class so I would know how much time I would have to devote to it over the weekend.

Tuesday night: Go to Contracts and Torts.

Wednesday night: Read the reading assignments for Thursday night's Contracts and Torts classes.

Thursday night: Attend classes.

Friday night: Meet up with a couple of friends in the library and work on the legal research assignment we were given on Monday night. (NEVER leaving the library until it was done.)

Saturday morning: Outline class notes every other week. (The off-week Saturdays were my one day to sleep late.) Saturday afternoon: Read in depth the legal writing assignment and draft whatever was required for the next Monday night's class.

Sunday afternoon and evening: Finish up the legal research assignment for Monday night and read the Contracts/Torts assignments for Tuesday night.

If Sunday's reading was light, I'd get a jump on the reading I normally did on Wednesdays, and vice versa. Friday night legal research was a must every week, as was Saturday for legal writing. Many times there was not a heavy-duty legal writing assignment, so I might have a few free hours.

If things were going on at home, I'd go to the library at school to do my reading. I carried my books with me everywhere. If I had a ten-minute break at work, I'd read. During my lunch hour, I'd read. Because I would take every free minute to get my reading assignments done for my various classes, I could usually block off Saturday evening for fun, Sunday morning for family (or church for those who attend), and Sunday evening for family time. It was tough, but doable.

Impressive! She was a student of mine long before I wrote the first edition, but she could have been a model for the C.R.E.D.O. chapter as applied to part-time evening students. Her most important piece of advice?

DO NOT PROCRASTINATE. I can't say that enough. When you are working full-time and raising a family and spending all your nights in class and are expected to be prepared, you simply cannot skip your reading for the week. *If you get behind, you'll never catch up.*

Hmm, there's that familiar theme again.

"Everybody's working for the weekend."[161] Poor night law students. For them, the lyrics to this classic rock

161. *See* LOVERBOY, WORKING FOR THE WEEKEND (Columbia 1981).

song about anticipated weekend fun from the eighties band, Loverboy, would have to be changed to "Everybody's working *on* the weekend." While many night students manage to squeeze some time for class preparation and legal writing assignments in during the week, it's not enough time to do all the work. If you can't stomach the thought of sacrificing weekends for law school, reconsider your decision to attend.

Asked for time-management suggestions, one night student said, "I mostly got my school work done during the weekends. You just learn that your decision to go to law school came with the additional decision to give up weekends. Those two days are the only times you can fit in school work." Another said, "I would go out either Friday or Saturday night, but I was always home at a reasonable hour so I could get an early start the next day. I would sit at home all day on Saturday and Sunday and read or write. I was never 'off' during that first year."

Unlike a lot of law school time-allocation decisions, this one doesn't really allow a choice for night students. Regular weekend work will be essential.

Steal minutes wherever they are available. Efficient night students learn to steal time whenever and wherever they can. "I would carry my books everywhere," said one student. "If I was getting my nails done or cooking, I was reading for Torts. If I was waiting for a doctor's appointment or waiting for class, I was reading Contracts." Other students mentioned reading cases while doing the laundry, at their kids' soccer games, or on the bus. Many night students listen to study aid CDs in their cars while commuting to and from work and law school.

Some jobs and employers allow students to get some studying done during the work day. Obviously, a lot depends on the flexibility of the particular job and employer. If you're working purely to earn extra money to go to law school (as opposed to working in a career-type job), look for a job that offers that kind of flexibility. Quite a few night law students work at law firms as receptionists, secretaries, or paralegals. Law firms may be more understanding and forgiving of law student employees trying to squeeze a little casebook reading in during the day. One student suggested fudging the workplace rules a bit: "If you have an office door, shut it and read when your boss isn't looking."

Second–Class Citizenship

Everywhere I've taught night students, they have complained about being treated as second-class citizens by the law school. The complaints are justified. Most services and institutional structures within law schools are set up to benefit full-time day students. The fact that this occurs for economic reasons, rather than any intent to disregard night students, doesn't lessen the impact on the students.

Important law school offices such as admissions, financial aid, career placement, and the registrar are staffed by 9–5 workers. Elective courses are fewer at night because it's expensive to double-up on course offerings. Courts operate during the day, which means night students are prevented from enrolling in litigation-based clinical courses, the most common type of law school legal clinic. Outside speakers brought in by student organizations or the law school usually present during the lunch hour. Law review, moot court, and other student organizations typically schedule their activities during the daytime, making it difficult for night students to participate.

In terms of law school social activities, most of them are organized by day students. While many of the activities occur at night, the day students rarely make it a point to invite night students, simply because they don't know them. At one school where I taught, the end of first-semester exams was celebrated with a grand tradition. Within literally minutes of finishing their last exam, the entire mass of 1L day students would pile into a chartered bus, stocked with their favorite beverages, and be chauffeured around the city, stopping at each of their 1L professor's homes to sing holiday carols to them. It was a fun, memorable event for all involved, which, unfortunately, never included the night students.

No wonder night students can feel left out, unappreciated, and under-loved. As a result, an unfortunate divide can arise between night and day students. Night students think the day students have it easy because all they have to do is study and go to class. Some day students think night students have it easy because of their reduced course schedule. One night student, asked to comment on ways being a night student made life harder, described the divide this way:

> One of the hardest parts is that the law school atmo-
> sphere makes part-time night students feel like second-

class citizens. When I began law school, the financial aid person went home at five. Night students get off work at five and start getting to school around five-thirty for classes that begin at six. So if we needed to do anything with financial aid, we had to try to find a way to take off work because we were *never* accommodated. Likewise, school clubs and organizations would meet at lunch during the day, effectively cutting all night students out of every social and support activity that existed. I was working a fifty-hour-a-week job when I began law school. I took my vacation from work so I could attend orientation week. I remember one particularly derisive day student cracking the comment to me, "Well, it must be nice to only take three classes when the rest of us have to take five." I replied, "Yeah, and I'd trade my fifty-plus hours a week that I work full-time for your extra two classes in a heartbeat!" All of this caused us to feel like we were never really a part of the school.

If you end up feeling similarly, keep in mind that the failure to support and include night students is not intentional, but the result of practicalities. That doesn't, however, necessarily excuse all of the behavior. Law schools have an obligation to provide important services to their evening-division students at feasible times, and, in fact, most schools have made progress in that regard. Transactional (non-litigation) legal clinics can operate at night because they don't require going to court, and law schools need more of them anyway since most lawyers do transactional work rather than courtroom work. Student organizations can and should be set up to accommodate both day and night students.

If you're at a law school which is falling short in these areas, pursue the issues with the administration. Take an interest in your Student Government Association. If you don't have time to participate, at least make an effort to elect a class representative who will push for improvements, including ways to bring day and night students together socially.

Toll on Outside Relationships

The next chapter is devoted to issues that can arise in outside relationships due to law school, so we won't go into the matter in great detail here. Study the chapter carefully. Much of what is said there could have a direct impact on you and your loved ones. To give you a preview (hopefully not a portent) of what's to come, consider these soul-searching comments from a former night student whose marriage ended in divorce:

> I was only married a year before I started law school and neither one of us was prepared for the toll it would take on the relationship. We got into bad habits and we got into them quickly because law school can overwhelm you from the start. Communication with my spouse devolved into a sort of short-hand speak (in order to save time, of course), which only led to miscommunication and one misunderstanding after another. Plus, my spouse felt constant rejection as she went to bed alone practically every night—leading to her understandable resentment.
>
> On the other side of the coin, I felt pressure from all sides (work/school/marriage/her family/my family). More often than not, my feelings of resentment came from feeling under-appreciated. I remember feeling guilty for going to law school, and being angry about feeling guilty. Dealing with the competing forces in my life was draining and I didn't have the tools at the time (and neither did she) to actually give a voice to the concerns so we could deal with them together. We grew further and further apart. I am convinced that the patterns of non-communication and resentment we both felt during that time period led to further problems later on in our marriage, which ultimately ended in divorce. Part of the artistry of being an effective attorney is being a good communicator. Start now and start at home.

Older but Wiser

Fortunately, there are also some strong positives to being a nontraditional law student. Too many fresh-out-of-college students come to law school for the wrong or uninspired reasons. Older students tend to be there because they really *want* to be in law school. Sometimes they want a law degree to further an existing career, but many have simply worked in other fields, figured out what they don't like, and made an informed decision that they'd rather be lawyers. Having a purpose for doing something is motivating. If someone joins a gym just because they think it would be "good to get more exercise," they aren't going to end up with the same results as someone who joins to train for an Iron Man competition. And they're certainly not going to be willing to sacrifice as much to get those results.

Night law students sacrifice a lot. As we've seen, for four years they have to work around the clock while putting the rest of their life on hold. This sacrifice and sense of purpose tends to make them more serious students than many day students. As one student who started law school at age forty explained:

> I had a much more serious perspective on things than the day students did. Oh, I played as hard as they did, but my play time took up much less time than theirs because the rest of my time was filled with family, work, and school. My experience gave me focus that I would not have had when I was in my early 20s. It also gave me a wider world view, which helped me see more facets of the issues we were covering in our classes. When you've had a mortgage, written a will, and been doing your own taxes for years, you just have a broader understanding of the realities of life (not to mention some of terminology in first-year Property!) than young day-student counterparts, some of whom never had a job or had to pay their own bills.

A related advantage of being an older student is that most nontraditional students don't have the time or inclination to engage in nonstop law school talk, obsess about grades and class rank, or become enmeshed in law school drama or the social scene. One former night student commented, "Having been out of school for ten years, I had sowed my wild oats and partied while in undergrad and grad school, so I was ready to settle down and study (for the most part!) in law school."

One nontraditional student explained another advantage to being older: more fully formed ethics, values, and judgment.

> By the time I started law school, my ethics and morals were set. Law is a powerful and heady career, and I firmly believe that many people go astray in the law ethically and morally because they come into it at a

time when they are still forming their ethics as adults. They're still deciding what's right and wrong. And while all of us will change and evolve, if you come into the practice of law without knowing *firmly* the difference between right and wrong, and then you're called on to handle client money, handed the responsibility to fully prepare a client's case, or ethically handle situations like candor before courts, etc., it is easy to spiral down into a mire of lying, sliding by as a mediocre attorney, and screwing with client funds (and maybe clients themselves).

More Tolerance From and Easier Relationships with Professors

I hadn't really thought about this point, but that's why I ask students for help. It surprised me that several students commented in a positive way on the unique nature of relationships between night students and professors. More than one student said that professors may be "easier" on night students. For example, one student listed as a "pro" of being a night student:

> PRO: Some professors will cut you more slack in class and respect you more for taking on such a heavy load. (Ex.: PROFESSOR: Ms. Smith, what were the facts in *Blank v. Blank*? ME: I'm sorry, professor, but I didn't get that far in the reading. PROFESSOR: It's the first case. ME: I know.)

There may be some truth to her observation, but let us pause to emphasize her use of the word "some." While law professors do respect and are sympathetic to the plight of night students, most hold them to the same high standards as day students. I've already emphasized my expectation that students be punctual. When they aren't, I give them "the evil eye" or call them out. One night while teaching a night Torts course in Miami, a student walked into class late. He was a busy surgeon, but everyone gets treated the same. I stopped class and said, "Dr. Bailey, you're late." "I'm sorry," he said sincerely. "I was in the middle of a kidney transplant operation and couldn't get out in time." What's the comeback to that? I said, "Well, alright then ... don't let it happen again." And we all had a good laugh. Dr. Bailey and I went on to become friends and co-authored a chapter in a medical textbook.

Another student commented that night students know that if they get called on once, "they may be able to slack," but added "unless they were lucky enough to take McClurg and get to *Palsgraf v. Long Island Railroad* and get grilled for two days (yeah, I'll never forget that McClurg)." Perhaps the moral of these stories is "Avoid McClurg!" No, the real moral is that night law students usually are held to the same high standards as day students, so prepare yourself. If you enter an evening-division law school program thinking it will be like an M.B.A. or other graduate school night program, you will be in for a rude awakening.

One interesting professor/student dynamic positively affecting night students is that, because they tend to be older and many of them already have successful careers, it is less likely they will tremble in the presence of their professors. As one student observed:

> I think older students can talk to the professors more easily because it's easier to see them as contemporaries. I remember a day student having an issue about a class, but she was reluctant to approach the professor. She couldn't see the professor as just another person in the world, one that would want to help her succeed. Older students just aren't as fearful of professors.

Professors recognize this "more equal footing" aspect as well, as noted by this student's comment: "I was only twenty-three when I started and quickly realized that the older students in my night classes had a lot more insights into a lot more topics. The professors seemed to realize this too. The jerky professors didn't seem to be nearly as jerky to the older students." That may be particularly true of young professors. It's harder to lower the Socratic hammer on students who are older than you are.

Unique Bonding/Less Competitiveness

All 1L classes develop close bonds and make deep friendships, but night students develop a unique bond because of their unusual shared circumstances. Their friendships are not better or deeper than the friendships that develop among day students. They're just different. Part of it is age-related, but the biggest difference is that night students are in survival mode their entire time in law school.

While most night students work hard to achieve academically, overall, they are less competitive than day students and more likely to adopt a collaborative approach to law school. One student described how she and her night comrades would work together in the library every Friday night on their legal research assignments (with the professor's permission, of course) before heading to the local pub to wind down. "No man was left behind," she said. "No one enjoyed their beer until everyone could enjoy their beer."

Other than time-management issues, comments about bonding with classmates dominated the answers of the former night students I surveyed. The below comment sums up the sentiments expressed by several students:

> It seemed to me that the younger/day students had a certain "me-centric" approach. As a very general statement, they seemed quite cutthroat in their dealings with one another. This was in contrast to the older students. I never had a problem obtaining notes or assistance from a classmate. It was as if we were all in the hull of a ship—a dark, dimly lit ship littered with delivery pizza boxes and empty coffee cups (don't question how pizza got delivered to a ship, just go with it)— all rowing in essentially the same direction, and all dependent upon each other. While we were weighed down by our common familial and personal sacrifices, we also had the bond of understanding those sacrifices in a way no one else could appreciate.

A Parting Note to Nontraditional Day Students

While this chapter has focused on part-time night students, nontraditional day students face several of the same hurdles, plus an added one: being accepted by and assimilated into the community of their younger peers. Nontraditional night students meld together easily, in part because most of their classmates also are nontraditional students. But in a large section of full-time day students, there may be, depending on the law school and particular entering class, only a couple of older students. Those students sometimes have a harder time developing a network of friends—one of the premier life-support systems for 1Ls.

An older day student, a really good guy, came to me and asked if I had any suggestions for how he could make friends with his younger peers. He said he felt isolated because they never invited him to join study groups or socialize. It broke my heart when he explained that he, a non-smoker, had taken to hanging out in front of the law school building where the smokers indulge their habit in the hope that some of them would talk to him. I offered to ask some of his classmates to include him in their activities, but he said that would embarrass him.

If you're an older day student, the extent of your social and other relations with your younger classmates will depend a lot on you and your personality. The student described above, for example, was an introverted person who sat in the back row and never volunteered in class. Much of his isolation was self-imposed. Compare him to this happy nontraditional day student who managed to seamlessly merge with the "kids" in her class:

> At fifty-five, I was the oldest person in my graduating class, but, as the saying goes, you're as young as you feel. In my case, while my body certainly looks middle-aged, I simply don't feel old. I think that having a young attitude together with a sense of humor about my age helped a lot. I jokingly referred to myself as "the old lady." I respected the young students and treated them as peers and they responded similarly. It may have helped that some of my interests were in sync with some of theirs. They were particularly impressed that I love to home-brew beer—an essential food group, of course, for law students. At the same time, there were occasions they seemed to welcome having a classmate who could impart some nonjudgmental, no strings-attached "motherly advice." Those very few students who were dismissive toward me acted stuck up toward others as well. The vast majority of my classmates were friendly and accepting. Like any other law school peers, we discussed school and exchanged outlines and notes, and supported each other in the extremely stressful law school environment. Some of the young students invited me to their parties, and I went, and we all had fun! I came to dearly love

some of those "youngsters," and we remain close friends today.

Making friends in law school, as we've discussed, usually is easy because of the co-extensiveness in the lives of law students. Everyone is taking the same classes from the same professors, feeling the same fears, bearing the same work-load, etc. But it's understandable that young adults in their early twenties might not know how to interact with substantially older classmates. The student quoted above, for example, was older than the parents of many traditional 1Ls. If you're feeling isolated, make an effort to put yourself out there a little bit, even if it takes you outside of your comfort zone. When 1L social gatherings are scheduled, show up. If you encounter a classmate in the student lounge, speak up. The same advice applies to all students, but older day students may have to do some extra work in making the first moves. Do it. It will be worth it.

* * *

This book establishes beyond peradventure—a commonly invoked judicial profundity meaning "without a doubt"—that attending law school is a unique, challenging experience, but attending law school as a nontraditional student, especially at night, is a particularly unusual and intense journey. The good news is that thousands of students do it successfully each year. The key is not just hard work. It will require a lot of that, but that won't be enough. *Careful advanced planning and sticking religiously to an organized schedule is the secret.*

CHAPTER 23

THE IMPACT OF LAW SCHOOL ON OUTSIDE RELATIONSHIPS

Conventional wisdom has it that law school is deadly for relationships, or at least very hard on them. That's one reason half of the nation's law schools offer special sessions during Orientation for married students or students with families. It is commonly said that law students suffer higher divorce rates than the rest of the population, although no reliable data exist to support that assertion. But even if law school doesn't kill outside relationships, there's no question it can add stress and conflict to them. Several factors contribute:

- Law schools train students to be argumentative and analytical with the result that even well-meaning students may approach relationships in off-putting ways.

- Law students wear down the people around them with nonstop talk about the law and law school.

- The workload and all-consuming nature of legal education can cause students to neglect loved ones.

- The foreign language and esoteric nature of law combined with the close relationships law students develop with each other can leave non-students feeling excluded and sometimes jealous.

- The stress of law school frequently spills over into outside relationships, causing friction.

- The time demands of law school may cause students to not uphold their share of everyday activities such as housekeeping or childcare.

- The high cost of legal education combined with the fact that the student is not generating income can cause money issues.

This chapter takes a look at each of these potential relationship bogies so you and your loved ones will be alert to spotting them if they come creeping into your lives. The chapter includes perspectives from both law students and their significant others, collected via surveys conducted at three law schools. Although the comments focus on partner relationships, most of what is said below applies to all close family and friendship relationships.

Symmetrical vs. Asymmetrical Relationships

First, some good news for readers whose significant other is or will also be a graduate student. Research shows that graduate students in "symmetrical" relationships have an easier time than students in "asymmetrical" relationships. As used by family relationship researchers, symmetrical relationships are relationships in which both partners are in graduate school; asymmetrical relationships are those where only one partner is in graduate school.

Several studies have found that students in symmetrical relationships have better quality marriages. In one study, graduate student couples scored higher on marital satisfaction tests.[162] Another study found that relationships in which both spouses were enrolled as college students "ranked significantly higher in quality of marriage than couples in which only one spouse was enrolled."[163] Another researcher found that graduate students in symmetrical relationships are more stable and satisfied with the relationships, while those in asymmetrical relationships "tend to be more volatile, conflictual, and dissatisfied."[164]

162. Rebecca Groves Brannock et al., *The Impact of Doctoral Study on Marital Satisfaction*, 3 J. COLLEGE COUNSELING 123, 127 (2000).

163. Gerald R. Bergen & M. Betsy Bergen, *Quality of Marriage of University Students in Relation to Sources of*

Financial Support and Demographic Characteristics, 27 FAM. COORDINATOR 245, 248 (1978).

164. Michele Scheinkman, *Graduate Student Marriages: An Organizational/Interactional View*, 27 FAM. PROCESS 351, 355 (1988).

What accounts for the difference? Partners in symmetrical relationships are more likely to share the same goals, interests, and lifestyles, all of which makes them more compatible.[165] Importantly, they *understand* each other better. They understand the academic pressures of exams and deadlines, erratic schedules, late-night studying, and other hallmarks of being a graduate student. Both partners are excited about what they are doing and working toward. They are more likely to be on equal footing, both intellectually and financially. It's much easier being dirt-poor when you're struggling together toward similar objectives.

Not so with many asymmetrical relationships. While the graduate student is soaring through an adventure filled with intellectual stimulation and dreams of better days, the non-student may be grinding away at a nine-to-five job—often an unfulfilling one—to support both of them. Whereas grad students need to spend much of their nights and weekends with noses in books or eyes locked on computer screens, non-students, like other normal human beings, want to get out and do things. When the non-student says "Let's PAR–TAY!" they don't want to hear back, "Sorry, have to STU–DAY!" Asymmetrical relationships also may be marked by feelings of inequality that can be manifested at several levels: in finances, educational attainment, and household responsibilities.[166]

Unscientific as they were, my surveys generated several comments from law students and their significant others in symmetrical relationships that supported the above propositions.

Sources of Law School Relationship Conflict

Most law students are not involved with other grad students and, even when they are, it doesn't mean their law school relationship experiences are going to be a day at the beach. Let's examine some major sources of potential conflict in relationships with law students.

Law students become overly argumentative and analytical.

Law school will literally train you to argue. Court cases are set for "argument." Not discussion, consideration, or

165. *See id.*   **166.** *Id.* at 357–59.

presentation, but *argument*. In the U.S. Supreme Court, the
proceedings in every case begin with the Chief Justice saying:
"We will hear *argument* today in [case number followed by
case name]."

Your intensive training in argumentation may begin on
the first day of classes. The Socratic method forces students
to argue and defend, not simply recite, their positions. Many
answers to professor questions will be followed up by "Why?"
Why, why, why? Every day for three years. In between
getting interrogated in class, students will be practicing for
and delivering their oral argument in the second semester of
Legal Research and Writing. For students who end up participating in moot court, arguing becomes the focus of their lives.
One insight into the relative importance that the U.S. legal
system places on resolving disputes peaceably rather than
adversarially is that only one national law student competition exists in negotiation skills compared to scores of competitions that champion argumentation skills.

Effective arguing is one of the most valuable tools of a
lawyer's trade, but it does not rank highly on lists of traits
considered helpful by psychotherapists to successful relationships. To a law student, the simplest assertion is an invita-
tion to a challenging response. If a mate complains, "You
don't give me enough attention," a law student might reply:

> First, we must define the word "attention." Attention
> comes in different degrees and forms and can reason-
> ably mean different things to different people. Let's
> assume A asks B for more attention. In response, B
> dumps a vase of water onto A's head. Would B be
> giving A attention? In one sense, yes, and yet the act
> probably would not fall within the scope of the reques-
> ter's original intent. And what about "give"? Does one
> really give attention? "Give" suggests a conveyance
> and since attention is not personal or real property, it
> cannot be conveyed. To discuss this intelligently, we
> first need to clarify the operative terms.

At this point, the non-law student may simply give up and
leave the room or perhaps pick up on B's idea and pour water
on the law student in rebuttal.

Several students recognized that their escalating propensi-
ty for argument had infiltrated their relationships:

- After my first year of law school, I was arguing with my wife in the car. I was pretty aggressive in my arguing and she got rather upset. She said, "Is this what they teach you in law school?"

- Much to the annoyance of my wife and family, I always present the other side of issues we are talking about, whether the subject is politics, sports, or whatever. I do this even if I don't agree with the side I'm arguing. They all say all I want to do is argue.

- I will argue with members of my family about anything. If they use an incorrect term, or write something on Facebook that is wrong, I will correct them. I don't like to—no, I *won't*—let an argument go. If I lose the argument on the facts, I will argue about the terms they used when making their arguments. This is a sad development.

Even more frustrating to outsiders will be the fact that law students learn to be *really good* at arguing, making it impossible for anyone to win a debate with them even when the student is wrong. Law students are trained to argue strong and weak positions equally well.

So tone it down, while also explaining to your loved ones that you do not intend to offend when "arguing" in legal-mindset mode. To a non-law student, "arguing" means "fighting." The constant questioning, clarifying, and asserting may feel like personal attacks. To a law student, "arguing" is synonymous with "discussing."

Law students also tend to become overly analytical, which is a great asset in law school and also helpful in making decisions in outside life, but can, like arguing, wear out the people around you. Asked to name his biggest change in personality after one year, a student said:

I analyze everything legally now. My friend told me he hit a deer the other day. My first question was "Was the deer in the road after you hit it?" "Yes." "Did you leave it there?" "Yes." "You had a duty to move it. You created an unreasonable risk." Last year I would have said, "Oh dang, that sucks. Did it mess up your car very much?"

Other students also recognized this change in their personalities:

- I'm sometimes unable to sufficiently enjoy what a person is saying because I have to analyze the entirety of the situation. I analyze even compliments because I have to determine if they are genuine or just situational. Although I think it's good to have an analytical mind, I worry that it's going to affect my ability to truly enjoy and develop my relationships.

- I have noticed I analyze everything about everything now. My fiancé always asks if we can just watch a show or drive down the street without me analyzing every fact about what is going on.

- I often find myself thinking that people's reasoning is faulty and many times I have let them know this. Typically, this situation arises in conversations with my wife and sometimes, if not most times, I come off as a jerk.

Developing an analytical mind is an asset in law and in life generally, but being *overly* analytical is not always the best course toward leading a full, spontaneous existence. In Torts, you will study Judge Learned Hand's famous economic cost-benefit formula for determining when conduct is negligent and, like many students, may adopt it, either consciously or unconsciously, as a guiding principle for making decisions.[167] Asked to name their biggest change in personality after one year of law school, several students replied with comments like this one: "I apply the Hand formula in every situation. I don't do this by choice. It is an automatic response, much like breathing or blinking." Judge Hand's formula is a handy tool for rational decision-making, but not all of life's decisions should be grounded exclusively in cost-benefit weighing.

---

167. In *U.S. v. Carroll Towing Co.*, 159 F.2d 169 (2d Cir. 1947), a case involving a barge that broke free and caused damage, Judge Hand set forth a famous algebraic economic cost-benefit formula for determining whether injury-causing conduct was *reasonable* or *unreasonable*. If reasonable, the defendant is off the hook. If unreasonable, the defendant is liable for negligence and must pay damages. The formula is $B < P \times L$. B stands for the burden of avoiding a risk of harm, P is the probability that the risk will actually cause harm, and L stands for the severity of the harm if it occurs. The formula states that if the burden of avoiding the risk is less than the probability of the harm multiplied by the severity of the potential harm, the conduct is unreasonable (i.e., negligent). Conversely, if the burden of avoiding the risk outweighs the probability times the severity of harm, the conduct is reasonable (i.e., non-negligent).

Suppose you and your partner are looking to rent or buy a house. You come across a house you both absolutely love. Being a law student, you naturally begin conducting a thorough cost-benefit analysis that includes weighing the cost against the square footage, floor plan, condition of the back fence, etc.—all worthy considerations, except they ignore what may be the most important factor of all: *that you love the house*!

Law students talk too much about the law and law school.

Law students, especially 1Ls, tend to overwhelm everyone around them by insisting on talking constantly about the law and law school. *Anything* can trigger a law-related, analytical response from a law student. If a partner says, "Honey, hold my hand," the student may respond: "Hand! Good old Judge Learned Hand. Now there was a great judge. Have I told you about the famous opinion he wrote in this case where a barge broke free and . . ."

Think I'm exaggerating? Check out the below comment, which made me laugh out loud, from a 1L explaining what she likes to talk about to her boyfriend:

> Recently, my boyfriend and I went to a wedding. It was very liturgical and the priest went on forever about promises. So naturally I started thinking enforceable promises—that is, contracts. I perked up in the ceremony and started listening very intently and my boyfriend was sitting there wondering why I was so interested (like most men, he was probably quaking in his boots that I was expecting to catch the bouquet). Seconds after the ceremony was over, I busted out with, "It's a contract! There was offer, acceptance, and the rings are consideration!"

> Sometimes I tell him "what I know" but I don't tell him the rule or anything. I guess I do this just to make him realize I really am learning a lot here. Like, for example, we passed a cat that was in the middle of the median on a country highway, fixing to catch a mouse. I told him I could tell him who the cat belongs to, even though it was a stray (law of capture, rules about wild animals on state property). Once I tickled him and he told me to stop, and I kept going and told him "You

know, this is a battery. I'm battering you right now." I also told him about the rules of engagement rings if an affianced pair of our friends happened to call it off before the wedding. I wore his robe and told him I was "trespassing on his chattels," and explained that if I took it home with me, it would be a conversion. Torts actually comes up a lot. But, come to think of it, I really don't tell him anything from Civil Procedure.

Poor bloke. I picture him shaking his head thinking, "Why couldn't she have gone for an M.B.A. instead?"

It's a great thing to be excited about law school! On the other hand, you have to keep in mind the non-legals around you. Imagine if the shoe were on the other foot. Imagine that your significant other enrolled in a Ph.D program studying a subject completely foreign to you, say, genetics. Every night after school, he or she waxes rapturously for hours about mitochondrial DNA and hematopoietic stem cells. When you suggest dinner and a movie one night, the response is: "Are you kidding? Not with my paper on gene-mapping due at the end of the week!" When you go out with your partner's new friends, instead of sports, music, or politics, the conversation turns immediately to homologous recombination and dishing about classmates and professors you don't know. How would you feel? Left out? Threatened? Unimportant?

This doesn't mean you shouldn't talk about law school, but moderate your conversations and focus on the good stuff. Generally speaking, subjects like the margin and font requirements for your legal writing memo do not command rapt attention. On the other hand, many loved ones find law school hypos, weird cases, and unusual doctrines to be interesting. Just be sure to give listeners a context for what you're talking about. One of the biggest complaints non-students have about law talk is that students don't take time to define their terms. As one significant other to a law student explained:

> I find any topic involving law school interesting if it is discussed in a manner courteous to those who are not in law school and who are unfamiliar with law school lingo. Law students love to talk about law school even around those who do not understand words and concepts usually only used in law school. To make law school interesting to non-students, you have to actually

consider those not in law school. This is the step most commonly skipped.

Law students can be neglectful.

No one in a relationship wants to feel like they rank anywhere except first place in the hearts, minds, and souls of their loved ones. Unfortunately, a variety of factors can combine to leave the loved ones of law students feeling neglected.

Neglect due to time demands. The time demands of law school can be a major source of discontent and disruption in relationships. One researcher of graduate student marriages observed that "[o]ver time, the graduate student's studies become like a lover to whom the student is totally devoted."[168] That made me laugh because of a comment received from a 1L at my current institution, The University of Memphis Cecil C. Humphreys School of Law: "My husband has asked me on numerous occasions if I am having an affair with someone, namely Cecil C. Humphreys." Here's what some other law students said about how the time demands of law school impacted their relationships:

- Lack of time spent together is the biggest problem, especially when I am at home but not really "there" because I'm doing homework. There have been times, such as studying for finals, that my wife hates my computer because I spend more time with it than with her. . . . She'd try to draw me away, and though I wanted to, I just had so much to do, the breaks would be short—to eat dinner or talk for a bit. I know this bothered her.

- Because my wife is the breadwinner and I am the student, I think we both felt going in that I would have more time, both practically and emotionally, to be available to help with our then infant daughter. She has regularly told our friends that she dreads my return to school after vacations, because I "disappear." Ironically, I have always felt like I could have invested so much more in law school and have held back because of my commitments at home.

168. Scheinkman, *supra*, at 359–60.

• I was in a long-distance relationship that did not survive beyond the winter break. We made it through the first semester, but my significant other was often hurt by the lack of time to talk on the phone, which was our only means of interacting. We only saw each other twice during the fall semester. We talked on the phone briefly each day and at night—but there never seemed to be enough time to truly nurture the relationship. The emotional and mental tug I felt from the relationship began to be too much.

Neglect due to preoccupation with law school. A common complaint from people who are close to law students is that even when law students are physically present they are mentally absent, preoccupied by law school. An anecdote from a law student recorded by researchers studying the effect of law school on marital relationships offers an amusing snapshot of the problem. The student was describing her thought process on occasions when her husband attempted to be amorous:

> There are times on a Saturday or something, he'll try to be all romantic. He'll come to my office, I'm studying, he'll put his arms around me and he'll be like would you come with me? Let's go to bed. And I have had days where, honestly and this is like kinda sick, ... I'm just like wondering how fast we can do this because I have reading to do.... I'm like, "oh my god ok, we gotta make this quick because I have this and this to do. My husband is trying to be romantic and I'm thinking about torts."[169]

Neglect due to exhaustion/lack of energy. A third cause of neglect is that law students simply get worn out physically and mentally from the burdens of law school, leaving them with insufficient energy to give to their outside relationships. Two students, one female and one male, respectively, explain:

• Law school was a big adjustment in my marriage. Although my husband is extremely supportive, he would get frustrated with me and school at times. Usually it would happen when I continued to break

---

169. Deanna Boyd McQuillan & Carrie Elizabeth Foote, *Law School and* *Marriage: Making It Work*, 42 MARRIAGE & FAM. REV. 7, 17 (2007).

our "date night" because I wanted to sit at home and watch TV or sleep when I had free time. Law school is very draining because of all of the attention to detail and stress students are under to properly prepare for class. So when I had free time, I did not want to do anything except be alone and not think about anything.

- Oftentimes when I get home I'm tired from a day of waking up early and stretching my brain to the breaking point. After my reading for the night is done, I usually just want to watch a mindless television show or stare at the wall for a few minutes. My wife, on the other hand, loves going outside and doing involved activities. Occasionally she gets frustrated because I'm boring and don't have the drive to do anything fun. I'm not boring! I'm just burned out!

But don't let these comments worry you too much. Maybe your partner is an optimistic soul who always looks at the bright side, like this husband of a 1L:

Law school hasn't really caused any stress or conflict. It's actually been a lot better for me because now she stays up all night studying, which means the bed is all mine. Then it gets even better when I wake up because she'll still be studying, meaning sometimes I get lucky and my breakfast will already be ready for me before I head out to work.

It's essential to find ways to carve out time away from law school, not only for your own sake as discussed in Chapter 20, but for the sanity of those around you. For couples, a common strategy is to reserve "date nights." But review your schedule carefully in advance to ensure you won't have to back out. Relationship research shows that scheduling and then cancelling date nights is worse than never scheduling them in the first place because it breeds anger and resentment.

I polled significant others of law students as to ways they managed to "get away from law school" with their student. They replied with a long list of great ideas, everything from go-carting to let off steam to "no computer days" to spending a night in a nearby hotel as a type of fantasy vacation. Most of their strategies did not involve or require expensive or excitement-filled vacations or other excursions. Often the simplest pleasures of together-time are the most fulfilling.

Law school can cause jealousy.

Subsumed within feelings of neglect can be feelings of jealousy arising from the fact that law students spend so much time absorbed in law school and with their new law school friends. This jealousy can assume the form of "priority jealousy," where a partner feels they've been supplanted in the hierarchy of importance in the other's life and/or "exclusivity jealousy," where a partner worries that the other is acting in ways that violate the exclusive compact of a romantic relationship.[170]

Priority jealousy can arise from both the student's fixation on law school itself and the close bonding that occurs among law students. Partners may resent that they are being made to take a backseat to law school and the student's new circle of friends. As one student wrote: "Jealousy is a problem. Spending so much time with students and books, and talking about them to loved ones, may lead the loved one to think that your highest priority is not your relationship but law school and law buddies."

Exclusivity jealousy, also called "romantic jealousy," arises from a concern that the student is engaging in behavior that threatens the exclusivity of an intimate relationship. It doesn't have to involve any kind of physical contact, although that may be part of the underlying fear. It includes any behavior that violates the jealous partner's understanding of his or her exclusive relationship rights, for lack of a better term, such as sharing personal information or going to lunch together.[171]

As an example, a student came to me asking for advice on how to handle a situation where his serious girlfriend was extremely jealous that he had begun studying with a female classmate. The girlfriend insisted he stop studying with her and he didn't know what to do. He insisted the study arrangement was innocent and that he loved his girlfriend. Of course, I didn't try to tell him what to do, but I did point out

---

170. Padmal De Silva, *Jealousy in Couple Relationships: Nature, Assessment and Therapy*, 35 BEHAV. RES. THERA-PY 973, 975 (1997) (describing these two types of jealousy).

171. *Id.*

that sometimes we have to do things that are important to our partners even if they seem irrational to us.

In my surveys, I received two interesting conflicting gender-based comments about jealousy. A female student said "the only instances where I have seen jealousy occur is with male students attending law school and their significant others becoming jealous of the women they are meeting in school." But a male student said exactly the opposite: "My gut opinion is that, as a general rule, female students have jealous boyfriends whereas male students generally do not appear to have jealous girlfriends." Who's right? My guess is both are half-right.

One point that stood out clearly from the student comments was that jealousy and feelings of neglect are much less of an issue for students who incorporate their partners into their new law school social lives. Several comments paralleled this one: "My boyfriend only expressed jealous feelings toward the beginning of the program when I was hanging out with new friends without him. Once he met my new friends and began attending law school social events with me, most of the jealous feelings seemed to drop off."

From this, we can derive an important piece of advice in maintaining outside relationships: Get your loved ones involved in your law school experience. Introduce them to your new law school friends early on and invite them to law school social events. Invite them to sit in on a class with you, which most professors will allow, so they can see what it's all about.

Law school stress spills over into relationships.

Researchers have long studied the "spillover effect" of work demands and pressures on non-work relationships. As the name suggests, spillover theory posits that negative aspects of work, including stress, are often brought home by the worker and can affect the worker's family. No big surprise there. While some are better at compartmentalizing than others, it's difficult to separate major portions of our lives and store them in neatly segregated boxes.

The spillover effect of stress from law school is real, as shown by these student comments:

- Like, right now I'm at about a seven on the stress scale. I overreact to small stimuli, like the other day

my boyfriend made a maneuver in a game we played
that virtually clinched that I would lose, and I started crying and told him we never played with that
rule before, which is unlike me. I'm usually a good
sport.

- Fights have stemmed from everything from "Are
  there any pretty girls in your class?" to "Is your
  memo more important than this relationship?" I'm,
  of course, not always innocent either. I remember
  losing it one night after a long week of classes when
  I had a light homework load and fell asleep on the
  couch watching TV. About fifteen minutes later my
  girlfriend came in and woke me up because she was
  bored and wanted to go do something. I wasn't
  happy about being woken up so I started yelling. We
  fought for about an hour.

- In general, I am on a very short fuse now, so a
  comment or suggestion that I would otherwise consider with a grain of salt can set me off or piss me
  off. There have been two instances where my emotional intelligence decreased to that of a shrieking
  three-year-old and a normal conversation with my
  boyfriend turned into an outlandish fight. I trans-
  formed from a normal person into a scary, scary
  beast.

In Chapter 20, we discussed strategies for lowering stress and
raising well-being. To borrow a legal term, your close friends
and other loved ones will be third-party beneficiaries of your
following those strategies.

Law students may ignore their fair share
of household responsibilities.

One of the most dramatic changes in role expectations,
and a frequent source of conflict in relationships with law
students, concerns the fair division of household responsibilities. In my surveys, this issue was raised almost exclusively
by women law students. Their comments included:

- Yes, law school has caused conflict. I feel like I need
  more help around the house and with general household matters. Prior to school I took care of everything, worked full time, and cooked dinner every
  night. Now, I still feel pressure to take care of the

house, but I don't have the time or energy. I definitely am stressed and I am trying to remember that I chose to do this.

- He mentioned that the house is a big mess and I haven't cooked in months. This made me feel really guilty. Then I got over it and went back to studying. Seriously, my priorities have shifted dramatically. Things that I used to take care of for my family have fallen to my spouse now.

- Stress has primarily come up for us in terms of household expectations. I feel like my husband should just *know* how stressed I am or what a hard day I had. But he *doesn't*. We have had all kinds of spats when I get home from twelve hours of studying and the dogs need a walk or the dishes need to be washed, and I expect him to just take care of it all. Communication is key. It's not fair for him to think that I will have the energy to do household chores at the end of the day, but it's not fair for me to expect that he will just take care of it all himself, despite his full-time job.

In her groundbreaking book, *The Second Shift*, first published in 1989, Arlie Hochschild documented the inequalities in the distribution of household responsibilities between working men and women. The book's title referred to the fact that many women in dual-career couples came home from a long day at work only to begin their second job: taking care of the household and family. With regard to higher education students, studies show that women students traditionally have experienced greater role conflict in this regard than men. Instead of adjusting or shifting their existing roles when they become students, many women attempt to simply add their new role as student on top of their other roles as worker, parent, and spouse, and attempt to perform all of them at the same high level; i.e., the "supermom."[172]

No research exists specific to law students, but whether you are a male or female student, if division of household labor is or becomes an issue in your relationships, the obvious solution is to discuss it and have each party agree to bear his or her fair share of the load. Of course, concurring on the definition of "fair share" can be a sticking point, in part

---

172. Patricia A.H. Dyk, *Graduate Student Management of Family and Ac-* *ademic Roles*, 36 FAM. REL. 329, 329 (1987) (discussing relevant studies).

because of what I call the "Who Has It Worse?" syndrome, a situation in which both the law student and the gainfully employed partner each think the other has the easier life.

Law students are often lost in and overwhelmed by their study carrel-size law school world. Particularly in the first year, students are so wrapped up in the workload and suffocated by the pressures that they can't imagine anything being worse. Meanwhile, non-law students who spend their days "workin' for a living" may have little sympathy for someone whose major life responsibility is simply attending "school." These opposing perceptions may cause both parties to end up stuck in competing thought processes like the following (which I made up):

Non-law student during the day: "Great. She's out sipping a caramel macchiato with her 'study group' while I have to work on these stupid reports all afternoon!"

Law student during the evening: "Nice. He's on the couch with a beer playing video games while I have to work on this stupid memo all night!"

As with most difficult issues in relationships, both sides have valid positions. To some extent, law school is a better, easier life than a full-time job, mainly because law students have flexible schedules and more free time during the day than most full-time workers. On the other hand, unlike most employees, a law student's work day doesn't end at 5 or 6 p.m. For many, the hardest parts of the day—reading and briefing cases, outlining, working on their memos—are just starting. For most students, this carries over to weekends and even holidays. And while some jobs are stressful and exhausting, many aren't. They may be boring and unfulfilling, but they aren't necessarily stressful or exhausting. Law students suffer abundant doses of both stress and exhaustion.

If you live with an intimate partner or with your family, the division of household responsibilities is an issue that should be thought about and discussed *prior* to law school, recognizing that everyone will have to be flexible in implementing the plan and making adjustments as events unfold.

Law student debt and lack of revenue can cause financial conflict.

Studies show that money is the most common issue about which couples fight. Particularly relevant to law students and their significant others, several studies have found that debt brought into a marriage can be a thorn in the union, and that worries about debt are linked to negative emotional outcomes, such as depression, for young couples.[173] One study of married college students found that couples with minor debt have much higher quality of marriage scores than couples who depend heavily on student loans for income.[174]

As one wife of a law student complained: "Law school is expensive. I really don't want his debt. I get mad because he is in law school and he jokes around saying things like, 'I want to be an importer-exporter.' Well, that is just great because you are in law school wasting away money and causing us financial strain."

This is all the more reason to pay attention to the advice in Chapter 20: stay determined and steadfast in doing everything possible to minimize your expenditures and keep a lid on your student loan debt.

* * *

When it comes to your outside relationships, here's the bottom line as summed up by a 2L: "Something I wish my family understood is that no matter how much they think they understand about everything I'm doing/going through, *they do not understand!*" Non-law students will never be able to fully understand law students or their lives, but that doesn't mean you shouldn't try to educate them.

Read this chapter with them. Even better, get them a copy of *The "Companion Text" to Law School: Understanding and Surviving Life with a Law Student* (2012). And you're thinking, "Well, duh, of course you would recommend your own book, McClurg." To assure you that this recommendation is completely unbiased, I solicited the opinions of others, including my literary agent and the trustee of my daughter's education fund, and they both said exactly the same thing. Seriously, dozens of books have been written to prepare students for law school, but *The "Companion Text" to Law School* is the only book devoted to preparing students' loved ones.

---

173. *Id.* (discussing studies).   **174.** Bergen & Bergen, *supra*, at 250.

CHAPTER 24
LAW REVIEW, MOOT COURT, AND OTHER CO- AND EXTRACUR-RICULAR ACTIVITIES

Your course work will consume most of your time, but a variety of co-curricular and extracurricular activities also take place in law schools. Some of them can be important to determining your future. While deep involvement in these activities is reserved largely for upper-level students, the first year is when students may face decisions as to which of these paths to follow.

The activities discussed in this chapter are voluntary, yet some of them require the dedication of hundreds of hours of labor. Wait! Don't flip ahead yet. While seeing "voluntary" and "hundreds of hours of labor" in the same sentence might seem like an excellent reason to skip this chapter, you'd be amazed by the large percentage of students who actively pursue these extensive commitments. Why do they do it? Because these activities give students opportunities to sharpen their lawyering skills, enrich their law school experience, find and create a distinct legal identity for themselves, meet and spend time with like-minded students, develop mentoring relationships with faculty, lawyers, and judges, and, importantly, bolster their resume credentials.

Law Review

Every law school publishes a "law review," a student-run, student-edited journal of scholarly legal articles written primarily by law professors, but also by judges, lawyers, and students. Law reviews typically publish four to six issues per year, with each issue containing a few primary articles by outside authors and a few works written by student members of the law review. Some law review articles become influential in the development of the law, while many others are read only by the authors and a few close relatives.

Being on law review has long been the holy grail of law school success. The law review stamp defines its holder as an elite academic performer. Traditionally, this was necessarily the case because the only students invited to participate on law review were those with high class ranks.

Today, most law reviews select members through a summer "write-on competition" at the conclusion of the first year. At some schools, any student can participate in the write-on competition, but many schools impose a minimum GPA requirement to participate. Some law reviews use a dual system combining automatic grade-on qualifiers and write-on participants.

Write-on competition details vary, but they typically include a time-limited writing assignment over a period of days, such as an analysis of a recent case, accompanied by a test on *Bluebook* citation style. One drawback of write-on competitions is that they discourage some worthy applicants from trying out, especially because the competitions take place shortly after the completion of first-year exams. Understandably, the last thing students want to take on immediately after concluding their exhausting first year is an intensive writing competition.

To achieve law review membership status—and, hence, the ability to list law review as a resume credential—students must successfully complete one and sometimes two major writing projects that travel under the names "casenote," "note," and "comment." A casenote is an extensive analysis of a significant case. Notes and comments (essentially the same thing with different labels) have a broader focus, addressing a topical legal issue rather than an individual case. They usually are thesis-driven works in which the writer makes a claim that some aspect of the law should be changed. Student law review works require in-depth research and a good deal of rewriting. They often reach fifty pages in length and usually contain more than two hundred footnotes. The best of these student works get selected for publication in the law review.

In addition to the writing requirements, staff members are required to do painstaking "cite-checking" of articles that have been accepted by the law review for publication. This involves verifying the accuracy of footnote citations as to both proper *Bluebook* format and substantive content. While anything but fun, these assignments force students to become masters of the *Bluebook*, a valuable, but underappreciated skill.

Particularly ambitious and well-qualified students go on to become law review editors (rather than just staff members), which is considered an especially high honor. The editor-in-chief of the law review occupies a law school status equivalent to being the captain of a starship.

Each year the current board of editors selects, through an application process, the editors for the next year. The student editors run the entire operation, much to the chagrin of law professors, who submit the bulk of article manuscripts for publication consideration. In the ultimate role reversal of legal education, students accustomed to being lorded over by law professors in every aspect of their law student existence suddenly have the upper-hand as professors from around the country—desperate to publish lest they perish—come begging to have their articles published. It's pretty hilarious.

Making matters even more topsy-turvy, once an article is accepted for publication, the students edit it. So now we have law students who only recently exited their first-year legal writing courses telling professors how to write. Classic. On the other hand, a lot of student law review editors prove to be much better researchers and writers than some of the professors and lawyers submitting articles.

Other than the devilish pleasure of telling law professors what do to, what does law review have to offer students other than a lot of hard work? Several things. Students earn some credit hours for law review. Many schools give full or partial tuition waivers or scholarships to editors, at least to the higher-ranking editors. Also, pursuant to an ABA-accreditation rule, law schools require upper-level students to complete one substantial writing project as a graduation requirement and law review student works usually satisfy that requirement. Law review helps members advance their skills as legal researchers and writers. A few members get their student works accepted for publication in the law review.

Graduating law school as a published legal scholar is a pretty neat deal.

But you may be thinking, "Yeah, I guess that stuff sounds okay, but I still can't see how it justifies voluntarily taking on hundreds of hours of extra work." I agree. Honestly, I found law review to be a tedious, largely unfulfilling experience. Cite-checking assignments were dreadful. Other important duties assigned to me included making coffee for the editors on Tuesday mornings and printing and collating student course outlines that the law review sold to other students for profit. The editing supervision I received on my casenote and note was unexceptional, not surprising since it came from untrained student editors with only slightly more experience than I had.

Would I do it all over if I had the chance? Absolutely, because of one benefit not described above: being able to write "law review" on your resume. Law review is still viewed as the ultimate academic credential of legal education. Law review status operates as a kind of VIP-admission ticket into the world of legal employment. I used to live and teach in Miami, home of many popular nightclubs in famous South Beach. At the trendy clubs, long lines of people form behind a rope each night and bouncers at the door pick and choose who gets to come inside. As my students explained it to me, the only ones invited past the rope are the "beautiful people." Well, being on law review makes you one of the beautiful people in the legal job market.

Many law firms, especially large ones, won't interview students who were not on law review. Most federal and many state judges limit consideration of applicants for judicial clerkships to law review members. While not always accurate, many employers use law review status as a litmus test for evaluating legal talent.

If you have the GPA necessary to qualify, you should definitely give the law review write-on competition a try. The odds might be in your favor depending on the size of the school. The smaller the school, the better the odds. At my current institution, roughly one out of every two competition participants makes the law review. And while it may be small comfort, even if you don't make law review, you'll improve your writing and *Bluebooking* skills by participating in the competition.

If you don't make or try out for the primary law review, consider participating on a "secondary journal" as they're called. In addition to the main law review, most law schools publish other journals focusing on particular subject areas. Large schools usually publish several secondary journals. Pick a legal topic and there's a good chance a law school is publishing a specialized journal devoted to it. Art law, civil rights law, elder law, health law, international law, media law, race, gender and sexual identity law, sports law, tax law, technology law—there are secondary journals devoted to those subjects and many more. At last count, U.S. law schools were publishing, in addition to their primary law reviews, a whopping 440 secondary journals.

The proliferation of secondary journals is good news for law students because they substantially increase the opportunities for students to serve on a scholarly journal. While being a member of a secondary journal is not considered as prestigious as serving on the primary law review, it still carries resume weight. Moreover, if the secondary journal focuses on a subject area in which you have a genuine interest, the experience might be more enjoyable and meaningful than serving on the primary law review. The selection process for secondary journal membership typically is similar to that for the primary law review: some combination of a write-on competition and minimum GPA, although the GPA requirement may be relaxed or eliminated.

Moot Court

Not considered as marketable as law review, but still an excellent resume credential and a whole lot more fun and exciting, is moot court. "Moot court" is basically "mock court" in an appellate setting, as opposed to a trial setting. Like law reviews, moot court has been around in legal education for a long time, beginning at Harvard Law School in the mid–1840s.

Most law schools have a moot court program. While they vary considerably in their structures and expansiveness, the programs sometimes begin at the ground level with a first-year intramural appellate argument competition. Students who show promise or interest or both can then apply to serve on the school's moot court board and moot court "travel teams" as upper-level students.

Moot court competitions, whether intramural or inter-school, operate similarly. Participants receive a package of materials containing an abbreviated appellate record of a fictitious case that is pending on appeal before a high court, often the U.S. Supreme Court. Intramural competitions usually involve teams of two. Each team argues the legal issues raised by the problem against other student teams in front of three-person panels of mock appellate judges, which might include law professors, lawyers, real judges, or law students. The problems usually raise two legal issues, enabling each student to argue one issue during the mock appellate proceeding. After each set of arguments, the panel of judges declares a winning team and that team advances to the next round. Competitions may be structured as either single- or double-elimination.

Members of moot court travel teams, which typically include three students, participate in regional and national moot court competitions, of which there are many, against teams from other law schools. The major competitions attract teams from more than 100 schools. Teams are judged both on their written briefs and oral arguments. In big competitions, the judges may include heavyweights from the U.S. Courts of Appeal and, occasionally, even U.S. Supreme Court justices.

Like law review, moot court requires a lot of work. Before even getting to the long rounds of practice arguments leading up to a competition, each competition team must research and write a lengthy appellate brief arguing one side of the issues. In oral argument, however, students must be able to argue both sides. Thus, in round one they may argue "on brief" (i.e., taking the same positions they argued in their written brief), while in round two they may be required to switch positions and argue "off brief." In judging practice rounds, I'm always amazed by the ability of students to accomplish this complete mind-switch in just the few minutes between arguments.

Moot court carries some of the same benefits as law review, along with some extras. Like law review, moot court participation, especially at the board level, usually carries some credit hours. Board members may get a full or partial tuition waiver or scholarship. A moot court brief often satisfies the law school's upper-level writing requirement. Additionally, moot court forces students to develop both writing *and* oral advocacy skills. It trains students to think on their feet and work as a part of a team. Accomplishments in moot court are more visible and easily recognized than law review accomplishments. Winning or placing highly in a moot court competition is a heady honor, one that schools feature prominently on their websites and in other marketing materials.

After reading about law review and moot court, you may be wondering, as many students do, "If I have to choose between law review and moot court, which one should I pick?" It is possible to do both, although I don't recommend it. A few remarkable students pull off the double-duty without a losing a step in either, but for most students something has to give because of the intense time commitments of both activities, not to mention ongoing school responsibilities.

From this reading, the choice may seem obvious: "Hmm, let's see. I could choose to spend my time writing and checking hundreds of footnotes or I could argue a case before the Supreme Court. I wonder which would be more fun." You couldn't go wrong with either choice, but if my daughter went to law school and came to me asking which activity to pursue, I'd go with law review because of the unique emphasis placed on law review by legal employers.

Other Competitions

In addition to moot court, law schools often sponsor teams in other types of skills competitions. Trial competitions are the most common type after moot court. Trial competitions generally involve two- or three-member student teams who compete against other student teams, either from the same school or other schools, in mock trial proceedings. Moot court, remember, involves appellate proceedings. Thus, instead of simply making legal arguments to judges, students examine and cross-examine witnesses, admit documentary evidence, and make opening and closing statements to juries.

Depending on your school, opportunities may also exist to participate in mock negotiation, arbitration, and client counseling competitions. The ABA sponsors national competitions in each of these areas. Negotiation competitions pit law students, acting as lawyers, against other students in attempting to resolve legal problems through negotiation, rather than adversarial legal proceedings. In arbitration competitions, student teams match up in a mock arbitration case, an increasingly common type of alternative dispute resolution proceeding that is much less formal than a traditional trial. Client counseling competitions involve students interacting with mock clients. The competitions simulate a first consultation with the client at which the student lawyers seek to extract legally relevant information related to the client's problem and analyze and discuss possible courses of action. These competitions offer several of the same rewards as moot court, although they are less prominent in law school landscapes.

Student Organizations

All law schools permit students to form organizations related to particular student interests. Student organizations enable students to explore and advance legal causes and subjects about which they are passionate, while providing a social outlet and opportunity to network with like-minded people. Joining a student organization is a great way to meet people and enrich your law school experience. Especially if you feel alienated or isolated, as many law students do, a student group can provide a real boost to your spirits and morale.

In the tough legal job market that descended after the 2008 recession, participating in extracurricular activities such as student organizations has acquired new importance. In any market, the top law students have always been and will always be able to find good jobs. But these days, a lot of students—including many excellent students who do not happen to be at the top of their class—are having a much harder time of it. A 1L explained the networking benefits she obtained from participating in student organizations:

> Even for 1Ls, extracurricular activities are important and give access to networking. They have given me a mentor, relationships with upper-level students, Alternative Spring Break experience, and now a clerk position on the executive board of Phi Alpha Delta. These things will hopefully distinguish me from my peers who do nothing but study, and will help me to continue to grow my networking base.

The range of law school student organizations is limited only by a lack of student interest in starting one and keeping it active. I asked a research assistant to do some quick surfing through law school websites and she returned with a list of more than 300 different types of student organizations. There's a little something for everyone out there. (Speaking of surfing, one California law school even has a Surf Club.) Student organizations exist representing just about every imaginable racial, ethnic, and religious group, political viewpoint (e.g., libertarianism, anarchy), social cause (e.g., animal rights, reproductive rights), and legal subject area (e.g., environmental law, national security law). Student organizations devoted to recreational pursuits include those appealing to interests in sports and hobbies (e.g., boxing, hockey), games (e.g., bridge, chess), and culinary tastes (e.g., cooking, single-malt whiskey).

Assuming sufficient student interest can be shown (usually by compiling a petition), it's feasible at most schools to start a student organization by following a few simple requirements such as drafting a constitution and compiling a proposed budget. One way to gauge the level of student engagement at a school is to check out the school's website for a list of student organizations, although be cognizant of the correlation between the number of student organizations and size of the law school. The larger the law school, the more student organizations it will have.

Most law schools also maintain active chapters of the two largest national law school fraternities: Phi Delta Phi and Phi Alpha Delta. Expect to have upper-level students hitting you up to join one or both of them. While both fraternities promote themselves as professional and social organizations, Phi Delta Phi is generally seen as the more academically oriented of the two, while Phi Alpha Delta is known more for its social activities. Visit their websites for more information: Phi Delta Phi, http://phideltaphi.org, and Phi Alpha Delta, http://www.pad.org.

One other student organization warrants special mention: student government. All law schools have a Student Government Association (SGA), also sometimes called the Student Bar Association (SBA). They are made up of elected officers, including a president, vice-president, treasurer, secretary, representatives from each class and, for 1Ls, each section of the first-year class. Depending on the particular officers and law school tradition, the SGA may be more concerned with organizing social events than with improving academic life or the reputation of the law school. When it comes time to vote for SGA officers, don't just vote for your friends, smooth talkers, or the candidates who hand out free candy. Vote for the folks you think will be truly committed to improving the quality of your law school.

Outside Speakers

Law schools and student organizations often bring in outside speakers, many of them prominent in their fields, to enrich the intellectual life of the school. These can be either individual speakers or groups of speakers brought in for an all-day symposium sponsored by the law review or a secondary journal. The Environmental Law Society, for example, may bring in an expert on climate change for a luncheon talk, while the Federalist Society may bring in a pro-gun rights speaker.

Regrettably, because law students are so busy, these events often are poorly attended, which doesn't reflect well on the school. Professors sometimes require students to attend presentations in lieu of class, both as a way to enrich the students and ensure a good turnout. Most individual presentations are held during lunch and include free food for attendees. If that's the case, take a break from your studies, go to the presentation and grab a bite and some extra knowledge.

CHAPTER 25

RECAPPING LAW SCHOOL'S FIRST YEAR IN THE WORDS OF STUDENTS

I think it's much easier to tell someone else that, to succeed in law school, "You've got to do this, you've got to do that, etc." than it is being the incoming student and having an appreciation for and actually listening to and implementing what someone else is telling you.

—1L nearing completion of the first year

One of the frustrating aspects about giving advice on how to succeed in law school is the certain knowledge that many students won't follow it. This is true no matter how great the advice. As we near the end of our figurative 1L ride, I thought the best way to reinforce the advice for law school success and well-being that you've been reading would be to hear it retold in the words of those who labored through the real 1L odyssey. Borrowing from humor writer Dave Barry, I'm hoping that reading the same advice coming from law students will assure you that "I was not making this stuff up" and help drive home the key points.

Shortly before the end of their first year, I posed some combination of the following questions to different groups of 1Ls:

- Name one thing you know now (other than the law) that you wish you had known when you started law school.

- As you near the end of your first year, what has surprised you the most about law school compared to your expectations going into it?
- Think back to when you were starting law school, specifically to your fears or concerns. In retrospect, which fear or concern do you think was the most exaggerated or overblown as compared to the reality of law school and which fear or concern do you think you most underestimated or overlooked?
- Imagine one of your closest friends or relatives is starting law school. What advice would you give them?
- What is your dominant feeling or sentiment (e.g., relief, nostalgia, frustration, exhaustion) as you near the end of law school's first year?

Below are select answers to each question, which I've grouped under subheadings to give them some structure. As you read the student advice, think back and try to connect it to the specific sections of this book where you first heard it. Specifically, think about the C.R.E.D.O. chapter and take note of how many of the tips relate to the habits of being Consistent, Rigorous, Efficient, Diligent, and Organized.

You'll note some overlap in the answers. For example, some students said the importance of not falling behind was the one thing they wished they had known when starting law school, while others listed it as the most important piece of advice they would give to a loved one who was starting law school. Contrarily, some students gave opposing comments about the same topic, which is also enlightening. For example, one student listed competitiveness as their most exaggerated fear, while another listed it as their most underestimated fear, showing once again that while many reliable generalizations can be made about law school and law students, no two law school experiences are identical.

QUESTION: Name one thing you know now (other than the law) that you wish you had known when you started law school.

Law School Will Be One of the Most Difficult Challenges of Your Life

- I think the one notion that students have about the law school experience is that it will be difficult. This is universal. I think students underestimate tremendously the type of difficulty that they will encounter. It is not necessarily that the material is always exceptionally difficult to understand, but that the process by which you learn and the sheer quantity of work required to learn—let alone master—the subject matter is overwhelming. I wish that I had some understanding of that before I started the whole deal.

- I wish I had known how mentally taxing law school was going to be. Beyond "learning the law" there is the stress of getting good grades, legal writing assignments, moot court, etc. Further, trying to balance this stress with the normal stress of life (family, relationships, money, etc.) is a challenge in and of itself.

- I wish I'd known how easy it is to fail out. I just assumed law school would be slightly harder than college—I was way off.

But It Can Be Done, So Take Heart

- I wish I'd had the confidence in my abilities at the beginning of the year that I have now. I'd stress to readers that if they have been accepted to law school, they are fully capable of doing well in law school. They didn't get there by some mistake in the admissions process. They didn't get someone else's letter of acceptance. I think there's a tendency to assume that because we've never done something, we "can't" do it. We say this sort of thing all the time. If a person has never learned to cook, they'll say, "I can't cook." In law school, it might be "I can't argue a case" because they've never done it. I'd recommend that new students do their best to put a stop to that way of thinking and say instead, "I haven't learned *yet* to cook" or "I haven't learned *yet* to argue a case" or whatever.

It's a Brave New World

- I wish I'd known that the way I'd studied in undergraduate school and graduate school would bear no resemblance to the way I needed to study in law school if I wanted to pass my exams.

- I wish I would have known just how different the whole law school experience was going to be from anything else I had ever done. I honestly feel that there is nothing in undergraduate school that could possibly have prepared me for law school. The only way to be successful is to try to adapt quickly.

- I wish I had known how to *study*. In undergrad I felt like things came fairly easy and other than writing papers I didn't actually have to sit down and dedicate my time to school material. I had never before *really* reviewed material from class or outlined and these are vital skills you need to apply in law school.

Everyone Has the Same Fears

- That everyone else was just as nervous about some aspect of the whole new experience as I was. Someone very well may have told me that before I started. If they did, I didn't believe them. But it's true. It has taken me two semesters of getting to know others well enough to realize that they are all nervous too. The basis for the nervousness varies drastically, but we all feel it. For some it will be about speaking in class or doing an oral argument. Others are nervous about not being liked, flunking out, or going broke. Amazingly to me, some of the most intelligent students seemed to struggle the most at first. Perhaps because they have always been the shiniest fish in their ponds, they were unaccustomed and uncomfortable with being surrounded by so many true peers. Everyone is struggling with some aspect of the law school experience!

Don't Fall Behind

- You have to stay on top of your obligations and responsibilities EVERY DAY. I don't just mean your reading assignments. You have to make sure to check your email daily and stay on top of other obligations such as signing up for Westlaw training and adding to your outlines on a regular basis. This was a big transition from my undergraduate experience. I would go weeks without checking my email and just cram for a few days before a big test without suffering any dire consequences. If your undergraduate experience was anything like mine, you cannot get away with adhering to the same habits once you start law school.

● I wish that I would have known that everything moves one step ahead in law school. If you are ahead in your readings/preparations, then you are where you need to be.

● If you are merely prepared for each class on a "just-in-time" strategy, you are behind. And if you fall behind, it is impossible to catch up. Although you can get notes from others, double a reading assignment for a class, etc., you simply cannot replace the learning process that comes from actual preparation in advance.

Conscientious Outlining and Periodic Review are Critical

● How important outlining is and how important it is to keep up with it as you go along. Outlining is a major part of the learning process for me and I did not realize how important it was until I really did it. It doesn't just help you study the material. It allows you to organize the concepts in a logical manner that helps you see the bigger picture.

● Fall semester would have been so much less stressful if I had kept a running outline that was updated biweekly, instead of waiting two weeks before exams to begin making the outline.

● I wish I would have known just how much time it took to study for exams. I wish I would have known that if I put just an hour into studying after class each day it would have made things easier.

Law School is Competitive

● I think that competition is the white elephant in the room in terms of discussion of the law school experience. Everyone is in a marathon race against the other. Everyone is aware of this—some simply care more than others. However, there is something to be said for being considerate and helpful to your peers. There are people who will go out of their way not to help you lest they give up some tiny thread of comparative advantage. Those students are rarely liked and respected even less. I think it would do our profession and our peers a great deal of good to realize that in the end it does not matter what grades you made or what awards you won. These are important, no doubt. But the relationships that you make now stay with you forever.

- To believe people when they warn how competitive law school is. Looking back, college was like running a 5K for a cause where everyone wanted you to succeed. People are there along the way giving you water and cheering you on. Even the slowest runner is praised for participation. Law school feels more like roller derby. While racing to the finish line, your competition is beating on you, intentionally tripping you up and pulling your hair out all in an effort to pass you by.

- I wish that I had known exactly how competitive law school is. I think that I kind of knew, but I had no real understanding of the fierceness of the whole system.

Being Organized and Managing Time Efficiently Will Make Your Life Easier

- I think the one thing that I wish I had a better working knowledge of when I started law school is that organization can make the most monumental task attainable.

- Organization makes work easy. It sounds simple, but I never realized I was disorganized. Your desk can be clean and everything can appear perfect, but if you don't know what the fourteen things you have to do at your computer are, then you're wasting time. Simply knowing what needs to be done and when makes it easy to crank out high-quality work quickly. So much time is wasted figuring out what to do and getting the tools to start.

Case Briefs Should Be Brief

- Case briefs should be concise! Really concise. Read the case carefully and underline/highlight important parts but don't waste your time typing every point into a brief. The professor will highlight in class the important points you should get out of the case. Then you can go back and copy anything into your brief that you may not have covered fully.

Don't Be a Transcriber

- Do not transcribe everything the professor says into class notes. The professors' words are important, of course, and if they make a point to slow down and state a specific point of law, transcribe it. But you need to filter their words into notes that you can understand.

Women Experience Law School Differently Than Men

- Women tend to underestimate their abilities, while men seem to overestimate theirs. Most girls are just not complimented on their intelligence that often. I'm trying to make a point of doing that more with my daughter and downplaying her appearance, but it's just so second-nature with girls to say "What a pretty dress!" or "Your hair looks so nice today!" and so on. The students who come to mind who I consider lacking in the confidence they fully deserve to have are all female. Many women students have said, "I want to be in a back office" or "I don't want to do litigation" and so on. There's certainly no more competence in being male, but there is definitely more confidence. Even with many law schools having a 50–50 gender balance, the de-emphasis on intelligence that girls experience in relation to the boys they later end up competing against has an effect. This brings us back to what I wished I'd known. Having made it through several scary things in law school (the final exams, the papers, the oral argument) and seeing now that I have the ability to do them, I could have spared myself a lot of needless stress if I'd had a bit of this confidence back in August.

Exercise!

- I wish I would have known how wide my backside was going to get from sitting around studying all the time (point: find time to exercise).

QUESTION: As you near the end of your first year, what has surprised you the most about law school compared to your expectations going into it?

How Much It Changed Me

- What most surprised me about law school is how much it has really changed me. Law school is one of those experiences that can't help but alter a person forever, but in a good way. I think about everything differently now. My perspective on life in general has shifted from what I've learned in law school. Law school has taught me to question and analyze everything, much to the annoyance of my family and friends.

- I am surprised how much law school has changed me. I don't know if that's a good thing or a bad thing.

- It changed how I think about even the most mundane things. I underestimated the impact this would have on the other people in my life. My wife is wonderful and has been very understanding, but law school has been hard on her too. Imagine living with someone who walks around and sees potential lawsuits everywhere he goes. In law school, every case you read is about something that went wrong, so, if you aren't careful, you can become a pessimist very quickly. You begin to approach situations by thinking about what the consequences could be and then taking those consequences to the extreme. I call it "hypothetical hell." My wife tried to tell me this was happening but I didn't believe her until one day when we were discussing how we were going to use our jet-ski the following summer. We had moved farther away from the lake we used to ride on for me to come to law school, so she suggested we rent a slip and keep the jet-ski in the water so that we wouldn't have to tow it every time we wanted to ride. I immediately begin to analyze the liability it could create for us to leave it in the water. "What if a friend wants to borrow it and has an accident?" "What if it gets stolen?" "What if someone hits a boat full of toddlers?" "We need insurance!"

How Much I Love It

- I don't know if I really expected to love law school so much. Before law school, I was excited about beginning a new phase of life, one that I knew would help determine my future professional life. I'm so pleasantly surprised to find that I love coming to school every day. I love reading a case and realizing that I really understand what it's about. Law school is challenging and difficult but there's something so beautiful and reassuring in knowing that I'm right where I'm supposed to be.

- I was surprised most by how much fun I actually had, as opposed to the misery I was expecting. The upper-level students (at orientation and such) do not do a good enough job telling incoming 1Ls to have fun with law school. I think it was due to my classmates' and my ability to enjoy the study of law that made the first year really special. After all, we chose to be here!

The Workload

- Everyone says this, but I really was surprised by the workload, assuming you intend to complete all of your assignments "properly." Before law school I heard everyone talk about how much work it is. I always thought to myself, "I was in the army and I deployed twice to Iraq. I know how to work hard." But I really underestimated the discipline required for law school. Maybe I'm just slower at doing homework than others, but if I did every single homework assignment properly, it would take me at least six hours a day during the week, not including class times. I would also have to put in another ten hours on the weekend to work on outlines and legal writing assignments, two areas I found really difficult to fit in during the week.

- I have been most surprised at how there just are not enough hours in the day to accomplish all the things that need to be done in a day. It is vitally important to streamline your life to remove any distraction that will prevent you from giving every bit of focus to law school. I have learned this the hard way.

How Supportive the Professors and Classmates Are

- I have been pleasantly surprised with how nice my fellow students and professors have been. I had preconceived notions coming into law school that the atmosphere would be cutthroat, competitive, and serious all of the time. In one year I have already met great people who I consider more than just regular friends because we had to rely on each other to get through the difficult times.

- I have been pleasantly surprised with how helpful the professors have been. I expected vicious professors who enjoy making first-year students look foolish in front of their peers. I have experienced nothing like that. My professors are all eager to help and meet after class to discuss any issues.

Lack of Feedback

- What surprised me most is the lack of feedback. Because we do not have tests throughout the semester, you don't really get a grasp of your level of understanding of the material. I think this is one the major reasons that law school is so stressful. There is no feedback, so no matter how much you study you always feel like there is more you should be doing or that you don't understand the material well enough.

How Competitive It Is

- The competitiveness. Grading against the curve changes everything. The college days of sharing notes, helping others, and all working together to get through a tough class are over. The competitive atmosphere of law school is almost hysterical. Point exactly: The last day of my Civil Procedure class the teacher said we were going to do something "fun." We began playing Jeopardy and getting quizzed on the Federal Rules of Civil Procedure (not my idea of fun!). Next thing you know, the entire class was accusing the other side of cheating or crying that the other side's questions were easier. Law school students will not miss any chance to unleash their inner-competiveness and do not mess around when it comes to getting a step ahead in the grades department.

QUESTION: Think back to when you were starting law school, specifically to your fears or concerns. In retrospect, which fear or concern do you think was the most exaggerated or overblown as compared to the reality of law school and which fear or concern do you think you most underestimated or overlooked?

Most Exaggerated Fear or Concern
The Socratic method/getting called on.

- The Socratic Method wasn't nearly as bad as I thought it was going to be. I definitely looked really dumb a few times, but it was not anything to go home crying about.

- Most exaggerated fear was definitely the Socratic method. Although it is scary the first time you get called on, the fear quickly diminishes when you realize that you are not expected to get every answer correct. Rather, the professors expect you to have read the material assigned for that class and be able to engage in an open discussion regarding its content. No student knows the correct answer to every question.

- I was extremely concerned with getting called on. There is something about having to respond on command in front of seventy other students and a professor that you do not know very well yet that makes a person lose sleep at night. That was my biggest fear and to be honest it was blown out of proportion. First of all, with a class as big as seventy students, getting called on is not an everyday occurrence even in courses where the professors call on multiple students each day. Second, even when I got called on, most of the time the answers to the questions came to me because I was always prepared for class. Third, I constantly reminded myself that as long as I prepared for class, the professors would not mind if I simply did not know an answer.

Failing/not understanding the material.

- My most exaggerated fear was my fear of failing out law school. I anticipated the material as being so difficult that no amount of work could overcome it. I have found that by reading the material, coming to class, taking good notes, and asking my professors for help when I don't understand something, the material is not insurmountable.

- My most overblown fear was that everyone would be infinitely more intelligent, more articulate, more competent, etc., than me, and that I would be revealed as an impostor and forced to endure the derision of the *real* future lawyers. This would all happen, of course, before I failed out of school. Fortunately, it hasn't played out this way, but the law school atmosphere *is* singularly intense and it intensified my prelaw and first-semester insecurities.

- I expected to not be able to understand the issues we would be discussing in class, especially at the beginning. However, I found that the professors genuinely care that you understand the material. The amount of time you must devote to reading and preparing is enormous, but as long as you are willing to put in that time and work, the information will not be difficult to understand.

Competitiveness.

- The most exaggerated concern was about the competitiveness between students. Before law school a lot of the conversations I had with lawyers and former students went like this: "Oh, it is fiercely competitive. When I was in law school we had a student that [insert ridiculous research sabotage story]." I have found students to be very helpful and amiable toward each other. The only time it feels competitive is when grades come out and some people get a little touchy.

Most Underestimated Fear or Concern
The workload.

- The fear or concern I most underestimated or overlooked was realizing there's not enough time in the day or week to get all the work done. The law school workload requires strict time management and organization. I have always been an organized student and able to handle schoolwork while participating in many other activities. But law school is at a completely different level in terms of the sheer volume of material. To anyone getting ready to start law school or thinking of going to law school, I would tell them to spend time organizing their lives outside of school because once law school starts, there is little time to do much else.

- It was more draining and challenging than I ever thought it would be. I always tell my friends and family that a student cannot be prepared enough for how grueling law school really is. When I was in high school, my teachers would always tell me how difficult college would be one day and that was not true for me personally. However, I am friends with many current attorneys who told me that law school was going to be a whole new ballgame and they could not have been more right. My family threw a party for me on the night before I moved for school and my uncle, a bankruptcy attorney, made a toast to me that ended with "Better you than me." We all laughed at the time but I did not realize how serious he really was when he made that statement.

- The fear I most underestimated was all the work necessary to prepare for exams my first semester. With all the outlining, reviewing, and collaborating, the time between class and exams quickly disappeared, leaving me more stressed. Time management is essential in law school, especially in that crunch before exams, and I had to learn that one the hard way.

Exams.

- The most underestimated fear was exams. While I knew the whole "one test" thing would be stressful, I did not expect the extreme level of stress I experienced. The two weeks of exams were likely the two most emotionally and physically exhausting weeks I have ever had. Then, to have to wait until the last couple of days before classes restarted to get the grades . . . absolute torture! The excruciating waiting for grades after exams should be deemed a violation of the Eighth Amendment prohibition on cruel and unusual punishment.

Competitiveness.

- One thing I overlooked was the type of students I would be interacting with on a daily basis. You do not get into law school by slacking off or being uninvolved in extracurricular activities. I still am surprised at how so many people are looking for extra ways to set themselves apart. For example, if there is a student government election, job, or scholarship opportunity, there will be intense competition by law students to get it.

- I didn't worry about the competitive atmosphere before coming to law school, and I suppose I should have more. By the competitive atmosphere, I mean the nature of the people who come to law school and how it affects me mentally. Maybe it is just the group of people I hang out with but I wasn't prepared for how much people worry about grades, moot court, summer jobs, etc. Being around highly stressed individuals all of the time is probably the thing I like least about law school. Being somewhat more laid-back, I have found it hard to adjust to people constantly "freaking out."

Strain on relationships.

- I underestimated the strain law school would place on my family. Not only is law school an overwhelming responsibility for me, but it places a heavier load on my dear wife to not only work to support us but then spend the majority of her free time caring for our two sons. Luckily, I married a saint and I have been able to strike somewhat of a balance between school and home. I have also found that time away from school with my family helps make me a better student.

Legal writing courses.

- The most underestimated fear was the time allocated toward my two-hour legal research and writing class. In no way was I aware of the time my legal writing class would take away from my core curriculum classes. I was not prepared for the extreme workload it required throughout the entire first year.

- Before school I was more worried about my substantive classes than legal writing. However, once school started I realized Legal Research and Writing was more than I had bargained for. If I knew then what I know now I would have researched legal writing more in my spare time before school started so that I would have been more prepared for the vast difference between writing papers in college and writing papers in law school.

QUESTION: Imagine one of your closest friends or relatives is starting law school. What advice would you give them?

Of all the questions I've used to survey law students, I think this one is my favorite. Casting students in the role of a trusted advisor to a close loved one forced them to think more deeply, advise more bluntly, and get to the heart of some important matters. Some of their answers fall into the realm of "soul searching," while most of their practical advice hammers home fundamental points made throughout this book.

Think Hard About Whether Law School Is Really the Place for You

- Talk to attorneys, consider the financial debt, sit in on a law school class, read a Supreme Court decision, pray/meditate/contemplate about it, understand the pressure involved, do a cost-benefit analysis (even though you may not understand that concept well yet), know that this will be far different from your undergraduate experience, consider the community you are moving to and will be living in for three years.
- I would advise anyone starting law school to make sure that it is truly where you want to be and that you are going *when* you want to be there. I was fortunate enough to take a year after graduating from college to work, relax, and refocus my energy. Several classmates of mine (including one who decided to withdraw after fall semester) regretted not taking time off.

- It is said so often that it sounds cliché, but you have to find in yourself the reason that you want to be here. You have to commit to yourself that you will do this, without fail, no matter what. Kind of like rescuing a baby from a burning building. Once you commit to do it, you follow through with it to the bitter end.

- Oh dear. Well, I don't know. First, I'd ask if they really wanted my advice. I wouldn't try to talk anyone out of it, but I'd advise that they sit in on some classes, talk to a lot of law students, talk to a lot of lawyers, if possible. I'd advise that if they do all those things, they can find out what law school entails and what a legal career entails, and then consider carefully whether it is something they would enjoy. I would say to ask themselves why they're going to law school. If they said something like, "It's all I can do with my degree," I would advise that they think about it some more.

- First I would say, "Are you crazy? You saw what I went through!" Ha ha. And then I would seriously tell them to really give law school a lot of thought. This isn't just something to do just because you can't get a job or you want to stay in school for another three years. If you want to get the most for your money and your time, law school really does become your life. But if law school is your dream, it is worth it. You can't just come to law school to get a quick and easy career, because it's not quick and it's not easy. Law school takes more work than you can imagine, as well as time and patience. There will be days when you want to quit. But if you're there for the right reasons, you will realize that in three years you will have fulfilled your dream and have a degree that will give you a better life. Then all the hard work will seem worth it and you can get right back to the books!

- I would think about giving the typical answer, "Don't go." However, I heard that from both my lawyer parents and all of my friends that I asked prior to law school. It was very discouraging to say the least. The best advice to give someone is if your heart is in law school then you can definitely accomplish it, but make sure to keep true to yourself. Do not let the pressures of law school or the intimidation factor of all the brilliant students surrounding you affect who you are.

Approach Law School Like a Job

• Remember that law school is a full-time job, which is not a bad thing. It requires commitment, and if you are ready for a full-time job that's more interesting than a lot of others, do it. It baffles me that some people complain about the workload when they walk out the door after class ends at 1:00 p.m. Granted, some of those people are doing work at home. But, when 2:30 rolls around and you think that it's time to go home, stop and remember that everyone else your age is either working until 5:00 or they're out looking for a job. Then come right back to your space and work until 5:00. Then enjoy the rest of your night!

• When I started law school, I was told to treat school as a 9 to 5 job and to just stay at school and work for that amount of time whether in class or not. This method didn't really work for me, because I like naps, breaks, etc., but the basic point was helpful. It made me realize that as long as I put in around seven to eight hours of work a day, whether it's preparing for class, being in class, or outlining, I would be fine.

Get Your Life in Order

• Get your life in order because you won't have time for disorganization once you start law school. Have a game plan in advance about when you are going to study, and be prepared to do it religiously.

• I would recommend to someone starting or considering law school to get their personal house in order prior to starting law school. As I observe others struggling with personal matters and difficulties, I feel blessed that my life has not been filled with any of these distractions. I think that learning the law—especially in the first year of law school—is too hard to have to deal with unnecessary distractions. As I

observe my peers I think that the two biggest distractions have been either relationships or financial
hardships. I would not start law school if I weren't
on firm financial footing.

- Make sure you are in a good place psychologically
  before you commit. The law school atmosphere is
  very intense and the pressure to excel (or even to
  just keep up) can be overwhelming at times. The
  best way to do this is to give yourself some time if
  you're in a bad place emotionally. Do NOT enroll on
  the tail end of an emotional crisis. It's important to
  remove anyone or anything from your life that could
  potentially distract you from your school work, as
  being unable to fully focus will greatly intensify any
  anxiety and stress you already have. Break off toxic
  romantic relationships and cut ties with unsupportive friends. This may seem brutal but it's absolutely
  necessary in order to fully face and handle the stress
  and anxiety of law school.

- I watch as some peers travel to see significant others
  on the weekends or pine away about someone who is
  away from them. I think this is a waste of time. I
  would probably not enter law school and hope that a
  long distance relationship would work out. I think I
  would probably just agree to go separate ways. Time
  is too valuable as a 1L to deal with relationship
  drama, especially long-distance relationship drama.

Pick a Law School in an Area Where
You Will Be Happy Living

- Pick an area that you would like to live in and then
  choose your law school based on that area. If you are
  not happy where you are living then you will not be
  happy in law school. School is going to take up most
  of your time, but you need to take some time away
  from the law to relax. It's important that there are
  things you enjoy doing in the town where you have
  chosen to go to school. There are good law schools
  everywhere, so if you like the beach, go to school
  near the beach; if you like the mountains, go to
  school near mountains; and if you can't live without
  seeing your mother every day, go to school near your
  mother.

Take a Year Off First

• Take a year off. Law School requires a *passionate devotion*. Working for a year will both give you the discipline to approach law school as a job and to know that coming here is the right decision.

Enjoy Your Time Before You Start

• Take a really long vacation before starting school.

Dress for Success

• Always look decent. Impressions are important and people judge you if you wear sweats and flip-flops and don't shower.

Everyone Struggles

• I would tell them that everyone struggles in their own way, be it a bad grade, getting called on when you are unprepared for class, showing up late, or just personal issues. No one's journey through law school is easy, so any struggles you have, remember there are many other students who feel the exact same way as you.

• I think the biggest thing to realize and remember is that there are going to be days when you have mental, physical, and emotional breakdowns. Trust me, I probably have two or three a month. And there are going to be days when you really want to hit that person who's ranked in the top ten who keeps talking about his or her grades in front of everyone not ranked in the top ten.

You'll Get Out What You Put Into It

• Law school really becomes what you make of it. If you start with a goal of finishing in the top 25 percent of your class, then you'd better accept that studying is going to be a continuous and very large part of your life. If you do, you'll probably meet your goal. If you start law school just as a way to get another degree and procrastinate the career-search process, then just do what you have to do to get by, but don't be disappointed when you aren't in the top of your class. I think every single person has a different perspective on law school and a different way of tackling it. You just have to make it your own!

Be Ready to Work Harder than Ever Before

- Study twice as hard as you think you need to be studying.

- Be ready to spend a lot of time to do a lot of work. Do not go into law school with the attitude that it is anything like undergraduate school. Anyone can do well if they are willing to put in the time and effort.

- Law school is going to be the most serious and difficult task you have ever taken on. You have to go into it wholeheartedly and devote most of your time to it.

- Take a quiet week before you start and try to find that one kernel of motivation that will get you through when you have no energy, desire, or drive left upon which to rely. You will need it.

Getting High Grades Is Not the Only Goal in Life

- Grades are important, but living your life is important also. Professors and deans will stress "grades, grades, grades" and make you feel bad about wanting to have a life. I don't think they do this on purpose, but most professors and deans were in the top ten percent of their class and feel that their sacrifices were worthwhile. The thought of a student actually making a conscious decision to be a *B* or *C* student is ludicrous to the faculty of a law school. Performing as a top 10 percent student can be extremely important depending on which type of job you want when you get out of law school, but it all rests on what YOU want out of life and out of your career. The difference in workload between a *B*- and an *A* is tremendous, and in my opinion, it was not worth the trade-off. I made a conscious decision to lower my goal so that I could participate in other law school activities, spend time hanging out with my husband and my dogs, visit with friends and family, and BBQ poolside. I don't feel bad about it and I don't think anyone else should either.

Relax, Try to Enjoy, and Do the Best You Can

• Relax. Don't worry about using six colors of highlighter to try to absorb every piece of every case. Do the work, try to understand the situation and the rule, and then be willing to put it down and watch a movie. Your ability to produce results is directly proportional to your ability to relax. One of my closest friends is busy burning herself out over law school. Another good friend of mine is doing the same thing at a different law school. They are making their lives hell, ruining their health, and they're frustrated with their understanding. There is a time for work and a time to stop and let your brain recover. Understand the difference.

• Relax. Although law school is a very stressful time, have fun with it. The classes are interesting, you will make amazing friends, and it really can be fun.

• Just do the best you can. Don't try to compare yourself with anyone else or stress too much about the competitive nature of law school because it will only wear you down. The only thing you really have control over is your own performance.

• Approach law school as a learning/training mission rather than as a contest for grades. The second I stopped trying to learn the material enthusiastically and started strategizing as to how to get the best grades, law school became less fun and the stress tripled.

• Have fun! Law school is an amazing journey that teaches one a great deal about themselves and their abilities.

Realize that Non–Law Students Aren't Interested in Hearing About the Law and Law School

• I'd probably tell them that they are about to have their entire lives consumed with the law and conversations about the law. Most of all I would remind them that no matter how interested everyone at the law school is in this stuff, nobody else really cares about it. Try to keep it to yourself because the law does not make for good conversations with friends and family. You'll just come off as boring and weird.

I mean outside of lawyers and judges, who could possibly care if a "dog sniff" constitutes a search within the meaning of the Fourth Amendment?

• Be careful about mixing your non-law school friends with your law school friends. Only mix your non-law school friends with law school friends who are capable of conversing about interests other than law school. No non-law school friend wants to be stuck at a table with five law students who only want to talk about law school.

Sort Through Advice Carefully

• Do not listen to anyone else's opinion about professors. Before each semester, I heard that Professor X was pure concentrated evil, or that you can sleep through Professor Y's class, etc. Some information has been helpful, such as what to expect in terms of assignments and exam prep, but most of the rest has been so far off base as to now seem comical.

• It's best to stick to the studying techniques that have worked for you in the past. The first semester I spent an inordinate amount of time perfecting *the* outline of my class notes because that's the studying/organizing technique that law students and professors emphasize the most. Every study advice panel discussion devoted a large portion to outlining success tips: "Have your outline done by this date or you'll probably fail," "By the time you're finished with your outline it should be condensed to x number of pages," "Constantly update and edit your outline so you can be the greatest law student in the world," etc. As a result, in my panic-stricken state of mind, I wasted an absurd amount of time formatting and crafting the perfect outline, and less time actually encoding and understanding the massive amount of information I'd been exposed to over the semester. (Although, I must say, I organized it beautifully.) During the second semester, I still created outlines for my classes but they did not follow the perfectly structured, linear "II, A, i, 1" format I thought was required in the first semester.

Don't Miss Classes

- Do not miss any classes. I have only missed one class since the beginning of the semester and it was for a court date for a traffic ticket. I felt really behind and confused missing just that one lecture. In undergrad it might have been fine to skip every now and then, but I would definitely advise anyone coming to law school not to miss any classes unless they absolutely have to.

Keep Your Emotions in Check

- You're not as smart as you think you are, nor are you as useless as you think you are. You'll go through periods of elation and periods of doubt. Both extremes are false and should be promptly dismissed.

- Don't be afraid of law school. While a little bit of fear is good motivation, too much can be crippling. There is no need to fear your professors, colleagues, or assignments. Most everyone is nice and helpful and most of the assignments and cases are straight-forward.

- Do not beat yourself up about things that you cannot control. You will walk into a class and, by design, not know all that you need to know. Recognize that you cannot win every battle. Most of all enjoy the experience.

Make Friends/Develop a Support Network

- Start introducing yourself to other students and try to make friends at orientation. Cliques begin forming then and cliques translate to study groups (which can be a very useful tool, depending on the group). When I say cliques, it's not so much a social thing as a way of finding others who have something in common with you and who, like you, also have no idea what they've gotten themselves into.

- Make as many friends as possible because in order to survive law school the best support system is people who know exactly what you are going through. Plus, friends are helpful for group study sessions and sharing outlines.

- Make friends because you need people who understand what you are going through to keep you sane.

- Get to know your classmates—they are not the enemy. Do not hide books or hoard outlines—share!

- Find one or two people you can really trust and spend large amounts of time studying and outlining with. There will be times when you might miss a class or even when you attend class where you might miss important bits of information from the professor. If you have a few people you can trust, you will be able to cover for each other as well as strengthen each other's notes and outlines, and hold each other accountable. But do not join a study group with too many people because then it becomes counterproductive.

Don't Make Enemies

- Don't make enemies. You know who you like and people you don't really get along with. However, you may very well have to work with these people one day. It is a lesson in humility and maturity that you can work with someone who you don't like.

Don't Fall Behind

- Be organized from day one and never let yourself fall behind. The destructive feelings of being overwhelmed and scared about having fallen behind will finish you off long before you ever have a chance to make a bad grade on an exam.

- I would tell them that when they have extra time, try to get ahead in their work. There is never enough time to get things done in law school, so what you think is free time, really isn't or shouldn't be. Mostly, I would just try to encourage them to stay focused and organized so that they won't get so stressed out.

- DO NOT GET BEHIND ON YOUR WORK. PLAN AHEAD. Six hours over two Saturdays is much better than six hours the weeknight before something is due.

- Keep up! Don't fall behind in your reading. Do your best work at all times. Don't ever cop out and just "phone in" a class hoping that the professor won't call on you.

- Start outlining ASAP. If you wait, you cannot catch back up. Seriously, you cannot catch back up.

Stay Organized

- Take the semester one week at a time and break that week down into days and organize what you need to accomplish that particular day. I am a list maker and that helped me tremendously this year. I placed a giant dry erase board in my room and made lists of assignments that I needed to accomplish that day. As I finished an assignment, I marked it off and moved to the next goal. This kept me organized and gave me satisfaction that I was accomplishing the things that needed to be accomplished.

- Organization is the key. Find a sound plan that works for you. Being able to plan for the seemingly millions of things going on requires attention to detail. Knowing you are well-organized will give you one less thing you have to worry about.

Start Outlines Early/Engage in Periodic Review

- Start outlining early. If you don't then it's almost impossible to do it at the end of the semester.

- If my little sister was starting law school, I would tell her to review her notes daily or weekly. My problem is that I waited until it was time to outline before I looked back at my notes, and was very unfamiliar with some of the concepts at that point.

- Outline early, at least two weeks before everyone else is starting. If you don't procrastinate, you'll have it all done with a week of class left and you won't be freaking out trying to desperately outline when you should be studying for exams.

Don't Take Short–Cuts

- Do not listen to any of the short-cuts your classmates as well as 2Ls and 3Ls will be all too willing to give. Shortcuts deprive you of the process of truly engaging the material, which is crucial to developing the skills of finding your way into a case and back out with rule in hand. Short-cut websites which provide case briefs do not help you develop the most important skills needed in law school, which are learning to analyze cases, finding the rules and sub-rules, and then applying them to entirely different sets of facts. DO NOT cheat yourself! Follow the C.R.E.D.O.! It worked for me.

Do Your Own Outlines

- "Legendary outlines" by former students do exist, but they won't get you an *A*. Going to class, reading the material, taking your own notes, and studying will do that. There is no cramming in law school. Spacing out in the back playing video games will earn you a fast ticket out.

Sit Up Front

- Sit in the front. This is productive for a couple of reasons. First, I tend to space out a lot and this prevents this. If you're in the first few rows you're visible to the entire class and to your professor. Not only will this ensure you're attentive at least most of the time, but also that you study hard so as not to be embarrassed by being called on. Another benefit is you get to know your professors a bit better and they get to know you. They're a lot less intimidating if you know them as someone other than just a professor. They're usually pretty cool.

Stay in Shape

- Drop the Ho–Ho's and back away from them. They are not your friend. True, they whisper nice, sweet things in your ear, and call out to you in the middle of the night, but when you have to get all gussied up for your oral argument, you're going to look like a fat man in a little suit.

Seek Help from Your Profs

- If something comes up that is beyond your control, go to your professors and ask for help. That's one thing I have always been too proud (or too dumb) to do. I always try to do things on my own. It's okay to sit down with someone and explain that you are overwhelmed.

Back Up Your Work

- Back up your computer work in many places!

Don't Give Up

- Keep your head down and plow through it. At times it will be fun, but at times it will really suck. If you really want to do it, it will be worth it. Just keep pushing through the difficult times.

- Never give up! Repeat after me: "This too shall pass!" And keep smiling.

Take Practice Exams Under Simulated Conditions

- To study for exams, use professors' old exams. Take them like real exams, including timing yourself.

Don't be a Know–It–All

- Don't become a know-it-all thinking you know everything about the law after a month of law school. Your friends will hate you if you do.

Use Study Aids to Clarify

- There are some teachers who are simply unclear about what they are teaching in class and what you should be learning in the course as a whole. If you find yourself with a teacher like that, don't hesitate to get a study aid or a canned outline to learn the material on your own. Read the assignments, because you need to be familiar with the material, but if the teacher is not getting the job done, make sure you get an understanding from somewhere else.

- My honest opinion: Get the study aids from the get-go and start outlining early! If you don't understand something, consult the professor and extract what you can from the study aids (but only if it falls in line with what the professor is teaching).

Don't Obsess about "Looking Stupid" in Class

- Don't freak out about getting called on in class. Everyone gets called on and everyone feels like they look stupid. However, no one ever remembers but you.

Don't Give Up Your Hobbies/Outside Life

- Law school is difficult and requires a lot of work, but you cannot give up every aspect of your life for law school. It's important to find something you enjoy outside of school with which to fill the limited free time you have. I would not have been able to make it as far as I have, and I realize I still have a long way to go, without being able to do something to relax when I have finished working for the day. I found that playing church-league basketball, playing a round of golf on the weekend, or just hanging out with my friends for a night made opening up my book and diving back into the intricacies of the law the next morning much easier to cope with.

- Make sure you have an outlet outside of school— whether it is tutoring a child, running, playing the guitar, yoga, sewing—just something to do other than study!

- Don't work ALL of the time, only most of it.

- Find time in every day to relax.

- Balance your academic life with your personal life. Don't give up all the things that make you who you are to provide more time for school. There is no way you can be happy if you completely sacrifice the things you do outside of school. If you are unhappy in general your performance in class will suffer.

QUESTION: What is your dominant feeling or sentiment (e.g., relief, nostalgia, frustration, exhaustion) as you near the end of law school's first year?

Two weeks before the end of the second semester, I posed the above question to a first-year class. Silly me. I naively expected cheerful answers, not taking into account the fact that with five exams still looming, the students weren't thinking—like I was—that they were at "the end" of the first year. Their answers disproportionately centered on anxiety and exhaustion. I'm sure if I asked the same question after exams, the answers would have been a lot more upbeat. Some students, however, were able to look ahead and feel excitement, relief, and a sense of accomplishment for what they'd been through. Overall, the answers reflected the entire spectrum of emotions inherent in being a 1L. Below I included one representative answer for each emotion.

Anxiety/Stress

- I'm full of anxiety. I didn't do well last semester and I have to do much better to remain in school for another year. For the last three weeks or so I have been waking up with nightmares and I have had a difficult time sleeping because I am so nervous about finals.

Despair

- "Dear God! I have two more years of this?" It's kind of like being sent to war and then getting wounded in battle. You start to think you are finally going to get sent home after you heal only to find out you're being sent back to the front line, with even less chance of survival because now you're wounded.

Exhaustion

- EXHAUSTION. I have reached a new level of mental exhaustion I did not know existed.

Frustration

- Frustration. Effort = Results. Plain and simple. I wish I would have spent more time studying and enjoying what I was learning—and less time analyzing what I could do to ensure a decent class rank.

Excitement

- I am energized. I feel excited that I now understand things better. Last semester I was planning a wedding, selling a house, etc. This semester I am focused on school only. That makes ALL the difference in the world. I now enjoy classes more, because I understand things more clearly. I am also at peace now that I have finally accepted the fact that I have no social life outside of classes. I am moving towards the realm of nerd-dom at a steady pace.

Indifference

- I guess I really feel kind of indifferent about it. I am relieved that the first year is coming to a close, but I know there are still two difficult years ahead. I don't really buy into the claim that school gets a lot easier after the first year. I think the students just become accustomed to the demands of the routine.

Numbness

● I am basically numb at this point. I'm looking forward to spending a summer away from law school so I will actually have time to reflect on and re-evaluate my choice to attend.

Pride

● As the year ends, I think I mainly feel proud. Proud of myself for moving across the state, living by myself for the first time, and taking on a world of new responsibilities. Proud for getting through the first year, doing well in my classes, and finding a way to balance school and studying and a social life. Proud to go back home this summer and tell everyone that I just finished my first year of law school ... and survived!

Relief

● Relief. It is impossible to believe that in just under three weeks I will have survived a WHOLE YEAR of law school. But at the same time there is definitely the end-of-the-year stress as exams approach.

Surprise

● Shock. I cannot believe it went by so fast. It doesn't feel like I'm one-third of the way prepared to be a lawyer.

All of the Above/Mixed feelings

● Such a mix of emotions ... Relief and exhaustion, but mostly a sense of accomplishment. So amazing to realize that, "Yes, I can do this!"

* * *

I also asked a group of students finishing up their first year whether they would do it all over again knowing what they know now. The vast majority of students said they would. Many said they would do so enthusiastically, as reflected by answers such as "Absolutely!," "Definitely!," and "Hell yes!" But not all. Some students said they wouldn't do it again and others were ambivalent.

One student who said he would *not* do law school again said: "Most of what I know now I had been told at the beginning of the first semester. The problem is I didn't put it to use. Therefore, I believe that I could fall into the same traps."

You now have the information and advice you'll need to avoid falling into those traps and succeeding in law school. It may seem far off, but it won't be long before you'll be finishing your own 1L adventure. Before you know it, you'll be *2L and Back*. Like the rest of life, your time in law school will fly by.

When you reach the end of your 1L ride, I hope you won't find yourself in the position of the student quoted above, bemoaning his unwillingness or inability to heed advice. I'd rather picture you smiling and thinking, "You know, that book I read about the first year gave some really good advice. I'm glad I followed it!"

Epilogue: The End of a Long and Grinding Road

I still remember the day of my last exam of my 1L year. What a feeling! It was like being released from prison. I walked out of the law school into bright sunshine and felt light as air. That night some of my non-law school friends staged a big party at a subterranean den called and painted to resemble Middle Earth, located beneath a block of dorms on the University of Florida campus. (Tolkien was popular on college campuses long before the *Lord of the Rings* movie trilogy.) We listened to music, watched a weird home movie some of my pals created, drank potent punch, and just hung out.

I was the only law student there. I doubt I mentioned law school the entire night, having learned months earlier that non-law students could care less about it. I did think about it though. I have a distinct memory of sitting in a chair watching the hubbub around me, sipping punch, and feeling blissfully happy, thinking: "I'm done! I can't believe I'm actually done!" Temporarily forgetting, I guess, that I still had two more years to go.

But human nature is funny that way. While I definitely would not want to repeat the first year, like many lawyers, I look back at it with nostalgia and fondness. For better or worse, there has never been another year of my life resembling my 1L experience. I've never learned as much or experienced as much camaraderie in any one year. There was a lot of stress too, but, fortunately, the human psyche seems designed to remember the good over the bad.

Your experience is likely to be similar. For most readers, the first year of law school may still be an abstraction. I hope I succeeded in giving it some shape in these pages, but when all is said and done, what I said at the beginning of the book is true. The only way to truly understand and appreciate the 1L experience is to live it yourself. Good luck on your journey. Here's to a smooth ride!

455

SAMPLE ISSUE–SPOTTING/ PROBLEM–SOLVING ESSAY QUESTION WITH MODEL ANSWER

Below is a classic "issue-spotting/problem-solving" law school essay question included on a recent Torts exam. Following the question is the model answer used to grade the exam. The question addresses a handful of issues in the arena of negligence law, which is more complex than the area of intentional torts from which most of the examples used in the book were drawn. Coincidentally, one of the issues is the child standard of care and adult-activity exception, with which you should be well-versed if you studied the case-briefing and outlining chapters.

The issues and legal standards are explained in the model answer, but don't worry about the specifics of the law at this point. The question and answer are included to give you an authentic advance feel for what law school essay questions and answers look like in terms of both content and structure. Study the question and answer in conjunction with Chapter 16, which details the most common mistakes students make on law school essay exams. Many of the points made in that chapter are illustrated in the question (e.g., specific instructions, combination of material and immaterial facts, "givens") and answer (e.g., clear organization, use of headings and subheadings, compartmentalized issue discussion, accurate and precise statements of the legal rules, rough IRAC framework).

NEGLIGENCE ESSAY QUESTION
(140 points/recommended time: 90 minutes)

Erwin Wizly is a very bright, precocious 10–year–old boy. He loves chemistry sets, even though he doesn't really know much about chemistry and is too lazy to read the instructions for most of the experiments. Mostly, he just loves having his corner of the family garage set up like a mad scientist's set from an old movie. He has rows of chemicals in vials, a microscope, and lots of test tubes and beakers. Often, he uses one of the beakers to heat instant soup over a Bunsen burner. The chemistry sets came by way of his parents, Dan and Helena, as birthday gifts.

Erwin's latest chemistry project was "bomb-making," at least that what's he called it. He found a recipe for gunpowder on the internet. Of the three essential ingredients— saltpeter (potassium nitrate), charcoal, and sulfur—only the first one presented any difficulty in obtaining. For the charcoal, he simply ground up some charcoal briquettes the family used for outdoor grilling. Sulfur was one of the standard chemicals that came with chemistry sets, so he had plenty of that. From the internet he discovered that saltpeter has certain medicinal uses. Calling around town, he found a local drug store that sold it. He used his allowance money to purchase a 16–ounce container of powdered saltpeter, explaining to the clerk that his grandmother used it for her sensitive teeth.

With that, Erwin was in business. He set about mixing up a batch of homemade gunpowder. He packed it into a plastic makeup container (2 inches wide × 2 inches deep × 4 inches long) he took from his sister, taped it up tight with duct tape, drilled a small hole in the side, and inserted a fuse from a firecracker. When finished, he admired his work as he enjoyed some instant chicken soup he had heated in a beaker in his "lab."

The next day after school while his parents were at work, Erwin decided to try out his new bomb. He and his pal, Stevie, took the device out to the middle of the Wizly's large backyard. Erwin brought his sister's old dollhouse with them, with the goal of blowing it up. He set the bomb inside the dollhouse.

"When I light the fuse, run to our back porch," Erwin said to Stevie. "That should be far enough."

Erwin lit the fuse, and he and Stevie ran quickly to the shelter of the Wizlys' back porch. But the bomb didn't explode. The type of gunpowder Erwin made and the fact that he used substandard home ingredients resulted in the device not being explosive. It did give off a great cloud of smoke though. Erwin had constructed—as it turned out—one heck of a big smoke bomb.

While disappointed by the lack of any explosion, both Erwin and Stevie were impressed by the thick clouds of smoke billowing from the dollhouse. As the boys watched in awe, the dense smoke drifted east toward neighboring houses. Two houses down from the Wizly's house, Nettie Narkle was working in her backyard garden when she became quickly engulfed by smoke. Thinking someone's house was on fire, she went to get her phone to call 911, but, because she could not see through the smoke, tripped over some bricks that her husband had been using to build an outdoor barbecue, falling and breaking her ankle.

Her husband drove her to the hospital. The break was a serious compound fracture. She was admitted to the hospital and scheduled for emergency surgery. Dr. Tippie, assisted by Nurses Slack and Crab, performed the surgery. The anesthesiologist was one Dr. Rump.

When Nettie woke up in her room after the surgery, her leg was in a plaster cast. Nurse Slack sat by her side and told her the surgery went well. Nettie, however, was having a hard time concentrating on the conversation because her head was hurting severely. She put her hand to her forehead and felt a large lump. She looked at her reflection in the stainless steel bowl sitting next to her bed and saw a large dark bruise on her forehead. She asked Nurse Slack about it, but the nurse claimed to have no knowledge how it got there.

It turned out that Nettie had a subdural hematoma (a gathering of blood beneath the surface) on her forehead. Experts agreed it was caused by some kind of blunt force trauma, but everyone at the hospital—including Tippie, Rump, Slack, and Crab—denied seeing or doing anything that would have caused Nettie's head injury. Nettie and her husband both swear the injury was not there before the surgery and none of the hospital records indicated that she arrived with a severe bruise on her head. Despite investigation, no explanation for how the injury occurred was ever determined. Nettie eventually recovered from the head injury, but only after an additional emergency surgery to relieve the pressure.

Poor Nettie, her troubles were not over yet. On leaving the hospital a week later, Nettie found that her husband wasn't there waiting to pick her up as he was supposed to (he got tied up in traffic). Nettie hailed a taxicab for the ride home. The cab was passing a horse and carriage coming from the opposite direction (one that ferried tourists around town), each in its proper lane, when two loud motorcycles negligently zoomed by, one on each side of the horse and carriage. Either of the motorcycles would have been sufficient to scare the horse and cause it to rear up, which it did. The horse's right hoof came crashing down onto the taxicab, breaking the window adjacent to where Nettie was sitting, sending a piece of glass into her left eye. Nettie had to make a return visit to the hospital to have her eye treated. Unfortunately, the glass caused permanent damage to the eye.

Instructions: Litigation ensued. Fully address the issues raised by the question facts as to these claims (and *only* these claims):

1.   Nettie sues Erwin for her broken ankle.

2.   Nettie sues Dr. Tippie, Dr. Rump, Nurse Slack, and Nurse Crab for her head injury (collectively "the hospital defendants").

3.   Nettie sues the two motorcycle drivers (Driver 1 and Driver 2) for her eye injury.

You may assume there are no issues of contributory/comparative negligence or duty in this question. Do not concern yourself with actors not mentioned in the numbered instructions above. To the extent proximate cause may be an issue, you may assume the events transpired in a "scope of the risk" jurisdiction. The question does not mention any statutes, so you should not discuss any. This is a negligence question. Do not discuss intentional torts.

* * *

Below is the grading key or "model answer" I used to grade the question, including notations of the maximum points available per issue. Most students, even those who earn very high grades, don't write with the precision and depth of analysis found in my model answers, although usually one curve-busting student in every class comes very close.

MODEL ANSWER

I will address the three claims from this series of unfortunate events in the order they appear in the question:

Nettie v. Erwin

Standard of Care (30 points)

Nettie is suing Erwin for negligently causing her broken ankle with his explosive device. The first issue is the standard of care to which Erwin will be held.

Child standard. Normally, as a 10–year–old child, Erwin would be subject to a child standard of care, which would evaluate his conduct by how a reasonable child of similar intelligence, experience, maturity, and training would have acted under the circumstances. As a "very bright" boy, it seems likely that Erwin would be found liable even under a child standard of care. A reasonable, very intelligent 10–year–old should know that it is unreasonable to build a bomb and set it off in the backyard of a residential neighborhood.

Adult standard. But we don't have to spend much time worrying about that because there is little question that Erwin will be held to an adult standard of care under these facts.

Jurisdictions are split on the test they apply to determine when a child will be held to an adult standard of care. Some jurisdictions apply an adult standard of care when the child is engaging in an "inherently dangerous activity" (*Robinson v. Lindsay*—Kid driving snowmobile). Other jurisdictions follow the *Restatement (Second) of Torts* and apply the adult standard when children engage in an activity normally undertaken by adults and for which adult qualifications are required. (The new *Restatement (Third) of Torts* combines the two approaches and applies an adult standard of care when the child engages in a dangerous activity normally undertaken by adults.)

Sometimes the standards can lead to different results for the same activity, but not in this case. There is no question that building and setting off bombs using a substantial quantity of gunpowder is both an activity that is inherently dangerous and an adult activity for which adult qualifications are normally required. Indeed, the activity requires expert qualifications beyond those of an ordinary reasonable adult.

Judge Hand Analysis (15 points)

Under an adult standard of care, Erwin would be found to have acted unreasonably. His conduct easily fails Judge

Hand's formula for negligence, which states that if the burden of avoiding a risk is less than the probability of the risk manifesting itself in harm times the gravity of the harm if it occurs, the actor is negligent. Here, the burden was much less than the risk.

The risk was substantial, both in terms of probability and severity. A bomb of the dimensions of Erwin's could have caused serious damage had it worked. A 2 × 2 × 4 inch demolition device would require a significant quantity of gunpowder to fill. If the bomb had worked as intended, it could have caused serious personal injury (to Erwin, Stevie, or others) or property damage. An explosion also could have triggered a large, expensive police response.

The burden of avoiding the risk was small. The conduct had no social utility other than Erwin's and Stevie's amusement and minor advancement of scientific understanding. Other equally entertaining and educational activities exist that present much less risk than bomb-making.

Proximate Cause (25 points)

Although Erwin acted unreasonably, Nettie may have an issue with proximate cause. (There is no factual causation issue as the facts clearly state that Nettie tripped because she could not see through the smoke.)

The question tells us we are in a jurisdiction that follows a "scope of the risk" approach to proximate cause. As we learned in *In re Wagon Mound*, this approach holds that one is negligent as to and liable only for the reasonably foreseeable consequences of their conduct. One way to approach this scope of the risk analysis is to ask: what was the risk that made Erwin's conduct negligent in the first place? The answer is physical injury to persons or property in the immediate area, which is what happened. While it's true that someone tripping in their backyard because of smoke from the bomb device is not the specific risk that comes to mind, it is not necessary that the precise manner in which the harm occurs be foreseeable, so long as the same general kind of harm was part of the foreseeable risk that made the conduct negligent.

A court most likely would find it foreseeable that a neighbor two houses away could be injured by an explosive device, especially when one remembers that proximate cause is a tool wielded by courts to decide whether it is fair to impose liability for the consequences of a negligent act. It seems fair to impose liability here for setting off a "bomb" in the backyard of a residential neighborhood.

Erwin should be liable to Nettie.

Nettie v. Hospital Defendants (Tippie, Rump, Slack, Crab)

Res Ipsa Loquitur (40 points)

Nettie went into the hospital and was put under anesthesia to get her ankle repaired. She woke up with a severe injury on her forehead and is suing the hospital defendants for negligence. What happened and who did it? Those are the questions. Since no definite answers exist (the question states that no cause was determined even after investigation), her only chance of prevailing will be to persuade the court to apply res ipsa loquitur (RIL).

This fact pattern is straight out of *Ybarra v. Spangard*, covered in class. If applied, *Ybarra* should allow Nettie to get to a jury and win her case.

First element. The first element of RIL is whether the injury is one that ordinarily (more likely than not) does not occur in the absence of negligence. RIL does not apply in most medical malpractice cases due to the complexity of the issues and multiple possible explanations for the patient's injury. But this case is an easy one. A head injury is an event that ordinarily does not happen while undergoing treatment for a broken ankle in the absence of negligence. Negligence is the most likely explanation. The first element is met.

Second element. More problematic for Nettie is the second element of RIL. To invoke RIL, the plaintiff must prove it is more likely than not that a *particular* defendant had exclusive control of the instrumentality causing the injury. Nettie cannot prove this element because she was unconscious, just as the plaintiff was in *Ybarra*. Also as in *Ybarra*, the hospital defendants are all asserting lack of knowledge.

Normally, in cases with multiple defendants where the plaintiff cannot prove the control element, the plaintiff will not be able to invoke RIL and will lose. But *Ybarra* created an exception in cases like this one based on the special relationship between healthcare providers and patients, stating it would be unfair to hold unconscious patients to a burden they could not meet. The court shifted the burden of going forward with the evidence to the defendants. If at trial one or more of the hospital defendants can prove they were not responsible for the head injury, those defendants would be off the hook. If not, each defendant will be jointly and severally liable to the plaintiff.

If this court follows *Ybarra* (some jurisdictions have rejected it), plaintiff should get to the jury under RIL against one or more of the defendants. If the court rejects *Ybarra*, plaintiff will lose because she lacks proof of negligence by a particular defendant.

Nettie v. Motorcycle Drivers

Concurrent Causes (30 points)

Nettie is suing the motorcycle drivers—Driver 1 and Driver 2—for negligently causing her eye injury. It is a given in the question that both drivers were negligent in roaring past the horse and carriage and also that either one of their acts alone would have caused the horse to rear up.

Factual causation. The only issue is factual causation. Normally, a plaintiff establishes factual causation by proving it is more likely than not that but for the negligence of a particular defendant, the plaintiff's injury would not have occurred. If held to this burden, Nettie would lose because she cannot satisfy but for causation as to either defendant. The question states that "[e]ither of the motorcycles would have been sufficient to scare the horse and cause it to rear up." Accordingly, Nettie will be unable to show it was more likely than not that but for the negligence of Driver 1 she would not have been injured. Similarly, she will be unable to show that but for the negligence of Driver 2 she would not have been injured. The negligence of either driver was sufficient to cause the entire harm.

Concurrent cause exception. Fortunately for Nettie, courts have created an exception to the but for rule in "concurrent cause" cases such as this one that will allow her to prevail. The seminal case is the *Anderson* or "twin fires" case, where the defendant's negligently started fire combined with a fire of unknown origin to burn down plaintiff's cottage. Either fire would have been sufficient to cause the entire harm. There, as here, plaintiff could not prove but for causation because his injury would have occurred even if the defendant had not been negligent.

In such cases, a plaintiff can show factual causation by proving that the defendant's conduct was a "substantial factor" in causing the injury. The rule of *Anderson* has been widely adopted, including by the *Restatement (Second) of Torts*. Here, since either motorcycle would have been sufficient to cause the horse to rear, both were substantial factors in causing the injury.

Nettie should prevail in her claim against the motorcycle drivers for her eye injury under the rule for concurrent causes.

Index

467

†